Pro HTML5 Games

Aditya Ravi Shankar

Apress®

ISBN-13 (pbk): 978-1-4302-4710-4

ISBN-13 (electronic): 978-1-4302-4711-1

President and Publisher: Paul Manning
Lead Editor: Louise Corrigan
Technical Reviewer: Richard Davey, Shane Hudson, Syd Lawrence, Josh Robinson
Editorial Board: Steve Anglin, Ewan Buckingham, Gary Cornell, Louise Corrigan, Morgan Ertel, Jonathan Gennick, Jonathan Hassell, Robert Hutchinson, Michelle Lowman, James Markham, Matthew Moodie, Jeff Olson, Jeffrey Pepper, Douglas Pundick, Ben Renow-Clarke, Dominic Shakeshaft, Gwenan Spearing, Matt Wade, Tom Welsh
Coordinating Editor: Anamika Panchoo
Copy Editors: William McManus, Kim Wimpsett
Compositor: SPi Global
Indexer: SPi Global
Artist: SPi Global
Cover Designer: Anna Ishchenko

Distributed to the book trade worldwide by Springer Science+Business Media New York, 233 Spring Street, 6th Floor, New York, NY 10013. Phone 1-800-SPRINGER, fax (201) 348-4505, e-mail orders-ny@springer-sbm.com, or visit www.springeronline.com.

For information on translations, please e-mail rights@apress.com, or visit www.apress.com.

Apress and friends of ED books may be purchased in bulk for academic, corporate, or promotional use. eBook versions and licenses are also available for most titles. For more information, reference our Special Bulk Sales–eBook Licensing web page at www.apress.com/bulk-sales.

Any source code or other supplementary materials referenced by the author in this text is available to readers at www.apress.com. For detailed information about how to locate your book's source code, go to www.apress.com/source-code.

For my father, who challenged me to learn game programming by first buying me a computer and then telling me that I could only play games on it if I made them myself.

For my mother, who had the unwavering confidence that I would complete this book even before I had written my first chapter.

And for my amazingly supportive sister, Arunima, who has always been my good luck charm.

Contents at a Glance

Contents

About the Author

Aditya Ravi Shankar started programming in 1993 when he was first introduced to the world of computers. With no access to the Internet or online tutorials at the time, he wrote his first game in GW-BASIC by painstakingly retyping code from a book he found at the local library.

After graduating from the Indian Institute of Technology – Madras in 2001, he spent nearly a decade working as a software consultant, developing trading and analytics systems for investment banks and large Fortune 100 companies, before eventually leaving his corporate life behind so he could focus on doing what he loved.

A self-confessed technology geek, he has spent the time since then working on his own projects and experimenting with every new language and technology that he could, including of course HTML5. During this time he became well known for singlehandedly re-creating the famous Command and Conquer RTS game entirely in HTML5.

Apart from programming, Aditya is passionate about billiards, salsa dancing, and learning to develop the subconscious mind. He maintains a personal website (`www.adityaravishankar.com`) where he writes articles on game programming, personal development, and billiards.

When he is not busy writing or working on his own projects, Aditya does consulting work with companies to help them launch new software products.

About the Technical Reviewers

Shane Hudson is a freelance web site developer with a focus on both bleeding-edge web technologies and web standards. He has extensive experience with JavaScript, having worked on a range of highly interactive web sites and side projects. He has a strong interest in the fields of artificial intelligence and computer vision. You can contact Shane by e-mailing shane@shanehudson.net.

Shane says, "Shankar has written the book that the industry has been waiting for: how to write and use JavaScript (and Node.js) effectively and with ease. The outcome of this book is a game, but it is not just a book about game development; it is a book about how to write very good JavaScript."

Josh Robinson is a code craftsman and freelance developer who thrives on cutting-edge technology. His love for coding began with the blue glow of a second-hand Commodore 64 and has continued into his career developing for the modern Web. In 2006, while working at a VoIP provider, he discovered the elegance of Ruby and Ruby on Rails, which led to the creation of several gems including the popular countries gem. He can be stalked at JoshRobinson.com or on Twitter: @JoshRobinson.

Josh says, "With *Pro HTML5 Games* you will be coding up games like a boss."

Syd Lawrence runs We Make Awesome Sh and is a developer evangelist for Twilio. He's previously been described as many things, some too rude to print but others less so. Geek.com once described him as a modern superhero, and The Next Web once described him as a social web guru.

Introduction

Welcome to *Pro HTML5 Games*.

In writing this book, I wanted to create the resource that I wish someone had given me when I was starting out learning game programming.

Unlike other books with abstract examples that you will never ever use, this book will show you firsthand how HTML5 can be used to make complete, working games.

I specifically chose a physics engine game and a real-time strategy game as examples because between the two, these genres encompass all the elements needed to build most of the game types that are popular today.

As you follow along, you will learn all the essential elements needed to create games in HTML5 and then see how these elements come together to form professional-looking games.

By the end of this book, I hope you will walk away with the confidence and the resources to start making amazing games of your own in HTML5.

Who This Book Is For

Pro HTML5 Games is meant for programmers who already have some HTML and JavaScript programming experience and who now want to learn to harness the power of HTML5 to build amazing-looking games but don't know where to begin.

Readers who have experience making games in other languages such as Flash and would like to move to HTML5 will also find a lot of useful information in this book.

If you do not feel confident about your game programming skills, don't worry. This book covers all the essentials needed to build these games so you can follow along and learn to design large, professional games in HTML5. The book will also point to resources and reference material for supplemental learning in case you are having trouble keeping up.

With dedicated chapters on HTML5 basics, the Box2D engine, pathfinding and steering, combat and effective enemy AI, and multiplayer using Node.JS with WebSockets, you should get a lot from this book no matter how much game programming experience you have.

How This Book Is Structured

Pro HTML5 Games takes you through the process of building two complete games over the course of 12 chapters.

In the first four chapters, you will build *Froot Wars*, a Box2D engine–based physics game similar to the very popular *Angry Birds*.

Chapter 1 discusses the basic elements of HTML5 needed to build games, such as drawing and animating on the canvas, playing audio, and using sprite sheets.

Chapter 2 covers building a basic game framework with splash screens, game menus, an asset loader, and a basic level with parallax scrolling.

Chapter 3 is a detailed introduction to the Box2D physics engine and shows how Box2D can be used to model a game world.

Chapter 4 shows how to integrate the game framework with the Box2D engine, add sounds, and add music to create a complete working physics game.

The second game in the book is an RTS game with both a single-player campaign mode and a multiplayer mode. You will build the single-player campaign over the next six chapters.

Chapter 5 covers building a basic game framework with splash screens, game menus, an asset loader, and a basic level with panning using the mouse.

Chapter 6 adds different entities such as vehicles, aircraft, and buildings to the game.

Chapter 7 shows how to add intelligent unit movement to the game using a combination of pathfinding and steering steps.

Chapter 8 adds some more elements such as an economy and a trigger-based system that allows scripting events.

Chapter 9 covers implementing a weapons and combat system in the game.

Chapter 10 wraps up the single-player by showing how to create several challenging single-player levels using the framework developed so far.

Finally, in the last two chapters, you will look at building the multiplayer component of the RTS game.

Chapter 11 discusses the basics of using the WebSocket API with Node.js and creating a multiplayer game lobby.

Chapter 12 covers implementing a framework for multiplayer gameplay using the lock-step networking model and compensating for network latency while maintaining game synchronization.

Downloading the Code

The code for the examples shown in this book is available on the Apress web site, `www.apress.com`. You can find a link on the book's information page on the Source Code/Downloads tab. This tab is located underneath the Related Titles section of the page.

Contacting the Author

Should you have any questions or feedback, you can contact the author through the dedicated page on his web site at `www.adityaravishankar.com/pro-html5-games/`. He can also be reached via e-mail at `prohtml5games@adityaravishankar.com`.

CHAPTER 1

■ ■ ■

HTML5 and JavaScript Essentials

HTML5, the latest version of the HTML standard, provides us with many new features for improved interactivity and media support. These new features (such as canvas, audio, and video) have made it possible to make fairly rich and interactive applications for the browser without requiring third-party plug-ins such as Flash.

The HTML5 specification is currently a work in progress, and browsers are still implementing some of its newer features. However, the elements that we need for building some very amazing games are already supported by most modern browsers (Google Chrome, Mozilla Firefox, Internet Explorer 9+, Safari, and Opera).

All you need to get started on developing your games in HTML5 are a good text editor to write your code (I use TextMate for the Mac—http://macromates.com/) and a modern, HTML5-compatible browser (I use Google Chrome—http://www.google.com/chrome).

The structure of an HTML5 file is very similar to that of files in previous versions of HTML except that it has a much simpler DOCTYPE tag at the beginning of the file. Listing 1-1 provides a skeleton for a very basic HTML5 file that we will be using as a starting point for the rest of this chapter.

Executing this code involves saving it as an HTML file and then opening the file in a web browser. If you do everything correctly, this file should pop up the message "Hello World!"

Listing 1-1. Basic HTML5 File Skeleton

```html
<!DOCTYPE html>
<html>
    <head>
        <meta http-equiv = "Content-type" content = "text/html; charset = utf-8">
        <title>Sample HTML5 File</title>
        <script type = "text/javascript" charset = "utf-8">
            // This function will be called once the page loads completely
            function pageLoaded(){
                alert('Hello World!');
            }
        </script>
    </head>
    <body onload = "pageLoaded();">

    </body>
</html>
```

■ **Note**   We use the body's onload event to call our function so that we can be sure that our page has completely loaded before we start working with it. This will become important when we start manipulating elements like canvas and image. Trying to access these elements before the browser has finished loading them will cause JavaScript errors.

Before we start developing games, we need to go over some of the basic building blocks that we will be using to create our games. The most important ones that we need are

- The canvas element, to render shapes and images

- The audio element, to add sounds and background music

- The image element, to load our game artwork and display it on the canvas

- The browser timer functions, and game loops to handle animation

The canvas Element

The most important element for use in our games is the new canvas element. As per the HTML5 standard specification, "The canvas element provides scripts with a resolution-dependent bitmap canvas, which can be used for rendering graphs, game graphics, or other visual images on the fly." You can find the complete specification at www.whatwg.org/specs/web-apps/current-work/multipage/the-canvas-element.html.

The canvas allows us to draw primitive shapes like lines, circles, and rectangles, as well as images and text, and has been optimized for fast drawing. Browsers have started enabling GPU-accelerated rendering of 2D canvas content, so that canvas-based games and animations run fast.

Using the canvas element is fairly simple. Place the < canvas > tag inside the body of the HTML5 file we created earlier, as shown in Listing 1-2.

Listing 1-2. Creating a Canvas Element

```
<canvas width = "640" height = "480" id = "testcanvas" style = "border:black 1px solid;">
    Your browser does not support HTML5 Canvas. Please shift to another browser.
</canvas>
```

The code in Listing 1-2 creates a canvas that is 640 pixels wide and 480 pixels high. By itself, the canvas shows up as a blank area (with a black border that we specified in the style). We can now start drawing inside this rectangle using JavaScript.

■ **Note** Browsers that do not support canvas will ignore the < canvas > tag and render anything inside the < canvas > tag. You can use this feature to show users on older browsers alternative fallback content or a message directing them to a more modern browser.

We draw on the canvas using its primary rendering context. We can access this context with the getContext() method in the canvas object. The getContext() method takes one parameter: the type of context that we need. We will be using the 2d context for our games.

Listing 1-3 shows how we can access the canvas and its context once the page has loaded.

Listing 1-3. Accessing the Canvas Context

```
<script type = "text/javascript" charset = "utf-8">
    function pageLoaded(){

        // Get a handle to the canvas object
        var canvas = document.getElementById('testcanvas');

        // Get the 2d context for this canvas
```

```
        var context = canvas.getContext('2d');

        // Our drawing code here...
    }
</script>
```

■ **Note**   All browsers support the 2d context that we need for 2D graphics. Browsers also implement other contexts with their own proprietary names, such as experimental-webgl for 3D graphics.

This context object provides us with a large number of methods that we can use to draw our game elements on the screen. This includes methods for the following:

- Drawing rectangles

- Drawing complex paths (lines, arcs, and so forth)

- Drawing text

- Customizing drawing styles (colors, alpha, textures, and so forth)

- Drawing images

- Transforming and rotating

We will look at each of these methods in more detail in the following sections.

Drawing Rectangles

The canvas uses a coordinate system with the origin (0,0) at the top-left corner, x increasing toward the right, and y increasing downward, as illustrated in Figure 1-1.

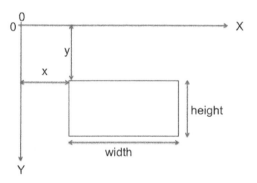

Figure 1-1. *Coordinate system for canvas*

We can draw a rectangle on the canvas using the context's rectangle methods:

- `fillRect(x, y, width, height)`: Draws a filled rectangle

- `strokeRect(x, y, width, height)`: Draws a rectangular outline

- `clearRect(x, y, width, height)`: Clears the specified rectangular area and makes it fully transparent

Listing 1-4. Drawing Rectangles Inside the Canvas

```
// FILLED RECTANGLES
// Draw a solid square with width and height of 100 pixels at (200,10)
context.fillRect (200,10,100,100);
// Draw a solid square with width of 90 pixels and height of 30 pixels at (50,70)
context.fillRect (50,70,90,30);

// STROKED RECTANGLES
// Draw a rectangular outline of width and height 50 pixels at (110,10)
context.strokeRect(110,10,50,50);
// Draw a rectangular outline of width and height 50 pixels at (30,10)
context.strokeRect(30,10,50,50);

// CLEARING RECTANGLES
// Clear a rectangle of width of 30 pixels and height 20 pixels at (210,20)
context.clearRect(210,20,30,20);
// Clear a rectangle of width 30 and height 20 pixels at (260,20)
context.clearRect(260,20,30,20);
```

The code in Listing 1-4 will draw multiple rectangles on the top-left corner of the canvas, as shown in Figure 1-2.

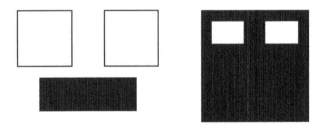

Figure 1-2. *Drawing rectangles inside the canvas*

Drawing Complex Paths

The context has several methods that allow us to draw complex shapes when simple boxes aren't enough:

- `beginPath()`: Starts recording a new shape

- `closePath()`: Closes the path by drawing a line from the current drawing point to the starting point

- `fill()`, `stroke()`: Fills or draws an outline of the recorded shape

- `moveTo(x, y)`: Moves the drawing point to x,y

- `lineTo(x, y)`: Draws a line from the current drawing point to x,y

- `arc(x, y, radius, startAngle, endAngle, anticlockwise)`: Draws an arc at x,y with specified radius

Using these methods, drawing a complex path involves the following steps:

1. Use `beginPath()` to start recording the new shape.

2. Use `moveTo()`, `lineTo()`, and `arc()` to create the shape.

3. Optionally, close the shape using `closePath()`.

4. Use either `stroke()` or `fill()` to draw an outline or filled shape. Using `fill()` automatically closes any open paths.

Listing 1-5 will create the triangles, arcs, and shapes shown in Figure 1-3.

Listing 1-5. Drawing Complex Shapes Inside the Canvas

```
// Drawing complex shapes
// Filled triangle
context.beginPath();
context.moveTo(10,120);     // Start drawing at 10,120
context.lineTo(10,180);
context.lineTo(110,150);
context.fill();     // close the shape and fill it out

// Stroked triangle
context.beginPath();
context.moveTo(140,160); // Start drawing at 140,160
context.lineTo(140,220);
context.lineTo(40,190);
context.closePath();
context.stroke();

// A more complex set of lines...
context.beginPath();
context.moveTo(160,160); // Start drawing at 160,160
context.lineTo(170,220);
context.lineTo(240,210);
context.lineTo(260,170);
context.lineTo(190,140);
context.closePath();
context.stroke();

// Drawing arcs

// Drawing a semicircle
context.beginPath();
// Draw an arc at (400,50) with radius 40 from 0 to 180 degrees,anticlockwise
context.arc(100,300,40,0,Math.PI,true);     //(PI radians = 180 degrees)
context.stroke();
```

```
// Drawing a full circle
context.beginPath();
// Draw an arc at (500,50) with radius 30 from 0 to 360 degrees,anticlockwise
context.arc(100,300,30,0,2*Math.PI,true); //(2*PI radians = 360 degrees)
context.fill();

// Drawing a three-quarter arc
context.beginPath();
// Draw an arc at (400,100) with radius 25 from 0 to 270 degrees,clockwise
context.arc(200,300,25,0,3/2*Math.PI,false); //(3/2*PI radians = 270 degrees) context.stroke();
```

The code in Listing 1-4 will create the triangles, arcs and shapes shown in Figure 1-3.

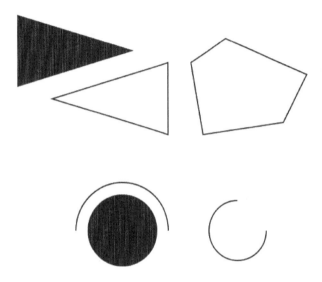

Figure 1-3. *Drawing complex shapes inside the canvas*

Drawing Text

The context also provides us with two methods for drawing text on the canvas:

- strokeText(text,x,y): Draws an outline of the text at (x,y)
- fillText(text,x,y): Fills out the text at (x,y)

Unlike text inside other HTML elements, text inside canvas does not have CSS layout options such as wrapping, padding, and margins. The text output, however, can be modified by setting the context font property as well as the stroke and fill styles, as shown in Listing 1-6. When setting the font property, you can use any valid CSS font property.

Listing 1-6. Drawing Text Inside the Canvas

```
// Drawing text
context.fillText('This is some text...',330,40);
```

```
// Modifying the font
context.font = '10 pt Arial';
context.fillText('This is in 10 pt Arial...',330,60);

// Drawing stroked text
context.font = '16 pt Arial';
context.strokeText('This is stroked in 16 pt Arial...',330,80);
```

The code in Listing 1-6 will draw the text shown in Figure 1-4.

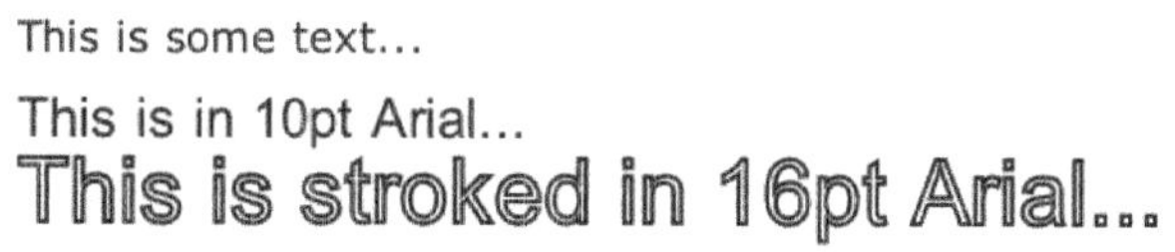

This is some text...

This is in 10pt Arial...

This is stroked in 16pt Arial...

Figure 1-4. *Drawing text inside the canvas*

Customizing Drawing Styles (Colors and Textures)

So far, everything we have drawn has been in black, but only because the canvas default drawing color is black. We have other options. We can style and customize the lines, shapes, and text on a canvas. We can draw using different colors, line styles, transparencies, and even fill textures inside the shapes

If we want to apply colors to a shape, there are two important properties we can use:

- fillStyle: Sets the default color for all future fill operations

- strokeStyle: Sets the default color for all future stroke operations

Both properties can take valid CSS colors as values. This includes rgb() and rgba() values as well as color constant values. For example, context.fillStyle = "red"; will define the fill color as red for all future fill operations (fillRect, fillText, and fill).

The code in Listing 1-7 will draw colored rectangles, as shown in Figure 1-5.

Listing 1-7. Drawing with Colors and Transparency

```
// Set fill color to red
context.fillStyle = "red";
// Draw a red filled rectangle
context.fillRect (310,160,100,50);

// Set stroke color to green
context.strokeStyle = "green";
// Draw a green stroked rectangle
context.strokeRect (310,240,100,50);

// Set fill color to red using rgb()
context.fillStyle = "rgb(255,0,0)";
// Draw a red filled rectangle
context.fillRect (420,160,100,50);
```

```
// Set fill color to green with an alpha of 0.5
context.fillStyle = "rgba(0,255,0,0.6)";
// Draw a semi transparent green filled rectangle
context.fillRect (450,180,100,50);
```

Figure 1-5. *Drawing with colors and transparency*

Drawing Images

Although we can achieve quite a lot using just the drawing methods we have covered so far, we still need to explore how to use images. Learning how to draw images will enable you to draw game backgrounds, character sprites, and effects like explosions that can make your games come alive.

We can draw images and sprites on the canvas using the drawImage() method. The context provides us with three different versions of this method:

- drawImage(image, x, y): Draws the image on the canvas at (x,y)

- drawImage(image, x, y, width, height): Scales the image to the specified width and height and then draws it at (x,y)

- drawImage(image, sourceX, sourceY, sourceWidth, sourceHeight, x, y, width, height): Clips a rectangle from the image (sourceX, sourceY, sourceWidth, sourceHeight), scales it to the specified width and height, and draws it on the canvas at (x, y)

Before we start drawing images, we need to load an image into the browser. For now, we will just add an < img > tag after the < canvas > tag in our HTML file:

```
<img src = "spaceship.png" id = "spaceship">
```

Once the image has been loaded, we can draw it using the code shown in Listing 1-8.

Listing 1-8. Drawing Images

```
// Get a handle to the image object
var image = document.getElementById('spaceship');

// Draw the image at (0,350)
context.drawImage(image,0,350);

// Scaling the image to half the original size
context.drawImage(image,0,400,100,25);

// Drawing part of the image
context.drawImage(image,0,0,60,50,0,420,60,50);
```

The code in Listing 1-8 will draw the images shown in Figure 1-6.

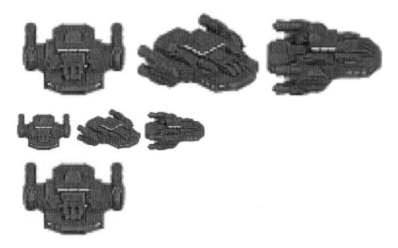

Figure 1-6. *Drawing images*

Transforming and Rotating

The `context` object has several methods for transforming the coordinate system used for drawing elements. These methods are

- `translate(x, y)`: Moves the canvas and its origin to a different point (x,y)
- `rotate(angle)`: Rotates the canvas clockwise around the current origin by angle (radians)
- `scale(x, y)`: Scales the objects drawn by a multiple of x and y

A common use of these methods is to rotate objects or sprites when drawing them. We can do this by

- Translating the canvas origin to the location of the object
- Rotating the canvas by the desired angle
- Drawing the object
- Restoring the canvas back to its original state

Let's look at rotating objects before drawing them, as shown in Listing 1-9.

Listing 1-9. Rotating Objects Before Drawing Them

```
//Translate origin to location of object
context.translate(250, 370);
//Rotate about the new origin by 60 degrees
context.rotate(Math.PI/3);
context.drawImage(image,0,0,60,50,-30,-25,60,50);
//Restore to original state by rotating and translating back
context.rotate(-Math.PI/3);
context.translate(-240, -370);

//Translate origin to location of object
context.translate(300, 370);
//Rotate about the new origin
context.rotate(3*Math.PI/4);
context.drawImage(image,0,0,60,50,-30,-25,60,50);
//Restore to original state by rotating and translating back
context.rotate(-3*Math.PI/4);
context.translate(-300, -370);
```

The code in Listing 1-9 will draw the two rotated ship images shown in Figure 1-7.

Figure 1-7. *Rotating images*

■ **Note** Apart from rotating and translating back, you can also restore the canvas state by first using the save() method before starting the transformations and then calling the restore() method at the end of the transformations.

The audio Element

Using the HTML5 audio element is the new standard way to embed an audio file into a web page. Until this element came along, most pages played audio files using embedded plug-ins (such as Flash).

The audio element can be created in HTML using the < audio > tag or in JavaScript using the Audio object. An example is shown in Listing 1-10.

Listing 1-10. The HTML5 < audio > Tag

```
<audio src = "music.mp3" controls = "controls">
    Your browser does not support HTML5 Audio. Please shift to a newer browser.
</audio>
```

▪ **Note**   Browsers that do not support audio will ignore the < audio > tag and render anything inside the
< audio > tag. You can use this feature to show users on older browsers alternative fallback content or a message direct-
ing them to a more modern browser.

The `controls` attribute included in Listing 1-10 makes the browser display a simple browser-specific interface for playing the audio file (such as a play/pause button and volume controls).

The `audio` element has several other attributes, such as the following:

- `preload`: Specifies whether or not the audio should be preloaded
- `autoplay`: Specifies whether or not to start playing the audio as soon as the object has loaded
- `loop`: Specifies whether to keep replaying the audio once it has finished

There are currently three popular file formats supported by browsers: MP3 (MPEG Audio Layer 3), WAV (Waveform Audio), and OGG (Ogg Vorbis). One thing to watch out for is that not all browsers support all audio formats. Firefox, for example, does not play MP3 files because of licensing issues, but it works with OGG files. Safari, on the other hand, supports MP3 but does not support OGG. Table 1-1 shows the formats supported by the most popular browsers.

Table 1-1. Audio Formats Supported by Different Browsers

Browser	MP3	WAV	OGG
Internet Explorer 9+	Yes	No	No
Firefox 3.6+	No	Yes	Yes
Chrome 3+	Yes	No	Yes
Safari 4+	Yes	Yes	No
Opera 9.5+	No	Yes	Yes

The way to work around this limitation is to provide the browser with alternative formats to play. The audio element allows multiple source elements within the < audio > tag, and the browser automatically uses the first recognized format (see Listing 1-11).

Listing 1-11. The < audio > Tag with Multiple Sources

```
<audio controls = "controls">
    <source src = "music.ogg" type = "audio/ogg" />
    <source src = "music.mp3" type = "audio/mpeg" />
    Your browser does not support HTML5 Audio. Please shift to a newer browser.
</audio>
```

Audio can also be loaded dynamically by using the Audio object in JavaScript. The Audio object allows us to load, play, and pause sound files as needed, which is what will be used for games (see Listing 1-12).

Listing 1-12. Dynamically Loading an Audio File

```
<script>
    //Create a new Audio object
    var sound = new Audio();

    // Select the source of the sound
    sound.src = "music.ogg";

    // Play the sound
    sound.play();
</script>
```

Again, as with the < audio > HTML tag, we need a way to detect which format the browser supports and load the appropriate format. The Audio object provides us with a method called canPlayType() that returns values of "", "maybe" or "probably" to indicate support for a specific codec. We can use this to create a simple check and load the appropriate audio format, as shown in Listing 1-13.

Listing 1-13. Testing for Audio Support

```
<script>
    var audio = document.createElement('audio');
    var mp3Support,oggSupport;
    if (audio.canPlayType) {
            // Currently canPlayType() returns: "", "maybe", or "probably"
        mp3Support = "" ! = myAudio.canPlayType('audio/mpeg');
        oggSupport = "" ! = myAudio.canPlayType('audio/ogg; codecs = "vorbis"');
    } else {
        //The audio tag is not supported
        mp3Support = false;
        oggSupport = false;
    }

    // Check for ogg, then mp3, and finally set soundFileExtn to undefined
    var soundFileExtn = oggSupport?".ogg":mp3Support?".mp3":undefined;

    if(soundFileExtn) {
        var sound = new Audio();
        // Load sound file with the detected extension
        sound.src = "bounce"+soundFileExtn;
        sound.play();
    }
</script>
```

The Audio object triggers an event called canplaythrough when the file is ready to be played. We can use this event to keep track of when the sound file has been loaded. Listing 1-14 shows an example.

Listing 1-14. Waiting for an Audio File to Load

```
<script>
    if(soundFileExtn) {
        var sound = new Audio();
        sound .addEventListener('canplaythrough', function(){
```

```
        alert('loaded');
        sound.play();
    });
    // Load sound file with the detected extension
    sound.src = "bounce"+soundFileExtn;
}
</script>
```

We can use this to design an audio preloader that will load all the game resources before starting the game. We will look at this idea in more detail in the next few chapters.

The image Element

The image element allows us to display images inside an HTML file. The simplest way to do this is by using the < image > tag and specifying an src attribute, as shown earlier and again here in Listing 1-15.

Listing 1-15. The < image > Tag

```
<img src = 'spaceship.png' id = 'spaceship' >
```

You can also load an image dynamically using JavaScript by instantiating a new Image object and setting it's src property, as shown in Listing 1-16.

Listing 1-16. Dynamically Loading an Image

```
var image = new Image();
image.src = 'spaceship.png';
```

You can use either of these methods to get an image for drawing on a canvas.

Image Loading

Games are usually programmed to wait for all the images to load before they start. A common thing for programmers to do is to display a progress bar or status indicator that shows the percentage of images loaded. The Image object provides us with an onload event that gets fired as soon as the browser finishes loading the image file. Using this event, we can keep track of when the image has loaded, as shown in the example in Listing 1-17.

Listing 1-17. Waiting for an Image to Load

```
image.onload = function() {
    alert('Image finished loading');
};
```

Using the onload event, we can create a simple image loader that tracks images loaded so far (see Listing 1-18).

Listing 1-18. Simple Image Loader

```
var imageLoader = {
    loaded:true,
    loadedImages:0,
    totalImages:0,
    load:function(url){
```

```
        this.totalImages++;
        this.loaded = false;
        var image = new Image();
        image.src = url;
        image.onload = function(){
            imageLoader.loadedImages++;
            if(imageLoader.loadedImages === imageLoader.totalImages){
                imageLoader.loaded = true;
            }
        }
        return image;
    }
}
```

This image loader can be invoked to load a large number of images (say in a loop). Checking to see if all the images are loaded can be done using imageLoader.loaded, and a percentage/progress bar can be drawn using loadedImages/totalImages.

Sprite Sheets

Another concern when your game has a lot of images is how to optimize the way the server loads these images. Games can require anything from tens to hundreds of images. Even a simple real-time strategy (RTS) game will need images for different units, buildings, maps, backgrounds, and effects. In the case of units and buildings, you might need multiple versions of images to represent different directions and states, and in the case of animations, you might need an image for each frame of the animation.

On my earlier RTS game projects, I used individual images for each animation frame and state for every unit and building, ending up with over 1,000 images. Since most browsers make only a few simultaneous requests at a time, downloading all these images took a lot of time, with an overload of HTTP requests on the server. While this wasn't a problem when I was testing the code locally, it was a bit of a pain when the code went onto the server. People ended up waiting 5 to 10 minutes (sometimes longer) for the game to load before they could actually start playing. This is where sprite sheets come in.

Sprite sheets store all the sprites (images) for an object in a single large image file. When displaying the images, we calculate the offset of the sprite we want to show and use the ability of the drawImage() method to draw only a part of an image. The spaceship.png image we have been using in this chapter is an example of a sprite sheet.

Looking at Listings 1-19 and 1-20, you can see examples of drawing an image loaded individually versus drawing an image loaded in a sprite sheet.

Listing 1-19. Drawing an Image Loaded Individually

```
//First: (Load individual images and store in a big array)

// Three arguments: the element, and destination (x,y) coordinates.
var image = imageArray[imageNumber];
context.drawImage(image,x,y);
```

Listing 1-20. Drawing an Image Loaded in a Sprite Sheet

```
// First: (Load single sprite sheet image)

// Nine arguments: the element, source (x,y) coordinates,
// source width and height (for cropping),
// destination (x,y) coordinates, and
// destination width and height (resize).
```

```
context.drawImage (this.spriteImage, this.imageWidth*(imageNumber), 0, this.imageWidth,
this.imageHeight, x, y, this.imageWidth, this.imageHeight);
```

The following are some of the advantages of using a sprite sheet:

- *Fewer HTTP requests*: A unit that has 80 images (and so 80 requests) will now be downloaded in a single HTTP request.

- *Better compression*: Storing the images in a single file means that the header information doesn't repeat and the combined file size is significantly smaller than the sum of the individual files.

- *Faster load times*: With significantly lower HTTP requests and file sizes, the bandwidth usage and load times for the game drop as well, which means users won't have to wait for a long time for the game to load.

Animation: Timer and Game Loops

Animating is just a matter of drawing an object, erasing it, and drawing it again at a new position. The most common way to handle this is by keeping a drawing function that gets called several times a second. In some games, there is also a separate control/animation function that updates movement of the entities within the game and is called less often than the drawing routine. Listing 1-21 shows a typical example.

Listing 1-21. Typical Animation and Drawing Loop

```
function animationLoop(){
    // Iterate through all the items in the game
    //And move them
}

function drawingLoop(){
    //1. Clear the canvas
    //2.  Iterate through all the items
    //3. And draw each item
}
```

Now we need to figure out a way to call `drawingLoop()` repeatedly at regular intervals. The simplest way of achieving this is to use the two timer methods `setInterval()` and `setTimeout()`. `setInterval(functionName, timeInterval)` tells the browser to keep calling a given function repeatedly at fixed time intervals until the `clearInterval()` function is called. When we need to stop animating (when the game is paused, or has ended), we use `clearInterval()`. Listing 1-22 shows an example.

Listing 1-22. Calling Drawing Loop with setInterval

```
// Call drawingLoop() every 20 milliseconds
var gameLoop = setInterval(drawingLoop,20);

// Stop calling drawingLoop() and clear the gameLoop variable
clearInterval(gameLoop);
```

`setTimeout(functionName, timeInterval)` tells the browser to call a given function once after a given time interval, as shown in the example in Listing 1-23.

Listing 1-23. Calling Drawing Loop with setTimeout

```
function drawingLoop(){
    //1. call the drawingLoop method once after 20 milliseconds
    var gameLoop = setTimeout(drawingLoop,20);

    //2. Clear the canvas

    //3. Iterate through all the items

    //4. And draw them
}
```

When we need to stop animating (when the game is paused, or has ended), we can use `clearTimeout()`:

```
// Stop calling drawingLoop() and clear the gameLoop variable
clearTimeout(gameLoop);
```

requestAnimationFrame

While using `setInterval()` or `setTimeout()` as a way to animate frames does work, browser vendors have come up with a new API specifically for handling animation. Some of the advantages of using this API instead of `setInterval()` are that the browser can do the following:

- Optimize the animation code into a single reflow-and-repaint cycle, resulting in smoother animation

- Pause the animation when the tab is not visible, leading to less CPU and GPU usage

- Automatically cap the frame rate on machines that do not support higher frame rates, or increase the frame rate on machines that are capable of processing them

Different browser vendors have their own proprietary names for the methods in the API (such as Microsoft's `msrequestAnimationFrame` and Mozilla's `mozRequestAnimationFrame`). However, there is a simple piece of code (see Listing 1-24) that acts as a cross-browser polyfill providing you with the two methods that you use: `requestAnimationFrame()` and `cancelAnimationFrame()`.

Listing 1-24. A Simple requestAnimationFrame Polyfill

```
(function() {
    var lastTime = 0;
    var vendors = ['ms', 'moz', 'webkit', 'o'];
    for(var x = 0; x < vendors.length && !window.requestAnimationFrame; ++x) {
        window.requestAnimationFrame = window[vendors[x]+'RequestAnimationFrame'];
        window.cancelAnimationFrame =
            window[vendors[x]+'CancelAnimationFrame'] ||
            window[vendors[x]+'CancelRequestAnimationFrame'];
    }

    if (!window.requestAnimationFrame)
        window.requestAnimationFrame = function(callback, element) {
            var currTime = new Date().getTime();
            var timeToCall = Math.max(0, 16 - (currTime - lastTime));
```

```
            var id = window.setTimeout(function() { callback(currTime+timeToCall); },
              timeToCall);
            lastTime = currTime+timeToCall;
            return id;
        };

    if (!window.cancelAnimationFrame)
        window.cancelAnimationFrame = function(id) {
            clearTimeout(id);
        };
}());
```

■ **Note**   Now that we have no guarantee of frame rate (the browser decides the speed at which it will call our drawing loop), we need to ensure that animated objects move at the same speed on the screen independent of the actual frame rate. We do this by calculating the time since the previous drawing cycle and using this calculation to interpolate the location of the object being animated.

Once this polyfill is in place, the requestAnimationFrame() method can be called from within the drawingLoop() method similar to setTimeout() (see Listing 1-25).

Listing 1-25. Calling Drawing Loop with requestAnimationFrame

```
function drawingLoop(nowTime){
    //1. call the drawingLoop method whenever the browser is ready to draw again
var gameLoop = requestAnimationFrame(drawingLoop);

    //2. Clear the canvas

    //3. Iterate through all the items

    //4. Optionally use nowTime and the last nowTime to interpolate frames

    //5. And draw them
}
```

When we need to stop animating (when the game is paused, or has ended), we can use cancelAnimationFrame():

```
// Stop calling drawingLoop()    and clear the gameLoop variable
cancelAnimationFrame(gameLoop);
```

This section has covered the primary ways to add animation to your games. We will be looking at actual implementations of these animation loops in the coming chapters.

Summary

In this chapter, we looked at the basic elements of HTML5 that are needed for building games. We covered how to use the canvas element to draw shapes, write text, and manipulate images. We examined how to use the audio element to load and play sounds across different browsers. We also briefly covered the basics of animation, preloading objects and using sprite sheets.

The topics we covered here are just a starting point and not exhaustive by any means. This chapter is meant to be a quick refresher on HTML5. We will be going into these topics in more detail, with complete implementations, as we build our games in the coming chapters.

If you have trouble keeping up and would like a more detailed explanation of the basics of JavaScript and HTML5, I would recommend reading introductory books on JavaScript and HTML5, such as *JavaScript for Absolute Beginners* by Terry McNavage and *The Essential Guide to HTML5* by Jeanine Meyer.

Now that we have the basics out of the way, let's get started building our first game.

CHAPTER 2

Creating a Basic Game World

The arrival of smartphones and handheld devices that support gaming has created a renewed interest in simple puzzle and physics-based games that can be played for short periods of time. Most of these games have a simple concept, small levels, and are easy to learn. One of the most popular and famous games in this genre is Angry Birds (by Rovio Entertainment), a puzzle/strategy game where players use a slingshot to shoot birds at enemy pigs. Despite a fairly simple premise, the game has been downloaded and installed on over 1 billion devices around the world. The game uses a physics engine to realistically model the slinging, collisions, and breaking of objects inside its game world.

Over the next three chapters, we are going to build our own physics-based puzzle game with complete playable levels. Our game, Froot Wars, will have fruits as protagonists, junk food as the enemy, and some breakable structures within the level.

We will be implementing all the essential components you will need in your own games—splash screens, loading screens and preloaders, menu screens, parallax scrolling, sound, realistic physics with the Box2D physics engine, and a scoreboard. Once you have this basic framework, you should be able to reuse these ideas in your own puzzle games.

So let's get started.

Basic HTML Layout

The first thing we need to do is to create the basic game layout. This will consist of several layers:

- *Splash screen*: Shown when the game page is loaded

- *Game start screen*: A menu that allows the player to start the game or modify settings

- *Loading/progress screen*: Shown whenever the game is loading assets (such as images and sound files)

- *Game canvas*: The actual game layer

- *Scoreboard*: An overlay above the game canvas to show a few buttons and the score

- *Ending screen*: A screen displayed at the end of each level

Each of these layers will be either a div element or a canvas element that we will display or hide as needed. We will be using jQuery (http://jquery.com/) to help us with some of these manipulation tasks. The code will be laid out with separate folders for images and JavaScript code.

Creating the Splash Screen and Main Menu

We start with a skeleton HTML file, similar to the first chapter, and add the markup for our containers, as shown in Listing 2-1.

Listing 2-1. Basic Skeleton (index.html) with the Layers Added

```
<!DOCTYPE html>
<html>
    <head>
        <meta http-equiv="Content-type" content="text/html; charset=utf-8">
        <title>Froot Wars</title>
        <script src="js/jquery.min.js" type="text/javascript" charset="utf-8"></script>
        <script src="js/game.js" type="text/javascript" charset="utf-8"></script>
        <link rel="stylesheet" href="styles.css" type="text/css" media="screen" charset="utf-8">
    </head>

    <body>
        <div id="gamecontainer">
            <canvas id="gamecanvas" width="640" height="480" class="gamelayer">
            </canvas>

            <div id="scorescreen" class="gamelayer">
                <img id="togglemusic" src="images/icons/sound.png">
                <img src="images/icons/prev.png">
                <span id="score">Score: 0</span>
            </div>

            <div id="gamestartscreen" class="gamelayer">
                <img src="images/icons/play.png" alt="Play Game"><br>
                <img src="images/icons/settings.png" alt="Settings">
            </div>

            <div id="levelselectscreen" class="gamelayer">
            </div>

            <div id="loadingscreen" class="gamelayer">
                <div id="loadingmessage"></div>
            </div>

            <div id="endingscreen" class="gamelayer">
                <div>
                    <p id="endingmessage">The Level Is Over Message</p>
                    <p id="playcurrentlevel"><img src="images/icons/prev.png">Replay Current
Level</p>

                    <p id="playnextlevel"><img src="images/icons/next.png">Play Next Level </p>
                    <p id="showLevelScreen"><img src="images/icons/return.png">Return to Level
Screen</p>
                </div>
            </div>
```

```
        </div>
    </body>
</html>
```

As you can see, we defined a main `gamecontainer` div element that contains each of the game layers: `gamestartscreen`, `levelselectscreen`, `loadingscreen`, `scorescreen`, `endingscreen`, and finally `gamecanvas`.

In addition, we will also add CSS styles for these layers in an external file called `styles.css`. We will start by adding styles for the game container and the starting menu screen, as shown in Listing 2-2.

Listing 2-2. CSS Styles for the Container and Start Screen (styles.css)

```css
#gamecontainer {
    width:640px;
    height:480px;
    background: url(images/splashscreen.png);
    border: 1px solid black;
}

.gamelayer {
    width:640px;
    height:480px;
    position:absolute;
    display:none;
}

/* Game Starting Menu Screen */
#gamestartscreen {
    padding-top:250px;
    text-align:center;
}

#gamestartscreen img {
    margin:10px;
    cursor:pointer;
}
```

We have done the following in this CSS style sheet so far:

- Define our game container and all game layers with a size of 640px by 480px.

- Make sure all game layers are positioned using absolute positioning (they are placed on top of each other) so that we can show/hide and superimpose layers as needed. Each of these layers is hidden by default.

- Set our game splash screen image as the main container background so it is the first thing a player sees when the page loads.

- Add some styling for our game start screen (the starting menu), which has options such as starting a new game and changing game settings.

■ **Note** All the images and source code are available in the Source Code/Download area of the Apress web site (www.apress.com). If you would like to follow along, you can copy all the asset files into a fresh folder and build the game on your own.

If we open in a browser the HTML file we have created so far, we see the game splash screen surrounded by a black border, as shown in Figure 2-1.

Figure 2-1. *The game splash screen*

We need to add some JavaScript code to start showing the main menu, the loading screen, and the game. To keep our code clean and easy to maintain, we will keep all our game-related JavaScript code in a separate file (js/game.js).

We start by defining a game object that will contain most of our game code. The first thing we need is an init() function that will be called after the browser loads the HTML document.

Listing 2-3. A Basic game Object (js/game.js)

```
var game = {
    // Start initializing objects, preloading assets and display start screen
    init: function(){

        // Hide all game layers and display the start screen
        $('.gamelayer').hide();
        $('#gamestartscreen').show();

        //Get handler for game canvas and context
        game.canvas = $('#gamecanvas')[0];
        game.context = game.canvas.getContext('2d');
    },
}
```

The code in Listing 2-3 defines a JavaScript object called game with an init() function. For now, this init() function just hides all game layers and shows the game start screen using the jQuery hide() and show() functions. It also saves pointers to the game canvas and context so we can refer to them more easily using game.context and game.canvas.

Trying to manipulate image and div elements before confirming that the page has loaded completely will result in unpredictable behavior (including JavaScript errors). We can safely call this game.init() method after the window has loaded by adding a small snippet of JavaScript code at the top of game.js (shown in Listing 2-4).

Listing 2-4. Calling game.init() Method Safely Using the load() Event

```
$(window).load(function() {
    game.init();
});
```

When we run our HTML code, the browser initially displays the splash screen and then displays the game start screen on top of the splash screen, as shown in Figure 2-2.

Figure 2-2. The game start screen and menu options

Level Selection

So far we have waited for the game HTML file to load completely and then show a main menu with two options. When the user clicks the Play button, ideally we would like to display a level selection screen that shows a list of available levels.

Before we can do this, we need to create an object for handling levels. This object will contain both the level data and some simple functions for handling level initialization. We will create this levels object inside game.js and place it after the game object, as shown in Listing 2-5.

Listing 2-5. Simple levels Object with Level Data and Functions

```
var levels = {
    // Level data
    data:[
        {   // First level
            foreground:'desert-foreground',
```

```
                background:'clouds-background',
                entities:[]
            },
            {   // Second level
                foreground:'desert-foreground',
                background:'clouds-background',
                entities:[]
            }
        ],
        // Initialize level selection screen
        init:function(){
            var html="";
            for (var i=0; i<levels.data.length; i++) {
                var level=levels.data[i];
                html+= '<input type="button" value="'+(i+1)+'">';
            };
            $('#levelselectscreen').html(html);

            // Set the button click event handlers to load level
            $('#levelselectscreen input').click(function(){
                levels.load(this.value-1);
                $('#levelselectscreen').hide();
            });
        },

        // Load all data and images for a specific level
        load:function(number){
        }
}
```

The levels object has a data array that contains information about each of the levels. For now, the only level information we store is a background and foreground image. However, we will be adding information about the hero characters, the villains, and the destructible entities within each level. This will allow us to add new levels very quickly by just adding new items to the array.

The next thing the levels object contains is an init() function that goes through the level data and dynamically generates buttons for each of the levels. The level button click event handlers are set to call the load() method for each level and then hide the level selection screen.

We will call levels.init() from inside the game.init() method to generate the level selection screen buttons. The game.init() method now looks as shown in Listing 2-6.

Listing 2-6. Initializing Levels from game.init()

```
init: function(){
    // Initialize objects
    levels.init();

    // Hide all game layers and display the start screen
    $('.gamelayer').hide();
    $('#gamestartscreen').show();
```

```
    //Get handler for game canvas and context
    game.canvas = $('#gamecanvas')[0];
    game.context = game.canvas.getContext('2d');
},
```

We also need to add some CSS styling for the buttons inside styles.css, as shown in Listing 2-7.

Listing 2-7. CSS Styles for the Level Selection Screen

```
/* Level Selection Screen */
#levelselectscreen {
    padding-top:150px;
    padding-left:50px;
}

#levelselectscreen input {
    margin:20px;
    cursor:pointer;
    background:url(images/icons/level.png) no-repeat;
    color:yellow;
    font-size: 20px;
    width:64px;
    height:64px;
    border:0;
}
```

The next thing we need to do is create inside the game object a simple game.showLevelScreen() method that hides the main menu screen and displays the level selection screen, as shown in Listing 2-8.

Listing 2-8. showLevelScreen Method Inside the game Object

```
showLevelScreen:function(){
    $('.gamelayer').hide();
    $('#levelselectscreen').show('slow');
},
```

This method first hides all the other game layers and then shows the levelselectscreen layer, using a slow animation.

The last thing we need to do is call the game.showLevelScreen() method when the user clicks the Play button. We do this by calling the method from the play image's onclick event:

```
<img src = "images/icons/play.png" alt = "Play Game"
onclick = "game.showLevelScreen()">
```

Now, when we start the game and click the Play button, the game detects the number of levels, hides the main menu, and shows buttons for each of the levels, as shown in Figure 2-3.

Figure 2-3. *The level selection screen*

Right now, we only have a couple of levels showing. However, as we add more levels, the code will automatically detect the levels and add the right number of buttons (formatted properly, thanks to the CSS). When the user clicks these buttons, the browser will call the levels.load() button that we have yet to implement.

Loading Images

Before we implement the levels themselves, we need to put in place the image loader and the loading screen. This will allow us to programmatically load the images for a level and start the game once all the assets have finished loading.

We are going to design a simple loading screen that contains an animated GIF with a progress bar image and some text above it showing the number of images loaded so far. First, we need to add the CSS in Listing 2-9 to styles.css.

Listing 2-9. CSS for the Loading Screen

```
/* Loading Screen */
#loadingscreen {
    background:rgba(100,100,100,0.3);
}

#loadingmessage {
    margin-top:400px;
    text-align:center;
    height:48px;
    color:white;
    background:url(images/loader.gif) no-repeat center;
    font:12px Arial;
}
```

This CSS adds a dim gray color over the game background to let the user know that the game is currently processing something and is not ready to receive any user input. It also displays a loading message in white text.

The next step is to create a JavaScript asset loader based on the code from Chapter 1. The loader will do the work of actually loading the assets and then updating the loadingscreen div.element. We will define a loader object inside game.js, as shown in Listing 2-10.

Listing 2-10. The Image/Sound Asset Loader

```
var loader = {
    loaded:true,
    loadedCount:0, // Assets that have been loaded so far
    totalCount:0, // Total number of assets that need to be loaded

    init:function(){
        // check for sound support
        var mp3Support,oggSupport;
        var audio = document.createElement('audio');
        if (audio.canPlayType) {
                // Currently canPlayType() returns: "", "maybe" or "probably"
            mp3Support = "" != audio.canPlayType('audio/mpeg');
            oggSupport = "" != audio.canPlayType('audio/ogg; codecs = "vorbis"');
        } else {
            //The audio tag is not supported
            mp3Support = false;
            oggSupport = false;
        }

        // Check for ogg, then mp3, and finally set soundFileExtn to undefined
        loader.soundFileExtn = oggSupport?".ogg":mp3Support?".mp3":undefined;
    },

    loadImage:function(url){
        this.totalCount++;
        this.loaded = false;
        $('#loadingscreen').show();
        var image = new Image();
        image.src = url;
        image.onload = loader.itemLoaded;
        return image;
    },
    soundFileExtn:".ogg",
    loadSound:function(url){
        this.totalCount++;
        this.loaded = false;
        $('#loadingscreen').show();
        var audio = new Audio();
        audio.src = url + loader.soundFileExtn;
        audio.addEventListener("canplaythrough", loader.itemLoaded, false);
        return audio;
    },
    itemLoaded:function(){
        loader.loadedCount++;
```

27

```
        $('#loadingmessage').html('Loaded '+loader.loadedCount+' of '+loader.totalCount);
        if (loader.loadedCount === loader.totalCount){
            // Loader has loaded completely..
            loader.loaded=true;
            // Hide the loading screen
            $('#loadingscreen').hide();
            //and call the loader.onload method if it exists
            if(loader.onload){
                loader.onload();
                loader.onload=undefined;
            }
        }
    }
}
}
```

The asset loader in Listing 2-10 has the same elements we discussed in Chapter 1, but it is built in a more modular way. It has the following components:

- An init() method that detects the supported audio file format and saves it.

- Two methods for loading images and audio files—loadImage() and loadSound(). Both methods increment the totalCount variable and show the loading screen when invoked.

- An itemLoaded() method that is invoked each time an asset finishes loading. This method updates the loaded count and the loading message. Once all the assets are loaded, the loading screen is hidden and an optional loader.onload() method is called (if defined). This lets us assign a callback function to call once the images are loaded.

■ **Note**　Using a callback method makes it easy for us to wait while the images are loading and start the game once all the images have loaded.

Before the loader can be used, we need to call the loader.init() method from inside game.init() so that the loader is initialized when the game is getting initialized. The game.init() method now looks as shown in Listing 2-11.

Listing 2-11. Initializing the Loader from game.init()

```
init: function(){
    // Initialize objects
    levels.init();
    loader.init();

    // Hide all game layers and display the start screen
    $('.gamelayer').hide();
    $('#gamestartscreen').show();

    //Get handler for game canvas and context
    game.canvas = $('#gamecanvas')[0];
    game.context = game.canvas.getContext('2d');
},
```

We will use the loader by calling one of the two load methods—loadImage() or loadSound(). When either of these load methods is called, the screen will display the loading screen shown in Figure 2-4 until all the images and sounds are loaded.

Figure 2-4. *The loading screen*

■ **Note**   You can optionally have different images for each of these screens by setting a different background property style for each div.

Loading Levels

Now that we have an image loader in place, we can work on getting the levels loaded. For now, let's start with loading the game background, foreground, and slingshot images by defining a load() method inside the levels object, as shown in Listing 2-12.

Listing 2-12. Basic Skeleton for the load() Method Inside the levels Object

```
// Load all data and images for a specific level
  load:function(number){

      // declare a new currentLevel object
      game.currentLevel ={number:number,hero:[]};
      game.score=0;
      $('#score').html('Score: '+game.score);
      var level=levels.data[number];
```

```
    //load the background, foreground, and slingshot images
    game.currentLevel.backgroundImage = loader.loadImage("images/backgrounds/" + level.background +
".png");
    game.currentLevel.foregroundImage = loader.loadImage("images/backgrounds/" + level.foreground +
".png");
    game.slingshotImage = loader.loadImage("images/slingshot.png");
    game.slingshotFrontImage = loader.loadImage("images/slingshot-front.png");

    //Call game.start() once the assets have loaded
    if(loader.loaded){
        game.start()
    } else {
        loader.onload = game.start;
    }
  }
}
```

The load() function creates a currentLevel object to store the loaded level data. So far we have only loaded three images. We will eventually use this method to load the heroes, villains, and blocks needed to build the game.

One last thing to note is that we call the game.start() method once the images are loaded by either calling it immediately or setting an onload callback. This start() method is where the actual game will be drawn.

Animating the Game

As discussed in Chapter 1, to animate our game, we will call our drawing and animation code multiple times a second using requestAnimationFrame. Before we can use requestAnimationFrame, we need to place the requestAnimation polyfill function from Chapter 1 at the top of game.js so that we can use it from our game code, as shown in Listing 2-13.

Listing 2-13. The requestAnimationFrame Polyfill

```
// Set up requestAnimationFrame and cancelAnimationFrame for use in the game code
(function() {
    var lastTime = 0;
    var vendors = ['ms', 'moz', 'webkit', 'o'];
    for(var x = 0; x < vendors.length && !window.requestAnimationFrame; ++x) {
        window.requestAnimationFrame = window[vendors[x] + 'RequestAnimationFrame'];
        window.cancelAnimationFrame =
          window[vendors[x] + 'CancelAnimationFrame'] ||
window[vendors[x] + 'CancelRequestAnimationFrame'];
    }

    if (!window.requestAnimationFrame)
        window.requestAnimationFrame = function(callback, element) {
            var currTime = new Date().getTime();
            var timeToCall = Math.max(0, 16 - (currTime - lastTime));
            var id = window.setTimeout(function() { callback(currTime + timeToCall); },
              timeToCall);
            lastTime = currTime + timeToCall;
            return id;
        };
```

```
        if (!window.cancelAnimationFrame)
            window.cancelAnimationFrame=function(id) {
                clearTimeout(id);
            };
}());
```

We next use the game.start() method to set up the animation loop, and then we draw the level inside the game.animate() method. The code is shown in Listing 2-14.

Listing 2-14. The start() and animate() Functions Inside the game Object

```
// Game mode
mode:"intro",
// X & Y Coordinates of the slingshot
slingshotX:140,
slingshotY:280,
start:function(){
    $('.gamelayer').hide();
    // Display the game canvas and score
    $('#gamecanvas').show();
    $('#scorescreen').show();

    game.mode="intro";
    game.offsetLeft=0;
    game.ended=false;
    game.animationFrame=window.requestAnimationFrame(game.animate,game.canvas);
},
handlePanning:function(){
    game.offsetLeft++; // Temporary placeholder - keep panning to the right
},
animate:function(){
    // Animate the background
  game.handlePanning();

  // Animate the characters

    //  Draw the background with parallax scrolling

game.context.drawImage(game.currentLevel.backgroundImage,game.offsetLeft/4,0,640,480,0,0,640,480);

game.context.drawImage(game.currentLevel.foregroundImage,game.offsetLeft,0,640,480,0,0,640,480);

    // Draw the slingshot
    game.context.drawImage(game.slingshotImage,game.slingshotX-game.offsetLeft,game.slingshotY);

    game.context.drawImage(game.slingshotFrontImage,game.slingshotX-game.offsetLeft,game.
slingshotY);

      if (!game.ended){
        game.animationFrame=window.requestAnimationFrame(game.animate,game.canvas);
    }
}
```

Again, the preceding code consists of two methods, game.start() and game.animate(). The start() method does the following:

- Initializes a few variables that we need in the game—offsetLeft and mode. offsetLeft will be used for panning the game view around the entire level, and mode will be used to store the current state of the game (intro, wait for firing, firing, fired).

- Hides all other layers and displays the canvas layer and the score layer that is a narrow bar on the top of the screen that contains.

- Sets the game animation interval to call the animate() function by using window.requestAnimationFrame.

The bigger method, animate(), will do all the animation and drawing within our game. The method starts with temporary placeholders for animating the background and characters. We will be implementing these later. We then draw the background and foreground image using the offsetLeft variable to offset the x axis of the images. Finally, we check if the game.ended flag has been set and, if not, use requestAnimationFrame to call animate() again. We can use the game.ended flag later to decide when to stop the animation loop.

One thing to note is that the background image and foreground image are moved at different speeds relative to the scroll left: the background image is moved only one-fourth of the distance that the foreground image is moved. This difference in movement speed of the two layers will give us the illusion that the clouds are further away once we start panning around the level.

Finally, we draw the slingshot in the foreground.

■ **Note**   Parallax scrolling is a technique used to create an illusion of depth by moving background images slower than foreground images. This technique exploits the fact that objects at a distance always appear to move slower than objects that are close by.

Before we can try out the code, we need to add a little more CSS styling inside styles.css to implement our score screen panel, as shown in Listing 2-15.

Listing 2-15. CSS for Score Screen Panel

```
/* Score Screen */
#scorescreen  {
    height:60px;
    font: 32px Comic Sans MS;
    text-shadow: 0 0 2px #000;
    color:white;
}

#scorescreen img{
    opacity:0.6;
    top:10px;
    position:relative;
    padding-left:10px;
    cursor:pointer;
}
```

```
#scorescreen #score {
    position:absolute;
    top:5px;
    right:20px;
}
```

The scorescreen layer, unlike the other layers, is just a narrow band at the top of our game. We also add some transparency to ensure that the images (for stopping music and restarting the level) do not distract from the rest of the game.

When we run this code and try to start a level, we should see a basic level with the Score bar in the top-right corner, as shown in Figure 2-5.

Figure 2-5. *A basic level with the score*

Our crude implementation of panning currently causes the screen to slowly pan toward the right until the image is no longer visible. Don't worry, we will be working on a better implementation soon.

As you can see, the clouds in the background move slower than the foreground. We could, potentially, add more layers and move them at different speeds to build more of an effect, but the two images illustrate this effect fairly well.

Now that we have a basic level in place, we will add the ability to handle mouse input and implement panning around the level with game states.

Handling Mouse Input

JavaScript has several events that we can use to capture mouse input—mousedown, mouseup, and mousemove. To keep things simple we will use jQuery to create a separate mouse object inside game.js to handle all the mouse events, as shown in Listing 2-16.

Listing 2-16. Handling Mouse Events

```
var mouse = {
    x:0,
    y:0,
    down:false,
    init:function(){
        $('#gamecanvas').mousemove(mouse.mousemovehandler);
        $('#gamecanvas').mousedown(mouse.mousedownhandler);
        $('#gamecanvas').mouseup(mouse.mouseuphandler);
        $('#gamecanvas').mouseout(mouse.mouseuphandler);
    },
    mousemovehandler:function(ev){
        var offset = $('#gamecanvas').offset();

        mouse.x = ev.pageX - offset.left;
        mouse.y = ev.pageY - offset.top;

        if (mouse.down) {
            mouse.dragging = true;
        }
    },
    mousedownhandler:function(ev){
        mouse.down = true;
        mouse.downX = mouse.x;
        mouse.downY = mouse.y;
        ev.originalEvent.preventDefault();
    },
    mouseuphandler:function(ev){
        mouse.down = false;
        mouse.dragging = false;
    }
}
```

This mouse object has an init() method that sets event handlers for when the mouse is moved, when a mouse button is pressed or released, and when the mouse leaves the canvas area. The following are the three handler methods that we use:

- mousemovehandler(): Uses jQuery's offset() method and the event object's pageX and pageY properties to calculate the x and y coordinates of the mouse relative to the top-left corner of the canvas and stores them. It also checks whether the mouse button is pressed down while the mouse is being moved and, if so, sets the dragging variable to true.

- mousedownhandler(): Sets the mouse.down variable to true and stores the location where the mouse button was pressed. It additionally contains an extra line to prevent the default browser behavior of the click button.

- mouseuphandler(): Sets the down and dragging variables to false. If the mouse leaves the canvas area, we call this same method.

Now that we have these methods in place, we can always add more code to interact with the game elements as needed. We also have access to the mouse.x, mouse.y, mouse.dragging, and mouse.down properties from anywhere within the game. As with all the previous init() methods, we call this method from game.init(), so it now looks as shown in Listing 2-17.

Listing 2-17. Initializing the Mouse from game.init()

```
init: function(){
    // Initialize objects
    levels.init();
    loader.init();
    mouse.init();

    // Hide all game layers and display the start screen
    $('.gamelayer').hide();
    $('#gamestartscreen').show();

    //Get handler for game canvas and context
    game.canvas = $('#gamecanvas')[0];
    game.context = game.canvas.getContext('2d');
},
```

With this bit of functionality in place, let's now implement some basic game states and panning.

Defining Our Game States

Remember the game.mode variable that we briefly mentioned earlier when we were creating game.start()? Well, this is where it comes into the picture. We will be storing the current state of our game in this variable. Some of the modes or states that we expect our game to go through are as follows:

- intro: The level has just loaded and the game will pan around the level once to show the player everything in the level.

- load-next-hero: The game checks whether there is another hero to load onto the slingshot and, if so, loads the hero. If we run out of heroes or all the villains have been destroyed, the level ends.

- wait-for-firing: The game pans back to the slingshot area and waits for the user to fire the "hero." At this point, we are waiting for the user to click the hero. The user may also optionally drag the canvas screen with the mouse to pan around the level.

- firing: This happens after the user clicks the hero but before the user releases the mouse button. At this point, we are waiting for the user to drag the mouse around to decide the angle and height at which to fire the hero.

- fired: This happens after the user releases the mouse button. At this point, we launch the hero and let the physics engine handle everything while the user just watches. The game will pan so that the user can follow the path of the hero as far as possible.

We may implement more states as needed. One thing to note about these different states is that only one of them is possible at a time, and there are clear conditions for transitioning from one state to another, and what is possible during each state. This construct is popularly known as a *finite state machine* in computer science. We will be using these states to create some simple conditions for our panning code, as shown in Listing 2-18. All of this code goes inside the game object after the start() method.

Listing 2-18. Implementing Panning Using the Game Modes

```
// Maximum panning speed per frame in pixels
maxSpeed:3,
```

```
// Minimum and Maximum panning offset
minOffset:0,
maxOffset:300,
// Current panning offset
offsetLeft:0,
// The game score
score:0,

//Pan the screen to center on newCenter
panTo:function(newCenter){
    if (Math.abs(newCenter-game.offsetLeft-game.canvas.width/4)>0
        && game.offsetLeft<= game.maxOffset && game.offsetLeft>= game.minOffset){

        var deltaX=Math.round((newCenter-game.offsetLeft-game.canvas.width/4)/2);
        if (deltaX && Math.abs(deltaX)>game.maxSpeed){
            deltaX=game.maxSpeed*Math.abs(deltaX)/(deltaX);
        }
        game.offsetLeft += deltaX;
    } else {

        return true;

    }
    if (game.offsetLeft<game.minOffset){
        game.offsetLeft=game.minOffset;
        return true;
    } else if (game.offsetLeft>game.maxOffset){
        game.offsetLeft=game.maxOffset;
        return true;
    }
    return false;
},
handlePanning:function(){
    if(game.mode=="intro"){
        if(game.panTo(700)){
            game.mode="load-next-hero";
        }
    }

    if(game.mode=="wait-for-firing"){
        if (mouse.dragging){
            game.panTo(mouse.x+game.offsetLeft)
        } else {
            game.panTo(game.slingshotX);
        }
    }

    if (game.mode=="load-next-hero"){
        // TODO:
        // Check if any villains are alive, if not, end the level (success)
        // Check if there are any more heroes left to load, if not end the level (failure)
```

```
            // Load the hero and set mode to wait-for-firing
            game.mode = "wait-for-firing";
        }

    if(game.mode == "firing"){
        game.panTo(game.slingshotX);
    }

    if (game.mode == "fired"){
        // TODO:
        // Pan to wherever the hero currently is
    }
},
```

We first create a method called panTo() that slowly pans the screen to a given x coordinate and returns true if the coordinate is near the center of the screen or if the screen has panned to the extreme left or right. It also caps the panning speed using maxSpeed so that the panning never becomes too fast. We have also improved the handlePanning() method so it implements a few of the game states we described earlier. We haven't implemented the load-current-hero, firing, and fired states yet.

If we run the code we have so far, we will see that as the level starts, the screen pans toward the right until we reach the right extreme and panTo() returns true (see Figure 2-6). The game mode then changes from intro to wait-for-firing and the screen slowly pans back to the starting position and waits for user input. We can also drag the mouse to the left or right of the screen to look around the level.

Figure 2-6. *The final result: panning around the level*

Summary

In this chapter we set out to develop the basic framework for our game.

We started by defining and implementing a splash screen and game menu. We then created a simple level system and an asset loader to dynamically load the images used by each level. We set up the game canvas and animation loop and implemented parallax scrolling to give the illusion of depth. We used game states to simplify our game flow and move around our level in an interesting way. Finally, we captured and used mouse events to let the user pan around the level.

At this point we have a basic game world that we can interact with, so we are ready to add the various game entities and game physics.

In the next chapter we will be learning the basics of the Box2D physics engine and using it to model the physics for our game. We will learn how to animate our characters using data from the physics engine. We will then integrate this engine with our existing framework so that the game entities move realistically within our game world, after which we can actually start playing the game.

CHAPTER 3

Physics Engine Basics

A physics engine is a program that provides an approximate simulation of a game world by creating a mathematical model for all the object interactions and collisions within the game. It accounts for gravity, elasticity, friction, and conservation of momentum between colliding objects so that the objects move in a believable way. For our game, we are going to be using an existing and very popular physics engine called Box2D.

The Box2D engine is a free, open source physics engine that was originally written in C++ by Erin Catto. It has been used in a lot of popular physics-based games, including *Crayon Physics Deluxe*, *Rolando*, and *Angry Birds*. The engine has since been ported to several other languages, including Java, ActionScript, C#, and JavaScript. We will be using a JavaScript port of Box2D known as Box2dWeb. You can find the latest source code and documentation for Box2dWeb at http://code.google.com/p/box2dweb/.

Before we start integrating the engine into our own game, let's go over some of the basic components of creating and simulating worlds using Box2D.

Box2D Fundamentals

Box2D uses a few basic objects to define and simulate the game world. The most important of these objects are as follows:

- *World*: The main Box2D object that contains all the world objects and simulates the game physics.

- *Body*: A rigid body that may consist of one or more shapes attached to the body via fixtures.

- *Shape*: A two-dimensional shape such as a circle or a polygon, which are the fundamental shapes used within Box2D.

- *Fixture*: Used to attach a shape to a body for collision detection. Fixtures hold additional, non-geometric data such as friction, collision and filters.

- *Joint*: Used to constrain two bodies together in different ways. For example, a revolute joint constrains two bodies to share a common point while they are free to rotate about the point.

When using Box2D in our game, we first need to define the game world. We then add bodies and their corresponding shapes using fixtures. Once this is done, we step through the world and let Box2D move the bodies around. Finally, we draw the bodies after each step. Most of the heavy lifting is done by the Box2D world object.

Now let's look at these steps in more detail as we use Box2D to create a simple world.

Setting Up Box2D

We will start with a simple HTML file just like in the previous chapters (box2d.html). The first thing we need to do is include a reference to the Box2dWeb library (Box2dWeb-2.1.a.3.min.js) in the head section of the HTML file (see Listing 3-1).

Listing 3-1. Basic HTML5 File for Box2D (box2d.html)

```html
<!DOCTYPE html>
<html>
    <head>
        <meta http-equiv="Content-type" content="text/html; charset=utf-8">
        <title>Box2d Test</title>
        <script src="Box2dWeb-2.1.a.3.min.js" type="text/javascript" charset="utf-8"></script>
        <script src="box2d.js" type="text/javascript" charset="utf-8"></script>
    </head>
    <body onload="init();">
        <canvas id="canvas" width="640" height="480" style="border:1px solid black;">Your browser
does not support HTML5 Canvas</canvas>
    </body>
</html>
```

As you see in Listing 3-1, the box2d.html file consists of only a single canvas element that we will be drawing on. We refer to two JavaScript files: the Box2dWeb library file and a second file that we will use to store all our JavaScript code (box2d.js). Once the HTML file has loaded completely, it will call an init() function that we will use to initialize the Box2D world and start animating.

Referencing the Box2dWeb JavaScript file gives us access to the Box2D object in our JavaScript code. This object contains all the objects that we will need, including the world (Box2D.Dynamics.b2World) and the body (Box2D.Dynamics.b2Body).

It is convenient to define the commonly used objects as variables to save us some typing effort when we reference them. The first thing we will do in our JavaScript file (box2d.js) is to declare these variables (see Listing 3-2).

Listing 3-2. Defining Commonly Used Objects as Variables

```javascript
// Declare all the commonly used objects as variables for convenience
var b2Vec2 = Box2D.Common.Math.b2Vec2;
var b2BodyDef = Box2D.Dynamics.b2BodyDef;
var b2Body = Box2D.Dynamics.b2Body;
var b2FixtureDef = Box2D.Dynamics.b2FixtureDef;
var b2Fixture = Box2D.Dynamics.b2Fixture;
var b2World = Box2D.Dynamics.b2World;
var b2PolygonShape = Box2D.Collision.Shapes.b2PolygonShape;
var b2CircleShape = Box2D.Collision.Shapes.b2CircleShape;
var b2DebugDraw = Box2D.Dynamics.b2DebugDraw;
var b2RevoluteJointDef = Box2D.Dynamics.Joints.b2RevoluteJointDef;
```

Once we define these variables as shortcuts, we can access the Box2D.Dynamics.b2World by using the b2World variable. Now, let's start defining our world.

Defining the World

The `Box2D.Dynamics.b2World` object is the heart of Box2D. It contains methods for adding and removing objects, methods for simulating physics in incremental steps, and even an option for drawing the world on a canvas. Before we can start using Box2D, we need to create the `b2World` object. We do this in an `init()` function that we create inside our JavaScript file (`box2d.js`), as shown in Listing 3-3.

Listing 3-3. Creating the b2World Object

```
var world;
var scale = 30; //30 pixels on our canvas correspond to 1 meter in the Box2d world
function init(){
    // Set up the Box2d world that will do most of the physics calculation
    var gravity = new b2Vec2(0,9.8); //declare gravity as 9.8 m/s^2 downward
    var allowSleep = true; //Allow objects that are at rest to fall asleep and be excluded from
calculations
    world = new b2World(gravity,allowSleep);
}
```

The `init()` function starts by defining `b2World` and passing the following two parameters to its constructor:

- `gravity`: Defined as a vector using a `b2Vec2` object, which takes two parameters, the x and y components. We set the world's gravity to be 9.8 meters per square second in the downward direction. The ability to set a custom gravity lets us simulate environments with different gravity fields, such as the moon or fantasy worlds with very low or very high gravity. We can also set `gravity` to 0 and use only the collision detection features of Box2D for games where we don't need gravity (space-based games or top-down view games like racing games).

- `allowSleep`: Used by `b2World` to decide whether or not to include objects that are at rest during its simulation calculations. Allowing objects that are at rest to be excluded from calculations reduces the number of unnecessary calculations and thus helps improve performance. Even if an object is asleep, it will wake up if a moving body collides with it.

One other thing that we do within our code is define a `scale` variable that we will use to convert between Box2D units (meters) and our game units (pixels).

▪ **Note** Box2D use the metric system for all its calculations. It works best with objects that are between 0.1 meter to 10 meters large. Since we use pixels when drawing on our canvas, we will need to convert between pixels and meters. A commonly used scale is 30 pixels to 1 meter.

Now that we have a basic world, we need to start adding bodies to it. The first body we will create is a static floor at the bottom of our world.

Adding Our First Body: The Floor

Creating any body in Box2D involves the following steps:

1. Declare a body definition in a `b2BodyDef` object. The `b2BodyDef` object contains details such as the position of the body (x and y coordinates) and the type of body (static or dynamic). Static bodies are not affected by gravity and collisions with other bodies.

2. Declare a fixture definition in a b2FixtureDef object. This is used to attach a shape to the body. A fixture definition also contains additional information such as density, friction coefficient, and the coefficient of restitution for the attached shape.

3. Set the shape of the fixture definition. The two types of shapes that are used in Box2D are polygons (b2PolygonShape) and circles (b2CircleShape).

4. Pass the body definition object to the createBody() method of the world and get back a body object.

5. Pass the fixture definition to the createFixture() method of the body object and attach the shape to the body.

Now that we know these basic steps, we will create our first body inside the world: the floor. We will do this by creating a createFloor() method right below the init() function we created earlier. This is shown in Listing 3-4.

Listing 3-4. Creating the Floor

```
function createFloor(){
    //A body definition holds all the data needed to construct a rigid body.
    var bodyDef = new b2BodyDef;
    bodyDef.type = b2Body.b2_staticBody;
    bodyDef.position.x = 640/2/scale;
    bodyDef.position.y = 450/scale;

    // A fixture is used to attach a shape to a body for collision detection.
    // A fixture definition is used to create a fixture.
    var fixtureDef = new b2FixtureDef;
    fixtureDef.density = 1.0;
    fixtureDef.friction = 0.5;
    fixtureDef.restitution = 0.2;

    fixtureDef.shape = new b2PolygonShape;
    fixtureDef.shape.SetAsBox(320/scale,10/scale); //640 pixels wide and 20 pixels tall

    var body = world.CreateBody(bodyDef);
    var fixture = body.CreateFixture(fixtureDef);
}
```

The first thing we do is define a bodyDef object. We set its type to be static (b2Body.b2_staticBody) since we want our floor to stay in the same place and not be affected by gravity or collisions with other bodies. We then set the position of the body near the bottom of our canvas (x = 320 pixels, y = 450 pixels) and use the scale variable to convert the pixels to meters for Box2D.

■ **Note** Unlike the canvas, where the position of rectangles is based on the top-left corner, the Box2D body position is based on the origin of the object. In the case of boxes created using SetAsBox(), this origin is at the center of the box.

The next thing we do is to define the fixture definition (fixtureDef). The fixture definition contains values like the density, the frictional coefficient, and the coefficient of restitution of its attached shape. The density is used to calculate the weight of the body, the frictional coefficient is used to make sure the body slides realistically, and the restitution is used to make the body bounce.

■ **Note**   The higher the coefficient of restitution, the more "bouncy" the object becomes. Values close to 0 mean that the body will not bounce and will lose most of its momentum in a collision (called an inelastic collision). Values close to 1 mean that the body retains most of its momentum and will bounce back as fast as it came (called an elastic collision).

We then set the shape for the fixture as a b2PolygonShape object. The b2PolygonShape object has a helper method called SetAsBox() that sets the polygon as a box which is centered on the origin of the parent body. The SetAsBox() method takes the half-width and half-height (the extents) of the box as parameters. Again, we use the scale variable to define a box that is 640 pixels wide and 20 pixels high.

Finally we create the body by passing bodyDef to world.CreateBody() and create the fixture by passing the fixtureDef to body.CreateFixture().

One other thing we need to do is call this newly created method from inside the init() function we declared earlier so that this body is created when the init() function is called. The init() function will now look like Listing 3-5.

Listing 3-5. Calling createFloor() from init()

```
function init(){
    // Set up the box2d World that will do most of the physics calculation
    var gravity = new b2Vec2(0,9.8); //declare gravity as 9.8 m/s^2 downward
    var allowSleep = true; //Allow objects that are at rest to fall asleep and be excluded from
calculations
    world = new b2World(gravity,allowSleep);

    createFloor();
}
```

Now that we have added our first body to the world, we need to learn how to draw the world so that we can see what we have created so far.

Drawing the World: Setting Up Debug Drawing

Box2D is primarily meant to be used only as an engine that handles physics calculations while we handle drawing all the objects in the world ourselves. However, the Box2D world object provides us with a simple DrawDebugData() method that we can use to draw the world on a given canvas.

The DrawDebugData() method draws a very simple representation of the bodies inside the world and is best used for helping us visualize the world while we are creating it.

Before we can use DrawDebugData(), we need to set up debug drawing by defining a b2DebugDraw() object and passing it to the world.SetDebugDraw() method. We do this in a setupDebugDraw() method that we will place below the createFloor() method inside box2d.js (see Listing 3-6).

Listing 3-6. Setting Up Debug Drawing

```
var context;
function setupDebugDraw(){
    context = document.getElementById('canvas').getContext('2d');

    var debugDraw = new b2DebugDraw();
```

```
    // Use this canvas context for drawing the debugging screen
    debugDraw.SetSprite(context);
    // Set the scale
    debugDraw.SetDrawScale(scale);
    // Fill boxes with an alpha transparency of 0.3
    debugDraw.SetFillAlpha(0.3);
    // Draw lines with a thickness of 1
    debugDraw.SetLineThickness(1.0);
    // Display all shapes and joints
    debugDraw.SetFlags(b2DebugDraw.e_shapeBit | b2DebugDraw.e_jointBit);

    // Start using debug draw in our world
    world.SetDebugDraw(debugDraw);
}
```

We first define a handle to the canvas context. We then create a new b2DebugDraw object and set a few attributes using its Set methods:

- SetSprite(): Used to provide a canvas context for the drawing.

- SetDrawScale(): Used to set the scale to convert between Box2D units and pixels.

- SetFillAlpha() and SetLineThickness(): Used to set drawing styles.

- SetFlags(): Used to choose which Box2D entities to draw. We have selected flags for drawing all shapes and joints, and we use logical OR operators to combine the two flags. Some of the other entities we can ask Box2D to draw are the center of mass (e_centerOfMassBit) and axis-aligned bounding boxes (e_aabbBit).

Finally, we pass the debugDraw object to the world.SetDebugDraw() method. After creating the function, we need to call it from inside the init() function. The init() function will now look like Listing 3-7.

Listing 3-7. Calling setupDebugDraw() from init()

```
function init(){
    // Set up the box2d World that will do most of the physics calculation
    var gravity = new b2Vec2(0,9.8); //declare gravity as 9.8 m/s^2 downward
    var allowSleep = true; //Allow objects that are at rest to fall asleep and be excluded from
calculations
    world = new b2World(gravity,allowSleep);

    createFloor();

    setupDebugDraw();
}
```

Now that debug drawing is set up, we can use the world.DrawDebugData() method to draw the current state of our Box2D world onto the canvas.

Animating the World

Animating a world using Box2D involves the following steps that we repeat within an animation loop:

1. Tell Box2D to run the simulation for a small time step (typically 1/60th of a second). We do this by using the world.Step() function.

2. Draw all the objects in their new positions using either world.DrawDebugData() or our own drawing functions.

3. Clear any forces that we have applied using world.ClearForces().

We can implement these steps in our own animate() function that we create inside box2d.js after init(), shown in Listing 3-8.

Listing 3-8. Setting Up a Box2D Animation Loop

```
var timeStep = 1/60;

//As per the Box2d manual, the suggested iteration count for Box2D is 8 for velocity and 3 for
position.
var velocityIterations = 8;
var positionIterations = 3;

function animate(){
    world.Step(timeStep,velocityIterations,positionIterations);
    world.ClearForces();

    world.DrawDebugData();

    setTimeout(animate, timeStep);

}
```

We first call world.step() and pass it three parameters: time step, velocity iterations, and position iterations.
Box2D uses a computational algorithm called an *integrator*. Integrators simulate the physics equations at discrete points of time. The time step is the amount of time we want Box2D to simulate. We set this to a value of 1/60th of a second.
In addition to the integrator, Box2D also uses a larger bit of code called a *constraint solver*. The constraint solver solves all the constraints in the simulation, one at a time. To get a good solution, we need to iterate over all constraints a number of times. There are two phases in the constraint solver: a velocity phase and a position phase. Each phase has its own iteration count, and we set these two values to 8 and 3, respectively.

■ **Note**   Generally, physics engines for games work well with a time step at least as fast as 60Hz or 1/60 second. As per Erin Catto's original C++ *Box2D v2.2.0 User Manual* (available at http://box2d.org/manual.pdf), it is preferable to keep the time step constant and not vary it with frame rate, as a variable time step produces variable results, which makes it difficult to debug.

Also as per the Box2d C++ manual, the suggested iteration count for Box2D is 8 for velocity and 3 for position. You can tune these numbers to your liking, but keep in mind that this has a trade-off between speed and accuracy. Using fewer iterations increases performance, but accuracy suffers. Likewise, using more iterations decreases performance but improves the quality of your simulation.

After stepping through the simulation, we call `world.ClearForces()` to clear any forces that are applied to the bodies. We then call `world.DrawDebugData()` to draw the world on the canvas.

Finally, we use `setTimeout()` to call our animation loop again after the timeout for the next time step. We use `setTimeout()` for now because it is simpler for us to use the `Box2d.Step()` function with a constant frame rate. In the next chapter, we will look at how to use `requestAnimationFrame()` and a variable frame rate when integrating Box2D with our game.

Now that the animation loop is complete, we can see the world we have created so far by calling these new methods from the `init()` function. The updated `init()` function will now look like Listing 3-9.

Listing 3-9. Updated init() Function

```
function init(){
    // Set up the box2d World that will do most of the physics calculation
    var gravity = new b2Vec2(0,9.8); //declare gravity as 9.8 m/s^2 downward
    var allowSleep = true; //Allow objects that are at rest to fall asleep and be excluded from
calculations
    world = new b2World(gravity,allowSleep);

    createFloor();

    setupDebugDraw();
    animate();
}
```

When we open `box2d.html` in the browser, we should see our world with the floor drawn, as shown in Figure 3-1.

Figure 3-1. Our first Box2D body: the floor

This doesn't look like much yet. The floor is a static body that just stays floating at the bottom of the canvas. However, now that we have set up everything to create our basic world and display it on the screen, we can start adding some more Box2D elements to our world.

More Box2D Elements

Box2D allows us to add different types of elements to our world, including the following:

- Simple bodies that are rectangular, circular, or polygon shaped

- Complex bodies that combine multiple shapes

- Joints such as revolute joints that connect multiple bodies

- Contact listeners that allow us to handle collision events

We will now look at each of these elements in turn in more detail.

Creating a Rectangular Body

We can create a rectangular body just like we created our floor—by defining a b2PolygonShape and using its SetAsBox() method. We will do this within a new method called createRectangularBody() that we will add to box2d.js (see Listing 3-10).

Listing 3-10. Creating a Rectangular Body

```
function createRectangularBody(){
    var bodyDef = new b2BodyDef;
    bodyDef.type = b2Body.b2_dynamicBody;
    bodyDef.position.x = 40/scale;
    bodyDef.position.y = 100/scale;

    var fixtureDef = new b2FixtureDef;
    fixtureDef.density = 1.0;
    fixtureDef.friction = 0.5;
    fixtureDef.restitution = 0.3;

    fixtureDef.shape = new b2PolygonShape;
    fixtureDef.shape.SetAsBox(30/scale,50/scale);

    var body = world.CreateBody(bodyDef);
    var fixture = body.CreateFixture(fixtureDef);
}
```

We create a body definition and place it near the top of the canvas at x = 40 pixels and y = 100 pixels. The one difference this time is that we define the body type as dynamic (b2Body.b2_dynamicBody). This means that the body will be affected by gravity and collisions. We then define the fixture with a polygon shape that is set as a box that is 60 pixels wide and 100 pixels tall. Finally, we add the body to our world.

We will need to add a call to createRectangularBody() inside the init() function so that it is called when the page loads. The init() function will now look like Listing 3-11.

Listing 3-11. Calling createRectangularBody() from init()

```
function init(){
    // Set up the box2d World that will do most of the physics calculation
    var gravity = new b2Vec2(0,9.8); //declare gravity as 9.8 m/s^2 downward
    var allowSleep = true; //Allow objects that are at rest to fall asleep and be excluded from
calculations
    world = new b2World(gravity,allowSleep);

    createFloor();
    // Create some bodies with simple shapes
    createRectangularBody();

    setupDebugDraw();
    animate();
}
```

When we run the code in the browser, we should see the new body that we just created, as shown in Figure 3-2.

Figure 3-2. *Our first dynamic body: a bouncing rectangle*

Since this body is dynamic, it will fall downward because of gravity until it hits the floor, and then it will bounce off the floor. The body rises to a lower height after each bounce until it finally settles down on the floor. If we want, we can change the coefficient of restitution to decide how bouncy the object is.

■ **Note** Once the body comes to rest, Box2D changes the color of the body and makes it darker. This is how Box2D tells us that the object is considered asleep. Box2D will wake a body up if another body collides with it.

Creating a Circular Body

The next body we will create is a simple circular body. We can define a circular shape by setting the shape property to a b2CircleShape object. We will do this within a new method called createCircularBody() that we will add to box2d.js, as shown in Listing 3-12.

Listing 3-12. Creating a Circular Shape

```
function createCircularBody(){
    var bodyDef = new b2BodyDef;
    bodyDef.type = b2Body.b2_dynamicBody;
    bodyDef.position.x = 130/scale;
    bodyDef.position.y = 100/scale;

    var fixtureDef = new b2FixtureDef;
    fixtureDef.density = 1.0;
    fixtureDef.friction = 0.5;
    fixtureDef.restitution = 0.7;

    fixtureDef.shape = new b2CircleShape(30/scale);

    var body = world.CreateBody(bodyDef);
    var fixture = body.CreateFixture(fixtureDef);
}
```

The b2CircleShape constructor takes one parameter, the radius of the circle. The rest of the code, defining a body, defining the fixture, and creating the body, remains very similar to the code for the rectangular body.

One change we have made is to increase the restitution value to 0.7, which is much higher than the value we used for our previous rectangular body. We need to call createCircularBody() from inside the init() function. The init() function will now look like Listing 3-13.

Listing 3-13. Calling createCircularBody() from init()

```
function init(){
    // Set up the box2d World that will do most of the physics calculation
    var gravity = new b2Vec2(0,9.8); //declare gravity as 9.8 m/s^2 downward
    var allowSleep = true; //Allow objects that are at rest to fall asleep and be excluded from
calculations
    world = new b2World(gravity,allowSleep);

    createFloor();
    // Create some bodies with simple shapes
    createRectangularBody();
    createCircularBody();

    setupDebugDraw();
    animate();
}
```

Once we do this and run the code, we should see the new circular body that we just created (as shown in Figure 3-3).

Figure 3-3. *A bouncier circular body*

You will notice that the circular body bounces much higher than the rectangular one, and takes a longer time to come to rest. This is because of the larger coefficient of restitution. When creating your own game, you can play around with these values until they feel right for your game.

Creating a Polygon-Shaped Body

The last simple shape we will create is the polygon. Box2D allows us to create any polygon we want by defining the coordinates of each of the points. The only restriction is that polygons need to be convex polygons.

To create a polygon, we first need to create an array of b2Vec2 objects with the coordinates of each of its points, and then we need to pass the array to the shape.SetAsArray() method. We will do this within a new method called createSimplePolygonBody() that we will add to box2d.js (see Listing 3-14).

Listing 3-14. Defining a Polygon Shape with Points

```
function createSimplePolygonBody(){
    var bodyDef = new b2BodyDef;
    bodyDef.type = b2Body.b2_dynamicBody;
    bodyDef.position.x = 230/scale;
    bodyDef.position.y = 50/scale;

    var fixtureDef = new b2FixtureDef;
    fixtureDef.density = 1.0;
    fixtureDef.friction = 0.5;
    fixtureDef.restitution = 0.2;
```

```
    fixtureDef.shape = new b2PolygonShape;
    // Create an array of b2Vec2 points in clockwise direction
    var points = [
        new b2Vec2(0,0),
        new b2Vec2(40/scale,50/scale),
        new b2Vec2(50/scale,100/scale),
        new b2Vec2(-50/scale,100/scale),
        new b2Vec2(-40/scale,50/scale),

    ];
    // Use SetAsArray to define the shape using the points array
    fixtureDef.shape.SetAsArray(points,points.length);

    var body = world.CreateBody(bodyDef);

    var fixture = body.CreateFixture(fixtureDef);
}
```

We defined a `points` array that contains the coordinates for each of the polygon points inside b2Vec2 objects. The following are a few things to note:

- All the coordinates are relative to the body origin. The first point (0,0) starts at the origin of the body and will be placed at the body position (230,50).

- We do not need to close out the polygon. Box2D will take care of this for us.

- All points must be defined in a clockwise direction.

■ **Tip**   If we define the coordinates in the counter-clockwise direction, Box2D will not be able to handle collisions correctly. If you find objects passing through each other, check to see whether you have defined points in the clockwise direction.

We then call the `SetAsArray()` method and pass it two parameters: the `points` array and the number of points. The rest of the code remains the same as it was for the previous shapes we covered.

Now we need to call `createSimplePolygonBody()` from the `init()` function. The `init()` function will now look like Listing 3-15.

Listing 3-15. Calling createSimplePolygonBody() from init()

```
function init(){
    // Set up the box2d World that will do most of the physics calculation
    var gravity = new b2Vec2(0,9.8); //declare gravity as 9.8 m/s^2 downward
    var allowSleep = true; //Allow objects that are at rest to fall asleep and be excluded from
calculations
    world = new b2World(gravity,allowSleep);
```

```
    createFloor();
    // Create some bodies with simple shapes
    createRectangularBody();
    createCircularBody();
    createSimplePolygonBody();

    setupDebugDraw();
    animate();
}
```

If we run this code, we should see our new polygon-shaped body (see Figure 3-4).

Figure 3-4. *A polygon-shaped body*

We now have created three simple bodies, with different shapes and properties. These simple shapes are usually enough to model a wide array of objects within our games (fruits, tires, crates, and so forth). Sometimes, however, these shapes are not enough. There are times when we need to create more complex objects that combine more than one shape.

Creating Complex Bodies with Multiple Shapes

So far we have been creating simple bodies with a single shape. However, as previously mentioned, Box2D lets us create bodies that contain multiple shapes.

To create a complex shape, all we need to do is attach multiple fixtures (each with its own shape) to the same body. Let's try to combine two of the shapes we just learned about into a single body: a circle and a polygon. We will do this within a new method called `createComplexPolygonBody()` that we will add to `box2d.js` (see Listing 3-16).

Listing 3-16. Creating a Body with Two Shapes

```
function createComplexBody(){
    var bodyDef = new b2BodyDef;
    bodyDef.type = b2Body.b2_dynamicBody;
    bodyDef.position.x = 350/scale;
    bodyDef.position.y = 50/scale;
    var body = world.CreateBody(bodyDef);

    //Create first fixture and attach a circular shape to the body
    var fixtureDef = new b2FixtureDef;
    fixtureDef.density = 1.0;
    fixtureDef.friction = 0.5;
    fixtureDef.restitution = 0.7;
    fixtureDef.shape = new b2CircleShape(40/scale);
    body.CreateFixture(fixtureDef);

    // Create second fixture and attach a polygon shape to the body
    fixtureDef.shape = new b2PolygonShape;
    var points = [
        new b2Vec2(0,0),
        new b2Vec2(40/scale,50/scale),
        new b2Vec2(50/scale,100/scale),
        new b2Vec2(-50/scale,100/scale),
        new b2Vec2(-40/scale,50/scale),
    ];
    fixtureDef.shape.SetAsArray(points,points.length);
    body.CreateFixture(fixtureDef);
}
```

We first create a body, and then two different fixtures—the first for a circular shape and the second for a polygon shape. We then attach both these fixtures to the body using the CreateFixture() method. Box2D will automatically take care of creating a single rigid body that includes both these shapes.

Now that we have created createComplexBody(), we need to call it from inside the init() function. The init() function will now look like Listing 3-17.

Listing 3-17. Calling createComplexBody() from init()

```
function init(){
    // Set up the box2d World that will do most of the physics calculation
    var gravity = new b2Vec2(0,9.8); //declare gravity as 9.8 m/s^2 downward
    var allowSleep = true; //Allow objects that are at rest to fall asleep and be excluded from
calculations
    world = new b2World(gravity,allowSleep);

    createFloor();

    // Create some bodies with simple shapes
    createRectangularBody();
    createCircularBody();
    createSimplePolygonBody();
```

```
    // Create a body combining two shapes
    createComplexBody();

    setupDebugDraw();
    animate();
}
```

When we run this code, we should see our new complex body, as shown in Figure 3-5.

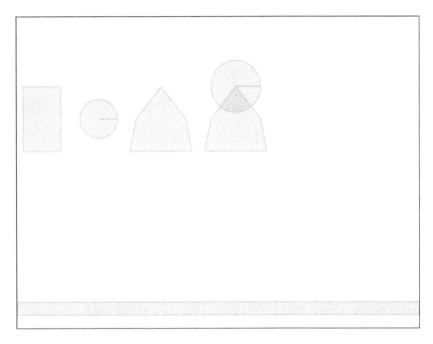

Figure 3-5. *A complex body with two shapes*

You will notice that the two shapes behave as one single unit. This is because Box2D treats these multiple shapes as a single rigid body. This ability to combine shapes allows us to emulate any kind of object we want, such as trees and tables.

It also allows us to get around the limitations on creating concave polygon shapes, since any concave polygon can be broken into multiple convex polygons.

Connecting Bodies with Joints

Now that we know how to make different types of bodies in Box2D, we will take a brief look at creating joints.

Joints are used to constrain bodies to the world or to each other. Box2D supports many different types of joints, including pulley, gear, distance, revolute, and weld joints.

Some of these joints restrict motion (for example, the distance joint and the weld joint), while others allow for interesting types of movement (for example, the pulley joint and the revolute joint). Some joints even provide motors that can be used to drive the joint at a specified speed. We will take a look at one of the simpler joints that Box2D offers: the revolute joint.

The revolute joint forces two bodies to share a common anchor point, often called a hinge point. What this means is that the bodies are attached to each other at this point, and can rotate about that point.

We can create a revolute joint by defining a b2RevoluteJointDef object and then passing it to the world.CreateJoint() method. This is illustrated in the createRevoluteJoint() method that we add to box2d.js (see Listing 3-18).

Listing 3-18. Creating a Revolute Joint

```
function createRevoluteJoint(){
    //Define the first body
    var bodyDef1 = new b2BodyDef;
    bodyDef1.type = b2Body.b2_dynamicBody;
    bodyDef1.position.x = 480/scale;
    bodyDef1.position.y = 50/scale;
    var body1 = world.CreateBody(bodyDef1);

    //Create first fixture and attach a rectangular shape to the body
    var fixtureDef1 = new b2FixtureDef;
    fixtureDef1.density = 1.0;
    fixtureDef1.friction = 0.5;
    fixtureDef1.restitution = 0.5;
    fixtureDef1.shape = new b2PolygonShape;
    fixtureDef1.shape.SetAsBox(50/scale,10/scale);

    body1.CreateFixture(fixtureDef1);

    // Define the second body
    var bodyDef2 = new b2BodyDef;
    bodyDef2.type = b2Body.b2_dynamicBody;
    bodyDef2.position.x = 470/scale;
    bodyDef2.position.y = 50/scale;
    var body2 = world.CreateBody(bodyDef2);

    //Create second fixture and attach a polygon shape to the body
    var fixtureDef2 = new b2FixtureDef;
    fixtureDef2.density = 1.0;
    fixtureDef2.friction = 0.5;
    fixtureDef2.restitution = 0.5;
    fixtureDef2.shape = new b2PolygonShape;
    var points = [
        new b2Vec2(0,0),
        new b2Vec2(40/scale,50/scale),
        new b2Vec2(50/scale,100/scale),
        new b2Vec2(-50/scale,100/scale),
        new b2Vec2(-40/scale,50/scale),
    ];
    fixtureDef2.shape.SetAsArray(points,points.length);
    body2.CreateFixture(fixtureDef2);

    // Create a joint between body1 and body2
    var jointDef = new b2RevoluteJointDef;
    var jointCenter = new b2Vec2(470/scale,50/scale);
```

```
        jointDef.Initialize(body1, body2, jointCenter);
        world.CreateJoint(jointDef);
}
```

In this code we first define two bodies, a rectangle (body1) and a polygon (body2), that are positioned on top of each other, and then we add them to the world.

We then create a b2RevolutionJointDef object and initialize it by passing three parameters to the Initialize() method: the two bodies (body1 and body2), and the joint center, which is the point around which the joints rotate.

Finally, we call world.CreateJoint() to add the joint to the world.

We need to call createRevoluteJoint() from our init() function. The init() function will now look like Listing 3-19.

Listing 3-19. Calling createRevoluteJoint() from init()

```
function init(){
    // Set up the box2d World that will do most of the physics calculation
    var gravity = new b2Vec2(0,9.8); //declare gravity as 9.8 m/s^2 downward
    var allowSleep = true; //Allow objects that are at rest to fall asleep and be excluded from
calculations
    world = new b2World(gravity,allowSleep);

    createFloor();

    // Create some bodies with simple shapes
    createRectangularBody();
    createCircularBody();
    createSimplePolygonBody();

    // Create a body combining two shapes
    createComplexBody();

    // Join two bodies using a revolute joint
    createRevoluteJoint();

    setupDebugDraw();
    animate();
}
```

When we run our code, we should see our revolute joint in action. You can see this in Figure 3-6.

Figure 3-6. *A revolute joint in action*

As you can see, the rectangular body rotates about its anchor point, almost like a windmill blade. This is very different from the complex body we created earlier, where the shapes acted like a single body.

Each of the joints in Box2D can be combined in different ways to create interesting motions and effects, such as pulleys, ragdolls, and pendulums. You can read more about these other types of joints in the Box2D reference API, which you can find at http://www.box2dflash.org/docs/2.1a/reference/. Note that this is for the Flash version of Box2D that our JavaScript version is based on. We can still refer to the method signatures and documentation in this Flash version when developing for the JavaScript version because the JavaScript version of Box2D was developed by directly converting the Flash version, and the method signatures remain the same across the two.

Tracking Collisions and Damage

One thing that you may have noticed in the previous few examples is that some of the bodies were colliding against each other and bouncing back and forth. It would be nice to be able to keep track of these collisions and the amount of impact they cause, and simulate a body getting damaged.

Before we can track the damage to an object, we need to be able to associate a life or health with it. Box2D provides us with methods that allow us to set custom properties for any body, fixture, or joint. We can assign any JavaScript object as a custom property for a body by calling its SetUserData() method, and retrieve the property later by calling its GetUserData() method.

Let's create another body that will have its own health unlike any of the previous bodies. We will do this inside a method called createSpecialBody() that we will add to box2d.js (see Listing 3-20).

Listing 3-20. Creating a Special Body with Its Own Properties

```
var specialBody;
function createSpecialBody(){
    var bodyDef = new b2BodyDef;
    bodyDef.type = b2Body.b2_dynamicBody;
    bodyDef.position.x = 450/scale;
    bodyDef.position.y = 0/scale;

    specialBody = world.CreateBody(bodyDef);
    specialBody.SetUserData({name:"special",life:250})

    //Create a fixture to attach a circular shape to the body
    var fixtureDef = new b2FixtureDef;
    fixtureDef.density = 1.0;
    fixtureDef.friction = 0.5;
    fixtureDef.restitution = 0.5;

    fixtureDef.shape = new b2CircleShape(30/scale);

    var fixture = specialBody.CreateFixture(fixtureDef);
}
```

The code for creating this body is similar to the code for creating a circular body that we looked at earlier. The only difference is that once we create the body, we call its SetUserData() method and pass it an object parameter with two custom properties, name and life.

We can add as many properties as we like to this object. Also, note that we saved a reference to the body in a variable called specialBody that we defined outside the function. This way, we can refer to this body outside of the function.

If we call createSpecialBody() from the init() function, we won't see anything exceptional—just another bouncing circle. We still want to be able to track collisions happening to this body. This is where contact listeners come in.

Contact Listeners

Box2D provides us with objects called contact listeners that let us define event handlers for several contact-related events. To do this, we must first define a b2ContactListener object and override one or more of the events we want to monitor. The b2ContactListener has four events we can use based on what we need:

- BeginContact(): Called when two fixtures begin to touch.

- EndContact(): Called when two fixtures cease to touch.

- PostSolve(): Lets us inspect a contact after the solver is finished. This is useful for inspecting impulses.

- PreSolve(): Lets us inspect a contact before it goes to the solver.

Once we override the methods that we need, we need to pass the contact listener to the world.SetContactListener() method. Since we want to track the damage a collision causes, we will listen to the PostSolve() event, which provides us with the impulse transferred during a collision (see Listing 3-21).

Listing 3-21. Implementing a Contact Listener

```
function listenForContact(){
    var listener = new Box2D.Dynamics.b2ContactListener;
    listener.PostSolve = function(contact,impulse){
        var body1 = contact.GetFixtureA().GetBody();
        var body2 = contact.GetFixtureB().GetBody();

        // If either of the bodies is the special body, reduce its life
        if (body1 == specialBody || body2 == specialBody){
            var impulseAlongNormal = impulse.normalImpulses[0];
            specialBody.GetUserData().life -= impulseAlongNormal;
            console.log("The special body was in a collision with impulse", impulseAlongNormal,"and
its life has now become ",specialBody.GetUserData().life);
        }
    };
    world.SetContactListener(listener);
}
```

As you can see, we create a b2ContactListener object and override its PostSolve() method with our own handler. The PostSolve() method provides us with two parameters: contact, which contains details of the fixtures that were involved in the collision, and impulse, which contains the normal and tangential impulse during the collision.

Within PostSolve(), we first extract the two bodies involved in the collision and check to see if our special body is one of them. If it is, we extract the impulse along the normal between the two bodies, and subtract life points from the body. We also log this event to the console so we can track each collision.

Obviously, this is a rather simplistic way of handling object damage, but it does what we need it to do. The greater the impulse in a collision, and the higher the number of collisions, the faster the body loses health.

■ **Note**　The PostSolve() method is called for every collision that takes place in the Box2D world, no matter how small. It is even called when an object is rolling on another. Be aware that this method will be called a lot.

Next we call both createSimpleBody() and listenForContact() from init(). The init() function will now look like Listing 3-22.

Listing 3-22. Calling createSpecialBody() and listenForContact() from init()

```
function init(){
    // Set up the box2d World that will do most of the physics calculation
    var gravity = new b2Vec2(0,9.8); //declare gravity as 9.8 m/s^2 downward
    var allowSleep = true; //Allow objects that are at rest to fall asleep and be excluded from
calculations
    world = new b2World(gravity,allowSleep);

    createFloor();

    // Create some bodies with simple shapes
    createRectangularBody();
    createCircularBody();
    createSimplePolygonBody();
```

```
    // Create a body combining two shapes
    createComplexBody();

    // Join two bodies using a revolute joint
    createRevoluteJoint();

    // Create a body with special user data
    createSpecialBody();

    // Create contact listeners and track events
    listenForContact();

    setupDebugDraw();
    animate();
}
```

If we run our code now, we should see the circle bouncing about, with a message in the browser console after each collision telling us how much the body's health has dropped, as shown in Figure 3-7.

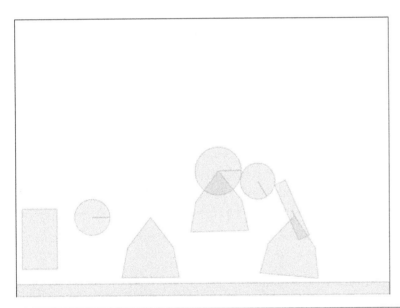

Figure 3-7. Watching collisions with Contact Listeners

It is nice to be able to track the life of our special body, but it would be nicer if we could do something when it runs out of life.

Now that we have access to `specialBody` and the `life` property, we can check after every iteration to see if the body life has reached 0 and, if so, remove it from the world using the `world.DestroyBody()` method. The easiest place to do this check is in the `animate()` method. The `animate()` function will now look like Listing 3-23.

Listing 3-23. Destroying the Body

```
function animate(){
    world.Step(timeStep,velocityIterations,positionIterations);
    world.ClearForces();

    world.DrawDebugData();

    //Kill Special Body if Dead
    if (specialBody && specialBody.GetUserData().life<=0){
        world.DestroyBody(specialBody);
        specialBody = undefined;
        console.log("The special body was destroyed");
    }

    setTimeout(animate, timeStep);
}
```

Once we finish calling `world.Step()` and drawing the world, we check to see whether `specialBody` is still defined and whether its life has reached 0. Once the life does reach 0, we remove the body from the world using `DestroyBody()` and then set `specialBody` to undefined.

This time when we run the code, the special body bounces around with its life dropping until it finally disappears. A message appears in the console telling us that the body was destroyed.

▓ **Note**   We can track all the bodies and elements in a game using a similar principle by iterating through an array of objects. The point where we destroy a body is the perfect place for us to add explosion sounds or visual effects in a game and maybe update the score.

Drawing Our Own Characters

We have played with a lot of Box2D features so far. However, we have only been drawing using the default `DrawDebugData()` method. While this method is fine when testing code, we can't really write an amazing game looking like this. We need to know how to draw our own characters using all the drawing methods we learned in the first chapter.

Every b2Body object has two methods, `GetPosition()` and `GetAngle()`, that provide us with the coordinates and rotation of the body inside the Box2D world. Using the scale variable we defined in this chapter and the canvas `translate()` and `rotate()` methods we explored in Chapter 1, we can draw our characters or sprites on the canvas at the location that Box2D calculates for us.

To illustrate this, we can draw the special body that we have been playing with so far inside a `drawSpecialBody()` method that we will add to `box2d.js` (see Listing 3-24).

Listing 3-24. Drawing Our Own Character

```
function drawSpecialBody(){
    // Get body position and angle
    var position = specialBody.GetPosition();
    var angle = specialBody.GetAngle();

    // Translate and rotate axis to body position and angle
    context.translate(position.x*scale,position.y*scale);
    context.rotate(angle);

    // Draw a filled circular face
    context.fillStyle = "rgb(200,150,250);";
    context.beginPath();
    context.arc(0,0,30,0,2*Math.PI,false);
    context.fill();

    // Draw two rectangular eyes
    context.fillStyle = "rgb(255,255,255);";
    context.fillRect(-15,-15,10,5);
    context.fillRect(5,-15,10,5);

    // Draw an upward or downward arc for a smile depending on life
    context.strokeStyle = "rgb(255,255,255);";
    context.beginPath();
    if (specialBody.GetUserData().life>100){
        context.arc(0,0,10,Math.PI,2*Math.PI,true);
    } else {
        context.arc(0,10,10,Math.PI,2*Math.PI,false);
    }
    context.stroke();

    // Translate and rotate axis back to original position and angle
    context.rotate(-angle);
    context.translate(-position.x*scale,-position.y*scale);
}
```

We start by translating the canvas to the body's position and rotating the canvas to the body's angle. This is very similar to the code we looked at in Chapter 1.

We then draw a filled circle for the face, two rectangular eyes, and a smile using an arc. Just for fun, when the body life goes below 100, we change the smile to a sad face.

Finally, we undo the rotation and translation.

Before we can see this method in action, we will need to call it from inside animate(). The finished animate() method will now look like Listing 3-25.

Listing 3-25. The Finished animate() Method

```
function animate(){
    world.Step(timeStep,velocityIterations,positionIterations);
    world.ClearForces();

    world.DrawDebugData();

    // Custom Drawing
    if (specialBody){
        drawSpecialBody();
    }

    //Kill Special Body if Dead
    if (specialBody && specialBody.GetUserData().life<=0){
        world.DestroyBody(specialBody);
        specialBody = undefined;
        console.log("The special body was destroyed");
    }

    setTimeout(animate, timeStep);
}
```

What we have done here is check whether specialBody is still defined and call drawSpecialBody() if it is. Once the body dies, specialBody will become undefined and we will stop trying to draw it. You will notice that we draw after DrawDebugData() has completed, so we end up drawing on top of the debug drawing.

When we run this finished code, we see our new version of specialBody with a smiley face that becomes sad after a while before finally disappearing (see Figure 3-8).

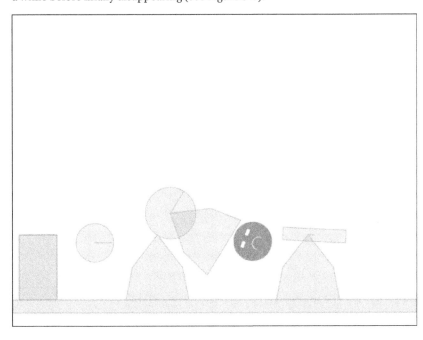

Figure 3-8. *Drawing our own character*

We have just animated our own character using the Box2D engine. This may not seem like much, but we now have all the building blocks that we need to build games using Box2D.

When you create your own game, you won't just be playing with boxes and circles. You will still use simple shapes that are similar in appearance to your game elements so that they seem to move realistically. However, you will be drawing all the characters yourself instead of using debug drawing.

Summary

In this chapter we took a crash course on the Box2D engine. We created a world in Box2D and drew different kinds of bodies within it. We made simple circular and rectangular shapes, polygons, and complex bodies that combined multiple shapes, and we used joints to combine shapes.

We animated the world realistically by letting Box2D handle the physics computations and drawing the world using `DrawDebugData()`. We used contact listeners to track collisions and slowly damage and destroy objects within the world. Finally, we drew our own character that was moved by Box2D.

We covered most of the elements of Box2D that we will be using in our game. If you would like to dive deeper into the Box2D API, you can look at the API reference available at `http://www.box2dflash.org/docs/`. You can also read the Box2D guide available at the same site.

In the next chapter, we will combine everything that we have learned so far to integrate Box2D into our game. We will create a framework to handle creation of our game entities inside Box2D. We will then use images and sprites to draw our characters over the parallax scrolling backgrounds that we built in Chapter 2. After that, we will spend some time polishing up our game by adding sound effects, and then wire everything together to create a finished, physics-based puzzle game.

CHAPTER 4

■ ■ ■

Integrating The Physics Engine

In Chapter 2, we developed the basic framework for our game, Froot Wars, and in Chapter 3, we looked at how to simulate a game world in Box2D. Now it is time to put together all the pieces to complete our game.

In this chapter, we will continue where we left off at the end of Chapter 2. We will add entities to our levels, use Box2D to simulate these entities, and then animate these entities within the game. We will use these entities to create a couple of working levels, and we will add mouse interactivity so that we can play the game. Once we have a working game, we will add sounds, background music, and a few other finishing touches to wrap up our game.

Now let's get started. We will be using the code from Chapter 2 as our starting point.

Defining Entities

So far, our game levels contain data for the background and foreground images and an empty array for entities. This entities array will eventually contain all the entities within our game: the heroes, the villains, the ground, and the blocks used to create the environment. We will then use this array to ask Box2D to create the corresponding Box2D shapes.

Typical entities will look like the examples shown in Listing 4-1.

Listing 4-1. Typical Entities

```
{type:"block", name:"wood", x:520,y:375,angle:90},
{type:"villain", name:"burger",x:520,y:200,calories:590},
```

The type property can contain values like "hero", "villain", "ground", and "block". We will use this property to decide how to handle an entity during creation and drawing operations.

The x, y, and angle properties are used to set the starting position and orientation of the entities. We can also store other custom properties (such as calories, which is the number of points scored for destroying a villain) within entities.

The name property tells us which sprite to use to draw the entity. All the images that we will use for the entities are stored in the images/entities folder.

The name property will also be used to refer to entity definitions. These definitions will include fixture data such as density and restitution, health data for destructible objects, and, in the case of heroes and villains, even details on the shape. Typical entity definitions will look like the examples shown in Listing 4-2.

Listing 4-2. Typical Entity Definitions

```
"burger":{
    shape:"circle",
    fullHealth:40,
    radius:25,
```

```
        density:1,
        friction:0.5,
        restitution:0.4,
    },
    "wood":{
        fullHealth:500,
        density:0.7,
        friction:0.4,
        restitution:0.4,
    },
```

Now that we have decided how we will be storing the entities, we also need a way to create them. We will start by creating an entities object in game.js that will handle all entity-related operations in our game. This object will contain all the entity definitions as well as the methods for creating and drawing entities (see Listing 4-3).

Listing 4-3. The entities Object with Definitions for Entities

```
var entities = {
    definitions:{
        "glass":{
            fullHealth:100,
            density:2.4,
            friction:0.4,
            restitution:0.15,
        },
        "wood":{
            fullHealth:500,
            density:0.7,
            friction:0.4,
            restitution:0.4,
        },
        "dirt":{
            density:3.0,
            friction:1.5,
            restitution:0.2,
        },
        "burger":{
            shape:"circle",
            fullHealth:40,
            radius:25,
            density:1,
            friction:0.5,
            restitution:0.4,
        },
        "sodacan":{
            shape:"rectangle",
            fullHealth:80,
            width:40,
            height:60,
            density:1,
```

```
                friction:0.5,
                restitution:0.7,
            },
            "fries":{
                shape:"rectangle",
                fullHealth:50,
                width:40,
                height:50,
                density:1,
                friction:0.5,
                restitution:0.6,
            },
            "apple":{
                shape:"circle",
                radius:25,
                density:1.5,
                friction:0.5,
                restitution:0.4,
            },
            "orange":{
                shape:"circle",
                radius:25,
                density:1.5,
                friction:0.5,
                restitution:0.4,
            },
            "strawberry":{
                shape:"circle",
                radius:15,
                density:2.0,
                friction:0.5,
                restitution:0.4,
            }
        },
    // take the entity, create a Box2D body, and add it to the world
    create:function(entity){

    },
    // take the entity, its position, and its angle and draw it on the game canvas
    draw:function(entity,position,angle){

    }
}
```

The entities object contains an array with definitions for all the material types (glass, wood, and dirt) and definitions for all the heroes and villains that we will have in the game (orange, apple, and burger).

The values for some of these properties (such as size, restitution, and fullHealth) were decided based on feel, by constantly tweaking them in an effort to make the game as much fun as possible. The correct values for these properties will vary with each game you make.

We also have placeholders for the create() and draw() functions that we need to implement. However, before we can implement these, we need to add Box2D to our code.

Adding Box2D

The first thing we need to do is add a reference to Box2dWeb-2.1.a.3.min.js in the <head> section of index.html before the reference to game.js. The <head> section of the file will now look like Listing 4-4.

Listing 4-4. Adding Box2D to the index.html <head> Section

```
<head>
    <meta http-equiv="Content-type" content="text/html; charset=utf-8">
    <title>Froot Wars</title>
    <script src="js/jquery.min.js" type="text/javascript" charset="utf-8"></script>
    <script src="js/Box2dWeb-2.1.a.3.min.js" type="text/javascript" charset="utf-8"></script>
    <script src="js/game.js" type="text/javascript" charset="utf-8"></script>
    <link rel="stylesheet" href="styles.css" type="text/css" media="screen" charset="utf-8">
</head>
```

One other thing that we will do is add references for all the commonly used Box2D objects to the beginning of game.js (see Listing 4-5).

Listing 4-5. Adding References to Commonly Used Box2D Objects

```
// Declare all the commonly used objects as variables for convenience
var b2Vec2 = Box2D.Common.Math.b2Vec2;
var b2BodyDef = Box2D.Dynamics.b2BodyDef;
var b2Body = Box2D.Dynamics.b2Body;
var b2FixtureDef = Box2D.Dynamics.b2FixtureDef;
var b2Fixture = Box2D.Dynamics.b2Fixture;
var b2World = Box2D.Dynamics.b2World;
var b2PolygonShape = Box2D.Collision.Shapes.b2PolygonShape;
var b2CircleShape = Box2D.Collision.Shapes.b2CircleShape;
var b2DebugDraw = Box2D.Dynamics.b2DebugDraw;
```

Now that we have the references set up, we can start using Box2D from within our game code. We will be creating a separate box2d object inside game.js to store all our Box2D-related methods (see Listing 4-6).

Listing 4-6. Creating a box2d Object

```
var box2d = {
    scale:30,
    init:function(){
        // Set up the Box2D world that will do most of the physics calculation
        var gravity = new b2Vec2(0,9.8); //declare gravity as 9.8 m/s^2 downward
        var allowSleep = true; //Allow objects that are at rest to fall asleep and be excluded from
calculations
        box2d.world = new b2World(gravity,allowSleep);
    },

    createRectangle:function(entity,definition){
            var bodyDef = new b2BodyDef;
            if(entity.isStatic){
                bodyDef.type = b2Body.b2_staticBody;
            } else {
                bodyDef.type = b2Body.b2_dynamicBody;
            }
```

```
            bodyDef.position.x = entity.x/box2d.scale;
            bodyDef.position.y = entity.y/box2d.scale;
            if (entity.angle) {
                bodyDef.angle = Math.PI*entity.angle/180;
            }

            var fixtureDef = new b2FixtureDef;
            fixtureDef.density = definition.density;
            fixtureDef.friction = definition.friction;
            fixtureDef.restitution = definition.restitution;

            fixtureDef.shape = new b2PolygonShape;
            fixtureDef.shape.SetAsBox(entity.width/2/box2d.scale,entity.height/2/box2d.scale);

            var body = box2d.world.CreateBody(bodyDef);
            body.SetUserData(entity);

            var fixture = body.CreateFixture(fixtureDef);
            return body;
    },

    createCircle:function(entity,definition){
            var bodyDef = new b2BodyDef;
            if(entity.isStatic){
                bodyDef.type = b2Body.b2_staticBody;
            } else {
                bodyDef.type = b2Body.b2_dynamicBody;
            }

            bodyDef.position.x = entity.x/box2d.scale;
            bodyDef.position.y = entity.y/box2d.scale;

            if (entity.angle) {
                bodyDef.angle = Math.PI*entity.angle/180;
            }
            var fixtureDef = new b2FixtureDef;
            fixtureDef.density = definition.density;
            fixtureDef.friction = definition.friction;
            fixtureDef.restitution = definition.restitution;

            fixtureDef.shape = new b2CircleShape(entity.radius/box2d.scale);

            var body = box2d.world.CreateBody(bodyDef);
            body.SetUserData(entity);

            var fixture = body.CreateFixture(fixtureDef);
            return body;
    },
}
```

The box2d object connects an init() method that initializes a new b2World object, just like we did in Chapter 3. The object also contains two helper methods, createRectangle() and createCircle(). Both methods accept two parameters, the entity and definition objects that we described earlier. The entity object contains details such as its position, angle, and whether or not the entity is static. The definition object contains details about the fixture, such as restitution and density. Using these parameters, the methods create Box2D bodies and fixtures and add them to the Box2D world.

One thing to note is that both these methods convert the position and size using box2d.scale and convert the angle from degrees to radians before they can be used by Box2D.

One other thing that these methods do is attach the entity object to the body using the SetUserData() method. This enables us to retrieve any of the entity-related data for a Box2D body using its GetUserData() method.

Creating Entities

Now that we have Box2D set up, we will implement the entities.create() method inside the entities object that we defined earlier. This method will take an entity object as a parameter and add it to the world (see Listing 4-7).

Listing 4-7. Defining the entities.create() Method

```
// take the entity, create a Box2D body, and add it to the world
create:function(entity){
    var definition = entities.definitions[entity.name];
    if(!definition){
        console.log ("Undefined entity name",entity.name);
        return;
    }
    switch(entity.type){
        case "block": // simple rectangles
            entity.health = definition.fullHealth;
            entity.fullHealth = definition.fullHealth;
            entity.shape = "rectangle";
            entity.sprite = loader.loadImage("images/entities/"+entity.name+".png");
            box2d.createRectangle(entity,definition);
            break;
        case "ground": // simple rectangles
            // No need for health. These are indestructible
            entity.shape = "rectangle";
            // No need for sprites. These won't be drawn at all
            box2d.createRectangle(entity,definition);
            break;
        case "hero":    // simple circles
        case "villain": // can be circles or rectangles
            entity.health = definition.fullHealth;
            entity.fullHealth = definition.fullHealth;
            entity.sprite = loader.loadImage("images/entities/"+entity.name+".png");
            entity.shape = definition.shape;
            if(definition.shape == "circle"){
                entity.radius = definition.radius;
                box2d.createCircle(entity,definition);
```

```
            } else if(definition.shape == "rectangle"){
                entity.width = definition.width;
                entity.height = definition.height;
                box2d.createRectangle(entity,definition);
            }
            break;
        default:
            console.log("Undefined entity type",entity.type);
            break;
    }
},
```

In this method, we use the entity type to decide how to handle the entity object and its properties:

- *Block*: For block entities, we set the entity health and fullHealth properties based on the entity definition, and set the shape property to "rectangle". We then load the sprite, and call the box2d.createRectangle() method.

- *Ground*: For ground entities, we set the entity object's shape property to "rectangle" and call the box2d.createRectangle() method. We do not load a sprite because we will be using the ground from the level foreground image and won't be drawing the ground separately.

- *Hero and villain*: For hero and villain entities, we set the entity health, fullHealth, and shape properties based on the entity definition. We then set either the radius or the height and width properties based on the shape of the entity. Finally, we call either box2d.createRectangle() or box2d.createCircle() based on the shape.

Now that we have a way to create entities, let's add some entities to our levels.

Adding Entities to Levels

The first thing we will do is add a few entities inside our levels.data array, as shown in Listing 4-8.

Listing 4-8. Adding Entities to the levels.data array

```
data:[
 {  // First level
    foreground:'desert-foreground',
    background:'clouds-background',
    entities:[
        {type:"ground", name:"dirt", x:500,y:440,width:1000,height:20,isStatic:true},
        {type:"ground", name:"wood", x:180,y:390,width:40,height:80,isStatic:true},

        {type:"block", name:"wood", x:520,y:375,angle:90,width:100,height:25},
        {type:"block", name:"glass", x:520,y:275,angle:90,width:100,height:25},
        {type:"villain", name:"burger",x:520,y:200,calories:590},

        {type:"block", name:"wood", x:620,y:375,angle:90,width:100,height:25},
        {type:"block", name:"glass", x:620,y:275,angle:90,width:100,height:25},
        {type:"villain", name:"fries", x:620,y:200,calories:420},
```

```
                {type:"hero", name:"orange",x:90,y:410},
                {type:"hero", name:"apple",x:150,y:410},
        ]
    },
    {   // Second level
        foreground:'desert-foreground',
        background:'clouds-background',
        entities:[
            {type:"ground", name:"dirt", x:500,y:440,width:1000,height:20,isStatic:true},
            {type:"ground", name:"wood", x:180,y:390,width:40,height:80,isStatic:true},
            {type:"block", name:"wood", x:820,y:375,angle:90,width:100,height:25},
            {type:"block", name:"wood", x:720,y:375,angle:90,width:100,height:25},
            {type:"block", name:"wood", x:620,y:375,angle:90,width:100,height:25},
            {type:"block", name:"glass", x:670,y:310,width:100,height:25},
            {type:"block", name:"glass", x:770,y:310,width:100,height:25},

            {type:"block", name:"glass", x:670,y:248,angle:90,width:100,height:25},
            {type:"block", name:"glass", x:770,y:248,angle:90,width:100,height:25},
            {type:"block", name:"wood", x:720,y:180,width:100,height:25},

            {type:"villain", name:"burger",x:715,y:160,calories:590},
            {type:"villain", name:"fries",x:670,y:400,calories:420},
            {type:"villain", name:"sodacan",x:765,y:395,calories:150},

            {type:"hero", name:"strawberry",x:40,y:420},
            {type:"hero", name:"orange",x:90,y:410},
            {type:"hero", name:"apple",x:150,y:410},
        ]
    }
],
```

The first level contains two background ground entities—one for the floor and the other for the slingshot. These entities are meant to be static objects that are not drawn by us.

The level also contains four rectangular block entities (glass and wood). These are destructible elements that we have positioned using their angle, x, and y properties.

Finally, the level contains two hero entities (orange and apple) and two villain entities (burger and fries). Note that the villains have an extra property called calories that we will use to increase the player score when they are destroyed.

The second level has a similar design, except with a few more entities.

Now that we have defined entities for each level, we need to load these entities when we load the level. To do this, we will modify the load() method of the levels object (see Listing 4-9).

Listing 4-9. Modifying levels.load() to Load the Entities

```
// Load all data and images for a specific level
load:function(number){
    //Initialize Box2D world whenever a level is loaded
    box2d.init();

    // declare a new current level object
    game.currentLevel = {number:number,hero:[]};
    game.score=0;
```

```
    $('#score').html('Score: '+game.score);
    game.currentHero = undefined;
    var level = levels.data[number];


    //load the background, foreground, and slingshot images
    game.currentLevel.backgroundImage =
loader.loadImage("images/backgrounds/"+level.background+".png");
    game.currentLevel.foregroundImage =
loader.loadImage("images/backgrounds/"+level.foreground+".png");
    game.slingshotImage = loader.loadImage("images/slingshot.png");
    game.slingshotFrontImage = loader.loadImage("images/slingshot-front.png");

    // Load all the entities
    for (var i = level.entities.length - 1; i >= 0; i--){
        var entity = level.entities[i];
        entities.create(entity);
    };

      //Call game.start() once the assets have loaded
    if(loader.loaded){
        game.start()
    } else {
        loader.onload = game.start;
    }
}
```

The first change we have made is the addition of a call to box2d.init() at the very beginning of the method. The other change is the addition of a for loop where we iterate through all the entities for a level and call entities. create() for each entity. Now when we load a level, Box2D will get initialized and all the entities will get loaded into the Box2D world.

We still can't see the bodies we have added. Let's use the Box2D debug drawing method introduced in Chapter 3 to see what we created.

Setting Up Box2D Debug Drawing

The first thing we will do is create another canvas element inside the HTML file and place it just before the end of the <body> tag:

```
<canvas id="debugcanvas" width="1000" height="480" style="border:1px solid black;"></canvas>
```

This canvas is larger than our game canvas, so we can see the entire level without any panning. We will be using this canvas and debug drawing only to design and test our levels. We can remove all traces of debug drawing once the game is complete.

The next thing we need to do is set up debug drawing when we are initializing Box2D. We will do this by modifying the box2d.init() method so that it looks as shown in Listing 4-10.

Listing 4-10. Modifying box2d.init() to Set Up Debug Draw

```
init:function(){
    // Set up the Box2D world that will do most of the physics calculation
    var gravity = new b2Vec2(0,9.8); //declare gravity as 9.8 m/s^2 downward
    var allowSleep = true; //Allow objects that are at rest to fall asleep and be excluded from
calculations
    box2d.world = new b2World(gravity,allowSleep);

    // Set up debug draw
    var debugContext = document.getElementById('debugcanvas').getContext('2d');
    var debugDraw = new b2DebugDraw();
    debugDraw.SetSprite(debugContext);
    debugDraw.SetDrawScale(box2d.scale);
    debugDraw.SetFillAlpha(0.3);
    debugDraw.SetLineThickness(1.0);
    debugDraw.SetFlags(b2DebugDraw.e_shapeBit | b2DebugDraw.e_jointBit);
    box2d.world.SetDebugDraw(debugDraw);
},
```

This newly added code is the same as the code in Chapter 3. Before we can see the results of debug draw, we need to call the world object's DrawDebugData() method. We will do this in a new method called drawAllBodies() inside the game object, as shown in Listing 4-11. We will call this method from the animate() method of the game object.

Listing 4-11. Modifying animate() and Creating drawAllBodies()

```
animate:function(){
    // Animate the background
    game.handlePanning();

    // TODO: Animate the characters

    //  Draw the background with parallax scrolling
    game.context.drawImage(game.currentLevel.backgroundImage,game.offsetLeft/4,0
,640,480,0,0,640,480);

game.context.drawImage(game.currentLevel.foregroundImage,game.offsetLeft,0,640,480,0,0,640,480);

    // Draw the slingshot
    game.context.drawImage(game.slingshotImage,game.slingshotX-game.offsetLeft,game.slingshotY);

    // Draw all the bodies
    game.drawAllBodies();

    // Draw the front of the slingshot
    game.context.drawImage(game.slingshotFrontImage,game.slingshotX-game.offsetLeft,game.slingshotY);
```

```
    if (!game.ended){
        game.animationFrame = window.requestAnimationFrame(game.animate,game.canvas);
    }
},
drawAllBodies:function(){
    box2d.world.DrawDebugData();
    // TODO: Iterate through all the bodies and draw them on the game canvas
}
```

For now, we have created a simple drawAllBodies() method that calls box2d.world.DrawDebugData(). We will eventually need to add code to iterate through all the bodies in the Box2D world and draw them on the game canvas. We call this new method from inside the game object's animate() method.

If we run our code now and load the first level, we should see the debug canvas with all the entities, as shown in Figure 4-1.

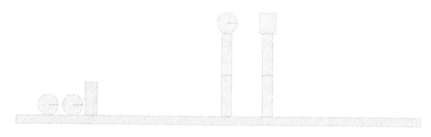

Figure 4-1. *First level drawn on the debug canvas*

The debug canvas view shows us all the game entities as circles and rectangles. We can also see the ground and slingshot blocks in a different color. We can use this view to quickly test our levels and make sure that all the entities are positioned correctly. Now that we can see that everything in the level looks alright, it's time to actually draw all the entities onto our game canvas.

Drawing the Entities

To draw an entity, we will define a method called draw() inside the entities object. This object will take the entity, its position, and its angle as parameters and draw it on the game canvas (see Listing 4-12).

Listing 4-12. The entities.draw() Method

```
// take the entity, its position, and its angle and draw it on the game canvas
draw:function(entity,position,angle){
    game.context.translate(position.x*box2d.scale-game.offsetLeft,position.y*box2d.scale);
    game.context.rotate(angle);
    switch (entity.type){
        case "block":
            game.context.drawImage(entity.sprite,0,0,entity.sprite.width,entity.sprite.height,
                    -entity.width/2-1,-entity.height/2-1,entity.width+2,entity.height+2);
        break;
        case "villain":
```

```
        case "hero":
            if (entity.shape=="circle"){

game.context.drawImage(entity.sprite,0,0,entity.sprite.width,entity.sprite.height,
                    -entity.radius-1,-entity.radius-1,entity.radius*2+2,entity.radius*2+2);
            } else if (entity.shape=="rectangle"){

game.context.drawImage(entity.sprite,0,0,entity.sprite.width,entity.sprite.height,
                    -entity.width/2-1,-entity.height/2-1,entity.width+2,entity.height+2);
            }
            break;
        case "ground":
            // do nothing... We will draw objects like the ground & slingshot separately
            break;
    }

    game.context.rotate(-angle);
    game.context.translate(-position.x*box2d.scale+game.offsetLeft,-position.y*box2d.scale);
}
```

This method first translates and rotates the context to the position and angle of the entity. It then draws the object on the canvas based on the entity type and shape. Finally, it rotates and translates the context back to the original position.

One thing to note is that the code stretches the image to a size of one pixel larger than the sprite definition in each direction when using drawImage(). This is so that small gaps between Box2D objects get covered up.

■ **Note** Box2D creates a "skin" around all polygons. The skin is used in stacking scenarios to keep polygons slightly separated. This allows continuous collision to work against the core polygon. When drawing Box2D objects, we need to compensate for this extra skin by drawing bodies slightly larger than their actual dimensions; otherwise, stacked objects will have unexplained gaps between them.

Now that we have defined an entities.draw() method, we need to call this method for every entity in our game world. We can iterate through every body in the game world by using the world object's GetBodyList() method. We will now modify the game object's drawAllBodies() method to do this, as shown in Listing 4-13.

Listing 4-13. Iterating Through All the Bodies and Drawing Them

```
drawAllBodies:function(){
    box2d.world.DrawDebugData();

    // Iterate through all the bodies and draw them on the game canvas
    for (var body = box2d.world.GetBodyList(); body; body = body.GetNext()) {
        var entity = body.GetUserData();

        if(entity){
            entities.draw(entity,body.GetPosition(),body.GetAngle())
        }
    }
}
```

The for loop initializes body using world.GetBodyList(), which returns the first body in the world. The body object's GetNext() method returns the next body in the list until it reaches the end of the list, at which point we exit the for loop. Within the loop, we check to see if the body has an attached entity; if it does, we call entities.draw(), passing it the body's entity object, position, and angle.

If we run our game and load the first level now, we should see all the entities drawn on the canvas, as shown in Figure 4-2.

Figure 4-2. *Drawing the game entities on the canvas*

Once the level loads, the game pans to the right so that we can see the bad guys clearly, and then it pans back to the slingshot. We can see all the entities drawn properly at the same locations as on the debug canvas. The extra pixel we added in our draw() method ensures that all the stacked objects are positioned tightly next to each other. Note that the canvas preserves image transparencies when drawing images, which is why we can see the background through the glass block.

Now that we have drawn all the elements in the Box2D world, we need to animate the Box2D world.

Animating the Box2D World

As in the previous chapter, we can animate the Box2D world by calling the world object's Step() method and passing it the time step interval as a parameter. However, this is where things get a little tricky.

As per the Box2D manual recommendation, ideally, we should use a fixed time step for best results because variable time steps are hard to debug. Also as per the manual, Box2D works best with a time step of around 1/60th of a second, and you should use a time step no larger than 1/30th of a second. If the time step becomes very large, Box2D starts having problems with collisions, and bodies start passing through each other.

The requestAnimationFrame API can vary the frequency at which it calls the animate() method across browsers and machines. One way to get around this is to measure the time elapsed since the last call to animate() and pass this difference as a time step to Box2D.

However, if we switch tabs on the browser and then return to the game tab, the browser will call the animate() method less often, and this time step may become much larger than the upper limit of 1/30th of a second. To avoid problems due to a large time step, we will need to actively cap the time step if it becomes larger than 1/30th of a second.

Armed with this information, we will first define a step() method inside the box2d object that takes a time interval as a parameter and calls the world object's Step() method (see Listing 4-14).

Listing 4-14. The box2d.step() Method

```
step:function(timeStep){
    // velocity iterations = 8
    // position iterations = 3
    if(timeStep >2/60){
        timeStep = 2/60
    }

    box2d.world.Step(timeStep,8,3);
},
```

The step() method takes a time step in seconds and passes it to the world.Step() method. If timeStep is too large, we cap it at 1/30th of a second. We use the Box2D manual recommended values of 8 and 3 for velocity and position iterations. We will call this method from the game.animate() method after calculating the time step. The game.animate() method will now look like Listing 4-15.

Listing 4-15. Calling box2d.step() from game.animate()

```
animate:function(){
    // Animate the background
    game.handlePanning();

    // Animate the characters
    var currentTime = new Date().getTime();
    var timeStep;
    if (game.lastUpdateTime){
        timeStep = (currentTime - game.lastUpdateTime)/1000;
        box2d.step(timeStep);
    }

    game.lastUpdateTime = currentTime;

    //  Draw the background with parallax scrolling

game.context.drawImage(game.currentLevel.backgroundImage,game.offsetLeft/4,0,640,480,0,0,640,480);

game.context.drawImage(game.currentLevel.foregroundImage,game.offsetLeft,0,640,480,0,0,640,480);

    // Draw the slingshot
    game.context.drawImage(game.slingshotImage, game.slingshotX-game.offsetLeft, game.slingshotY);
    game.drawAllBodies();

    // Draw the front of the slingshot
    game.context.drawImage(game.slingshotFrontImage,game.slingshotX-game.offsetLeft,game.slingshotY);
```

```
    if (!game.ended){
        game.animationFrame = window.requestAnimationFrame(game.animate,game.canvas);
    }
},
```

We calculate timeStep as the difference between lastUpdateTime and currentTime and then call the box2d.step() method. We then save the current time into the game.lastUpdateTime variable.

The first time animate() is called, game.lastUpdateTime will be undefined, so we will not calculate timeStep or call box2d.step().

Loading the Hero

Now that the animation and engine are in place, it's time to implement some more game states (a.k.a. game modes). The first state that we will implement is the load-next-hero state. When in this state, the game needs to count the number of heroes and villains left in the game, check how many are left, and act accordingly, as follows:

- If all the villains are gone, the game switches to the state level-success.

- If all the heroes are gone, the game switches to the state level-failure.

- If there are still heroes remaining, the game places the first hero on top of the slingshot and then switches to the state wait-for-firing.

We will do this by creating a method called game.countHeroesAndVillains() and modifying the game.handlePanning() method, as shown in Listing 4-16.

Listing 4-16. Handling the load-next-hero State

```
countHeroesAndVillains:function(){
    game.heroes = [];
    game.villains = [];
    for (var body = box2d.world.GetBodyList(); body; body = body.GetNext()) {
        var entity = body.GetUserData();
        if(entity){
            if(entity.type == "hero"){
                game.heroes.push(body);
            } else if (entity.type =="villain"){
                game.villains.push(body);
            }
        }
    }
},
handlePanning:function(){
    if (game.mode=="intro"){
        if(game.panTo(700)){
            game.mode = "load-next-hero";
        }
    }

    if (game.mode=="wait-for-firing"){
        game.panTo(game.slingshotX);
    }
```

```
    if (game.mode == "firing"){
        game.panTo(game.slingshotX);
    }

    if (game.mode == "fired"){
        // TODO:
        // Pan to wherever the hero currently is
    }

    if (game.mode == "load-next-hero"){
        game.countHeroesAndVillains();

        // Check if any villains are alive, if not, end the level (success)
        if (game.villains.length == 0){
            game.mode = "level-success";
            return;
        }

        // Check if there are any more heroes left to load, if not end the level (failure)
        if (game.heroes.length == 0){
            game.mode = "level-failure"
            return;
        }

        // Load the hero and set mode to wait-for-firing
        if(!game.currentHero){
            game.currentHero = game.heroes[game.heroes.length-1];
            game.currentHero.SetPosition({x:180/box2d.scale,y:200/box2d.scale});
            game.currentHero.SetLinearVelocity({x:0,y:0});
            game.currentHero.SetAngularVelocity(0);
            game.currentHero.SetAwake(true);
        } else {
            // Wait for hero to stop bouncing and fall asleep and then switch to wait-for-firing
            game.panTo(game.slingshotX);
            if(!game.currentHero.IsAwake()){
                game.mode = "wait-for-firing";
            }
        }
    }
},
```

The countHeroesAndVillains() method iterates through all the bodies in the world and stores the heroes in the game.heroes array and the villains in the game.villains array.

Inside the handlePanning() method, when game.mode is load-next-hero, we first call countHeroesandVillains(). We then check to see if the villain or hero count is 0 and, if so, set game.mode to level-success or level-failure, respectively. If not, we save the last hero in the game.heroes array into the game.currentHero variable and set its position to a point in the air above the slingshot. We set its angular and linear velocity to 0. We also wake up the body in case it is asleep.

When the body drops on to the slingshot, it will keep bouncing until it finally comes to rest and falls asleep again. Once the body goes back to sleep, we set game.mode to wait-for-firing. If we run the game and start the first level, we will see the first hero bounce on the slingshot and come to rest, as shown in Figure 4-3.

Figure 4-3. *First hero loaded on slingshot and waiting to be fired*

Now that we have the hero ready to be fired, we need to handle firing the hero from the slingshot.

Firing the Hero

We will implement firing the hero using three states:

- wait-for-firing: The game pans over the slingshot and waits for the mouse to be clicked and dragged while the pointer is above the hero. When this happens, it shifts to the firing state.

- firing: The game moves the hero with the mouse until the mouse button is released. When this happens, it pushes the hero with an impulse based on its distance from the slingshot and shifts to the fired state.

- fired: The game pans to follow the hero until it either comes to rest or goes outside the level bounds. Then game then removes the hero from the game world and goes back to the load-next-hero state.

We will first implement a method called mouseOnCurrentHero() inside the game object to test if the mouse pointer is positioned on the current hero (see Listing 4-17).

Listing 4-17. The mouseOnCurrentHero() Method

```
mouseOnCurrentHero:function(){
    if(!game.currentHero){
        return false;
    }
```

```
        var position = game.currentHero.GetPosition();
        var distanceSquared = Math.pow(position.x*box2d.scale - mouse.x-game.offsetLeft,2) +
Math.pow(position.y*box2d.scale-mouse.y,2);
        var radiusSquared = Math.pow(game.currentHero.GetUserData().radius,2);
        return (distanceSquared<= radiusSquared);
    },
```

This method calculates the distance between the current hero center and the mouse location and compares it with the radius of the current hero to check if the mouse is positioned over the hero. If the distance is less than the radius, the mouse pointer is positioned on the hero.

We can get away with using this simple check since all our heroes are circular. If you want to implement heroes with different shapes, you might need a more complex method.

Now that we have this method in place, we can implement the three states inside the handlePanning() method, as shown in Listing 4-18.

Listing 4-18. Handling the Firing States Inside the handlePanning() Method

```
if (game.mode=="wait-for-firing"){
    if (mouse.dragging){
        if (game.mouseOnCurrentHero()){
            game.mode = "firing";
        } else {
            game.panTo(mouse.x + game.offsetLeft)
        }
    } else {
        game.panTo(game.slingshotX);
    }
}

if (game.mode == "firing"){
    if(mouse.down){
        game.panTo(game.slingshotX);

game.currentHero.SetPosition({x:(mouse.x+game.offsetLeft)/box2d.scale,y:mouse.y/box2d.scale});
    } else {
        game.mode = "fired";
        var impulseScaleFactor = 0.75;
        var impulse = new b2Vec2((game.slingshotX+35-mouse.x-game.offsetLeft)*impulseScaleFactor,
(game.slingshotY+25-mouse.y)*impulseScaleFactor);
        game.currentHero.ApplyImpulse(impulse,game.currentHero.GetWorldCenter());
    }
}

if (game.mode == "fired"){
    //pan to wherever the current hero is...
    var heroX = game.currentHero.GetPosition().x*box2d.scale;
    game.panTo(heroX);

    //and wait till he stops moving or is out of bounds
    if(!game.currentHero.IsAwake() || heroX<0 || heroX >game.currentLevel.foregroundImage.width ){
```

```
        // then delete the old hero
        box2d.world.DestroyBody(game.currentHero);
        game.currentHero = undefined;
        // and load next hero
        game.mode = "load-next-hero";
    }
}
```

When the state is wait-for-firing and the mouse is being dragged, we change the state to firing if the mouse pointer is positioned on the hero; if the mouse pointer is not positioned on the hero, we pan the screen toward the cursor. If the mouse is not being dragged, we pan toward the slingshot.

When the state is firing and the mouse button is down, we set the position of the hero to the mouse position and pan toward the slingshot. When the mouse button is released, we set the state to fired and apply an impulse to the hero using the b2Body object's ApplyImpulse() method. This method takes the impulse as a parameter in the form of a b2Vec2 object. We set the x and y values of the impulse vector as a multiple of the x and y distance of the hero from the top of the slingshot. (The impulse scaling factor is a number that I came up with by experimenting with different values.)

When the state is fired, we pan the screen toward the hero and wait for the hero to either come to rest or fall outside of the game bounds. When it does either, we remove the hero from the world using the DestroyBody() method and change the state back to load-next-hero.

When we run this finished code and load the level, we should be able to fire the hero at the blocks and knock them down, as shown in Figure 4-4.

Figure 4-4. *Firing the hero at the blocks and knocking them over*

Once the hero either stops rolling or goes outside the bounds of the level, it is removed from the game and the next hero is loaded onto the slingshot. At this point, once all the heroes are gone, the game just stops and waits. So, the last thing that we need to do is implement ending the level.

Ending the Level

Once a level ends, we will stop the game animation loop and display a level ending screen. This screen will give the user options to replay the current level, proceed to the next level, or return to the level selection screen.

The first thing we need to do is add onclick event handlers to the endingscreen div element and place it in the index.html file after the other game layers. The final markup will look like Listing 4-19.

Listing 4-19. Finished endingscreen div Element

```
<div id="endingscreen" class="gamelayer">
    <div>
        <p id="endingmessage">The Level Is Over Message</p>
        <p id="playcurrentlevel" onclick="game.restartLevel();"><img src="images/icons/prev.png">
Replay Current Level</p>
        <p id="playnextlevel" onclick="game.startNextLevel();"><img src="images/icons/next.png">
Play Next Level </p>
        <p id="returntolevelscreen"onclick="game.showLevelScreen();"><img
src="images/icons/return.png"> Return to Level Screen</p>
    </div>
</div>
```

We also need to add the corresponding CSS into styles.css, as shown in Listing 4-20.

Listing 4-20. CSS for the endingscreen div Element

```
/* Ending Screen */
endingscreen {
    text-align:center;
}

#endingscreen div {
    height:430px;
    padding-top:50px;
    border:1px;
    background:rgba(1,1,1,0.5);
    text-align:left;
    padding-left:100px;
}

#endingscreen p  {
    font: 20px Comic Sans MS;
    text-shadow: 0 0 2px #000;
    color:white;
}

#endingscreen p img{
    top:10px;
    position:relative;
    cursor:pointer;
}
```

```css
#endingscreen #endingmessage  {
    font: 32px Comic Sans MS;
    text-shadow: 0 0 2px #000;
    color:white;
}
```

Now that the ending screen is ready, we will implement a method called showEndingScreen() inside the game object that will display the endingscreen div element (see Listing 4-21).

Listing 4-21. The game.showEndingScreen() Method

```javascript
showEndingScreen:function(){
    if (game.mode=="level-success"){
        if(game.currentLevel.number<levels.data.length-1){
            $('#endingmessage').html('Level Complete. Well Done!!!');
            $("#playnextlevel").show();
        } else {
            $('#endingmessage').html('All Levels Complete. Well Done!!!');
            $("#playnextlevel").hide();
        }
    } else if (game.mode=="level-failure"){
        $('#endingmessage').html('Failed. Play Again?');
        $("#playnextlevel").hide();
    }

    $('#endingscreen').show();
},
```

The showEndingScreen() method shows different messages based on the value of game.mode. The option to play the next level is shown if the player was successful and the current level was not the final level of the game. If the player was unsuccessful or the current level was the final level, the option is hidden.

We will now handle level-success and level-failure within the handlePanning() method of the game object by adding the code shown in Listing 4-22 to the bottom of the method.

Listing 4-22. Implementing the Level Ending States

```javascript
if(game.mode=="level-success" || game.mode=="level-failure"){
    if(game.panTo(0)){
        game.ended = true;

        game.showEndingScreen();
    }
}
```

When game.mode is either level-success or level-failure, the game first pans back to the left, then sets the game.ended property to true, and finally displays the ending screen shown in Figure 4-5.

Figure 4-5. *The level ending screen*

Of course, since we haven't yet implemented collision damage, the villains cannot die and we can never win. Therefore, the next thing we will implement is collision damage.

Collision Damage

The first thing we need to do is track collisions by using a contact listener and overriding its PostSolve() method, just like we did in Chapter 3. We will add this listener to the world immediately after it has been created in the init() method of the box2d object, as shown in Listing 4-23.

Listing 4-23. Handling Collisions Using a Contact Listener

```
init:function(){
    // Set up the Box2D world that will do most of the physics calculation
    var gravity = new b2Vec2(0,9.8); //declare gravity as 9.8 m/s^2 downward
    var allowSleep = true; //Allow objects that are at rest to fall asleep and be excluded from
calculations
    box2d.world = new b2World(gravity,allowSleep);

    var debugContext = document.getElementById('debugcanvas').getContext('2d');
    var debugDraw = new b2DebugDraw();
    debugDraw.SetSprite(debugContext);
    debugDraw.SetDrawScale(box2d.scale);
    debugDraw.SetFillAlpha(0.3);
    debugDraw.SetLineThickness(1.0);
    debugDraw.SetFlags(b2DebugDraw.e_shapeBit | b2DebugDraw.e_jointBit);
    box2d.world.SetDebugDraw(debugDraw);
```

```
    var listener = new Box2D.Dynamics.b2ContactListener;
    listener.PostSolve = function(contact,impulse){
        var body1 = contact.GetFixtureA().GetBody();
        var body2 = contact.GetFixtureB().GetBody();
        var entity1 = body1.GetUserData();
        var entity2 = body2.GetUserData();

        var impulseAlongNormal = Math.abs(impulse.normalImpulses[0]);
        // This listener is called a little too often. Filter out very tiny impulses.
        // After trying different values, 5 seems to work well
        if(impulseAlongNormal>5){
            // If objects have a health, reduce health by the impulse value
            if (entity1.health){
                entity1.health -= impulseAlongNormal;
            }

            if (entity2.health){
                entity2.health -= impulseAlongNormal;
            }
        }
    };
    box2d.world.SetContactListener(listener);
},
```

Within the PostSolve() method, if either of the bodies involved in the collision has a health property, we reduce the health by the value of the impulse along the normal. Since the PostSolve() method is called for every little collision, we ignore any collision where impulseAlongNormal is less than a threshold.

The next thing we will do is add some code in the game object's drawAllBodies() method to check if a body's health property is less than zero or the body has gone outside the level bounds. If either is true, we will remove the body from the world. The drawAllBodies() method now looks like Listing 4-24.

Listing 4-24. Removing Dead Bodies from the World

```
drawAllBodies:function(){
    box2d.world.DrawDebugData();

    // Iterate through all the bodies and draw them on the game canvas
    for (var body = box2d.world.GetBodyList(); body; body = body.GetNext()) {
        var entity = body.GetUserData();

        if(entity){
            var entityX = body.GetPosition().x*box2d.scale;
            if(entityX<0|| entityX>game.currentLevel.foregroundImage.width||(entity.health &&
entity.health <0)){
                box2d.world.DestroyBody(body);
                if (entity.type=="villain"){
                    game.score += entity.calories;
                    $('#score').html('Score: '+game.score);
                }
```

```
            } else {
                entities.draw(entity,body.GetPosition(),body.GetAngle())
            }
        }
    }
}
```

If the code finds that the body has gone outside the level bounds or the entity has lost all its health, we use the world object's DestroyBody() method to remove the body. Additionally, if the entity is a villain, we add the entity's calorie value to the game score.

When we run the game, the villains do get destroyed and the score increases, as shown in Figure 4-6.

Figure 4-6. *The score increases after a bad guy gets destroyed*

Now that we have a working level, let's add a few finishing touches. The first thing we will do is draw a slingshot band when the hero is being fired.

Drawing the Slingshot Band

The slingshot band is going to be a thick brown line from the end of the slingshot to the extreme end of the hero. We will draw the band only when the game is in firing mode. We will do this in a drawSlingshotBand() method inside the game object, as shown in Listing 4-25.

Listing 4-25. Drawing the Slingshot Band

```
drawSlingshotBand:function(){
    game.context.strokeStyle = "rgb(68,31,11)"; // Darker brown color
    game.context.lineWidth = 6; // Draw a thick line

    // Use angle hero has been dragged and radius to calculate coordinates of edge of hero wrt.
hero center
    var radius = game.currentHero.GetUserData().radius;
    var heroX = game.currentHero.GetPosition().x*box2d.scale;
    var heroY = game.currentHero.GetPosition().y*box2d.scale;
    var angle = Math.atan2(game.slingshotY+25-heroY,game.slingshotX+50-heroX);

    var heroFarEdgeX = heroX - radius * Math.cos(angle);
    var heroFarEdgeY = heroY - radius * Math.sin(angle);

    game.context.beginPath();
    // Start line from top of slingshot (the back side)
    game.context.moveTo(game.slingshotX+50-game.offsetLeft, game.slingshotY+25);

    // Draw line to center of hero
    game.context.lineTo(heroX-game.offsetLeft,heroY);
    game.context.stroke();

    // Draw the hero on the back band

entities.draw(game.currentHero.GetUserData(),game.currentHero.GetPosition(),game.currentHero.
GetAngle());

    game.context.beginPath();
    // Move to edge of hero farthest from slingshot top
    game.context.moveTo(heroFarEdgeX-game.offsetLeft,heroFarEdgeY);

    // Draw line back to top of slingshot (the front side)
    game.context.lineTo(game.slingshotX-game.offsetLeft +10,game.slingshotY+30)
    game.context.stroke();
},
```

We start by setting the drawing color to a dark brown using the strokeStyle property. We next set the line drawing width to 6 pixels using the lineWidth property. We then draw a band from the back of the slingshot to the hero, draw the hero on top of the band, and, finally, draw a band from the front of the slingshot to the edge of the hero furthest from the slingshot.

We will call this method from the game.animate() method right after we draw all the other bodies. The final game.animate() method will look like Listing 4-26.

Listing 4-26. Calling the drawSlingshotBand() Method from animate()

```
animate:function(){
    // Animate the background
    game.handlePanning();

    // Animate the characters
        var currentTime = new Date().getTime();
```

```
        var timeStep;
        if (game.lastUpdateTime){
            timeStep = (currentTime - game.lastUpdateTime)/1000;
            if(timeStep >2/60){
                timeStep = 2/60
            }
            box2d.step(timeStep);
        }
        game.lastUpdateTime = currentTime;

    // Draw the background with parallax scrolling

game.context.drawImage(game.currentLevel.backgroundImage,game.offsetLeft/4,0,640,480,0,0,640,480);

game.context.drawImage(game.currentLevel.foregroundImage,game.offsetLeft,0,640,480,0,0,640,480);

    // Draw the slingshot
    game.context.drawImage(game.slingshotImage,game.slingshotX-game.offsetLeft,game.slingshotY);

    // Draw all the bodies
    game.drawAllBodies();

    // Draw the band when we are firing a hero
    if(game.mode == "firing"){
        game.drawSlingshotBand();
    }

    // Draw the front of the slingshot
    game.context.drawImage(game.slingshotFrontImage,game.slingshotX-game.offsetLeft,
game.slingshotY);

    if (!game.ended){
        game.animationFrame = window.requestAnimationFrame(game.animate,game.canvas);
    }
},
```

When we run this code, we should see a brown band around the hero, as shown in Figure 4-7.

Figure 4-7. *Drawing the slingshot band*

This isn't a complete solution. The band might look a little unnatural at certain extreme angles. You might consider improving this method by superimposing some extra images on top of the band to cover up these edge effects. For now, this simple implementation will suffice.

Now that we have the artwork for the level wrapped up, let's implement the buttons for changing and restarting levels.

Changing Levels

We have already implemented one way to traverse levels, using the level selection screen. Now we will implement the buttons for restarting a level and proceeding to the next level.

We start by implementing the restartLevel() and startNextLevel() methods inside the game object, as shown in Listing 4-27.

Listing 4-27. Implementing restartLevel() and startNextLevel()

```
restartLevel:function(){
    window.cancelAnimationFrame(game.animationFrame);
    game.lastUpdateTime = undefined;
    levels.load(game.currentLevel.number);
},
startNextLevel:function(){
    window.cancelAnimationFrame(game.animationFrame);
    game.lastUpdateTime = undefined;
    levels.load(game.currentLevel.number+1);
},
```

The methods are fairly simple. Both of them cancel any existing `animationFrame` loops, reset the `game.lastUpdateTime` variable, and finally call the `levels.load()` method with the appropriate level number. We need to call these methods from the `onclick` event of the corresponding images in the `scorescreen` and `endingscreen` layers, as shown in Listing 4-28.

Listing 4-28. Setting the onclick Events for Changing Levels

```
<div id="scorescreen" class="gamelayer">
    <img id="togglemusic" src="images/icons/sound.png">
    <img src="images/icons/prev.png" onclick="game.restartLevel();">
    <span id="score">Score: 0</span>
</div>

<div id="endingscreen" class="gamelayer">
    <div>
        <p id="endingmessage">The Level Is Over Message</p>
        <p id="playcurrentlevel" onclick="game.restartLevel();"><img
src="images/icons/prev.png"> Replay Current Level</p>
        <p id="playnextlevel" onclick="game.startNextLevel();"><img
src="images/icons/next.png"> Play Next Level </p>
        <p id="returntolevelscreen"onclick="game.showLevelScreen();"><img
src="images/icons/return.png"> Return to Level Screen</p>
    </div>
</div>
```

If we run the game, we should now be able to restart a level or proceed to the next level using the provided buttons.

We now have a working game with complete levels. We also have a simple way to build new levels. However, there is still one last element missing: sound.

Adding Sound

Adding sound makes a game much more immersive. We will start by adding a few sound effects for when the slingshot is released, for when a hero or villain bounces, and for when one of the blocks gets destroyed. We will also add some background music, along with the capability to turn it off if we want.

The sounds files for each of these effects are available in the audio folder (in both MP3 and OGG format).

We will start by loading these sound files in the game object's `init()` method, as shown in Listing 4-29.

Listing 4-29. Loading Sound and Background Music

```
init: function(){
    // Initialize objects
    levels.init();
    loader.init();
    mouse.init();

    // Load All Sound Effects and Background Music

    //"Kindergarten" by Gurdonark
    //http://ccmixter.org/files/gurdonark/26491 is licensed under a Creative Commons license
    game.backgroundMusic = loader.loadSound('audio/gurdonark-kindergarten');
```

```
game.slingshotReleasedSound = loader.loadSound("audio/released");
game.bounceSound = loader.loadSound('audio/bounce');
game.breakSound = {
    "glass":loader.loadSound('audio/glassbreak'),
    "wood":loader.loadSound('audio/woodbreak')
};

// Hide all game layers and display the start screen
$('.gamelayer').hide();
$('#gamestartscreen').show();

//Get handler for game canvas and context
game.canvas = document.getElementById("gamecanvas");
game.context = game.canvas.getContext('2d');
},
```

The code loads the different sound files using the `loader.loadSound()` method and saves them for later reference. We store the break sounds in an associative array so that we can easily add sounds for more entities and reference them by name. The background music is an excellent Creative Common–licensed tune called "Kindergarten" by Gurdonark.

■ **Tip** You can find some amazing free music for your own games at the ccMixter website, located at http://www.ccmixter.com.

Adding Break and Bounce Sounds

Now that we have loaded these sounds, we need to associate these sound effects with the entities and play them at the right time. We will modify the `entities.create()` method and set the break and bounce sounds in the entity definitions, as shown in Listing 4-30.

Listing 4-30. Assigning Sounds to Entities During Creation

```
create:function(entity){
    var definition = entities.definitions[entity.name];
    if(!definition){
        console.log ("Undefined entity name",entity.name);
        return;
    }
    switch(entity.type){
        case "block": // simple rectangles
            entity.health = definition.fullHealth;
            entity.fullHealth = definition.fullHealth;
            entity.shape = "rectangle";
            entity.sprite = loader.loadImage("images/entities/"+entity.name+".png");
            entity.breakSound = game.breakSound[entity.name];
            box2d.createRectangle(entity,definition);
            break;
```

```
        case "ground": // simple rectangles
            // No need for health. These are indestructible
            entity.shape = "rectangle";
            // No need for sprites. These won't be drawn at all
            box2d.createRectangle(entity,definition);
            break;
        case "hero":    // simple circles
        case "villain": // can be circles or rectangles
            entity.health = definition.fullHealth;
            entity.fullHealth = definition.fullHealth;
            entity.sprite = loader.loadImage("images/entities/"+entity.name+".png");
            entity.shape = definition.shape;
            entity.bounceSound = game.bounceSound;
            if(definition.shape == "circle"){
                entity.radius = definition.radius;
                box2d.createCircle(entity,definition);
            } else if(definition.shape == "rectangle"){
                entity.width = definition.width;
                entity.height = definition.height;
                box2d.createRectangle(entity,definition);
            }
            break;
        default:
            console.log("Undefined entity type",entity.type);
            break;
    }
},
```

The advantage of attaching sounds to entities during creation like this is that every entity can have its own custom "break" sound and "bounce" sound. Now, all we need to do is play the sounds when the events actually occur. First, we play the bounce sound whenever we detect a collision, inside the b2ContactListener object we defined earlier, as shown in Listing 4-31.

Listing 4-31. Playing the Bounce Sound During a Collision

```
var listener = new Box2D.Dynamics.b2ContactListener;
listener.PostSolve = function(contact,impulse){
    var body1 = contact.GetFixtureA().GetBody();
    var body2 = contact.GetFixtureB().GetBody();
    var entity1 = body1.GetUserData();
    var entity2 = body2.GetUserData();

    var impulseAlongNormal = Math.abs(impulse.normalImpulses[0]);
    // This listener is called a little too often. Filter out very tiny impulses.
    // After trying different values, 5 seems to work well
    if(impulseAlongNormal>5){
        // If objects have a health, reduce health by the impulse value
        if (entity1.health){
            entity1.health -= impulseAlongNormal;
        }
```

```
        if (entity2.health){
            entity2.health -= impulseAlongNormal;
        }

        // If objects have a bounce sound, play the sound
        if (entity1.bounceSound){
            entity1.bounceSound.play();
        }

        if (entity2.bounceSound){
            entity2.bounceSound.play();
        }
    }
};
```

During a collision, we check if the entity has a bounceSound property defined and, if so, we play the sound. If we define bounce sounds for any entity, this code will automatically play it. Next, we play the break sound any time an object gets destroyed, inside the drawAllBodies() method of the game object (see Listing 4-32).

Listing 4-32. Playing the Break Sound when an Object Is Destroyed

```
drawAllBodies:function(){
    box2d.world.DrawDebugData();

    // Iterate through all the bodies and draw them on the game canvas
    for (var body = box2d.world.GetBodyList(); body; body = body.GetNext()) {
        var entity = body.GetUserData();

        if(entity){
            var entityX = body.GetPosition().x*box2d.scale;
            if(entityX<0|| entityX>game.currentLevel.foregroundImage.width||(entity.health &&
entity.health <0)){
                box2d.world.DestroyBody(body);
                if (entity.type=="villain"){
                    game.score += entity.calories;
                    $('#score').html('Score: '+game.score);
                }
                if (entity.breakSound){
                    entity.breakSound.play();
                }
            } else {
                entities.draw(entity,body.GetPosition(),body.GetAngle())
            }
        }
    }
},
```

Again, we check to see if the entity being destroyed has a breakSound property and, if so, we play the sound. So far we have defined break sounds for the glass and wood blocks, but we can easily extend the code to add sounds for the other entities.

Finally, we play the slingshotReleasedSound when game.mode changes from firing to fired inside the handlePanning() method (see Listing 4-33).

Listing 4-33. Playing the Slingshot Released Sound when the Hero Is Fired

```
if (game.mode == "firing"){
    if(mouse.down){
        game.panTo(game.slingshotX);

game.currentHero.SetPosition({x:(mouse.x+game.offsetLeft)/box2d.scale,y:mouse.y/box2d.scale});
    } else {
        game.mode = "fired";
        game.slingshotReleasedSound.play();
        var impulseScaleFactor = 0.75;
        // Coordinates of center of slingshot (where the band is tied to slingshot)
        var slingshotCenterX = game.slingshotX + 35;
        var slingshotCenterY = game.slingshotY+25;
        var impulse = new b2Vec2((slingshotCenterX -mouse.x-game.offsetLeft)*impulseScaleFactor,
(slingshotCenterY-mouse.y)*impulseScaleFactor);
        game.currentHero.ApplyImpulse(impulse, game.currentHero.GetWorldCenter());


    }
}
```

Now when you run the game, you should hear sound effects when the hero is fired, when it bumps against something, or when the blocks get destroyed. The last thing we will be adding is the background music.

Adding Background Music

We have already loaded the background music file along with the other sound files in the game.init() method. Now we need to create a few methods for starting, stopping, and toggling the background music. We will add these methods to the game object, as shown in Listing 4-34.

Listing 4-34. Methods for Controlling Background Music

```
startBackgroundMusic:function(){
    var toggleImage = $("#togglemusic")[0];
    game.backgroundMusic.play();
    toggleImage.src="images/icons/sound.png";
},
stopBackgroundMusic:function(){
    var toggleImage = $("#togglemusic")[0];
    toggleImage.src="images/icons/nosound.png";
    game.backgroundMusic.pause();
    game.backgroundMusic.currentTime = 0; // Go to the beginning of the song
},
toggleBackgroundMusic:function(){
    var toggleImage = $("#togglemusic")[0];
    if(game.backgroundMusic.paused){
        game.backgroundMusic.play();
        toggleImage.src="images/icons/sound.png";
    } else {
        game.backgroundMusic.pause();
```

```
        $("#togglemusic")[0].src="images/icons/nosound.png";
    }
},
```

The startBackgroundMusic() method first calls the backgroundMusic object's play() method and then sets the toggle music button image to show a speaker with sound coming out.

The stopBackgroundMusic() method sets the toggle music button image to show a speaker with no sound. It then calls the backgroundMusic object's pause() method and sets the audio back to the beginning of the song by setting its currentTime property to 0.

Finally, the toggleBackgroundMusic() method checks to see whether or not the music is currently paused, calls either the pause() or play() method, and then sets the toggle image appropriately.

Now that we have these methods in place, we need to call them. We will call the startBackgroundMusic() method when the game starts from inside the game.start() method, as shown in Listing 4-35.

Listing 4-35. Starting the Background Music

```
start:function(){
    $('.gamelayer').hide();
    // Display the game canvas and score
    $('#gamecanvas').show();
    $('#scorescreen').show();

    game.startBackgroundMusic();

    game.mode = "intro";
    game.offsetLeft = 0;
    game.ended = false;
    game.animationFrame = window.requestAnimationFrame(game.animate,game.canvas);
},
```

Next, we will call the stopBackgroundMusic() method whenever the level ends by adding it to the showEndingScreen() method, as shown in Listing 4-36.

Listing 4-36. Stopping the Background Music

```
showEndingScreen:function(){
    game.stopBackgroundMusic();
    if (game.mode=="level-success"){
        if(game.currentLevel.number<levels.data.length-1){
            $('#endingmessage').html('Level Complete. Well Done!!!');
            $("#playnextlevel").show();
        } else {
            $('#endingmessage').html('All Levels Complete. Well Done!!!');
            $("#playnextlevel").hide();
        }
    } else if (game.mode=="level-failure"){
        $('#endingmessage').html('Failed. Play Again?');
        $("#playnextlevel").hide();
    }

    $('#endingscreen').show();
},
```

Finally, we will call the toggleBackgroundMusic() method from the onclick event of the toggle music button inside the scorescreen layer, as shown in Listing 4-37.

Listing 4-37. Toggling the Background Music

```
<div id="scorescreen" class="gamelayer">
    <img id="togglemusic" src="images/icons/sound.png" onclick="game.toggleBackgroundMusic()">
    <img src="images/icons/prev.png" onclick="game.restartLevel();">
    <span id="score">Score: 0</span>
</div>
```

Now when we run the game, the background music starts playing every time a level starts. If we click the toggle button, the music pauses and the button changes to the no-sound icon, as shown in Figure 4-8.

Figure 4-8. *The finished game with the background music switched off*

With this last change, our game is finally complete. We now can select a level and play the game by slinging across the hero fruits to attack the evil junk food while listening to sound effects and background music. Take some time to enjoy the game and come up with your own ideas for levels.

Summary

Over the past three chapters, we created our first physics engine–based HTML5 game. We started in Chapter 2 by creating a basic game framework with menus, a level system, and an asset loader and setting up game animation. We then covered the basics of Box2D in Chapter 3. Finally, in this chapter we integrated Box2D into our existing game framework and wrapped up our game by adding menu options, sounds effects, and music.

Of course, there is still a lot of room for us to expand the functionality of this game. Some of the obvious next steps would be to add animations for different entities, add more levels, tweak the game physics parameters, and add more heroes and villains with different characteristics.

However, the game has all the essential elements that people have come to expect from a good HTML5 game. You can use the code in this game as a starting point for any of your own physics engine–based games and take it wherever you would like.

Now that we have made our first game, we will take on a slightly more challenging project in the next few chapters: building a complete, multiplayer, real-time strategy game. So let's keep going.

CHAPTER 5

Creating the RTS Game World

Real-time strategy (RTS) games combine fast-paced tactical combat, resource management, and economy building within a defined game world.

A typical RTS game consists of a map of a world with different units, buildings, and terrain, as well as an interface to control and manipulate these elements. The player uses the interface to handle tasks such as gathering resources, constructing buildings, and creating an army, and then manages the army to achieve a set of goals defined for each level.

Although these games have an extensive history, the RTS genre was largely popularized by the games released by Westwood Studios and Blizzard Entertainment in the 1990s. Westwood's *Dune II* and *Command & Conquer* series are considered classics that helped define the genre. With its engaging story line and addictive multiplayer, Blizzard's *Starcraft* went on to elevate RTS gaming to an e-sport with professional competitive tournaments held around the world.

HTML5 now makes it possible to bring this genre to the browser in a way that wasn't possible earlier. In fact, one of my better known game programming–related achievements in the last year was single-handedly re-creating the original *Command & Conquer* entirely in HTML5. While generating a lot of buzz on the Web, this project proved beyond a doubt that HTML5 is ready for the next generation of games.

Over the next few chapters, we will use what we learned in previous chapters and build upon it to create our own RTS game. We will define a game world with buildings, units, and an overarching story line to create an engaging single-player campaign. We will then use HTML5 websockets to add real-time multiplayer support to our game.

Most of the artwork for this game has been provided by Daniel Cook (www.lostgarden.com), who originally designed this art for an unreleased RTS title called *Hard Vacuum*. We will be reusing the artwork that he has graciously shared but will create our own game concept. Our game, *Last Colony*, will be about a small band of survivors on a planet that has just been attacked. We will explore the story and gameplay in more detail over the next few chapters.

While developing this game, we will keep the code as generic and customizable as possible so that you can later reuse this code to build your own ideas.

So, let's get started.

Basic HTML Layout

Like the previous game, our RTS game will consist of several layers. The following are the first few layers that we will define:

- *Splash screen and main menu*: Shown when the game loads and allows the player to select campaign or multiplayer mode

- *Loading screen*: Shown whenever the game is loading assets

- *Mission screen*: Shown before a mission starts, with instructions for the mission

- *Game interface screen*: The main game screen that includes the map area and a dashboard for controlling the game

We will define more screens as needed in later chapters. We will be organizing all of the artwork inside an images folder. Unlike the previous game, we will break the JavaScript code into several files (such as buildings.js, vehicles.js, levels.js, and common.js) inside the js folder so as to make the code easier to maintain.

Creating the Splash Screen and Main Menu

We will start by creating an HTML file and adding the markup for our containers, as shown in Listing 5-1.

Listing 5-1. Basic Skeleton (index.html) with Layers Added

```html
<!DOCTYPE html>
<html>
    <head>
        <meta http-equiv="Content-type" content="text/html; charset=utf-8">
        <title>Last Colony</title>
        <script src="js/common.js" type="text/javascript" charset="utf-8"></script>
        <script src="js/jquery.min.js" type="text/javascript" charset="utf-8"></script>
        <script src="js/game.js" type="text/javascript" charset="utf-8"></script>
        <script src="js/mouse.js" type="text/javascript" charset="utf-8"></script>
        <script src="js/singleplayer.js" type="text/javascript" charset="utf-8"></script>
        <script src="js/maps.js" type="text/javascript" charset="utf-8"></script>
        <link rel="stylesheet" href="styles.css" type="text/css" media="screen" charset="utf-8">
    </head>
    <body>
        <div id="gamecontainer">
            <div id="gamestartscreen" class="gamelayer">
                <span id="singleplayer" onclick = "singleplayer.start();">Campaign</span><br>
                <span id="multiplayer" onclick = "multiplayer.start();">Multiplayer</span><br>
            </div>
            <div id="loadingscreen" class="gamelayer">
                <div id="loadingmessage"></div>
            </div>
        </div>
    </body>
</html>
```

The code first refers to the external JavaScript and CSS files we will be using. We will be creating and implementing all these JavaScript files (other than the jQuery code) over the course of this game. We also define a gamecontainer div that contains our first two game layers: gamestartscreen and loadingscreen.

The next thing we will do is define the initial style for the game container inside styles.css, as shown in Listing 5-2.

Listing 5-2. Initial Style Sheet (styles.css) for Game Container and Layer

```css
#gamecontainer {
    width:640px;
    height:480px;
    background: url(images/splashscreen.png);
    border: 1px solid black;
}
```

```
.gamelayer {
    width:640px;
    height:480px;
    position:absolute;
    display:none;
}
```

In this code, we set the width and height for the game container and layers and assign a background splash screen, just like we did in our previous game.

When we load index.html in the browser, we should now see our new splash screen, as shown in Figure 5-1.

Figure 5-1. *The initial game splash screen*

Now that the splash screen is in place, we can implement the main menu screen and the game loading screen.

We will start by setting up requestAnimationFrame and the asset loader using the same code as we did in our previous game. We will place this code inside a separate file called common.js, as shown in Listing 5-3.

Listing 5-3. Setting Up requestAnimationFrame and Image Loader (common.js)

```
// Setup requestAnimationFrame and cancelAnimationFrame for use in the game code
(function() {
    var lastTime = 0;
    var vendors = ['ms', ';', 'webkit', 'o'];
    for(var x = 0; x < vendors.length && !window.requestAnimationFrame; ++x) {
        window.requestAnimationFrame = window[vendors[x]+'RequestAnimationFrame'];
        window.cancelAnimationFrame =
          window[vendors[x]+'CancelAnimationFrame'] || window[vendors[x]+'CancelRequestAnimationFrame'];
    }
```

```javascript
        if (!window.requestAnimationFrame)
            window.requestAnimationFrame = function(callback, element) {
                var currTime = new Date().getTime();
                var timeToCall = Math.max(0, 16 - (currTime - lastTime));
                var id = window.setTimeout(function() { callback(currTime + timeToCall); },
                  timeToCall);
                lastTime = currTime + timeToCall;
                return id;
            };

        if (!window.cancelAnimationFrame)
            window.cancelAnimationFrame = function(id) {
                clearTimeout(id);
            };
}());

var loader = {
    loaded:true,
    loadedCount:0, // Assets that have been loaded so far
    totalCount:0, // Total number of assets that need to be loaded

    init:function(){
        // check for sound support
        var mp3Support,oggSupport;
        var audio = document.createElement('audio');
        if (audio.canPlayType) {
                // Currently canPlayType() returns: "", "maybe" or "probably"
              mp3Support = "" != audio.canPlayType('audio/mpeg');
              oggSupport = "" != audio.canPlayType('audio/ogg; codecs="vorbis"');
        } else {
            //The audio tag is not supported
            mp3Support = false;
            oggSupport = false;
        }

        // Check for ogg, then mp3, and finally set soundFileExtn to undefined
        loader.soundFileExtn = oggSupport?".ogg":mp3Support?".mp3":undefined;
    },
    loadImage:function(url){
        this.totalCount++;
        this.loaded = false;
        $('#loadingscreen').show();
        var image = new Image();
        image.src = url;
        image.onload = loader.itemLoaded;
        return image;
    },
    soundFileExtn:".ogg",
    loadSound:function(url){
        this.totalCount++;
        this.loaded = false;
        $('#loadingscreen').show();
```

```javascript
        var audio = new Audio();
        audio.src = url+loader.soundFileExtn;
        audio.addEventListener("canplaythrough", loader.itemLoaded, false);
        return audio;
    },
    itemLoaded:function(){
        loader.loadedCount++;
        $('#loadingmessage').html('Loaded '+loader.loadedCount+' of '+loader.totalCount);
        if (loader.loadedCount === loader.totalCount){
            loader.loaded = true;
            $('#loadingscreen').hide();
            if(loader.onload){
                loader.onload();
                loader.onload = undefined;
            }
        }
    }
}
```

Next, we will define our game object inside game.js, as shown in Listing 5-4.

Listing 5-4. Defining the Game Object init() Method (game.js)

```javascript
$(window).load(function() {
    game.init();
});

var game = {
    // Start preloading assets
    init: function(){
        loader.init();

        $('.gamelayer').hide();
        $('#gamestartscreen').show();
    },
}
```

In this code, we create a game object with an init() method that first initializes our asset loader and then uses jQuery to display the game start screen. We also use the window load handler to call game.init() once the window has loaded completely.

Finally, we need to append the CSS for the game starting screen and loading screen in styles.css, as shown in Listing 5-5.

Listing 5-5. Style for the Game Starting Screen and Loading Screen (styles.css)

```css
/* Game Starting Menu Screen */
#gamestartscreen {
    padding-top:320px;
    text-align:left;
    padding-left:50px;
    width:590px;
    height:160px;
}
```

```css
#gamestartscreen span {
    margin:20px;
    font-family: 'Courier New', Courier, monospace;
    font-size: 48px;
    cursor:pointer;
    color:white    ;
    text-shadow: -2px 0 purple, 0 2px purple, 2px 0 purple, 0 -2px purple;
}

#gamestartscreen span:hover {
    color:yellow;
}

/* Loading Screen */
#loadingscreen {
    background:rgba(100,100,100,0.7);
    z-index:10;
}

#loadingmessage {
    margin-top:400px;
    text-align:center;
    height:48px;
    color:white;
    background:url(images/loader.gif) no-repeat center;
    font:12px Arial;
}
```

When we open the game in the browser, we should see the starting screen with the main menu, as shown in Figure 5-2.

Figure 5-2. *The starting screen with the main menu*

The menu currently offers options for campaign, which is our story-based single-player mode, and multiplayer, which is our player-versus-player mode. You may have noticed in Listing 5-1 that the onclick handler for these two options call the singleplayer.start() and multiplayer.start() methods, respectively. Right now, clicking the Campaign option won't do anything since we haven't yet implemented the singleplayer object. Before we can do this, however, we need to create our first level.

Creating Our First Level

There are many viable approaches to defining maps or levels, for our game. One approach is to store all the information about the map terrain as metadata and then draw the map by assembling all the necessary images for the terrain on the browser at runtime.

The other approach, which is slightly simpler, is to store the basic map as a large image with the terrain drawn out using our own level-designing tool. We then need to store only the location of the map image along with metadata such as game entities and mission objectives. This is the approach that we will be using for our game.

Map images can be designed very quickly by using general-purpose tile map–editing software such as Tiled (www.mapeditor.org). Tiled is an excellent free tool that is available for several operating systems including Windows, Mac, and Linux. Once you start the application, you can load the sprite sheet for the terrain as a tile set and then use it to draw the map as if you were using a painting application (see Figure 5-3).

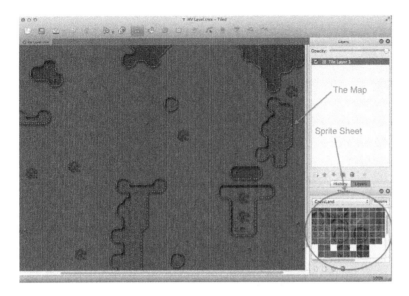

Figure 5-3. *Drawing a map using Tiled*

Once you draw the map, you can export it to several different file formats such as PNG images or JSON metadata. You won't need to use this the tool to follow along with this book since all the maps we will need have already been generated. However, if you are considering developing your own game, I strongly recommend exploring the tool's features.

■ **Note**   The Tiled editor's JSON format contains references to the sprite sheet and offsets for all the tiles it uses. This means you can use the JSON files to create maps that are assembled at runtime (instead of the preassembled ones we are creating).

Once we have our first map image designed, we will need to create the basic metadata describing the level. We will do this inside maps.js, as shown in Listing 5-6.

Listing 5-6. Defining the Basic Level Metadata (maps.js)

```
var maps = {
    "singleplayer":[
        {
            "name":"Introduction",
            "briefing": "In this level you will learn how to pan across the map.\n\nDon't worry! We
will be implementing more features soon.",

            /* Map Details */
            "mapImage":"images/maps/level-one-debug-grid.png",
            "startX":4,
            "startY":4,

        },
    ]
};
```

We define a maps object that contains a singleplayer array. This array currently contains details for only one map. This array will eventually contain all our single-player campaign maps in chronological order. When the single-player campaign is started, the singleplayer object will load the first map in this array and then proceed down the list as the player completes each level.

The details that we store for the level include the level name and a mission briefing that we will display before we start the level. We then store the map image and the starting map coordinates (startX, startY).

The map image is broken down into a grid of squares 20 pixels wide by 20 pixels high (based on the size of the tiles we are using). For now, we are using a "debug" version of the level that has this grid drawn on the map. This will make it easier for us to position elements inside the level while we are building the game.

The starting map coordinates let us decide where to position the screen on the map when we start the level using the grid coordinates.

Now that we have a simple map defined, we will set up the singleplayer object and display the mission briefing screen.

Loading the Mission Briefing Screen

The first thing we will do is add the HTML code for the mission screen into the body of our HTML file (index.html). The body of the HTML will now look like Listing 5-7.

Listing 5-7. Adding the Mission Screen

```
<body>
    <div id="gamecontainer">
        <div id="gamestartscreen" class="gamelayer">
            <span id="singleplayer" onclick = "singleplayer.start();">Campaign</span><br>
            <span id="multiplayer" onclick = "multiplayer.start();">Multiplayer</span><br>
        </div>

        <div id="missionscreen" class="gamelayer">
            <input type="button" id="entermission" onclick = "singleplayer.play();">
            <input type="button" id="exitmission" onclick = "singleplayer.exit();">
            <div id="missonbriefing"></div>
        </div>

        <div id="loadingscreen" class="gamelayer">
            <div id="loadingmessage"></div>
        </div>
    </div>
</body>
```

The missionscreen div contains two buttons; they are for entering the mission and exiting the mission screen. It also contains a missionbriefing div that we will use to display the briefing message.

Now that we have the HTML markup in place, we need to add the CSS styles for the mission screen into styles.css, as shown in Listing 5-8.

Listing 5-8. CSS Style for Mission Screen

```
/* Mission Briefing Screen */
#missionscreen {
    background: url(images/missionscreen.png) no-repeat;
}
```

```css
#missionscreen #entermission {
    position:absolute;
    top:79px;
    left:6px;
    width:246px;
    height:68px;
    border-width:0px;
    background-image: url(images/buttons.png);
    background-position: 0px 0px;
}

#missionscreen #entermission:disabled, #missionscreen #entermission:active {
    background-image: url(images/buttons.png);
    background-position: -251px 0px;
}

#missionscreen #exitmission {
    position:absolute;
    top:79px;
    left:380px;
    width:98px;
    height:68px;
    border-width:0px;
    background-image: url(images/buttons.png);
    background-position: 0px -76px;
}

#missionscreen #exitmission:disabled,#missionscreen #exitmission:active{
    background-image: url(images/buttons.png);
    background-position: -103px -76px;
}

#missionscreen #missonbriefing {
    position:absolute;
    padding:10px;
    top:160px;
    left:20px;
    width:410px;
    height:300px;
    color:rgb(130,150,162);
    font-size: 13px;
    font-family: 'Courier New', Courier, monospace;
}
```

We define a new background for the mission briefing screen that looks like a futuristic console. We then position the button and div elements to fit into the background. We keep different images for the enabled and disabled states of the buttons but store all of these sprites in a single image file (buttons.png).

Now that the mission briefing layer is in place, we will implement the singleplayer object with the start() and exit() methods inside singleplayer.js, as shown in Listing 5-9.

Listing 5-9. Implementing the Basic Singleplayer Object (singleplayer.js)

```
var singleplayer = {
    // Begin single player campaign
    start:function(){
        // Hide the starting menu layer
        $('.gamelayer').hide();

        // Begin with the first level
        singleplayer.currentLevel = 0;
        game.type = "singleplayer";
        game.team = "blue";

        // Finally start the level
        singleplayer.startCurrentLevel();
    },
    exit:function(){
        // Show the starting menu layer
        $('.gamelayer').hide();
        $('#gamestartscreen').show();
    },
    currentLevel:0,
    startCurrentLevel:function(){
        // Load all the items for the level
        var level = maps.singleplayer[singleplayer.currentLevel];

        // Don't allow player to enter mission until all assets for the level are loaded
        $("#entermission").attr("disabled", true);

        // Load all the assets for the level
        game.currentMapImage = loader.loadImage(level.mapImage);
        game.currentLevel = level;

        // Enable the enter mission button once all assets are loaded
        if (loader.loaded){
            $("#entermission").removeAttr("disabled");
        } else {
            loader.onload = function(){
                $("#entermission").removeAttr("disabled");
            }
        }

        // Load the mission screen with the current briefing
        $('#missonbriefing').html(level.briefing.replace(/\n/g,'<br><br>'));
        $("#missionscreen").show();
    },
};
```

We define a `singleplayer` object with three methods: `start()`, `exit()`, and `startCurrentLevel()`.

The `start()` method first hides all game layers and sets `singleplayer.currentLevel` to 0, which refers to the first level in the `maps.singleplayer` array that we defined earlier. It then sets the `game.type` and `game.team` variables to `singleplayer` and `blue`, respectively. We will use these values later once the game starts running. Finally, it calls the `singleplayer.startCurrentLevel()` method that we will call every time we want to load a level.

The `exit()` method hides all the game layers and takes us back to the main menu.

The `startCurrentLevel()` method first creates a `level` object that contains the metadata for our level.

It then temporarily disables the Enter Mission button on the screen and starts loading the level assets. For now, the only asset we are loading is the map image. Once the assets are loaded, the Enter Mission button is enabled so that the player can click it and enter the game.

Finally, the method puts the level briefing inside the `missionbriefing` div and displays the `missionscreen` div.

■ **Note** We replace carriage returns with `<br>` tags so that they show up in the HTML. This way, we can easily break out the mission briefing into multiple paragraphs if we want.

When we load the game in the browser and click the Campaign option, we should see the mission briefing screen for the first level, as shown in Figure 5-4.

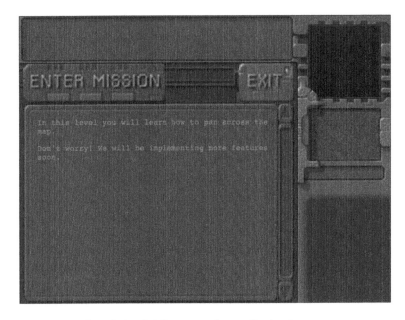

Figure 5-4. *The mission briefing screen for our first level*

The advantage of displaying the briefing screen while loading the assets in the background is that players can spend their time reading the mission briefing while waiting for all the assets to load.

Clicking the Exit button should take us back to the main menu. We still can't enter the mission until we implement the actual game interface and the game animation and drawing loops.

Implementing the Game Interface

The first thing we will do is add the HTML markup for the game interface screen into the body of our HTML file (index.html). The body will now look like Listing 5-10.

Listing 5-10. Adding the Game Interface Layer (index.html)

```
<body>
    <div id="gamecontainer">
        <div id="gamestartscreen" class="gamelayer">
            <span id="singleplayer" onclick = "singleplayer.start();">Campaign</span><br>
            <span id="multiplayer" onclick = "multiplayer.start();">Multiplayer</span><br>
        </div>
        <div id="missionscreen" class="gamelayer">
            <input type="button" id="entermission" onclick = "singleplayer.play();">
            <input type="button" id="exitmission" onclick = "singleplayer.exit();">
            <div id="missonbriefing">Welcome to your first mission.
            </div>
        </div>
        <div id="gameinterfacescreen" class="gamelayer">
            <div id="gamemessages"></div>
            <div id="callerpicture"></div>
            <div id="cash"></div>
            <div id="sidebarbuttons">
            </div>
            <canvas id="gamebackgroundcanvas" height="400" width="480"></canvas>
            <canvas id="gameforegroundcanvas" height="400" width="480"></canvas>
        </div>
        <div id="loadingscreen" class="gamelayer">
            <div id="loadingmessage"></div>
        </div>
    </div>
</body>
```

Our game interface layer consists of several different areas within it.

- *Game area*: This is where the player can see the map and interact with the buildings, units, and other entities within the game. This is implemented using two canvas elements: gamebackgroundcanvas for the map and gameforegroundcanvas for the entities inside the level (such as buildings and units).

- *Game messages*: This is where the player can see system notifications or story-driven messages.

- *Caller picture*: This is where the player will see profile pictures of the person sending story-driven messages.

- *Cash*: This is where players will see their cash reserves.

- *Sidebar buttons*: This is where players will see buttons they can use for creating units and buildings within the game.

Now that the HTML is in place, we will add the CSS for the game interface screen to styles.css, as shown in Listing 5-11.

Listing 5-11. CSS for the Game Interface Screen

```css
/* Game Interface Screen */
#gameinterfacescreen {
    background: url(images/maininterface.png) no-repeat;
}

#gameinterfacescreen #gamemessages{
    position:absolute;
    padding-left:10px;
    top:5px;
    left:5px;
    width:450px;
    height:60px;
    color:rgb(130,150,162);
    overflow:hidden;
    font-size: 13px;
    font-family: 'Courier New', Courier, monospace;
}
#gameinterfacescreen #gamemessages span {
    color:white;
}

#gameinterfacescreen #callerpicture {
    position:absolute;
    left:498px;
    top:154px;
    width:126px;
    height:88px;
    overflow:none;
}

#gameinterfacescreen #cash {
    width:120px;
    height:22px;
    position:absolute;
    left:498px;
    top:256px;
    color:rgb(130,150,162);
    overflow:hidden;
    font-size: 13px;
    font-family: 'Courier New', Courier, monospace;
    text-align:right;
}

#gameinterfacescreen canvas{
    position:absolute;
    top:79px;
    left:0px;
}
```

```css
#gameinterfacescreen #foregroundcanvas{
    z-index:1;
}

#gameinterfacescreen #backgroundcanvas{
    z-index:0;
}
```

We start by defining a separate background for the gameinterfacescreen div and then positioning the various other divs at the appropriate location above the interface area. Both game canvas elements are positioned at the same location with foregroundcanvas on top of backgroundcanvas by setting a higher z-index value for the foregroundcanvas. Elements with a higher z-index value are displayed above elements with a lower z-index value.

Next we will modify the game object inside game.js to initialize the canvas elements and define animation and drawing loops. The modified game object will now look like Listing 5-12.

Listing 5-12. Adding Animation and Drawing Loops to the Game Object (game.js)

```javascript
var game = {
    // Start preloading assets
    init: function(){
        loader.init();

        $('.gamelayer').hide();
        $('#gamestartscreen').show();

        game.backgroundCanvas = document.getElementById('gamebackgroundcanvas');
        game.backgroundContext = game.backgroundCanvas.getContext('2d');

        game.foregroundCanvas = document.getElementById('gameforegroundcanvas');
        game.foregroundContext = game.foregroundCanvas.getContext('2d');

        game.canvasWidth = game.backgroundCanvas.width;
        game.canvasHeight = game.backgroundCanvas.height;
    },
    start:function(){
        $('.gamelayer').hide();
        $('#gameinterfacescreen').show();
        game.running = true;
        game.refreshBackground= true;

        game.drawingLoop();
    },

    // The map is broken into square tiles of this size (20 pixels x 20 pixels)
    gridSize:20,

    // Store whether or not the background moved and needs to be redrawn
    backgroundChanged:true,

    // A control loop that runs at a fixed period of time
    animationTimeout:100, // 100 milliseconds or 10 times a second
    offsetX:0,      // X & Y panning offsets for the map
```

```
        offsetY:0,
        animationLoop:function(){

            // Animate each of the elements within the game
        },
        drawingLoop:function(){
            // Handle Panning the Map
            // Since drawing the background map is a fairly large operation,
            // we only redraw the background if it changes (due to panning)
            if (game.refreshBackground){
                game.backgroundContext.drawImage(game.currentMapImage,game.offsetX,game.offsetY,
                game.canvasWidth,game.canvasHeight, 0,0,game.canvasWidth,game.canvasHeight);
                game.refreshBackground = false;
            }

            // Call the drawing loop for the next frame using request animation frame
            if (game.running){
                requestAnimationFrame(game.drawingLoop);
            }
        },
}
```

We modified the init() method to save the canvas elements, their 2D context objects, and their width and height into variables.

We define a start() method that hides other layers and displays the game interface screen. It then sets the game. running and game.backgroundChanged variables to true for later use. Finally, we call the drawingLoop() method for the first time.

We also define two different methods called animationLoop() and drawingLoop().

The animationLoop() method handles all control- and animation-related logic and needs to be run at a fixed interval (defined in animationTimeout). An animation timeout of 100 milliseconds is usually sufficient for a fairly smooth game. For now the animationLoop() method is empty with placeholders for handling map panning and animating the game elements.

The reason we break out the code into two different timer loops is because the animation code will contain logic such as pathfinding, processing commands, and changing the animation states of sprites, which will not need to be executed as often as the drawing code.

The animation code will also control the actual movement of units. By keeping this code independent of the drawing code, we ensure that units will move the same amount after each animation cycle. This will become very important when we handle multiplayer and need the game state to be synchronized across different machines. If we aren't careful, slight calculation differences between browsers and machines can cause unexpected results such as a bullet hitting an enemy unit in one browser but missing the enemy in the other browser.

In case the code takes longer than 100 milliseconds to run, the next interval loop will not be executed until the current loop has completed. This may result in the game skipping and stuttering slightly on slower machines. Some games use a time-delta-based code to work around this by extrapolating unit movement. However, since we are going to be developing our game to handle multiplayer, extrapolation can get a little tricky. For now, we will assume that the player has a machine capable of running the game smoothly.

The drawingLoop() method handles the actual drawing of all the game elements onto the two game canvas objects. The method is called using requestAnimationFrame() and can run as often as the browser allows.

The first thing that the drawingLoop() method does is check whether the background has changed and needs to be redrawn. If so, it draws the map image (stored in currentMapImage when the map was loaded) using the panning offsets (offsetX, offsetY) and the canvas dimensions. It then resets the backgroundChanged flag. We use this optimization so that we don't need to redraw the entire background after each refresh. Finally, the drawingLoop() method calls itself using requestAnimationFrame() as long as the game is still running.

Now that the game animation state is in place, we will need to implement the singleplayer.play() method inside singleplayer.js, as shown in Listing 5-13.

Listing 5-13. The singleplayer.play() Method (singleplayer.js)

```
play:function(){
    game.animationLoop();
    game.animationInterval = setInterval(game.animationLoop,game.animationTimeout);
    game.start();
},
```

This method is fairly simple. It calls the game.animationLoop() method for first time and then uses the setInterval() method to call the method every 100 milliseconds (set in game.animationTimeout). Finally, it calls the game.start() method. The gameAnimationLoop() method is currently empty, but we will start using it when we add entities to our game in the next chapter.

If we run the game code we have so far, we should be able to click the Enter Mission button at the mission briefing screen and then see the game interface screen with the map loaded, as shown in Figure 5-5.

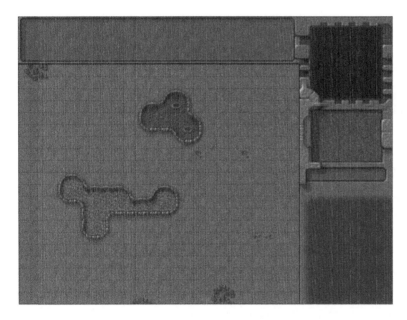

Figure 5-5. *The game interface screen with the first map loaded*

One thing you might notice is that the game starts off at the top-left corner of the map. To use the initial map offset settings that we provided in map.js, we will need to load the offset values when we start the level. We will do this by modifying the startCurrentLevel() method in singleplayer.js, as shown in Listing 5-14.

Listing 5-14. Setting the Map Offset Inside startCurrentLevel() (singleplayer.js)

```
startCurrentLevel:function(){
    // Load all the items for the level
    var level = maps.singleplayer[singleplayer.currentLevel];
```

```
    // Don't allow player to enter mission until all assets for the level are loaded
    $("#entermission").attr("disabled", true);

    // Load all the assets for the level
    game.currentMapImage = loader.loadImage(level.mapImage);
    game.currentLevel = level;

    game.offsetX = level.startX * game.gridSize;
    game.offsetY = level.startY * game.gridSize;

    // Enable the enter mission button once all assets are loaded
    if (loader.loaded){
        $("#entermission").removeAttr("disabled");
    } else {
        loader.onload = function(){
            $("#entermission").removeAttr("disabled");
        }
    }

    // Load the mission screen with the current briefing
    $('#missonbriefing').html(level.briefing.replace('\n','<br><br>'));
    $("#missionscreen").show();
},
```

We added just two new lines to set game.offsetX and game.offsetY based on level.startX and level.startY. This time when we load the map, it loads at the offset we defined in the map. Now that we have finished loaded the map, we will implement panning around the map using the mouse.

Implementing Map Panning

The first thing we will do is set up mouse input by creating a mouse object inside mouse.js (see Listing 5-15).

Listing 5-15. Setting Up the Mouse Object

```
var mouse = {
    // x,y coordinates of mouse relative to top left corner of canvas
    x:0,
    y:0,
    // x,y coordinates of mouse relative to top left corner of game map
    gameX:0,
    gameY:0,
    // game grid x,y coordinates of mouse
    gridX:0,
    gridY:0,
    // whether or not the left mouse button is currently pressed
    buttonPressed:false,
    // whether or not the player is dragging and selecting with the left mouse button pressed
    dragSelect:false,
    // whether or not the mouse is inside the canvas region
    insideCanvas:false,
```

```
    click:function(ev,rightClick){
        // Player clicked inside the canvas
    },

    draw:function(){
        if(this.dragSelect){
            var x = Math.min(this.gameX,this.dragX);
            var y = Math.min(this.gameY,this.dragY);
            var width = Math.abs(this.gameX-this.dragX)
            var height = Math.abs(this.gameY-this.dragY)
            game.foregroundContext.strokeStyle = 'white';
            game.foregroundContext.strokeRect(x-game.offsetX,y-game.offsetY, width, height);
        }
    },
    calculateGameCoordinates:function(){
        mouse.gameX = mouse.x + game.offsetX ;
        mouse.gameY = mouse.y + game.offsetY;

        mouse.gridX = Math.floor((mouse.gameX) / game.gridSize);
        mouse.gridY = Math.floor((mouse.gameY) / game.gridSize);
    },
    init:function(){
        var $mouseCanvas = $("#gameforegroundcanvas");
        $mouseCanvas.mousemove(function(ev) {
            var offset = $mouseCanvas.offset();
            mouse.x = ev.pageX - offset.left;
            mouse.y = ev.pageY - offset.top;

            mouse.calculateGameCoordinates();

            if (mouse.buttonPressed){
                if  ((Math.abs(mouse.dragX - mouse.gameX) > 4 || Math.abs(mouse.dragY - mouse.gameY)
> 4)){
                    mouse.dragSelect = true
                }
            } else {
                mouse.dragSelect = false;
            }
        });

        $mouseCanvas.click(function(ev) {
            mouse.click(ev,false);
            mouse.dragSelect = false;
            return false;
        });

        $mouseCanvas.mousedown(function(ev) {
            if(ev.which == 1){
                mouse.buttonPressed = true;
                mouse.dragX = mouse.gameX;
```

```
                    mouse.dragY = mouse.gameY;
                    ev.preventDefault();
                }
            return false;
        });

        $mouseCanvas.bind('contextmenu',function(ev){
            mouse.click(ev,true);
            return false;
        });

        $mouseCanvas.mouseup(function(ev) {
            var shiftPressed = ev.shiftKey;
            if(ev.which==1){
                //Left key was released
                mouse.buttonPressed = false;
                mouse.dragSelect = false;
            }
            return false;
        });

        $mouseCanvas.mouseleave(function(ev) {
            mouse.insideCanvas = false;
        });

        $mouseCanvas.mouseenter(function(ev) {
            mouse.buttonPressed = false;
            mouse.insideCanvas = true;
        });
    }
}
```

There is a lot happening inside this object. First, we declare a mouse object and start by defining variables to store the mouse coordinates relative to the canvas (x, y), relative to the map (gameX, gameY) and in terms of the map grid (gridX, gridY). We also define several variables to store the mouse state (buttonPressed, dragSelect, and insideCanvas).

Next we define the click() method as a placeholder that gets called any time the mouse is clicked inside the canvas region. We will implement this method later.

Next we define a draw() method that checks whether the mouse is being dragged across the canvas and, if so, draws a white rectangle from the top-left corner to the bottom-right corner of the selected area. We subtract the map offset when calculating the coordinates of the rectangle so that it is drawn relative to the game map and it does not move even if the map is panned around.

We also define a method called calculateGameCoordinates() that converts the mouse x and y coordinates to game coordinates.

Finally, we define the init() method, which is the heart of the mouse object. This method sets up all the necessary mouse event listeners for the foreground canvas:

- mousemove: Whenever the mouse is moved, we calculate the different mouse coordinates and store them. We also check whether the mouse button is pressed and whether the mouse has been dragged at least 4 pixels and, if so, set the dragSelect option. The 4-pixel threshold prevents the game from confusing every click with a drag selection operation.

- click: Whenever a click operation is completed, we call our mouse.click() method and clear the dragSelect flag.

120

- mousedown: If the left mouse button is pressed down, we set the buttonPressed flag and save the coordinates into dragX and dragY. In addition, we prevent the default mouse click behavior (such as browser context menus when the right mouse button is pressed).

- contextmenu: We call the mouse.click() method and pass the rightClick parameter as true.

- mouseup: If the left mouse button is released, we clear the dragSelect and buttonPressed flags.

- mouseleave: When the mouse leaves the canvas area, we set the insideCanvas flag to false.

- mouseenter: Whenever the mouse reenters the canvas area, we set the insideCanvas flag to true and clear the buttonPressed flag.

Now that we have set up our mouse object, we will modify our game object inside game.js to use the mouse. The first thing we need to do is call the mouse.init() method from inside the game.init() method. The updated game.init() method will look like Listing 5-16.

Listing 5-16. Calling mouse.init() from Inside game.init() (game.js)

```
init: function(){
    loader.init();
    mouse.init();

    $('.gamelayer').hide();
    $('#gamestartscreen').show();

    game.backgroundCanvas = document.getElementById('gamebackgroundcanvas');
    game.backgroundContext = game.backgroundCanvas.getContext('2d');

    game.foregroundCanvas = document.getElementById('gameforegroundcanvas');
    game.foregroundContext = game.foregroundCanvas.getContext('2d');

    game.canvasWidth = game.backgroundCanvas.width;
    game.canvasHeight = game.backgroundCanvas.height;
},
```

Next we will define a handlePanning() method inside the game object. (See Listing 5-17.)

Listing 5-17. Defining the handlePanning() Method Inside the Game Object (game.js)

```
// A control loop that runs at a fixed period of time
animationTimeout:100, // 100 milliseconds or 10 times a second
offsetX:0,      // X & Y panning offsets for the map
offsetY:0,
panningThreshold:60, // Distance from edge of canvas at which panning starts
panningSpeed:10, // Pixels to pan every drawing loop
handlePanning:function(){
    // do not pan if mouse leaves the canvas
    if (!mouse.insideCanvas){
        return;
    }
```

```
    if(mouse.x<=game.panningThreshold){
        if (game.offsetX>=game.panningSpeed){
            game.refreshBackground = true;
            game.offsetX -= game.panningSpeed;
        }
    } else if (mouse.x>= game.canvasWidth - game.panningThreshold){
        if (game.offsetX + game.canvasWidth + game.panningSpeed <= game.currentMapImage.width){
            game.refreshBackground = true;
            game.offsetX += game.panningSpeed;
        }
    }

    if(mouse.y<=game.panningThreshold){
        if (game.offsetY>=game.panningSpeed){
            game.refreshBackground = true;
            game.offsetY -= game.panningSpeed;
        }
    } else if (mouse.y>= game.canvasHeight - game.panningThreshold){
        if (game.offsetY + game.canvasHeight + game.panningSpeed <= game.currentMapImage.height){
            game.refreshBackground = true;
            game.offsetY += game.panningSpeed;
        }
    }

    if (game.refreshBackground){
        // Update mouse game coordinates based on game offsets
        mouse.calculateGameCoordinates();
    }
},
```

We start by defining two new variables, panningThreshold and panningSpeed, that store how close to the canvas edge the mouse cursor needs to be for panning to occur and how fast the panning should be. The handlePanning() method itself checks to see whether the mouse is near any of the edges of the canvas and whether there is still any map left to pan in that direction. If there is, we adjust the offset in that direction by the panning threshold and set the background changed flag. Finally, if the map did pan, we refresh the mouse game coordinates since they will change any time the map pans.

The last change we will make to the game object is calling the handlePanning() and mouse.draw() method from inside game.drawingLoop(). The final drawingLoop() method will look like Listing 5-18.

Listing 5-18. Calling mouse.draw() from Inside game.drawingLoop() (game.js)

```
drawingLoop:function(){
    // Handle Panning the Map
    game.handlePanning();

    // Since drawing the background map is a fairly large operation,
    // we only redraw the background if it changes (due to panning)
    if (game.refreshBackground){
        game.backgroundContext.drawImage(game.currentMapImage, game.offsetX, game.offsetY,
        game.canvasWidth, game.canvasHeight, 0,0,game.canvasWidth,game.canvasHeight);
        game.refreshBackground = false;
    }
```

```
        // Clear the foreground canvas
        game.foregroundContext.clearRect(0,0,game.canvasWidth,game.canvasHeight);

        // Start drawing the foreground elements

        // Draw the mouse
        mouse.draw()

        // Call the drawing loop for the next frame using request animation frame
        if (game.running){
            requestAnimationFrame(game.drawingLoop);
        }
    },
```

We start by calling the game.handlePanning() method that we defined just now. Next we clear the foreground canvas by resetting the canvas width. We then leave a placeholder for drawing the foreground elements such as buildings and units that we will implement later. Finally, we call the mouse.draw() method just before the end of the drawing loop.

At this point, if we run the game, we should be able to pan around the map by moving the mouse near the edges of the canvas so that we can explore the entire map, as shown in Figure 5-6.

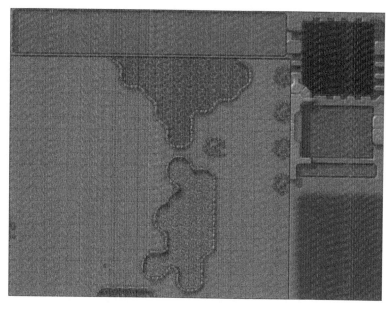

Figure 5-6. Panning around the map

Summary

In this chapter, we set out to develop the basic framework for our RTS game.

Just like in Chapter 2, we implemented a splash screen and a starting menu. We then created our first level by combining a map image and some basic level metadata.

We implemented a single-player object that loaded map data and displayed a mission briefing screen. We then created the game interface screen and set up the animation and drawing loop for the game so we could load and see the initial map on the canvas. Finally, we captured and used mouse events to let the user pan around the level.

While we have a lot of the essential elements of our game world, we are still missing the actual entities to interact with, such as buildings and vehicles.

In the next chapter, we will start adding these different entities to our level. We will draw them on the screen using sprite sheets and animation states. We will then set up a framework for selecting these entities so we can interact with them.

■ ■ ■

CHAPTER 6

Adding Entities to Our World

In the previous chapter, we put together the basic framework for our RTS game. We loaded a level and panned around using the mouse.

In this chapter, we will build upon that by adding entities to our game world. We will build a general framework that will allow us to easily add entities such as buildings and units to a level. Finally, we will add the ability for the player to select these entities using the mouse.

Let's get started. We will use the code from Chapter 5 as our starting point.

Defining Entities

These are the game entities we will be adding to our game:

- *Buildings*: Our game will have four types of buildings.

    - *Base*: Primary structure used to construct other buildings

    - *Starport*: Used to teleport in both ground vehicles and aircraft

    - *Harvester*: Used to extract resources from oil fields

    - *Ground turret*: Defensive structure used to guard against ground vehicles

- *Vehicles*: Our game will have four types of vehicles.

    - *Transport*: An unarmed vehicle used to transport supplies and people

    - *Harvester*: A mobile unit that deploys into the harvester building at an oil field

    - *Scout tank*: A light, fast-moving tank used for scouting

    - *Heavy tank*: A slower tank with heavier armor and weaponry

- *Aircraft*: Our game will have two types of aircraft.

    - *Chopper*: A slow-moving craft that can attack both land and air

    - *Wraith*: A fast-moving jet aircraft that can attack only in the air

- *Terrain*: Apart from the terrain already integrated in our map, we will define two additional types of terrain.

    - *Oil field*: Source of mineral resources that can be extracted for cash by deploying a harvester

    - *Rocks*: Interesting rock formations

We will store our entity types in separate JavaScript files to make the code easier to maintain. The first thing we will do is add references to the new JavaScript files inside the head section of our HTML file. The modified head section will now look like Listing 6-1.

Listing 6-1. Adding References to Entities (index.html)

```
<head>
    <meta http-equiv="Content-type" content="text/html; charset=utf-8">
    <title>Last Colony</title>
    <script src="js/common.js" type="text/javascript" charset="utf-8"></script>
    <script src="js/jquery.min.js" type="text/javascript" charset="utf-8"></script>
    <script src="js/game.js" type="text/javascript" charset="utf-8"></script>
    <script src="js/mouse.js" type="text/javascript" charset="utf-8"></script>
    <script src="js/singleplayer.js" type="text/javascript" charset="utf-8"></script>
    <script src="js/maps.js" type="text/javascript" charset="utf-8"></script>

    <!-- Definitions for game entities -->
    <script src="js/buildings.js" type="text/javascript" charset="utf-8"></script>
    <script src="js/vehicles.js" type="text/javascript" charset="utf-8"></script>
    <script src="js/aircraft.js" type="text/javascript" charset="utf-8"></script>
    <script src="js/terrain.js" type="text/javascript" charset="utf-8"></script>

    <link rel="stylesheet" href="styles.css" type="text/css" media="screen" charset="utf-8">
</head>
```

With this code in place, we are now ready to start defining our first set of entities, the buildings, to the game.

Defining Our First Entity: The Main Base

The first building we will define is the main base. Unlike other buildings in the game that can be constructed by the player, the main base will always be preconstructed before the level starts. The base allows the player to teleport in other buildings as long as the player has sufficient resources.

The base will consist of a single sprite sheet image that contains different animation states for the base (see Figure 6-1).

Figure 6-1. Sprite sheet for the base

As you can see, the sheet consists of two different rows of frames for the blue and green teams. The sprites in this case consist of a default animation (four frames), a damaged base (one frame), and finally an animation for when the base is constructing a building (three frames). We will be using similar sprite sheets and a common loading and drawing mechanism for all the entitites within our game.

The first thing we will do is define a `buildings` object inside `buildings.js`, as shown in Listing 6-2.

Listing 6-2. Defining the buildings Object with the First Building Type (buildings.js)

```
var buildings = {
list:{
    "base":{
        name:"base",
        // Properties for drawing the object
        pixelWidth:60,
        pixelHeight:60,
        baseWidth:40,
        baseHeight:40,
        pixelOffsetX:0,
        pixelOffsetY:20,
        // Properties for describing structure for pathfinding
        buildableGrid:[
            [1,1],
            [1,1]
        ],
        passableGrid:[
            [1,1],
            [1,1]
        ],
        sight:3,
        hitPoints:500,
        cost:5000,
        spriteImages:[
            {name:"healthy",count:4},
            {name:"damaged",count:1},
            {name:"contructing",count:3},
        ],
    },
},
defaults:{
    type:"buildings",
    animationIndex:0,
    direction:0,
    orders:{ type:"stand" },
    action:"stand",
    selected:false,
    selectable:true,
    // Default function for animating a building
    animate:function(){
    },
    // Default function for drawing a building
    draw:function(){
    }
},
load:loadItem,
add:addItem,
}
```

The buildings object has four important items.

- The list property will contain the definitions for all our buildings. For now, we define the base building along with properties that we will need later. These include properties for drawing the object (such as pixelWidth), properties for pathfinding (buildableGrid), general properties such as hitPoints and cost, and finally the list of sprite images.

- The defaults property contains properties and definitions common for all buildings. This includes a placeholder for the animate() and draw() methods that are commonly used by all buildings. We will implement these methods later.

- The load() method points to a common method for all the entities called loadItem() that we still need to define. This method will load the sprite sheet and definitions for a given entity.

- The add() method points to another common method for all the entities called addItem() that we need to define. This method will create a new instance of a given entity to be added to the game.

Now that we have a basic building definition in place, we will define the loadItem() and addItem() methods inside common.js so that they can be used by all the entities (see Listing 6-3).

Listing 6-3. Defining the loadItem() and addItem() Methods (common.js)

```
/* The default load() method used by all our game entities*/
function loadItem(name){
    var item = this.list[name];
    // if the item sprite array has already been loaded then no need to do it again
    if(item.spriteArray){
        return;
    }
    item.spriteSheet = loader.loadImage('images/'+this.defaults.type+'/'+name+'.png');
    item.spriteArray = [];
    item.spriteCount = 0;

    for (var i=0; i < item.spriteImages.length; i++){
        var constructImageCount = item.spriteImages[i].count;
        var constructDirectionCount = item.spriteImages[i].directions;
        if (constructDirectionCount){
            for (var j=0; j < constructDirectionCount; j++) {
                var constructImageName = item.spriteImages[i].name +"-"+j;
                item.spriteArray[constructImageName] = {
                    name:constructImageName,
                    count:constructImageCount,
                    offset:item.spriteCount
                };
                item.spriteCount += constructImageCount;
            };
        } else {
            var constructImageName = item.spriteImages[i].name;
            item.spriteArray[constructImageName] = {
                name:constructImageName,
                count:constructImageCount,
                offset:item.spriteCount
            };
```

```
            item.spriteCount += constructImageCount;
        }

    }
}

/* The default add() method used by all our game entities*/
function addItem(details){
    var item = {};
    var name = details.name;
    $.extend(item,this.defaults);
    $.extend(item,this.list[name]);
    item.life = item.hitPoints;
    $.extend(item,details);
    return item;
}
```

The loadItem() method uses the image loader to load the sprite sheet image into the spriteSheet property. It then goes through the spriteImages definition and creates a spriteArray object that stores the starting offsets for each of the sprite animations.

You will notice that the code checks for the existence of count and directions properties when creating the array. This allows us to define multidirectional sprites, which will be needed for drawing entities like turrets and vehicles.

The addItem() method first applies the defaults for the entity type (for example, buildings) and then extends it with properties for the specific entity (for example, base), sets the life for the item, and finally applies any additional properties passed into the details parameter.

This interesting way of creating objects gives us our own implementation of multiple inheritance, allowing us to define and override properties at three different levels: building properties, base properties, and item-specific details (such as position and team color).

Now that we have defined our first entity, we need a simple way of adding entities into a level.

Adding Entities to the Level

The first thing we will do is modify our map definition to include a list of entity types required to be loaded and a list of items to add to the level before it starts. We will modify the first map that we created in maps.js, as shown in Listing 6-4.

Listing 6-4. Loading and Adding Entities Inside the Map (maps.js)

```
var maps = {
    "singleplayer":[
        {
            "name":"Entities",
            "briefing": "In this level you will add new entities to the map.\nYou will also select
them using the mouse",

            /* Map Details */
            "mapImage":"images/maps/level-one-debug-grid.png",
            "startX":4,
            "startY":4,
```

```
        /* Entities to be loaded */
        "requirements":{
            "buildings":["base"],
            "vehicles":[],
            "aircraft":[],
            "terrain":[]
        },

        /* Entities to be added */
        "items":[
            {"type":"buildings","name":"base","x":11,"y":14,"team":"blue"},
            {"type":"buildings","name":"base","x":12,"y":16,"team":"green"},
            {"type":"buildings","name":"base","x":15,"y":15,"team":"green", "life":50}
        ]

    }
  ]
}
```

The map is very similar to the map from Chapter 5. We have added two new sections: requirements and items.

The requirements property contains the buildings, vehicles, aircraft, and terrain to preload for this level. For now, we load only buildings of type base.

The items array contains details of the entities we want to add to the level. The details we provide include the item type and name, the x and y grid coordinates, and the color of the team. These are the bare-minimum properties that we need in order to uniquely define an entity.

We have added three base buildings with random positions and teams. The last building in the items array also contains an additional property: life. Because of the way we defined the addItem() method earlier, this life property will override the default value of life for the base. This way, we will also have an example of a damaged building.

Next we will modify the singleplayer.startCurrentLevel() method in singleplayer.js to load and add the entities when the game starts (see Listing 6-5).

Listing 6-5. Loading and Adding Entities inside the startCurrentLevel() Method (singleplayer.js)

```
startCurrentLevel:function(){
    // Load all the items for the level
    var level = maps.singleplayer[singleplayer.currentLevel];

    // Don't allow player to enter mission until all assets for the level are loaded
    $("#entermission").attr("disabled", true);
    // Load all the assets for the level
    game.currentMapImage = loader.loadImage(level.mapImage);
    game.currentLevel = level;

    game.offsetX = level.startX * game.gridSize;
    game.offsetY = level.startY * game.gridSize;

    // Load level Requirements
    game.resetArrays();
    for (var type in level.requirements){
        var requirementArray = level.requirements[type];
        for (var i=0; i < requirementArray.length; i++) {
            var name = requirementArray[i];
```

```
        if (window[type]){
            window[type].load(name);
        } else {
            console.log('Could not load type :',type);
        }
    };
}

for (var i = level.items.length - 1; i >= 0; i--){
    var itemDetails = level.items[i];
    game.add(itemDetails);
};

// Enable the enter mission button once all assets are loaded
if (loader.loaded){
    $("#entermission").removeAttr("disabled");
} else {
    loader.onload = function(){
        $("#entermission").removeAttr("disabled");
    }
}

// Load the mission screen with the current briefing
$('#missonbriefing').html(level.briefing.replace(/\n/g,'<br><br>'));
$("#missionscreen").show();
},
```

We do three things in the newly added code. We first initialize the game arrays by calling the game.resetArrays() method. We then iterate through the requirements object and call the appropriate load() method for each entity. The load() methods in turn will call the loader to asynchronously load all the images for the entity in the background and enable the entermission button once all the images have been loaded.

Finally, we iterate through the items array and pass the details to the game.add() method.

Next we will add the resetArrays(), add(), and remove() methods to the game object inside game.js (see Listing 6-6).

Listing 6-6. Adding resetArrays(), add(), and remove() to the Game Object (game.js)

```
resetArrays:function(){
    game.counter = 1;
    game.items = [];
    game.sortedItems = [];
    game.buildings = [];
    game.vehicles = [];
    game.aircraft = [];
    game.terrain = [];
    game.triggeredEvents = [];
    game.selectedItems = [];
    game.sortedItems = [];
},
add:function(itemDetails) {
    // Set a unique id for the item
    if (!itemDetails.uid){
        itemDetails.uid = game.counter++;
    }
```

131

```
        var item = window[itemDetails.type].add(itemDetails);

        // Add the item to the items array
        game.items.push(item);
        // Add the item to the type specific array
        game[item.type].push(item);
        return item;
},
remove:function(item){
        // Unselect item if it is selected
        item.selected = false;
        for (var i = game.selectedItems.length - 1; i >= 0; i--){
                if(game.selectedItems[i].uid == item.uid){
                        game.selectedItems.splice(i,1);
                        break;
                }
        };

        // Remove item from the items array
        for (var i = game.items.length - 1; i >= 0; i--){
                if(game.items[i].uid == item.uid){
                        game.items.splice(i,1);
                        break;
                }
        };

        // Remove items from the type specific array
        for (var i = game[item.type].length - 1; i >= 0; i--){
                if(game[item.type][i].uid == item.uid){
                        game[item.type].splice(i,1);
                        break;
                }
        };
},
```

The resetArrays() method merely initializes all the game-specific arrays and the counter variable.

The add() method generates a unique identifier (UID) for an item using the counter, invokes the appropriate entity's add() method, and finally saves the item in the appropriate game arrays. For the base building, this method would first call buildings.add() and then add the new building to the game.items and game.buildings arrays.

The remove() method removes a specified item from the selectedItems, items, and entity-specific arrays. This way, any time an item is removed from the game (for example, when it is destroyed), it is automatically removed from the selection and the items array.

Now that we have set up the code for both defining the entity and adding entities to the level, we are ready to start drawing them on the screen.

Drawing the Entities

To draw the entities, we need to implement the animate() and draw() methods inside the entity object and then call these methods from the game animationLoop() and drawingLoop() methods.

We start by implementing the draw() and animate() methods inside the buildings object in buildings.js. The buildings object's default draw() and animate() methods will now look like Listing 6-7.

Listing 6-7. Implementing the Default draw() and animate() Methods (buildings.js)

```
animate:function(){
    // Consider an item healthy if it has more than 40% life
    if (this.life>this.hitPoints*0.4){
        this.lifeCode = "healthy";
    } else if (this.life <= 0){
        this.lifeCode = "dead";
        game.remove(this);
        return;
    } else {
        this.lifeCode = "damaged";
    }

    switch (this.action){
        case "stand":
            this.imageList = this.spriteArray[this.lifeCode];
            this.imageOffset = this.imageList.offset + this.animationIndex;
            this.animationIndex++;
            if (this.animationIndex>=this.imageList.count){
                this.animationIndex = 0;
            }
            break;
        case "construct":
            this.imageList = this.spriteArray["contructing"];
            this.imageOffset = this.imageList.offset + this.animationIndex;
            this.animationIndex++;
            // Once constructing is complete go back to standing
            if (this.animationIndex>=this.imageList.count){
                this.animationIndex = 0;
                this.action = "stand";
            }
            break;
    }
},
// Default function for drawing a building
draw:function(){
    var x = (this.x*game.gridSize)-game.offsetX-this.pixelOffsetX;
    var y = (this.y*game.gridSize)-game.offsetY-this.pixelOffsetY;

    // All sprite sheets will have blue in the first row and green in the second row
    var colorIndex = (this.team == "blue")?0:1;
    var colorOffset = colorIndex*this.pixelHeight;
    game.foregroundContext.drawImage(this.spriteSheet,
    this.imageOffset*this.pixelWidth,colorOffset, this.pixelWidth, this.pixelHeight,
    x,y,this.pixelWidth,this.pixelHeight);
}
```

In the animate() method, we first set the lifeCode property of the item based on its health and hitPoints. Any time an item's health drops below 0, we set lifeCode to dead and remove it from the game.

Next we implement behavior based on the item's action property. For now, we implement only the stand and construct actions.

133

For the stand action, we choose either the "healthy" or "damaged" sprite animation and increment the animationIndex property. In case the animationIndex exceeds the number of frames in the sprite, we roll the value back to 0. This way, the animation rotates through every frame in the sprite again and again.

For the construct action, we display the constructing sprites and roll over into the stand action once it has completed.

The draw() method is relatively simpler. We calculate the absolute x and y pixel coordinates of the building by converting the grid x and y coordinates. We then calculate the correct image offset (based on animationIndex) and the image color row (based on team). Finally, we draw the appropriate image on the foreground canvas by using the foregroundContext.drawImage() method.

Now that the draw() and animate() methods are in place, we need to call them from the game object. We will modify the game.animationLoop() and game.drawingLoop() methods inside game.js, as shown in Listing 6-8.

Listing 6-8. Calling draw() and animate() from the Game Loops (game.js)

```
animationLoop:function(){
    // Animate each of the elements within the game
    for (var i = game.items.length - 1; i >= 0; i--){
        game.items[i].animate();
    };

    // Sort game items into a sortedItems array based on their x,y coordinates
    game.sortedItems = $.extend([],game.items);
    game.sortedItems.sort(function(a,b){
        return b.y-a.y + ((b.y==a.y)?(a.x-b.x):0);
    });
},
drawingLoop:function(){
    // Handle Panning the Map
    game.handlePanning();

    // Since drawing the background map is a fairly large operation,
    // we only redraw the background if it changes (due to panning)
    if (game.refreshBackground){
game.backgroundContext.drawImage(game.currentMapImage,game.offsetX,game.offsetY,
game.canvasWidth, game.canvasHeight, 0,0,game.canvasWidth,game.canvasHeight);
        game.refreshBackground = false;
    }

    // Clear the foreground canvas
    game.foregroundContext.clearRect(0,0,game.canvasWidth,game.canvasHeight);

    // Start drawing the foreground elements
    for (var i = game.sortedItems.length - 1; i >= 0; i--){
        game.sortedItems[i].draw();
    };

    // Draw the mouse
    mouse.draw();
```

```
        // Call the drawing loop for the next frame using request animation frame
    if (game.running){
        requestAnimationFrame(game.drawingLoop);
    }
},
```

Within the `animationLoop()` method, we first iterate through all the game items and call their `animate()` methods. We then sort all the items by y and then x values and store them in the `game.sortedItems` array.

The new code inside the `drawingLoop()` method merely iterates through the `sortedItems` array and calls the `draw()` method of each item. We use the `sortedItems` array so that items are drawn in order from back to front based on their y coordinates. This is a simple implementation of depth sorting that ensures that items closer to the player obscure items behind them, giving the illusion of depth.

With this last change, we are now ready to see our first game entity drawn on the screen. If we open the game in the browser and load the first level, we should see the three base buildings we defined in the map drawn next to each other (see Figure 6-2).

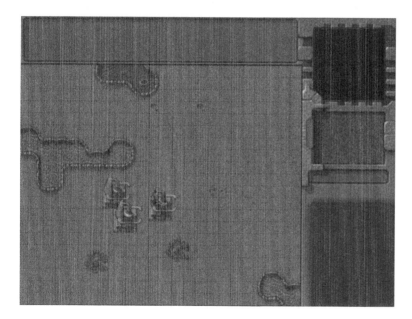

Figure 6-2. *The three base buildings*

As you can see, the first "blue" team base is shown with a a flashing blue light using the "healthy" animation.

The second "green" team base is drawn on top of the first one and partially obscures it. This is a result of our depth-sorting step and lets the player clearly see that the second base is in front of the first one.

Finally, the third base with a lower value of life looks damaged. This is because we automatically use the "damaged" animation whenever the life of the building is less than 40 percent of its maximum hit points.

Now that we have the framework for showing buildings within the game, let's add the remaining buildings, starting with the starport.

Adding the Starport

The starport is used to purchase both land and air units. The starport sprite sheet has a few interesting animations that the base did not have: a teleporting animation sequence that we will use when the building is first created and an opening and closing animation sequence that we will use when we transport in new units.

The first thing we will do is add the starport definition to the buildings list just below the base definition inside buildings.js (see Listing 6-9).

Listing 6-9. Definition for Starport Building (buildings.js)

```
"starport":{
    name:"starport",
    pixelWidth:40,
    pixelHeight:60,
    baseWidth:40,
    baseHeight:55,
    pixelOffsetX:1,
    pixelOffsetY:5,
    buildableGrid:[
        [1,1],
        [1,1],
        [1,1]
    ],
    passableGrid:[
        [1,1],
        [0,0],
        [0,0]
    ],
    sight:3,
    cost:2000,
    hitPoints:300,
    spriteImages:[
        {name:"teleport",count:9},
        {name:"closing",count:18},
        {name:"healthy",count:4},
        {name:"damaged",count:1},
    ],
},
```

Apart from the two new sprite sets, the starport definition is very similar to the base definition. Next, we will need to account for animating the opening, closing, and teleporting animation states. We will do this by modifying the default animate() method for the buildings inside buildings.js, as shown in Listing 6-10.

Listing 6-10. Modifying animate() to Handle Teleporting, Opening, and Closing

```
animate:function(){
    // Consider an item healthy if it has more than 40% life
    if (this.life>this.hitPoints*0.4){
        this.lifeCode = "healthy";
    } else if (this.life <= 0){
        this.lifeCode = "dead";
        game.remove(this);
```

```
        return;
    } else {
        this.lifeCode = "damaged";
    }

switch (this.action){
    case "stand":
        this.imageList = this.spriteArray[this.lifeCode];
        this.imageOffset = this.imageList.offset + this.animationIndex;
        this.animationIndex++;
        if (this.animationIndex>=this.imageList.count){
            this.animationIndex = 0;
        }
        break;
    case "construct":
        this.imageList = this.spriteArray["contructing"];
        this.imageOffset = this.imageList.offset + this.animationIndex;
        this.animationIndex++;
        // Once contructing is complete go back to standing
        if (this.animationIndex>=this.imageList.count){
            this.animationIndex = 0;
                this.action = "Stand";
        }
        break;
    case "teleport":
        this.imageList = this.spriteArray["teleport"];
        this.imageOffset = this.imageList.offset + this.animationIndex;
        this.animationIndex++;
        // Once teleporting is complete, move to either guard or stand mode
        if (this.animationIndex>=this.imageList.count){
            this.animationIndex = 0;
            if (this.canAttack){
                this.action = "guard";
            } else {
                this.action = "stand";
            }
        }
        break;
    case "close":
        this.imageList = this.spriteArray["closing"];
        this.imageOffset = this.imageList.offset + this.animationIndex;
        this.animationIndex++;
        // Once closing is complete go back to standing
        if (this.animationIndex>=this.imageList.count){
            this.animationIndex = 0;
            this.action = "stand";
        }
        break;
    case "open":
        this.imageList = this.spriteArray["closing"];
        // Opening is just the closing sprites running backwards
```

```
            this.imageOffset = this.imageList.offset + this.imageList.count - this.animationIndex;
            this.animationIndex++;
            // Once opening is complete, go back to close
            if (this.animationIndex>=this.imageList.count){
                this.animationIndex = 0;
                this.action = "close";
            }
            break;
    }
},
```

Like the construct animation state, the teleport, close, and open animation states do not keep repeating once they end. The teleport animation rolls over into the stand animation state (or the guard animation state for buildings that can attack such as the gun turret). The open animation (which is merely the close animation state running backward) rolls over into the close animation state, which then rolls over into the stand animation state.

This way, we can initialize the starport with a teleport or open animation state, knowing that it will eventually move back to the stand animation state once the current animation completes.

Now, we can add the starport to the map by modifying the requirements and items inside maps.js, as shown in Listing 6-11.

Listing 6-11. Adding the Starport to the Map

```
/* Entities to be loaded */
"requirements":{
    "buildings":["base","starport"],
    "vehicles":[],
    "aircraft":[],
    "terrain":[]
},

/* Entities to be added */
"items":[
    {"type":"buildings","name":"base","x":11,"y":14,"team":"blue"},
    {"type":"buildings","name":"base","x":12,"y":16,"team":"green"},
    {"type":"buildings","name":"base","x":15,"y":15,"team":"green", "life":50},

    {"type":"buildings","name":"starport","x":18,"y":14,"team":"blue"},
    {"type":"buildings","name":"starport","x":18,"y":10,"team":"blue", "action":"teleport"},
    {"type":"buildings","name":"starport","x":18,"y":6,"team":"green", "action":"open"},
]
```

When we open the game in the browser and start the level, we should see three new starport buildings, as shown in Figure 6-3.

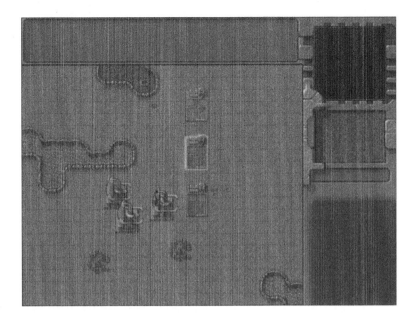

Figure 6-3. *The three starport buildings*

The first green team starport opens and then closes. The second blue team starport first glows and comes into existence and then switches to stand mode, while the last blue team starport merely waits in stand mode.

Now that the starport has been added, the next building we will look at is the harvester.

Adding the Harvester

The harvester is a unique entity in the sense that it is both a building and a vehicle. Unlike the other buildings in the game, the harvester is created by deploying a harvester vehicle at an oil field where it turns into the building (see Figure 6-4).

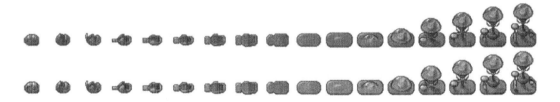

Figure 6-4. *Harvester deploying into building form*

The first thing we will do is add the harvester definition to the buildings list just below the starport definition inside `buildings.js` (see Listing 6-12).

Listing 6-12. Definition for Harvester Building (buildings.js)

```
"harvester":{
    name:"harvester",
    pixelWidth:40,
```

```
        pixelHeight:60,
        baseWidth:40,
        baseHeight:20,
        pixelOffsetX:-2,
        pixelOffsetY:40,
        buildableGrid:[
            [1,1]
        ],
        passableGrid:[
            [1,1]
        ],
        sight:3,
        cost:5000,
        hitPoints:300,
        spriteImages:[
            {name:"deploy",count:17},
            {name:"healthy",count:3},
            {name:"damaged",count:1},
        ],
    },
},
```

Next, we will need to account for the deploying animation state. We will do this by adding the deploy case to the default animate() method inside buildings.js, as shown in Listing 6-13.

Listing 6-13. Handling the deploy Animation State (buildings.js)

```
case "deploy":
    this.imageList = this.spriteArray["deploy"];
    this.imageOffset = this.imageList.offset + this.animationIndex;
    this.animationIndex++;
    // Once deploying is complete, go back to stand
    if (this.animationIndex>=this.imageList.count){
        this.animationIndex = 0;
        this.action = "stand";
    }
    break;
```

The deploy state, like the teleport state we defined earlier, automatically rolls into the stand animation state once it completes.

Now, we can add the harvester to the map by modifying the requirements and items inside maps.js, as shown in Listing 6-14.

Listing 6-14. Adding the Harvester to the Map

```
/* Entities to be loaded */
"requirements":{
    "buildings":["base","starport","harvester"],
    "vehicles":[],
    "aircraft":[],
    "terrain":[]
},
```

```
/* Entities to be added */
"items":[
    {"type":"buildings","name":"base","x":11,"y":14,"team":"blue"},
    {"type":"buildings","name":"base","x":12,"y":16,"team":"green"},
    {"type":"buildings","name":"base","x":15,"y":15,"team":"green", "life":50},


    {"type":"buildings","name":"starport","x":18,"y":14,"team":"blue"},
    {"type":"buildings","name":"starport","x":18,"y":10,"team":"blue", "action":"teleport"},
    {"type":"buildings","name":"starport","x":18,"y":6,"team":"green", "action":"open"},

    {"type":"buildings","name":"harvester","x":20,"y":10,"team":"blue"},
    {"type":"buildings","name":"harvester","x":22,"y":12,"team":"green", "action":"deploy"},

]
```

When we open the game in the browser and start the level, we should see two new harvester buildings, as shown in Figure 6-5.

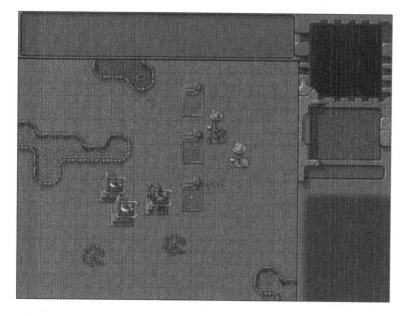

Figure 6-5. *The two harvester buildings*

The blue harvester is in the default stand mode, while the green harvester in deploy mode transforms into a building and then switches to stand mode.

Now that the harvester has been added, the last building we will look at the ground turret.

Adding the Ground Turret

The ground turret is a defensive structure that attacks only ground-based threats.

It is the only building that uses direction-based sprites. Also, unlike the other buildings, it has a default animation state of guard, which takes the turret's direction into account during animation and drawing.

The direction property can take values ranging from 0 to 7 increasing in the clockwise direction, with 0 pointing toward the north and 7 pointing in the northwest direction, as shown in Figure 6-6.

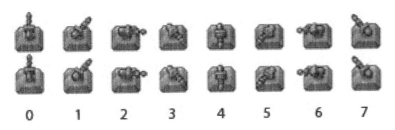

Figure 6-6. *Direction sprites for the gun turret ranging from 0 to 7*

The first thing we will do is add the gun turret definition to the buildings list just below the harvester definition inside buildings.js (see Listing 6-15).

Listing 6-15. Definition for Harvester Building (buildings.js)

```
"ground-turret":{
    name:"ground-turret",
    canAttack:true,
    canAttackLand:true,
    canAttackAir:false,
    weaponType:"cannon-ball",
    action:"guard", // Default action is guard unlike other buildings
    direction:0, // Face upward (0) by default
    directions:8, // Total of 8 turret directions allowed (0-7)
    orders:{type:"guard"},
    pixelWidth:38,
    pixelHeight:32,
    baseWidth:20,
    baseHeight:18,
    cost:1500,
    pixelOffsetX:9,
    pixelOffsetY:12,
    buildableGrid:[
        [1]
    ],
    passableGrid:[
        [1]
    ],
    sight:5,
    hitPoints:200,
    spriteImages:[
        {name:"teleport",count:9},
        {name:"healthy",count:1,directions:8},
        {name:"damaged",count:1},
    ],
}
```

The gun turret has a few additional properties that indicate whether it can be used to attack the enemy, the direction the turret is pointing, and the type of weapon it uses. We will use these properties later when we implement combat in our game.

The healthy sprites have an additional directions property that is used by the itemLoad() method to generate sprites for each direction.

Next, we will add the guard case to the animate() method inside buildings.js, as shown in Listing 6-16.

Listing 6-16. Handling the guard Animation State (buildings.js)

```
case "guard":
    if (this.lifeCode == "damaged"){
        // The damaged turret has no directions
        this.imageList = this.spriteArray[this.lifeCode];
    } else {
        // The healthy turret has 8 directions
        this.imageList = this.spriteArray[this.lifeCode+"-"+this.direction];
    }
    this.imageOffset = this.imageList.offset;
    break;
```

Unlike the previous animation states, the guard state does not use animationIndex and instead uses the turret direction to pick the appropriate image offset.

Now, we can add the turret to the map by modifying the requirements and items inside maps.js, as shown in Listing 6-17.

Listing 6-17. Adding the Ground Turret to the Map

```
/* Entities to be loaded */
"requirements":{
    "buildings":["base","starport","harvester","ground-turret"],
    "vehicles":[],
    "aircraft":[],
    "terrain":[]
},

/* Entities to be added */
"items":[
    {"type":"buildings","name":"base","x":11,"y":14,"team":"blue"},
    {"type":"buildings","name":"base","x":12,"y":16,"team":"green"},
    {"type":"buildings","name":"base","x":15,"y":15,"team":"green", "life":50},

    {"type":"buildings","name":"starport","x":18,"y":14,"team":"blue"},
    {"type":"buildings","name":"starport","x":18,"y":10,"team":"blue", "action":"teleport"},
    {"type":"buildings","name":"starport","x":18,"y":6,"team":"green", "action":"open"},

    {"type":"buildings","name":"harvester","x":20,"y":10,"team":"blue"},
    {"type":"buildings","name":"harvester","x":22,"y":12,"team":"green", "action":"deploy"},

    {"type":"buildings","name":"ground-turret","x":14,"y":9,"team":"blue", "direction":3},
    {"type":"buildings","name":"ground-turret","x":14,"y":12,"team":"green", "direction":1},
    {"type":"buildings","name":"ground-turret","x":16,"y":10,"team":"blue", "action":"teleport"},
]
```

We specify a starting direction property for the first two turrets and set the action property to `teleport` for the third. When we open the game in the browser and start the level, we should see three new turrets, as shown in Figure 6-7.

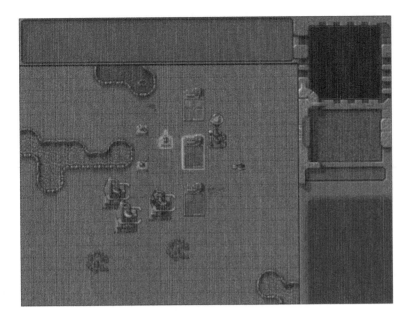

Figure 6-7. *The three ground turret buildings*

The first two turrets are in guard mode and face two different directions, while the third one teleports in facing the default direction and switches to guard mode after teleporting in.

At this point, we have implemented all the buildings that we need. Now it's time to start adding a few vehicles to our game.

Adding the Vehicles

All the vehicles in our game including the transport will have a simple sprite sheet with the vehicle pointing in eight directions similar to the ground turret, as shown in Figure 6-8.

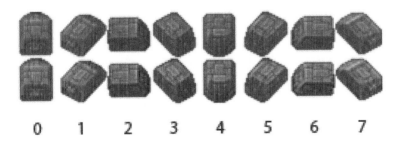

Figure 6-8. *The transport sprite sheet*

We will set up the code for our vehicles by defining a new vehicles object inside vehicles.js, as shown in Listing 6-18.

Listing 6-18. Defining the vehicles Object (vehicles.js)

```
var vehicles = {
    list:{
        "transport":{
            name:"transport",
            pixelWidth:31,
            pixelHeight:30,
            pixelOffsetX:15,
            pixelOffsetY:15,
            radius:15,
            speed:15,
            sight:3,
            cost:400,
            hitPoints:100,
            turnSpeed:2,
            spriteImages:[
                {name:"stand",count:1,directions:8}
            ],
        },
        "harvester":{
            name:"harvester",
            pixelWidth:21,
            pixelHeight:20,
            pixelOffsetX:10,
            pixelOffsetY:10,
            radius:10,
            speed:10,
            sight:3,
            cost:1600,
            hitPoints:50,
            turnSpeed:2,
            spriteImages:[
                {name:"stand",count:1,directions:8}
            ],
        },
        "scout-tank":{
            name:"scout-tank",
            canAttack:true,
            canAttackLand:true,
            canAttackAir:false,
            weaponType:"bullet",
            pixelWidth:21,
            pixelHeight:21,
            pixelOffsetX:10,
            pixelOffsetY:10,
            radius:11,
            speed:20,
            sight:4,
```

```
                cost:500,
                hitPoints:50,
                turnSpeed:4,
                spriteImages:[
                    {name:"stand",count:1,directions:8}
                ],
        },
        "heavy-tank":{
            name:"heavy-tank",
            canAttack:true,
            canAttackLand:true,
            canAttackAir:false,
            weaponType:"cannon-ball",
            pixelWidth:30,
            pixelHeight:30,
            pixelOffsetX:15,
            pixelOffsetY:15,
            radius:13,
            speed:15,
            sight:5,
            cost:1200,
            hitPoints:50,
            turnSpeed:4,
            spriteImages:[
                {name:"stand",count:1,directions:8}
            ],
        }
    },
    defaults:{
        type:"vehicles",
        animationIndex:0,
        direction:0,
        action:"stand",
        orders:{type:"stand"},
        selected:false,
        selectable:true,
        directions:8,
        animate:function(){
            // Consider an item healthy if it has more than 40% life
            if (this.life>this.hitPoints*0.4){
                this.lifeCode = "healthy";
            } else if (this.life <= 0){
                this.lifeCode = "dead";
                game.remove(this);
                return;
            } else {
                this.lifeCode = "damaged";
            }
```

```
            switch (this.action){
                case "stand":
                    var direction = this.direction;
                    this.imageList = this.spriteArray["stand-"+direction];
                    this.imageOffset = this.imageList.offset + this.animationIndex;
                    this.animationIndex++;

                    if (this.animationIndex>=this.imageList.count){
                        this.animationIndex = 0;
                    }

                break;
            }
        },
        draw:function(){
            var x = (this.x*game.gridSize)-game.offsetX-this.pixelOffsetX;
            var y = (this.y*game.gridSize)-game.offsetY-this.pixelOffsetY;
            var colorIndex = (this.team == "blue")?0:1;
            var colorOffset = colorIndex*this.pixelHeight;
            game.foregroundContext.drawImage(this.spriteSheet, this.imageOffset*this.pixelWidth,
colorOffset, this.pixelWidth, this.pixelHeight, x, y, this.pixelWidth, this.pixelHeight);
        }
    },
    load:loadItem,
    add:addItem,
}
```

The structure of our vehicles object is very similar to the buildings object. We have a list property where we define the four vehicle types: the transport, the harvester, the scout tank, and the heavy tank.

All of the vehicle sprites have the directions property and the default stand animation implementation inside animate(), which uses the vehicle's direction to select the sprite to draw. We use animationIndex to handle multiple images within a sprite so that we can add vehicles with animation if needed.

The vehicles also have properties such as speed, sight, and cost. The transport and harvester do not have any weapons, while the two tanks have weapon-based properties similar to the ground turret building we defined earlier. We will use all of these properties in later chapters to implement movement and combat.

Now, we can add these vehicles to the map by modifying the requirements and items properties inside maps.js, as shown in Listing 6-19.

Listing 6-19. Adding the Vehicles to the Map

```
/* Entities to be loaded */
"requirements":{
    "buildings":["base","starport","harvester","ground-turret"],
    "vehicles":["transport","harvester","scout-tank","heavy-tank"],
    "aircraft":[],
    "terrain":[]
},

/* Entities to be added */
"items":[
    {"type":"buildings","name":"base","x":11,"y":14,"team":"blue"},
    {"type":"buildings","name":"base","x":12,"y":16,"team":"green"},
    {"type":"buildings","name":"base","x":15,"y":15,"team":"green", "life":50},
```

```
{"type":"buildings","name":"starport","x":18,"y":14,"team":"blue"},
{"type":"buildings","name":"starport","x":18,"y":10,"team":"blue", "action":"teleport"},
{"type":"buildings","name":"starport","x":18,"y":6,"team":"green", "action":"open"},

{"type":"buildings","name":"harvester","x":20,"y":10,"team":"blue"},
{"type":"buildings","name":"harvester","x":22,"y":12,"team":"green", "action":"deploy"},

{"type":"buildings","name":"ground-turret","x":14,"y":9,"team":"blue", "direction":3},
{"type":"buildings","name":"ground-turret","x":14,"y":12,"team":"green", "direction":1},
{"type":"buildings","name":"ground-turret" ,"x":16,"y":10, "team":"blue", "action":"teleport"},

{"type":"vehicles","name":"transport","x":26,"y":10,"team":"blue","direction":2},
{"type":"vehicles","name":"harvester","x":26,"y":12,"team":"blue","direction":3},
{"type":"vehicles","name":"scout-tank","x":26,"y":14,"team":"blue", "direction":4},
{"type":"vehicles","name":"heavy-tank","x":26,"y":16,"team":"blue", "direction":5},
{"type":"vehicles","name":"transport","x":28,"y":10,"team":"green", "direction":7},
{"type":"vehicles","name":"harvester","x":28,"y":12,"team":"green", "direction":6},
{"type":"vehicles","name":"scout-tank","x":28,"y":14,"team":"green", "direction":1},
{"type":"vehicles","name":"heavy-tank","x":28,"y":16,"team":"green", "direction":0},
]
```

When we open the game in the browser and start the level, we should see the vehicles, as shown in Figure 6-9.

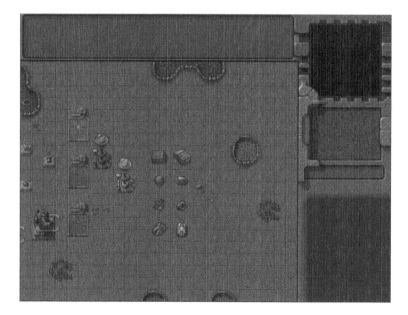

Figure 6-9. *Adding vehicles to the level*

The vehicles point in different directions based on the properties we set when adding them to the items list. With the vehicles implemented, it's time to add the aircraft to our game.

Adding the Aircraft

The aircraft in our game have a sprite sheet similar to vehicles except for one difference: shadows. The aircraft sprite sheet has a third row with shadows in it. Also, the chopper sprite sheet has multiple images for each direction, as shown in Figure 6-10.

Figure 6-10. *The chopper sprite sheet with shadows*

We will set up the code for our aircraft by defining a new `aircraft` object inside `aircraft.js`, as shown in Listing 6-20.

Listing 6-20. Defining the aircraft Object (aircraft.js)

```
var aircraft = {
    list:{
        "chopper":{
            name:"chopper",
            cost:900,
            pixelWidth:40,
            pixelHeight:40,
            pixelOffsetX:20,
            pixelOffsetY:20,
            weaponType:"heatseeker",
            radius:18,
            sight:6,
            canAttack:true,
            canAttackLand:true,
            canAttackAir:true,
            hitPoints:50,
            speed:25,
            turnSpeed:4,
            pixelShadowHeight:40,
            spriteImages:[
                {name:"fly",count:4,directions:8}
            ],
        },
        "wraith":{
            name:"wraith",
            cost:600,
            pixelWidth:30,
```

```
            pixelHeight:30,
            canAttack:true,
            canAttackLand:false,
            canAttackAir:true,
            weaponType:"fireball",
            pixelOffsetX:15,
            pixelOffsetY:15,
            radius:15,
            sight:8,
            speed:40,
            turnSpeed:4,
            hitPoints:50,
            pixelShadowHeight:40,
            spriteImages:[
                {name:"fly",count:1,directions:8}
            ],
        }
    },
    defaults:{
        type:"aircraft",
        animationIndex:0,
        direction:0,
        directions:8,
        action:"fly",
        selected:false,
        selectable:true,
        orders:{type:"float"},
        animate:function(){
            // Consider an item healthy if it has more than 40% life
            if (this.life>this.hitPoints*0.4){
                this.lifeCode = "healthy";
            } else if (this.life <= 0){
                this.lifeCode = "dead";
                game.remove(this);
                return;
            } else {
                this.lifeCode = "damaged";
            }
            switch (this.action){
                case "fly":
                    var direction = this.direction;
                     this.imageList = this.spriteArray["fly-"+ direction];
                    this.imageOffset = this.imageList.offset + this.animationIndex;
                    this.animationIndex++;
                    if (this.animationIndex>=this.imageList.count){
                        this.animationIndex = 0;
                    }
                break;
            }
        },
        draw:function(){
            var x = (this.x*game.gridSize)-game.offsetX-this.pixelOffsetX;
```

```
        var y = (this.y*game.gridSize)-game.offsetY-this.pixelOffsetY-this.pixelShadowHeight;
        var colorIndex = (this.team == "blue")?0:1;
        var colorOffset = colorIndex*this.pixelHeight;
        var shadowOffset = this.pixelHeight*2; // The aircraft shadow is on the second row of
the sprite sheet

            game.foregroundContext.drawImage(this.spriteSheet, this.imageOffset*this.pixelWidth,
colorOffset, this.pixelWidth, this.pixelHeight, x, y, this.pixelWidth,this.pixelHeight);
            game.foregroundContext.drawImage(this.spriteSheet, this.imageOffset*this.pixelWidth,
shadowOffset, this.pixelWidth, this.pixelHeight, x, y+this.pixelShadowHeight, this.pixelWidth,
this.pixelHeight);
        }
    },
    load:loadItem,
    add:addItem,
}
```

The structure of our aircraft object is similar to the vehicles object. We have a list property where we define the two aircraft types: the chopper and the wraith.

All of the aircraft sprites have the directions property. The default fly animation implementation inside animate() uses the aircraft's direction to select the sprite to draw. In the case of the chopper, we also use animationIndex to handle multiple images for each direction.

The one big difference is in the way the draw() method is implemented. We draw a shadow at the location of the aircraft and draw the actual aircraft pixelShadowHeight pixels above the location of the aircraft. This way, the aircraft looks like it is floating above the ground and the shadow is on the ground below it.

Now, we can add these aircraft to the map by modifying the requirements and items properties inside maps.js, as shown in Listing 6-21.

Listing 6-21. Adding the Aircraft to the Map

```
/* Entities to be loaded */
"requirements":{
    "buildings":["base","starport","harvester","ground-turret"],
    "vehicles":["transport","harvester","scout-tank","heavy-tank"],
    "aircraft":["chopper","wraith"],
    "terrain":[]
},

/* Entities to be added */
"items":[
    {"type":"buildings","name":"base","x":11,"y":14,"team":"blue"},
    {"type":"buildings","name":"base","x":12,"y":16,"team":"green"},
    {"type":"buildings","name":"base","x":15,"y":15,"team":"green", "life":50},

    {"type":"buildings","name":"starport","x":18,"y":14,"team":"blue"},
    {"type":"buildings","name":"starport","x":18,"y":10,"team":"blue", "action":"teleport"},
    {"type":"buildings","name":"starport","x":18,"y":6,"team":"green", "action":"open"},

    {"type":"buildings","name":"harvester","x":20,"y":10,"team":"blue"},
    {"type":"buildings","name":"harvester","x":22,"y":12,"team":"green", "action":"deploy"},
```

```
{"type":"buildings","name":"ground-turret","x":14,"y":9,"team":"blue", "direction":3},
{"type":"buildings","name":"ground-turret","x":14,"y":12,"team":"green", "direction":1},
{"type":"buildings","name":"ground-turret","x":16,"y":10,"team":"blue", "action":"teleport"},

{"type":"vehicles","name":"transport","x":26,"y":10,"team":"blue","direction":2},
{"type":"vehicles","name":"harvester","x":26,"y":12,"team":"blue","direction":3},
{"type":"vehicles","name":"scout-tank","x":26,"y":14,"team":"blue", "direction":4},
{"type":"vehicles","name":"heavy-tank","x":26,"y":16,"team":"blue", "direction":5},
{"type":"vehicles","name":"transport","x":28,"y":10,"team":"green", "direction":7},
{"type":"vehicles","name":"harvester","x":28,"y":12,"team":"green", "direction":6},
{"type":"vehicles","name":"scout-tank","x":28,"y":14,"team":"green", "direction":1},
{"type":"vehicles","name":"heavy-tank","x":28,"y":16,"team":"green", "direction":0},
{"type":"aircraft","name":"chopper","x":20,"y":22,"team":"blue", "direction":2},
{"type":"aircraft","name":"wraith","x":23,"y":22,"team":"green", "direction":3},
]
```

When we open the game in the browser and start the level, we should see the aircraft hovering above the ground, as shown in Figure 6-11.

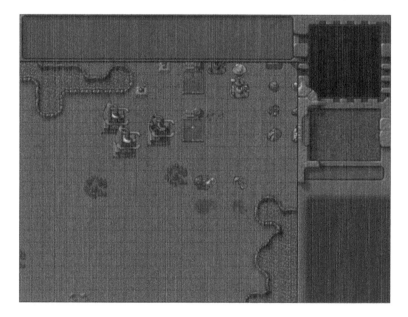

Figure 6-11. *The aircraft floating above the ground*

The shadows help create the illusion that the aircraft are floating above the ground and also mark their exact position on the ground. The chopper blades and their shadow on the ground seem to rotate because of the animation.

With the aircraft implemented, we will now add the terrain to our game.

Adding the Terrain

With the exception of the oil field, the terrain entities in our game are static bodies intended only for cosmetic use. The oil field is a special entity above which the harvester vehicle can deploy into the harvester building. The oil field sprite sheet includes two versions: a default version and a "hint" version that shows a blurry harvester above it as a hint for the player.

We will set up the code for our terrain by defining a new terrain object inside `terrain.js`, as shown in Listing 6-22.

Listing 6-22. Defining the Terrain Object (terrain.js)

```
var terrain = {
    list:{
        "oilfield":{
            name:"oilfield",
            pixelWidth:40,
            pixelHeight:60,
            baseWidth:40,
            baseHeight:20,
            pixelOffsetX:0,
            pixelOffsetY:40,
            buildableGrid:[
                [1,1]
            ],
            passableGrid:[
                [1,1]
            ],
            spriteImages:[
                {name:"hint",count:1},
                {name:"default",count:1},
            ],
        },
        "bigrocks":{
            name:"bigrocks",
            pixelWidth:40,
            pixelHeight:70,
            baseWidth:40,
            baseHeight:40,
            pixelOffsetX:0,
            pixelOffsetY:30,
            buildableGrid:[
                [1,1],
                [0,1]
            ],
            passableGrid:[
                [1,1],
                [0,1]
            ],
            spriteImages:[
                {name:"default",count:1},
            ],
        },
        "smallrocks":{
            name:"smallrocks",
            pixelWidth:20,
            pixelHeight:35,
            baseWidth:20,
            baseHeight:20,
```

```
                    pixelOffsetX:0,
                    pixelOffsetY:15,
                    buildableGrid:[
                        [1]
                    ],
                    passableGrid:[
                        [1]
                    ],
                    spriteImages:[
                        {name:"default",count:1},
                    ],
                },
            },
        defaults:{
            type:"terrain",
            animationIndex:0,
            action:"default",
            selected:false,
            selectable:false,
            animate:function(){
                switch (this.action){
                    case "default":
                        this.imageList = this.spriteArray["default"];
                        this.imageOffset = this.imageList.offset + this.animationIndex;
                        this.animationIndex++;
                        if (this.animationIndex>=this.imageList.count){
                            this.animationIndex = 0;
                        }
                    break;
                    case "hint":
                        this.imageList = this.spriteArray["hint"];
                        this.imageOffset = this.imageList.offset + this.animationIndex;
                        this.animationIndex++;
                        if (this.animationIndex>=this.imageList.count){
                            this.animationIndex = 0;
                        }
                    break;
                }
            },
            draw:function(){
                var x = (this.x*game.gridSize)-game.offsetX-this.pixelOffsetX;
                var y = (this.y*game.gridSize)-game.offsetY-this.pixelOffsetY;

                var colorOffset = 0; // No team based colors
                game.foregroundContext.drawImage(this.spriteSheet, this.imageOffset*this.pixelWidth,
colorOffset, this.pixelWidth, this.pixelHeight, x, y, this.pixelWidth, this.pixelHeight);
            }
        },
    load:loadItem,
    add:addItem,
}
```

The structure of our terrain object is similar to the buildings object. We have a list property where we define the terrain types: the oil field, the big rocks, and the small rocks. We implement a default and a hint animation state inside the animate() method. We also implement a simpler draw() method that does not use team-based colors.

Now, we can add these terrain to the map by modifying the requirements and items inside maps.js, as shown in Listing 6-23.

Listing 6-23. Adding the Terrain to the Map

```
/* Entities to be loaded */
"requirements":{
    "buildings":["base","starport","harvester","ground-turret"],
    "vehicles":["transport","harvester","scout-tank","heavy-tank"],
    "aircraft":["chopper","wraith"],
    "terrain":["oilfield","bigrocks","smallrocks"]
},

/* Entities to be added */
"items":[
    {"type":"buildings","name":"base","x":11,"y":14,"team":"blue"},
    {"type":"buildings","name":"base","x":12,"y":16,"team":"green"},
    {"type":"buildings","name":"base","x":15,"y":15,"team":"green", "life":50},

    {"type":"buildings","name":"starport","x":18,"y":14,"team":"blue"},
    {"type":"buildings","name":"starport","x":18,"y":10,"team":"blue", "action":"teleport"},
    {"type":"buildings","name":"starport","x":18,"y":6,"team":"green", "action":"open"},

    {"type":"buildings","name":"harvester","x":20,"y":10,"team":"blue"},
    {"type":"buildings","name":"harvester","x":22,"y":12,"team":"green", "action":"deploy"},

    {"type":"buildings","name":"ground-turret","x":14,"y":9,"team":"blue","direction":3},
    {"type":"buildings","name":"ground-turret","x":14,"y":12,"team":"green","direction":1},
    {"type":"buildings","name":"ground-turret","x":16,"y":10,"team":"blue","action":"teleport"},

    {"type":"vehicles","name":"transport","x":26,"y":10,"team":"blue", "direction":2},
    {"type":"vehicles","name":"harvester","x":26,"y":12,"team":"blue", "direction":3},
    {"type":"vehicles","name":"scout-tank","x":26,"y":14,"team":"blue","direction":4},
    {"type":"vehicles","name":"heavy-tank","x":26,"y":16,"team":"blue","direction":5},
    {"type":"vehicles","name":"transport","x":28,"y":10,"team":"green", "direction":7},
    {"type":"vehicles","name":"harvester","x":28,"y":12,"team":"green", "direction":6},
    {"type":"vehicles","name":"scout-tank","x":28,"y":14,"team":"green","direction":1},
    {"type":"vehicles","name":"heavy-tank","x":28,"y":16,"team":"green","direction":0},

    {"type":"aircraft","name":"chopper","x":20,"y":22,"team":"blue", "direction":2},
    {"type":"aircraft","name":"wraith","x":23,"y":22,"team":"green", "direction":3},

    {"type":"terrain","name":"oilfield","x":5,"y":7},
    {"type":"terrain","name":"oilfield","x":8,"y":7,"action":"hint"},

    {"type":"terrain","name":"bigrocks","x":5,"y":3},
    {"type":"terrain","name":"smallrocks","x":8,"y":3},
]
```

We add two oil fields, one of which has the action property set to hint. When we open the game in the browser and start the level, we should see the rocks and the oil fields, as shown in Figure 6-12.

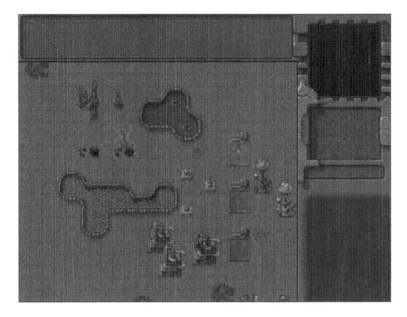

Figure 6-12. *Adding the rocks and the oil fields*

The oil field on the right with the hint has a subtle glowing image of a harvester to let the player know that a harvester can be deployed there. This hint version of the oil field can be used in the earlier levels of our campaign when the player has just been introduced to the idea of harvesting.

With this, we have implemented all the important entities in the game. Of course, at this point all we can do is look at them. The next thing we would like to do is interact with them by selecting them.

Selecting Game Entities

We will allow players to select entities either by clicking them or by dragging a selection box across them.

We will enable click selection by modifying the mouse object inside mouse.js, as shown in Listing 6-24.

Listing 6-24. Enabling Selection by Clicking (mouse.js)

```
click:function(ev,rightClick){
    // Player clicked inside the canvas

    var clickedItem = this.itemUnderMouse();
    var shiftPressed = ev.shiftKey;

    if (!rightClick){ // Player left clicked
        if (clickedItem){
            // Pressing shift adds to existing selection. If shift is not pressed, clear
existing selection
            if(!shiftPressed){
                game.clearSelection();
            }
            game.selectItem(clickedItem,shiftPressed);
        }
```

```
    } else { // Player right clicked
        // Handle actions like attacking and movement of selected units
    }
},
itemUnderMouse:function(){
    for (var i = game.items.length - 1; i >= 0; i--){
        var item = game.items[i];
        if (item.type=="buildings" || item.type=="terrain"){
            if(item.lifeCode != "dead"
                && item.x<= (mouse.gameX)/game.gridSize
                && item.x >= (mouse.gameX - item.baseWidth)/game.gridSize
                && item.y<= mouse.gameY/game.gridSize
                && item.y >= (mouse.gameY - item.baseHeight)/game.gridSize
                ){
                    return item;
            }
        } else if (item.type=="aircraft"){
            if (item.lifeCode != "dead" &&
                Math.pow(item.x-mouse.gameX/game.gridSize,2) + Math.pow(item.y-(mouse.gameY+item.
pixelShadowHeight)/game.gridSize,2) < Math.pow((item.radius)/game.gridSize,2)){
                return item;
            }
        }else {
            if (item.lifeCode != "dead" && Math.pow(item.x-mouse.gameX/game.gridSize,2) + Math.
pow(item.y-mouse.gameY/game.gridSize,2) < Math.pow((item.radius)/game.gridSize,2)){
                return item;
            }
        }
    }
},
```

The mouse.click() method first checks whether there is an item under the mouse during the click using the itemUnderMouse() method. In case an item was under the mouse and the left button was clicked, we call the game. selectItem() method. The game.clearSelection() method is called before selecting the new item unless the Shift key is pressed during the click. This way, users can select multiple items by holding down the Shift key while selecting.

The itemUnderMouse() method iterates through all the items in the list and returns the first item that is under the mouse gameX and gameY coordinates using different criteria for different item types.

- In the case of buildings and terrain, we check whether the base of the item is under the mouse. This way, the player can click the base of a building to select it but won't have problems selecting vehicles behind the building.

- In the case of vehicles, we check whether the mouse is within a radius from the vehicle center.

- In the case of aircraft, we check whether the mouse is within a radius from the aircraft center and not the shadow by using the pixelShadowHeight property.

Next we will handle drag selection by modifying the mouseup event handler inside the init() method of the mouse object (see Listing 6-25).

Listing 6-25. Implementing Drag Selection in the mouseup Event Handler (mouse.js)

```
$mouseCanvas.mouseup(function(ev) {
    var shiftPressed = ev.shiftKey;
    if(ev.which==1){
    //Left key was released
        if (mouse.dragSelect){
            if (!shiftPressed){
                // Shift key was not pressed
                game.clearSelection();
            }

            var x1 = Math.min(mouse.gameX,mouse.dragX)/game.gridSize;
            var y1 = Math.min(mouse.gameY,mouse.dragY)/game.gridSize;
            var x2 = Math.max(mouse.gameX,mouse.dragX)/game.gridSize;
            var y2 = Math.max(mouse.gameY,mouse.dragY)/game.gridSize;
            for (var i = game.items.length - 1; i >= 0; i--){
                var item = game.items[i];
                if (item.type != "buildings" && item.selectable && item.team==game.team && x1<=
item.x && x2 >= item.x){
                    if ((item.type == "vehicles" && y1<= item.y && y2 >= item.y)
                    || (item.type == "aircraft" && (y1 <= item.y-item.pixelShadowHeight/game.
gridSize) && (y2 >= item.y-item.pixelShadowHeight/game.gridSize))){
                        game.selectItem(item,shiftPressed);
                    }

                }
            };
        }
        mouse.buttonPressed = false;
        mouse.dragSelect = false;
    }
    return false;
});
```

Inside the mouseup event, we check whether the mouse had been dragged and, if so, iterate through every game item and check whether it lies within the bounds of the dragged rectangle. We then select the appropriate items.

Most importantly, we only allow drag selection for our own vehicles and aircraft and not for enemy entities or our own buildings. This is because drag selection is typically used to select groups of units to move them or attack with them quickly, and selecting enemy units or our own buildings does not really help the player.

Next, we will add some selection-related code to the game object inside game.js, as shown in Listing 6-26.

Listing 6-26. Adding Selection-Related Code to Game Object (game.js)

```
/* Selection Related Code */
selectionBorderColor:"rgba(255,255,0,0.5)",
selectionFillColor:"rgba(255,215,0,0.2)",
healthBarBorderColor:"rgba(0,0,0,0.8)",
healthBarHealthyFillColor:"rgba(0,255,0,0.5)",
healthBarDamagedFillColor:"rgba(255,0,0,0.5)",
lifeBarHeight:5,
clearSelection:function(){
```

```
        while(game.selectedItems.length>0){
            game.selectedItems.pop().selected = false;
        }
    },
    selectItem:function(item,shiftPressed){
        // Pressing shift and clicking on a selected item will deselect it
        if (shiftPressed && item.selected){
            // deselect item
            item.selected = false;
            for (var i = game.selectedItems.length - 1; i >= 0; i--){
                if(game.selectedItems[i].uid == item.uid){
                    game.selectedItems.splice(i,1);
                    break;
                }
            };
            return;
        }

        if (item.selectable && !item.selected){
            item.selected = true;
            game.selectedItems.push(item);
        }
    },
```

We start by defining a few common selection-based properties related to colors and life bars. We then define the two methods used for selection.

- The clearSelection() method iterates through the game.selectedItems array, clears the selected flag from each item, and removes the item from the array.

- The selectItem() method either adds a selectable item to the selectedItems() array or removes it from the array depending on whether the Shift key is pressed. This way, players can unselect a selected item by clicking it with the Shift key pressed.

At this point, we have all the code we need to select items inside the game. However, we still need a way to highlight selected items so we can identify them visually. This is what we will implement next.

Highlighting Selected Entities

When the player selects an item, we will detect it using the item's selected property and draw an enclosing selection boundary around the item. We will also add an indicator to show us how much life the item has.

We will do this by defining two default methods, drawSelection() and drawLifeBar(), for each of the entities and modify the draw() method to call them.

First, we will implement these methods in the buildings object (see Listing 6-27).

Listing 6-27. Implementing drawSelection() and drawLifeBar() for Buildings (buildings.js)

```
drawLifeBar:function(){
    var x = this.drawingX+ this.pixelOffsetX;
    var y = this.drawingY - 2*game.lifeBarHeight;
```

```
        game.foregroundContext.fillStyle = (this.lifeCode == "healthy") ?
game.healthBarHealthyFillColor: game.healthBarDamagedFillColor;

        game.foregroundContext.fillRect(x,y,this.baseWidth*this.life/this.hitPoints,game.lifeBarHeight)

            game.foregroundContext.strokeStyle = game.healthBarBorderColor;
            game.foregroundContext.lineWidth = 1;
            game.foregroundContext.strokeRect(x,y,this.baseWidth,game.lifeBarHeight)
        },
        drawSelection:function(){
            var x = this.drawingX + this.pixelOffsetX;
            var y = this.drawingY + this.pixelOffsetY;
            game.foregroundContext.strokeStyle = game.selectionBorderColor;
            game.foregroundContext.lineWidth = 1;
            game.foregroundContext.fillStyle = game.selectionFillColor;
            game.foregroundContext.fillRect(x-1,y-1,this.baseWidth+2,this.baseHeight+2);
            game.foregroundContext.strokeRect(x-1,y-1,this.baseWidth+2,this.baseHeight+2);
        },
        // Default function for drawing a building
        draw:function(){
            var x = (this.x*game.gridSize)-game.offsetX-this.pixelOffsetX;
            var y = (this.y*game.gridSize)-game.offsetY-this.pixelOffsetY;
            this.drawingX = x;
            this.drawingY = y;
            if (this.selected){
                this.drawSelection();
                this.drawLifeBar();
            }
            // All sprite sheets will have blue in the first row and green in the second row
            var colorIndex = (this.team == "blue")?0:1;
            var colorOffset = colorIndex*this.pixelHeight;
            game.foregroundContext.drawImage(this.spriteSheet, this.imageOffset*this.pixelWidth,
colorOffset, this.pixelWidth, this.pixelHeight, x, y, this.pixelWidth, this.pixelHeight);
        }
```

The drawLifeBar() method merely draws a bar slightly above the building with a green or red color depending on the life of the building. The length of the bar is proportional to the life of the building. The drawSelection() method draws a yellow rectangle around the base of the building. Finally, we call both these methods if the item is selected from inside the draw() method.

Next we will implement these methods for the vehicles object (see Listing 6-28).

Listing 6-28. Implementing drawSelection() and drawLifeBar() for Vehicles (vehicles.js)

```
drawLifeBar:function(){
    var x = this.drawingX;
    var y = this.drawingY - 2*game.lifeBarHeight;
    game.foregroundContext.fillStyle = (this.lifeCode == "healthy")?game.
healthBarHealthyFillColor:game.healthBarDamagedFillColor;

game.foregroundContext.fillRect(x,y,this.pixelWidth*this.life/this.hitPoints,game.lifeBarHeight)
    game.foregroundContext.strokeStyle = game.healthBarBorderColor;
    game.foregroundContext.lineWidth = 1;
    game.foregroundContext.strokeRect(x,y,this.pixelWidth,game.lifeBarHeight)
},
```

```
drawSelection:function(){
    var x = this.drawingX + this.pixelOffsetX;
    var y = this.drawingY + this.pixelOffsetY;
    game.foregroundContext.strokeStyle = game.selectionBorderColor;
    game.foregroundContext.lineWidth = 1;
    game.foregroundContext.beginPath();
    game.foregroundContext.arc(x,y,this.radius,0,Math.PI*2,false);
    game.foregroundContext.fillStyle = game.selectionFillColor;
    game.foregroundContext.fill();
    game.foregroundContext.stroke();
},
draw:function(){
    var x = (this.x*game.gridSize)-game.offsetX-this.pixelOffsetX;
    var y = (this.y*game.gridSize)-game.offsetY-this.pixelOffsetY;
    this.drawingX = x;
    this.drawingY = y;
    if (this.selected){
        this.drawSelection();
        this.drawLifeBar();
    }
    var colorIndex = (this.team == "blue")?0:1;
    var colorOffset = colorIndex*this.pixelHeight;
    game.foregroundContext.drawImage(this.spriteSheet,
    this.imageOffset*this.pixelWidth,colorOffset,
    this.pixelWidth,this.pixelHeight,x,y,this.pixelWidth,this.pixelHeight);
}
```

This time, the drawSelection() method draws a yellow, lightly filled circle under the selected vehicle. Like before, the drawLifeBar() method draws a life bar above the vehicle.

Lastly, we will implement these methods for the aircraft object (see Listing 6-29).

Listing 6-29. Implementing drawSelection() and drawLifeBar() for Aircraft (aircraft.js)

```
drawLifeBar:function(){
    var x = this.drawingX;
    var y = this.drawingY - 2*game.lifeBarHeight;
    game.foregroundContext.fillStyle = (this.lifeCode ==
    "healthy")?game.healthBarHealthyFillColor:game.healthBarDamagedFillColor;

game.foregroundContext.fillRect(x,y,this.pixelWidth*this.life/this.hitPoints,game.lifeBarHeight)
    game.foregroundContext.strokeStyle = game.healthBarBorderColor;
    game.foregroundContext.lineWidth = 1;
    game.foregroundContext.strokeRect(x,y,this.pixelWidth,game.lifeBarHeight)
},
drawSelection:function(){
    var x = this.drawingX + this.pixelOffsetX;
    var y = this.drawingY + this.pixelOffsetY;
    game.foregroundContext.strokeStyle = game.selectionBorderColor;
    game.foregroundContext.lineWidth = 2;
    game.foregroundContext.beginPath();
    game.foregroundContext.arc(x,y,this.radius,0,Math.PI*2,false);
    game.foregroundContext.stroke();
    game.foregroundContext.fillStyle = game.selectionFillColor;
    game.foregroundContext.fill();
```

```
    game.foregroundContext.beginPath();
    game.foregroundContext.arc(x,y+this.pixelShadowHeight,4,0,Math.PI*2,false);
    game.foregroundContext.stroke();

    game.foregroundContext.beginPath();
    game.foregroundContext.moveTo(x,y);
    game.foregroundContext.lineTo(x,y+this.pixelShadowHeight);
    game.foregroundContext.stroke();
},
draw:function(){
    var x = (this.x*game.gridSize)-game.offsetX-this.pixelOffsetX;
    var y = (this.y*game.gridSize)-game.offsetY-this.pixelOffsetY-this.pixelShadowHeight;
    this.drawingX = x;
    this.drawingY = y;
    if (this.selected){
        this.drawSelection();
        this.drawLifeBar();
    }
    var colorIndex = (this.team == "blue")?0:1;
    var colorOffset = colorIndex*this.pixelHeight;
    var shadowOffset = this.pixelHeight*2; // The aircraft shadow is on the second row of the sprite
sheet

    game.foregroundContext.drawImage(this.spriteSheet, this.imageOffset*this.pixelWidth,
colorOffset, this.pixelWidth, this.pixelHeight, x, y, this.pixelWidth, this.pixelHeight);
    game.foregroundContext.drawImage(this.spriteSheet, this.imageOffset*this.pixelWidth,
shadowOffset, this.pixelWidth, this.pixelHeight, x, y+this.pixelShadowHeight,
this.pixelWidth,this.pixelHeight);
}
```

This time, the drawLifeBar() method adjusts for the shadow height when drawing the life bar. The drawSelection() method draws a yellow circle around the aircraft, a straight line from the aircraft to the shadow, and finally a small circle at the center of the shadow.

With this last change, we have implemented drawing selections for all the entities. We don't need to implement selections for the terrain since it cannot be selected within the game.

If we run the game in our browser, we should now be able to select items by either clicking them or dragging the mouse over multiple units. These selected items should then show up highlighted, as shown in Figure 6-13.

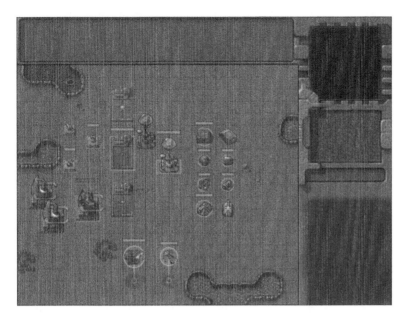

Figure 6-13. *Selected items show up highlighted*

Notice that the life bar above the damaged building clearly shows us how badly damaged it is. You can add or subtract items from the selection by clicking them with the Shift key pressed. We have now completely implemented entity selection in our game.

Summary

We covered a lot of ground in this chapter. Starting with an empty level from the previous chapter, we developed a general framework for animating and drawing items within the game by implementing draw() and animate() methods for these entities.

We handled depth sorting before drawing the items so that items closer to the screen obscured items that were farther away. Using this framework, we then added buildings, vehicles, aircraft, and terrain to our game.

Finally, we implemented the ability to select these entities using the mouse and highlight these selected entities.

In the next chapter, we will implement sending commands to these entities starting with the most important one: movement. We will also look at using pathfinding and steering algorithms so that units navigate intelligently around buildings and other obstacles.

So, let's keep going.

CHAPTER 7

■ ■ ■

Intelligent Unit Movement

In the previous chapter, we built a framework for animating and drawing entities within our game and then added different types of buildings, vehicles, aircraft, and terrain to it. Finally, we added the ability to select these entities.

In this chapter, we will add a framework to give selected units commands and to get the entities to follow orders. We will then implement the most basic of these orders: unit movement by using a combination of pathfinding and steering algorithms to move our units intelligently.

Now let's get started. We will use the code from Chapter 6 as a starting point.

Commanding Units

We will command units using a convention that has now become standard within most modern RTS games. We will select units using left-clicks and command them by using right-clicks.

Right-clicking a navigable spot on the map will command selected units to move to the spot. Right-clicking an enemy unit or building will command all selected units that can attack to attack the enemy. Right-clicking a friendly unit will tell all selected units to follow it around and protect it. And finally, right-clicking an oil field with a harvester vehicle selected will tell the harvester to move to the oil field and deploy on it.

The first thing we need to do is modify the mouse object's click() method inside mouse.js to handle right-click events, as shown in Listing 7-1.

Listing 7-1. Modifying click() to Handle Commands on Right-Click (mouse.js)

```
click:function(ev,rightClick){
    // Player clicked inside the canvas

    var clickedItem = this.itemUnderMouse();
    var shiftPressed = ev.shiftKey;

    if (!rightClick){ // Player left clicked
        if (clickedItem){
            // Pressing shift adds to existing selection. If shift is not pressed, clear
existing selection
            if(!shiftPressed){
                game.clearSelection();
            }
            game.selectItem(clickedItem,shiftPressed);
        }
    } else { // Player right-clicked
        // Handle actions like attacking and movement of selected units
        var uids = [];
```

```
        if (clickedItem){ // Player right-clicked on something
            if (clickedItem.type != "terrain"){
                if (clickedItem.team != game.team){ // Player right-clicked on an enemy item
                    // Identify selected items from players team that can attack
                    for (var i = game.selectedItems.length - 1; i >= 0; i--){
                        var item = game.selectedItems[i];
                        if(item.team == game.team && item.canAttack){
                            uids.push(item.uid);
                        }
                    };
                    // then command them to attack the clicked item
                    if (uids.length>0){
                        game.sendCommand(uids,{type:"attack",toUid:clickedItem.uid});
                    }
                } else  { // Player right-clicked on a friendly item
                    //identify selected items from players team that can move
                    for (var i = game.selectedItems.length - 1; i >= 0; i--){
                        var item = game.selectedItems[i];
                        if(item.team == game.team && (item.type == "vehicles" ||
item.type == "aircraft")){
                            uids.push(item.uid);
                        }
                    };
                    // then command them to guard the clicked item
                    if (uids.length>0){
                        game.sendCommand(uids,{type:"guard", toUid:clickedItem.uid});
                    }
                }
            } else if (clickedItem.name == "oilfield"){ // Player right licked on an oilfield
                // identify the first selected harvester from players team (since only one can
deploy at a time)
                for (var i = game.selectedItems.length - 1; i >= 0; i--){
                    var item = game.selectedItems[i];
                    if(item.team == game.team && (item.type == "vehicles" && item.name ==
"harvester")){
                        uids.push(item.uid);
                        break;
                    }
                };
                // then command it to deploy on the oilfield
                if (uids.length>0){
                    game.sendCommand(uids,{type:"deploy",toUid:clickedItem.uid});
                }
            }
        } else { // Player clicked on the ground
            //identify selected items from players team that can move
            for (var i = game.selectedItems.length - 1; i >= 0; i--){
                var item = game.selectedItems[i];
                if(item.team == game.team && (item.type == "vehicles" || item.type == "aircraft")){
                    uids.push(item.uid);
                }
            };
```

```
                // then command them to move to the clicked location
                if (uids.length>0){
                    game.sendCommand(uids, {type:"move", to:{x:mouse.gameX/game.gridSize,
y:mouse.gameY/game.gridSize}});
                }
            }
        }
    }
},
```

When the player right-clicks inside the game map, we first check to see whether the mouse is above an object.

If the player has not clicked an object, we call the game.sendCommand() method to send a move order to all friendly vehicles and aircraft that are selected.

If the player has clicked an object, we similarly send either an attack, guard, or deploy command to the appropriate units. We also pass the UID of the clicked item as a parameter called toUid within the order.

With the right-click logic in place, we now have to implement methods for sending and receiving game commands.

Sending and Receiving Commands

We could have implemented sending commands by modifying the orders property of selected items inside the click() method that we modified earlier. However, we are going to use a slightly more complex implementation.

Any clicking action that generates a command will call the game.sendCommand() method. The sendCommand() method will pass the call to either the singleplayer or multiplayer object. These objects will then send the command details back to the game.processCommand() method. Within the game.processCommand() method, we will update the orders for all the appropriate objects. We will start by adding these methods to the game object inside game.js, as shown in Listing 7-2.

Listing 7-2. Implementing sendCommand() and processCommand() (game.js)

```
// Send command to either singleplayer or multiplayer object
sendCommand:function(uids,details){
    if (game.type=="singleplayer"){
        singleplayer.sendCommand(uids,details);
    } else {
        multiplayer.sendCommand(uids,details);
    }
},
getItemByUid:function(uid){
    for (var i = game.items.length - 1; i >= 0; i--){
        if(game.items[i].uid == uid){
            return game.items[i];
        }
    };
},
// Receive command from singleplayer or multiplayer object and send it to units
processCommand:function(uids,details){
    // In case the target "to" object is in terms of uid, fetch the target object
    var toObject;
    if (details.toUid){
        toObject = game.getItemByUid(details.toUid);
        if(!toObject || toObject.lifeCode=="dead"){
```

```
                // To object no longer exists. Invalid command
                return;
            }
        }

    for (var i in uids){
        var uid = uids[i];
        var item = game.getItemByUid(uid);
        //if uid is a valid item, set the order for the item
        if(item){
            item.orders = $.extend([],details);
            if(toObject) {
                item.orders.to = toObject;
            }
        }
    };
},
```

The sendCommand() method passes the call to either the singleplayer or multiplayer object's sendCommand() method based on the game type. Using this layer of abstraction allows us to use the same code for both single-player and multiplayer while handling the commands differently.

While the single-player version of sendCommand() will just call processCommand() back immediately, the multiplayer version will send the command to the server, which will then forward the command to all the players at the same time.

We also implement the getItemByUid() method that looks up item UIDs and returns entity objects.

We pass UIDs instead of actual game objects to the sendCommand() method because of the multiplayer version of the game. A typical item object contains a lot of details for animating and drawing the objects such as methods, sprite sheet images, and all the item properties. While needed for drawing the item, transmitting this extra data to the server and getting it back is a waste of bandwidth and quite unnecessary, especially since the entire object can be replaced by a single integer (the UID).

The processCommand() method first looks up any toUid property and gets the resulting item. If no item with the UID exists, it assumes the command is invalid and ignores the command. The method then looks up the items passed in the uids array and sets their orders object to a copy of the order details provided in the parameters.

The next thing we will do is implement the singlePlayer object's sendCommand() method inside singleplayer.js, as shown in Listing 7-3.

Listing 7-3. Implementing the Single-Player sendCommand() Method (singleplayer.js)

```
sendCommand:function(uids,details){
    game.processCommand(uids,details);
}
```

As you can see, the implementation of sendCommand() is fairly simple. We merely forward the call right to game.processCommand(). However, if we wanted, we could also use this method to add functionality for saving game commands, along with details about the currently running animation cycle, to implement the ability to replay saved games.

Now that we have set up a mechanism for commanding units and setting their orders, we need to set up a way for the units to process these orders and execute them.

Processing Orders

Our implementation for processing orders will be fairly simple. We will implement a method called processOrders() for every entity that needs it and call the processOrders() method for all game items from inside the game animation loop.

We will start by modifying the game object's animationLoop() method inside game.js, as shown in Listing 7-4.

Listing 7-4. Calling processOrders() from Inside the Animation Loop (game.js)

```
animationLoop:function(){
    // Process orders for any item that handles it
    for (var i = game.items.length - 1; i >= 0; i--){
        if(game.items[i].processOrders){
            game.items[i].processOrders();
        }
    };

    // Animate each of the elements within the game
    for (var i = game.items.length - 1; i >= 0; i--){
        game.items[i].animate();
    };

    // Sort game items into a sortedItems array based on their x,y coordinates
    game.sortedItems = $.extend([],game.items);
    game.sortedItems.sort(function(a,b){
     return b.y-a.y + ((b.y==a.y)?(a.x-b.x):0);
    });
},
```

The code iterates through every game item and calls the item's processOrders() method if it exists. Now, we can implement the processOrders() method for the game entities one by one and watch as these entities start obeying our commands.

Let's start by implementing movement for aircraft.

Implementing Aircraft Movement

Unlike land vehicles, moving aircraft is fairly simple since aircraft are not affected by terrain, buildings, or other vehicles. When an aircraft is given a move order, it will just turn toward the destination and then move forward in a straight line. Once the aircraft nears its destination, it will go back to its float state.

We will implement this as a default processOrders() method for aircraft inside aircraft.js, as shown in Listing 7-5.

Listing 7-5. Movement in the Aircraft Object's Default processOrders() Method (aircraft.js)

```
processOrders:function(){
    this.lastMovementX = 0;
    this.lastMovementY = 0;
    switch (this.orders.type){
        case "move":
```

```
            // Move towards destination until distance from destination is less than aircraft radius
            var distanceFromDestinationSquared = (Math.pow(this.orders.to.x-this.x,2) +
Math.pow(this.orders.to.y-this.y,2));
                if (distanceFromDestinationSquared < Math.pow(this.radius/game.gridSize,2)) {
                    this.orders = {type:"float"};
                } else {
                    this.moveTo(this.orders.to);
                }
                break;
        }
    }
},
```

We first reset two variables related to movement that we will use later. We then check the order type inside a case statement.

In case the order type is move, we call the moveTo() method until the aircraft's distance from the destination (stored in the to parameter) is less than the aircraft's radius. Once the aircraft has reached its destination, we change the order back to float.

Right now, we have implemented only one order. Any time the aircraft gets an order it doesn't know how to handle, it will continue floating at its current location. We will be implementing more orders as we go along.

The next thing we will do is implement a default moveTo() method that will be used by both the aircraft (see Listing 7-6).

Listing 7-6. The Aircraft Object's Default moveTo() Method (aircraft.js)

```
moveTo:function(destination){
    // Find out where we need to turn to get to destination
    var newDirection = findAngle(destination,this,this.directions);
    // Calculate difference between new direction and current direction
    var difference = angleDiff(this.direction,newDirection,this.directions);
    // Calculate amount that aircraft can turn per animation cycle
    var turnAmount = this.turnSpeed*game.turnSpeedAdjustmentFactor;
    if (Math.abs(difference)>turnAmount){
        this.direction = wrapDirection(this.direction+turnAmount*Math.abs
(difference)/difference,this.directions);
    } else {
        // Calculate distance that aircraft can move per animation cycle
        var movement = this.speed*game.speedAdjustmentFactor;
        // Calculate x and y components of the movement
        var angleRadians = -(Math.round(this.direction)/this.directions)*2*Math.PI ;
        this.lastMovementX = - (movement*Math.sin(angleRadians));
        this.lastMovementY = - (movement*Math.cos(angleRadians));
        this.x = (this.x +this.lastMovementX);
        this.y = (this.y +this.lastMovementY);
    }
},
```

We first calculate the angle from the aircraft to its destination using the findAngle() method and the difference between the current and new direction using the angleDiff() method. The newDirection variable will have a value between 0 and 7 (to reflect the directions that the aircraft can take), while the difference variable will have a value between -4 and 4, with a negative sign indicating an anticlockwise turn is shorter than a clockwise turn.

We then calculate the amount the aircraft can turn based on its turnSpeed property and check to see whether the item needs to turn more by comparing the angle difference with the turn amount.

In case the aircraft still needs to turn, we add the turnAmount value to its direction while keeping the sign of the difference variable. We use the wrapDirection() method to ensure that the final aircraft direction is still between 0 and 7.

In case the aircraft has turned toward its destination, we calculate the movement distance based on its speed. We then calculate the x and y components of the movement and add it to the aircraft's x and y coordinates.

Of course, now that the aircraft direction can take noninteger values, we need to modify the aircraft object's default animate() method to ensure it rounds the direction before selecting the sprite (see Listing 7-7).

Listing 7-7. Modifying animate() to Handle Noninteger Direction Values (aircraft.js)

```
animate:function(){
    // Consider an item healthy if it has more than 40% life
    if (this.life>this.hitPoints*0.4){
        this.lifeCode = "healthy";
    } else if (this.life <= 0){
        this.lifeCode = "dead";
        game.remove(this);
        return;
    } else {
        this.lifeCode = "damaged";
    }
    switch (this.action){
        case "fly":
            var direction = wrapDirection(Math.round(this.direction),this.directions);
            this.imageList = this.spriteArray["fly-"+ direction];
            this.imageOffset = this.imageList.offset + this.animationIndex;
            this.animationIndex++;
            if (this.animationIndex>=this.imageList.count){
                this.animationIndex = 0;
            }
            break;
    }
},
```

We first round the aircraft direction and then call wrapDirection() to ensure that the direction lies between 0 and 7. The rest of the method remains the same.

Next we will add the findAngle(), angleDiff(), and wrapDirection() methods to common.js, as shown in Listing 7-8.

Listing 7-8. Implementing findAngle(), angleDiff(), and wrapDirection() (common.js)

```
/* Common functions for turning and movement */

// Finds the angle between two objects in terms of a direction (where 0 <= angle < directions)
function findAngle(object,unit,directions){
    var dy = (object.y) - (unit.y);
    var dx = (object.x) - (unit.x);
    //Convert Arctan to value between (0 - directions)
    var angle = wrapDirection(directions/2-(Math.atan2(dx,dy)*directions/(2*Math.PI)),directions);
    return angle;
}
```

```
// returns the smallest difference (value ranging between -directions/2 to +directions/2)
// between two angles (where 0 <= angle < directions)
function angleDiff(angle1,angle2,directions){
    if (angle1>=directions/2){
        angle1 = angle1-directions;
    }
    if (angle2>=directions/2){
        angle2 = angle2-directions;
    }

    diff = angle2-angle1;

    if (diff<-directions/2){
        diff += directions;
    }
    if (diff>directions/2){
        diff -= directions;
    }

    return diff;
}

// Wrap value of direction so that it lies between 0 and directions-1
function wrapDirection(direction,directions){
    if (direction<0){
        direction += directions;
    }
    if (direction >= directions){
        direction -= directions;
    }
    return direction;
}
```

The last change we need to make is defining two movement-related properties within the game object inside game.js (see Listing 7-9).

Listing 7-9. Adding Movement-Related Properties to the game Object (game.js)

```
//Movement related properties
speedAdjustmentFactor:1/64,
turnSpeedAdjustmentFactor:1/8,
```

These two factors are used to convert an entity's speed and turnSpeed values into in-game units for movement and turning.

We are now ready to start moving our aircraft within the game, but before we do that, let's simplify our level by removing all the unnecessary items from the map. The new maps.js will look like Listing 7-10.

Listing 7-10. Removing Unnecessary Items from the Map (maps.js)

```
var maps = {
    "singleplayer":[
        {
            "name":"Entities",
            "briefing": "In this level you will start commanding units and moving them around the map.",

            /* Map Details */
            "mapImage":"images/maps/level-one-debug-grid.png",
            "startX":2,
            "startY":3,

            /* Entities to be loaded */
            "requirements":{
                "buildings":["base","starport","harvester","ground-turret"],
                "vehicles":["transport","harvester","scout-tank","heavy-tank"],
                "aircraft":["chopper","wraith"],
                "terrain":["oilfield","bigrocks","smallrocks"]
            },

            /* Entities to be added */
            "items":[
                {"type":"buildings","name":"base","x":11,"y":14,"team":"blue"},
                {"type":"buildings","name":"starport","x":18,"y":14, "team":"blue"},
                {"type":"buildings","name":"harvester","x":20,"y":10, "team":"blue"},
                {"type":"buildings","name":"ground-turret","x":24,"y":7,
"team":"blue","direction":3},

                {"type":"vehicles","name":"transport","x":24,"y":10, "team":"blue","direction":2},
                {"type":"vehicles","name":"harvester","x":16,"y":12, "team":"blue","direction":3},
                {"type":"vehicles","name":"scout-tank","x":24,"y":14, "team":"blue","direction":4},
                {"type":"vehicles","name":"heavy-tank","x":24,"y":16, "team":"blue","direction":5},

                {"type":"aircraft","name":"chopper","x":7,"y":9, "team":"blue","direction":2},
                {"type":"aircraft","name":"wraith","x":11,"y":9, "team":"blue","direction":3},

                {"type":"terrain","name":"oilfield","x":3,"y":5, "action":"hint"},
                {"type":"terrain","name":"bigrocks","x":19,"y":6},
                {"type":"terrain","name":"smallrocks","x":8,"y":3}
            ]
        }
    ]
}
```

When you run the game in the browser, you should be able to select the two aircraft and move them around on the new map shown in Figure 7-1.

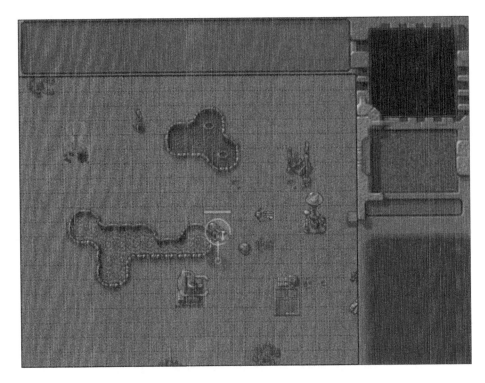

Figure 7-1. *Moving aircraft around the new map*

When you select an aircraft and right-click the map somewhere, the aircraft should turn and move toward the destination. You will notice that the wraith aircraft moves faster than the chopper because we specified a higher value for speed in the wraith entity's properties.

You may also notice that right-clicking a building or a friendly unit doesn't do anything. This is because right-clicking a friendly item generates the guard order, which we have not yet implemented.

Implementing movement for our aircraft was fairly simple because we took the creative liberty of assuming that aircraft could avoid buildings, vehicles, and other aircraft by virtue of adjusting their height.

However, when it comes to vehicles, we can no longer do that. We need to worry about finding the shortest path between a vehicle and its destination while driving around obstacles such as buildings and terrain. This is where pathfinding comes in.

Pathfinding

Pathfinding, or pathing, is the process of finding the shortest path between two points. Typically it involves the use of various algorithms to traverse a graph of nodes starting at one vertex and exploring adjacent nodes until the destination node is reached.

Two of the most commonly used algorithms for graph-based pathfinding are Dijkstra's algorithm and its variant called the A* (pronounced "A star") algorithm.

A* uses an additional distance heuristic that helps it find paths faster than Dijkstra. Because of its performance and accuracy, it is widely used in games. You can read more about the algorithm at http://en.wikipedia.org/wiki/A*. We will also be using A* for the vehicle pathing in our game.

We will use an excellent MIT-licensed JavaScript implementation of A* by Andrea Giammarchi. The code has been optimized for JavaScript, and its performance even on large graphs is fairly good. You can see the latest code as well as play with a live demo at http://devpro.it/javascript_id_137.html. We will add a reference to the A* implementation (stored in astar.js) to the head section of index.html, as shown in Listing 7-11.

Listing 7-11. Adding Reference to the A* Implementation (index.html)

```
<!-- A* Implementation by Andrea Giammarchi -->
<script src="js/astar.js" type="text/javascript" charset="utf-8"></script>
```

The implementation, while fairly complex, is relatively easy to use. The code gives us access to an Astar() method that accepts four parameters: the map graph for us to use, the starting coordinates, the ending coordinates, and optionally a name for the heuristic to use.

The method returns either an array with all the intermediate steps of the shortest path or an empty array in case there is no possible path.

Now that we have our A* algorithm in place, we need to provide it with a graph or grid for pathfinding.

Defining Our Pathfinding Grid

We have already broken our map into a grid of squares with the dimensions 20 pixels by 20 pixels. We will store the pathfinding grid as a two-dimensional array with values of 0 and 1 for passable and impassable squares, respectively.

Before we can create this array, we will need to modify our map to define all the impassable areas of terrain on the map. We will do this by adding a few new properties to the first level in maps.js, as shown in Listing 7-12.

Listing 7-12. Adding Properties for Pathfinding to the Level (maps.js)

```
/* Map coordinates that are obstructed by terrain*/
"mapGridWidth":60,
"mapGridHeight":40,
"mapObstructedTerrain":[
    [49,8], [50,8], [51,8], [51,9], [52,9], [53,9], [53,10], [53,11], [53,12], [53,13], [53,14],
    [53,15], [53,16], [52,16], [52,17], [52,18], [52,19], [51,19], [50,19], [50,18], [50,17], [49,17],
    [49,18], [48,18], [47,18], [47,17], [47,16], [48,16], [49,16], [49,15], [49,14], [48,14], [48,13],
    [48,12], [49,12], [49,11], [50,11], [50,10], [49,10], [49,9], [44,0], [45,0], [45,1], [45,2],
    [46,2], [47,2], [47,3], [48,3], [48,4], [48,5], [49,5], [49,6], [49,7], [50,7], [51,7], [51,6],
    [51,5], [51,4], [52,4], [53,4], [53,3], [54,3], [55,3], [55,2], [56,2], [56,1], [56,0], [55,0],
    [43,19], [44,19], [45,19], [46,19], [47,19], [48,19], [48,20], [48,21], [47,21], [46,21], [45,21],
    [44,21], [43,21], [43,20], [41,22], [42,22], [43,22], [44,22], [45,22], [46,22], [47,22], [48,22],
    [49,22], [50,22], [50,23], [50,24], [49,24], [48,24], [47,24], [47,25], [47,26], [47,27], [47,28],
    [47,29], [47,30], [46,30], [45,30], [44,30], [43,30], [43,29], [43,28], [43,27], [43,26], [43,25],
    [43,24], [42,24], [41,24], [41,23], [48,39], [49,39], [50,39], [51,39], [52,39], [53,39], [54,39],
    [55,39], [56,39], [57,39], [58,39], [59,39], [59,38], [59,37], [59,36], [59,35], [59,34], [59,33],
    [59,32], [59,31], [59,30], [59,29], [0,0], [1,0], [2,0], [1,1], [2,1], [10,3], [11,3], [12,3],
    [12,2], [13,2], [14,2], [14,3], [14,4], [15,4], [15,5], [15,6], [14,6], [13,6], [13,5], [12,5],
    [11,5], [10,5], [10,4], [3,9], [4,9], [5,9], [5,10], [6,10], [7,10], [8,10], [9,10], [9,11],
    [10,11], [11,11], [11,10], [12,10], [13,10], [13,11], [13,12], [12,12], [11,12], [10,12], [9,12],
    [8,12], [7,12], [7,13], [7,14], [6,14], [5,14], [5,13], [5,12], [5,11], [4,11], [3,11], [3,10],
    [33,33], [34,33], [35,33], [35,34], [35,35], [34,35], [33,35], [33,34], [27,39], [27,38], [27,37],
    [28,37], [28,36], [28,35], [28,34], [28,33], [28,32], [28,31], [28,30], [28,29], [29,29], [29,28],
    [29,27], [29,26], [29,25], [29,24], [29,23], [30,23], [31,23], [32,23], [32,22], [32,21], [31,21],
    [30,21], [30,22], [29,22], [28,22], [27,22], [26,22], [26,21], [25,21], [24,21], [24,22], [24,23],
    [25,23], [26,23], [26,24], [25,24], [25,25], [24,25], [24,26], [24,27], [25,27], [25,28], [25,29],
    [24,29], [23,29], [23,30], [23,31], [24,31], [25,31], [25,32], [25,33], [24,33], [23,33], [23,34],
```

```
[23,35], [24,35], [24,36], [24,37], [23,37], [22,37], [22,38], [22,39], [23,39], [24,39], [25,39],
[26,0], [26,1], [25,1], [25,2], [25,3], [26,3], [27,3], [27,2], [28,2], [29,2], [29,3], [30,3],
[31,3], [31,2], [31,1], [32,1], [32,0], [33,0], [32,8], [33,8], [34,8], [34,9], [34,10], [33,10],
[32,10], [32,9], [8,29], [9,29], [9,30], [17,32], [18,32], [19,32], [19,33], [18,33], [17,33],
[18,34], [19,34], [3,27], [4,27], [4,26], [3,26], [2,26], [3,25], [4,25], [9,20], [10,20], [11,20],
[11,21], [10,21], [10,19], [19,7], [15,7], [29,12], [30,13], [20,14], [21,14], [34,13], [35,13],
[36,13], [36,14], [35,14], [34,14], [35,15], [36,15], [16,18], [17,18], [18,18], [16,19], [17,19],
[18,19], [17,20], [18,20], [11,19], [58,0], [59,0], [58,1], [59,1], [59,2], [58,3], [59,3], [58,4],
[59,4], [59,5], [58,6], [59,6], [58,7], [59,7], [59,8], [58,9], [59,9], [58,10], [59,10], [59,11],
[52,6], [53,6], [54,6], [52,7], [53,7], [54,7], [53,8], [54,8], [44,17], [46,32], [55,32], [54,28],
[26,34], [34,34], [4,10], [6,11], [6,12], [6,13], [7,11], [8,11], [12,11], [27,0], [27,1], [26,2],
[28,1], [28,0], [29,0], [29,1], [30,2], [30,1], [30,0], [31,0], [33,9], [46,0], [47,0], [48,0],
[49,0], [50,0], [51,0], [52,0], [53,0], [54,0], [55,1], [54,1], [53,1], [52,1], [51,1], [50,1],
[49,1], [48,1], [47,1], [46,1], [48,2], [49,2], [50,2], [51,2], [52,2], [53,2], [54,2], [52,3],
[51,3], [50,3], [49,3], [49,4], [50,4], [50,5], [50,6], [50,9], [51,10], [52,10], [51,11], [52,11],
[50,12], [51,12], [52,12], [49,13], [50,13], [51,13], [52,13], [50,14], [51,14], [52,14], [50,15],
[51,15], [52,15], [50,16], [51,16], [51,17], [48,17], [51,18], [44,20], [45,20], [46,20], [47,20],
[42,23], [43,23], [44,23], [45,23], [46,23], [47,23], [48,23], [49,23], [44,24], [45,24], [46,24],
[44,25], [45,25], [46,25], [44,26], [45,26], [46,26], [44,27], [45,27], [46,27], [44,28], [45,28],
[46,28], [44,29], [45,29], [46,29], [11,4], [12,4], [13,4], [13,3], [14,5], [25,22], [31,22],
[27,23], [28,23], [27,24], [28,24], [26,25], [27,25], [28,25], [25,26], [26,26], [27,26], [28,26],
[26,27], [27,27], [28,27], [26,28], [27,28], [28,28], [26,29], [27,29], [24,30], [25,30], [26,30],
[27,30], [26,31], [27,31], [26,32], [27,32], [26,33], [27,33], [24,34], [25,34], [27,34], [25,35],
[26,35], [27,35], [25,36], [26,36], [27,36], [25,37], [26,37], [23,38], [24,38], [25,38], [26,38],
[26,39], [2,25], [9,19], [36,31]
],
```

We first define two properties called mapGridWidth and mapGridHeight and finally an extremely large and scary-looking array called mapObstructedTerrain. This array merely contains the x and y coordinates for every grid inside our map that is impassable. This includes areas with trees, mountains, water, craters, and lava.

■ **Note**   If you plan to add a lot of levels to your game, you should take the time to design a level editor that generates this array for you automatically instead of trying to create it by hand.

Now that we have these properties in place, we need to generate a terrain grid from this data when we load the level. We will do this within the singleplayer object's startCurrentLevel() method inside singleplayer.js (see Listing 7-13).

Listing 7-13. Creating the Terrain Grid When Starting Level (singleplayer.js)

```
startCurrentLevel:function(){
    // Load all the items for the level
    var level = maps.singleplayer[singleplayer.currentLevel];

    // Don't allow player to enter mission until all assets for the level are loaded
    $("#entermission").attr("disabled", true);

    // Load all the assets for the level
    game.currentMapImage = loader.loadImage(level.mapImage);
    game.currentLevel = level;
```

```
        game.offsetX = level.startX * game.gridSize;
        game.offsetY = level.startY * game.gridSize;

        // Load level Requirements
        game.resetArrays();
        for (var type in level.requirements){
            var requirementArray = level.requirements[type];
            for (var i=0; i < requirementArray.length; i++) {
                var name = requirementArray[i];
                if (window[type]){
                    window[type].load(name);
                } else {
                    console.log('Could not load type :',type);
                }
            };
        }

        for (var i = level.items.length - 1; i >= 0; i--){
            var itemDetails = level.items[i];
            game.add(itemDetails);
        };

        // Create a grid that stores all obstructed tiles as 1 and unobstructed as 0
        game.currentMapTerrainGrid = [];
        for (var y=0; y < level.mapGridHeight; y++) {
            game.currentMapTerrainGrid[y] = [];
            for (var x=0; x< level.mapGridWidth; x++) {
                game.currentMapTerrainGrid[y][x] = 0;
            }
        };
        for (var i = level.mapObstructedTerrain.length - 1; i >= 0; i--){
            var obstruction = level.mapObstructedTerrain[i];
            game.currentMapTerrainGrid[obstruction[1]][obstruction[0]] = 1;
        };
        game.currentMapPassableGrid = undefined;

        // Enable the enter mission button once all assets are loaded
        if (loader.loaded){
            $("#entermission").removeAttr("disabled");
        } else {
            loader.onload = function(){
                $("#entermission").removeAttr("disabled");
            }
        }

        // Load the mission screen with the current briefing
        $('#missonbriefing').html(level.briefing.replace(/\n/g,'<br><br>'));
        $("#missionscreen").show();
    },
```

We initialize an array called currentMapTerrainGrid inside the game object and set it to the dimensions of our map using mapGridWidth and mapGridHeight. We then set all the obstructed squares to 1 and leave the unobstructed tiles as 0.

If we were to highlight the obstructed squares in currentMapTerrainGrid on our map, it would look like Figure 7-2.

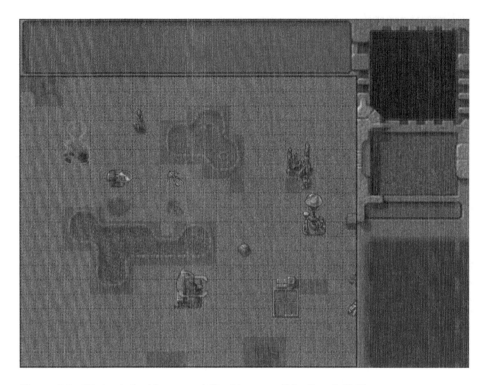

Figure 7-2. *Obstructed grid squares defined in currentMapTerrainGrid*

While currentMapTerrainGrid marks out all the obstacles in the map terrain, it still does not include the buildings and terrain entities on the map.

We will keep another array inside the game object called currentMapPassableGrid that will combine the building and terrain entities and the currentMapTerrainGrid array we defined earlier. This array will need to be re-created every time buildings or terrain get added to or removed from the game. We will do this in a rebuildPassableGrid() method within the game object (see Listing 7-14).

Listing 7-14. rebuildPassableGrid() Method in game Object (game.js)

```
rebuildPassableGrid:function(){
    game.currentMapPassableGrid = $.extend(true,[],game.currentMapTerrainGrid);
    for (var i = game.items.length - 1; i >= 0; i--){
        var item = game.items[i];
        if(item.type == "buildings" || item.type == "terrain"){
            for (var y = item.passableGrid.length - 1; y >= 0; y--){
                for (var x = item.passableGrid[y].length - 1; x >= 0; x--){
```

```
                    if(item.passableGrid[y][x]){
                        game.currentMapPassableGrid[item.y+y][item.x+x] = 1;
                    }
                };
            };
        }
    };
},
```

We first copy the currentMapTerrainGrid array into currentMapPassableGrid. We then iterate through all the game items and use the passableGrid property that we defined for all buildings and terrain to mark out grid squares that are not passable. If we were to highlight the obstructed squares in our map based on the currentMapPassableGrid, it would look like Figure 7-3.

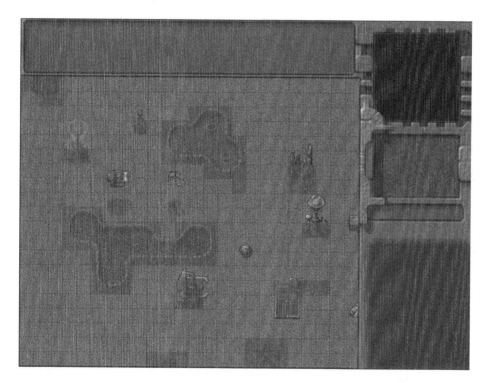

Figure 7-3. *Obstructed grid squares defined in currentMapPassableGrid*

Because of the way we define passableGrid for each building, it is possible to allow portions of buildings to be passable (for example, the lower portion of the starport).

We will need to ensure that game.currentMapPassableGrid is reset anytime a building is added or removed from the game. We do this by adding an extra condition inside the add() and remove() methods of the game object, as shown in Listing 7-15.

Listing 7-15. Clearing currentMapPassableGrid Inside add() and remove() (game.js)

```
add:function(itemDetails) {
    // Set a unique id for the item
    if (!itemDetails.uid){
        itemDetails.uid = game.counter++;
    }

    var item = window[itemDetails.type].add(itemDetails);

    // Add the item to the items array
    game.items.push(item);
    // Add the item to the type specific array
    game[item.type].push(item);

    if(item.type == "buildings" || item.type == "terrain"){
        game.currentMapPassableGrid = undefined;
    }
    return item;
},
remove:function(item){
    // Unselect item if it is selected
    item.selected = false;
    for (var i = game.selectedItems.length - 1; i >= 0; i--){
            if(game.selectedItems[i].uid == item.uid){
                game.selectedItems.splice(i,1);
                break;
            }
        };

    // Remove item from the items array
    for (var i = game.items.length - 1; i >= 0; i--){
        if(game.items[i].uid == item.uid){
            game.items.splice(i,1);
            break;
        }
    };

    // Remove items from the type specific array
    for (var i = game[item.type].length - 1; i >= 0; i--){
        if(game[item.type][i].uid == item.uid){
            game[item.type].splice(i,1);
            break;
        }
    };

    if(item.type == "buildings" || item.type == "terrain"){
        game.currentMapPassableGrid = undefined;
    }
},
```

Within both methods, we check whether the item being added or removed is a building or terrain type and, if so, reset the currentMapPassableGrid variable.

Now that we have defined the movement grid for our A* algorithm, we are ready to implement vehicle movement.

Implementing Vehicle Movement

We will start by adding a default processOrders() method for the vehicles object inside vehicles.js, as shown in Listing 7-16.

Listing 7-16. The Default processOrders() Method for Vehicles (vehicles.js)

```
processOrders:function(){
    this.lastMovementX = 0;
    this.lastMovementY = 0;
    switch (this.orders.type){
        case "move":
            // Move towards destination until distance from destination is less than vehicle radius
            var distanceFromDestinationSquared = (Math.pow(this.orders.to.x-this.x,2) +
Math.pow(this.orders.to.y-this.y,2));
            if (distanceFromDestinationSquared < Math.pow(this.radius/game.gridSize,2)) {
                this.orders = {type:"stand"};
                return;
            } else {
                // Try to move to the destination
                var moving = this.moveTo(this.orders.to);
                if(!moving){
                    // Pathfinding couldn't find a path so stop
                    this.orders = {type:"stand"};
                    return;
                }
            }
            break;
    }
},
```

The method is fairly similar to the processOrders() method that we defined for aircraft. The one subtle difference is that we check whether the moveTo() method returns a value of true indicating it is able to move toward the destination and reset the order to stand in case it does not. We do this because it is possible for the pathfinding algorithm to not find a valid path, and moveTo() will return a value indicating this.

Next, we will implement the default moveTo() method for vehicles, as shown in Listing 7-17.

Listing 7-17. The Default moveTo() Method for Vehicles (vehicles.js)

```
moveTo:function(destination){
    if(!game.currentMapPassableGrid){
        game.rebuildPassableGrid();
    }
```

```
    // First find path to destination
    var start = [Math.floor(this.x),Math.floor(this.y)];
    var end = [Math.floor(destination.x),Math.floor(destination.y)];

    var grid = $.extend(true,[],game.currentMapPassableGrid);
    // Allow destination to be "movable" so that algorithm can find a path
    if(destination.type == "buildings"||destination.type == "terrain"){
        grid[Math.floor(destination.y)][Math.floor(destination.x)] = 0;
    }

    var newDirection;
    // if vehicle is outside map bounds, just go straight towards goal
    if (start[1]<0 || start[1]>=game.currentLevel.mapGridHeight || start[0]<0 ||
start[0]>= game.currentLevel.mapGridWidth){
        this.orders.path = [this,destination];
        newDirection = findAngle(destination,this,this.directions);
    } else {
        //Use A* algorithm to try and find a path to the destination
        this.orders.path = AStar(grid,start,end,'Euclidean');
        if (this.orders.path.length>1){
            var nextStep = {x:this.orders.path[1].x+0.5,y:this.orders.path[1].y+0.5};
            newDirection = findAngle(nextStep,this,this.directions);
        } else if(start[0]==end[0] && start[1] == end[1]){
            // Reached destination grid;
            this.orders.path = [this,destination];
            newDirection = findAngle(destination,this,this.directions);
        } else {
            // There is no path
            return false;
        }
    }

    // Calculate turn amount for new direction
    var difference = angleDiff(this.direction,newDirection,this.directions);
    var turnAmount = this.turnSpeed*game.turnSpeedAdjustmentFactor;

    // Move forward, but keep turning as needed
    var movement = this.speed*game.speedAdjustmentFactor;
    var angleRadians = -(Math.round(this.direction)/this.directions)*2*Math.PI;
    this.lastMovementX = - (movement*Math.sin(angleRadians));
    this.lastMovementY = - (movement*Math.cos(angleRadians));
    this.x = (this.x +this.lastMovementX);
    this.y = (this.y +this.lastMovementY);

    if (Math.abs(difference)>turnAmount){
        this.direction = wrapDirection(this.direction + turnAmount*Math.abs(difference)/difference,
this.directions);
    }

    return true;
},
```

We start by checking whether `game.currentMapPassableGrid` is defined and calling `game.rebuildPassableGrid()` if it is not defined. We then define the start and end values for our path by truncating the vehicle and destination locations.

Next, we copy the `game.currentMapPassableGrid` into a grid variable and define the destination grid square as passable in case the destination is a building or terrain. This hack lets the A* algorithm find a path to a building even though the destination is impassable.

The next step is calculating the path and new direction. We first check whether the vehicle is outside the map bounds and, if so, head straight toward the destination by defining the start and end locations of our path using the vehicle and destination and calculating `newDirection` using the `findAngle()` method. We do this because the `AStar()` method would fail if we passed it starting coordinates that were outside the grid.

If the vehicle is within the map bounds, we call the `AStar()` method while passing it values of `start`, `end`, and the grid. We specify a heuristic method of `Euclidean`, which allows diagonal movement and seems to work well for our game.

If the `AStar()` method returns a path with at least two elements, we calculate `newDirection` by finding the angle from the vehicle to the middle of the next grid.

If the path does not contain at least two elements, we check whether this is because we have reached the destination grid square and, if so, aim toward the final destination. If not, we assume this is because `AStar()` could not find a path and return false.

Finally, we use the `newDirection` and `turnSpeed` and `speed` values to both move the vehicle forward and turn it toward `newDirection`. Unlike our aircraft, vehicles should not be able to turn in place, and we implement this by making both movement and turning happen simultaneously.

With the heart of our pathfinding method implemented, we will need to make one last change to the `vehicles` object. We will modify the default `animate()` method to account for noninteger values of direction, as shown in Listing 7-18.

Listing 7-18. Modifying animate() to Handle Noninteger Direction Values (vehicles.js)

```
animate:function(){
    // Consider an item healthy if it has more than 40% life
    if (this.life>this.hitPoints*0.4){
        this.lifeCode = "healthy";
    } else if (this.life <= 0){
        this.lifeCode = "dead";
        game.remove(this);
        return;
    } else {
        this.lifeCode = "damaged";
    }

    switch (this.action){
        case "stand":
            var direction = wrapDirection(Math.round(this.direction),this.directions);
            this.imageList = this.spriteArray["stand-"+direction];
            this.imageOffset = this.imageList.offset + this.animationIndex;
            this.animationIndex++;

            if (this.animationIndex>=this.imageList.count){
                this.animationIndex = 0;
            }
            break;
    }
},
```

If you run the game now, you should be able to select vehicles and move them around the map by right-clicking a spot on the map. The vehicles will move along a path that avoids all the terrain and building obstacles. Figure 7-4 illustrates a typical path returned by the pathfinding algorithm.

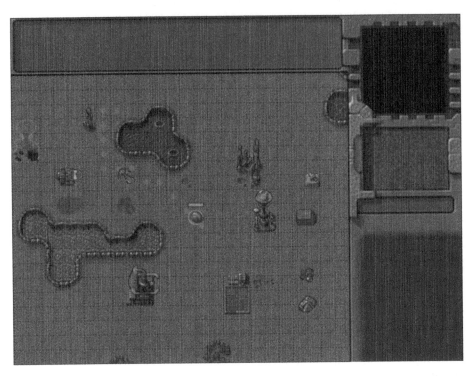

Figure 7-4. *Typical movement path using pathfinding algorithm*

One thing that you will notice is that while the vehicles avoid unpassable terrain, they still drive over other vehicles.

One simple way to fix this is to just mark all squares occupied by any vehicle as unpassable. However, this simplistic approach might end up blocking very large portions of the map since vehicles often move across multiple grid squares. The other disadvantage of this method is that if we try to move a bunch of vehicles through a narrow passage, the first vehicle will block the passage, causing the pathfinding for the vehicles behind to try to find a longer alternate route or, worse, assume there is no possible path and give up.

A better alternative is to implement a steering step that checks for collisions with other objects and modifies the vehicle's direction while still trying to maintain the original path as far as possible.

Collision Detection and Steering

Steering, like pathfinding, is a fairly vast AI subject. The idea of applying steering behavior in games has been around for a long time, but it was popularized by the work of Craig Reynolds in the mid to late 1980s. His paper "Steering Behaviors for Autonomous Characters" and his Java demos are still considered the basic starting point for developing steering mechanisms in games. You can read more about his research and look at demos of various steering mechanisms at http://www.red3d.com/cwr/steer/.

We will use a fairly simple implementation for our game. We will first check to see whether moving a vehicle along its present direction will result in collisions with any object. If there are colliding objects, we will create repulsive forces from any colliding objects to our vehicle and a mild attractive force toward the next grid square in the pathfinding path.

We will then combine all of these forces as vectors to see which direction the vehicle will need to move to get away from the collisions. We will steer the vehicle toward this direction until the vehicle is no longer colliding with any object, at which point the vehicle will return to the basic pathfinding mode.

We will distinguish between hard and soft collisions based on the distance from colliding objects. A vehicle that is about to have a soft collision may still move while turning; however, a vehicle about to have hard collision will not move forward at all and will only turn away.

We will start by implementing a default checkCollisionsObject() method for the vehicle object inside vehicles.js, as shown in Listing 7-19.

Listing 7-19. The Default checkCollisionObjects() Method (vehicles.js)

```
// Make a list of collisions that the vehicle will have if it goes along present path
checkCollisionObjects:function(grid){
    // Calculate new position on present path
    var movement = this.speed*game.speedAdjustmentFactor;
    var angleRadians = -(Math.round(this.direction)/this.directions)*2*Math.PI;
    var newX = this.x - (movement*Math.sin(angleRadians));
    var newY = this.y - (movement*Math.cos(angleRadians));

    // List of objects that will collide after next movement step
    var collisionObjects = [];

    var x1 = Math.max(0,Math.floor(newX)-3);
    var x2 = Math.min(game.currentLevel.mapGridWidth-1,Math.floor(newX)+3);
    var y1 = Math.max(0,Math.floor(newY)-3);
    var y2 = Math.min(game.currentLevel.mapGridHeight-1,Math.floor(newY)+3);
    // Test grid upto 3 squares away
    for (var j=x1; j <= x2;j++){
        for(var i=y1; i<= y2 ;i++){
            if(grid[i][j]==1){ // grid square is obsutructed
                if (Math.pow(j+0.5-newX,2)+Math.pow(i+0.5-newY,2) <
Math.pow(this.radius/game.gridSize+0.1,2)){
                    // Distance of obstructed grid from vehicle is less than hard collision threshold
                    collisionObjects.push({collisionType:"hard", with:{type:"wall",x:j+0.5,y:i+0.5}});
                } else if (Math.pow(j+0.5-newX,2)+Math.pow(i+0.5-newY,2) <
Math.pow(this.radius/game.gridSize+0.7,2)){
                    // Distance of obstructed grid from vehicle is less than soft collision
threshold
                    collisionObjects.push({collisionType:"soft", with:{type:"wall",x:j+0.5,y:i+0.5}});
                }
            }
        };
    };

    for (var i = game.vehicles.length - 1; i >= 0; i--){
        var vehicle = game.vehicles[i];
        // Test vehicles that are less than 3 squares away for collisions
        if (vehicle != this && Math.abs(vehicle.x-this.x)<3 && Math.abs(vehicle.y-this.y)<3){
            if (Math.pow(vehicle.x-newX,2) + Math.pow(vehicle.y-newY,2) <
Math.pow((this.radius+vehicle.radius)/game.gridSize,2)){
```

```
                    // Distance between vehicles is less than hard collision threshold (sum of vehicle
radii)
                         collisionObjects.push({collisionType:"hard",with:vehicle});
                } else if (Math.pow(vehicle.x-newX,2) + Math.pow(vehicle.y-newY,2) <
Math.pow((this.radius*1.5+vehicle.radius)/game.gridSize,2)){
                    // Distance between vehicles is less than soft collision threshold (1.5 times
vehicle radius + colliding vehicle radius)
                         collisionObjects.push({collisionType:"soft",with:vehicle});
                }
            }
        };

    return collisionObjects;
},
```

We first calculate the new position of the vehicle if it moves along its current direction. We then check to see whether there are any impassable grid squares nearby that might collide with the vehicle in its new position by comparing the distances between their centers with certain threshold values based on the vehicle radius. We mark collisions as "hard" if they are colliding or "soft" if they are almost ready to collide. All collisions are then added to the collisionObjects array.

We then repeat this process with the vehicles array by testing all vehicles that are close by for possible collisions using the sum of their radii as a threshold distance.

Now that we have a list of colliding objects, we will modify the default moveTo() method we defined earlier to handle collisions (see Listing 7-20).

Listing 7-20. Handling Collisions Inside the default moveTo() Method (vehicles.js)

```
moveTo:function(destination){
    if(!game.currentMapPassableGrid){
        game.rebuildPassableGrid();
    }

    // First find path to destination
    var start = [Math.floor(this.x),Math.floor(this.y)];
    var end = [Math.floor(destination.x),Math.floor(destination.y)];

    var grid = $.extend(true,[],game.currentMapPassableGrid);
    // Allow destination to be "movable" so that algorithm can find a path
    if(destination.type == "buildings"||destination.type == "terrain"){
        grid[Math.floor(destination.y)][Math.floor(destination.x)] = 0;
    }

    var newDirection;
    // if vehicle is outside map bounds, just go straight towards goal
    if (start[1]<0 || start[1]>=game.currentLevel.mapGridHeight || start[0]<0 ||
start[0]>= game.currentLevel.mapGridWidth){
        this.orders.path = [this,destination];
        newDirection = findAngle(destination,this,this.directions);
    } else {
        //Use A* algorithm to try and find a path to the destination
        this.orders.path = AStar(grid,start,end,'Euclidean');
```

```
        if (this.orders.path.length>1){
            var nextStep = {x:this.orders.path[1].x+0.5,y:this.orders.path[1].y+0.5};
            newDirection = findAngle(nextStep,this,this.directions);
        } else if(start[0]==end[0] && start[1] == end[1]){
            // Reached destination grid square
            this.orders.path = [this,destination];
            newDirection = findAngle(destination,this,this.directions);
        } else {
            // There is no path
            return false;
        }
    }

    // check if moving along current direction might cause collision..
    // If so, change newDirection
    var collisionObjects = this.checkCollisionObjects(grid);
    this.hardCollision = false;
    if (collisionObjects.length>0){
        this.colliding = true;

        // Create a force vector object that adds up repulsion from all colliding objects
        var forceVector = {x:0,y:0}
        // By default, the next step has a mild attraction force
        collisionObjects.push({collisionType:"attraction", with:{x:this.orders.path[1].x+0.5,
y:this.orders.path[1].y+0.5}});
        for (var i = collisionObjects.length - 1; i >= 0; i--){
            var collObject = collisionObjects[i];
            var objectAngle = findAngle(collObject.with,this,this.directions);
            var objectAngleRadians = -(objectAngle/this.directions)* 2*Math.PI;
            var forceMagnitude;
            switch(collObject.collisionType){
                case "hard":
                    forceMagnitude = 2;
                    this.hardCollision = true;
                    break;
                case "soft":
                    forceMagnitude = 1;
                    break;
                case "attraction":
                    forceMagnitude = -0.25;
                    break;
            }

            forceVector.x += (forceMagnitude*Math.sin(objectAngleRadians));
            forceVector.y += (forceMagnitude*Math.cos(objectAngleRadians));
        };
        // Find a new direction based on the force vector
        newDirection = findAngle(forceVector,{x:0,y:0},this.directions);
    } else {
        this.colliding = false;
    }
```

```
    // Calculate turn amount for new direction
    var difference = angleDiff(this.direction,newDirection,this.directions);
    var turnAmount = this.turnSpeed*game.turnSpeedAdjustmentFactor;

    // Either turn or move forward based on collision type
    if (this.hardCollision){
        // In case of hard collision, do not move forward, just turn towards new direction
        if (Math.abs(difference)>turnAmount){
            this.direction = wrapDirection(this.direction+
turnAmount*Math.abs(difference)/difference, this.directions);
        }
    } else {
        // Otherwise, move forward, but keep turning as needed
        var movement = this.speed*game.speedAdjustmentFactor;
        var angleRadians = -(Math.round(this.direction)/this.directions)* 2*Math.PI ;
        this.lastMovementX = - (movement*Math.sin(angleRadians));
        this.lastMovementY = - (movement*Math.cos(angleRadians));
        this.x = (this.x +this.lastMovementX);
        this.y = (this.y +this.lastMovementY);
        if (Math.abs(difference)>turnAmount){
            this.direction = wrapDirection(this.direction+
turnAmount*Math.abs(difference)/difference, this.directions);
        }
    }
    return true;
},
```

After the initial pathfinding step, we call the checkCollisionObjects() method and get a list of objects that the vehicle will collide with.

We then iterate through this list of objects and define a repulsive force for each with a magnitude of either 1 or 2 based on whether the collision is "soft" or "hard." We also define an attractive force toward the next pathfinding grid square. Finally, we add up all these forces into a forceVector object and use it to calculate the direction that would take the vehicle the farthest away from all the forces and assign it to the newDirection variable.

What this means is as long as there are no colliding objects, the vehicle will head toward the next grid square defined in its path. The moment the vehicle senses a collision, its primary motivation will be to avoid the collision by taking evasive action. Once the collision threat has been averted, the vehicle will return to its original path-following behavior.

We add an extra check to prevent the vehicle from moving forward if movement will result in a hard collision. As a result, the vehicle will stop completely rather than actually collide with another object.

If you run the game now and try to move a vehicle, you will find that it steers around other vehicles to avoid colliding with them.

One problem that you might notice is that if you try to move multiple vehicles to the same spot, the first one stops at the correct location, while the others keep circling around trying in vain to reach the occupied stop. We will need to fix this by adding some intelligence to the way a vehicle handles trying to move to a blocked spot.

The ideal behavior would be to stop at a little distance from the destination if the destination is blocked and to stop even farther away if the vehicle has been colliding for a long time without reaching its destination.

We will implement this by modifying the default processOrders() method, as shown in Listing 7-21.

Listing 7-21. Modifying processOrders() to Handle Stopping (vehicles.js)

```
processOrders:function(){
    this.lastMovementX = 0;
    this.lastMovementY = 0;
    switch (this.orders.type){
        case "move":
            // Move towards destination until distance from destination is less than vehicle radius
            var distanceFromDestinationSquared = (Math.pow(this.orders.to.x-this.x,2) +
Math.pow(this.orders.to.y-this.y,2));
                if (distanceFromDestinationSquared < Math.pow(this.radius/game.gridSize,2)) {
                    //Stop when within one radius of the destination
                    this.orders = {type:"stand"};
                    return;
                } else if (distanceFromDestinationSquared <Math.pow(this.radius*3/game.gridSize,2)) {
                    //Stop when within 3 radius of the destination if colliding with something
                    this.orders = {type:"stand"};
                    return;
                } else {
                    if (this.colliding && (Math.pow(this.orders.to.x-this.x,2) +
Math.pow(this.orders.to.y-this.y,2))<Math.pow(this.radius*5/game.gridSize,2)) {
                        // Count collsions within 5 radius distance of goal
                        if (!this.orders.collisionCount){
                            this.orders.collisionCount = 1
                        } else {
                            this.orders.collisionCount ++;
                        }
                        // Stop if more than 30 collisions occur
                        if (this.orders.collisionCount > 30) {
                            this.orders = {type:"stand"};
                            return;
                        }
                    }
                    var moving = this.moveTo(this.orders.to);
                    // Pathfinding couldn't find a path so stop
                    if(!moving){
                        this.orders = {type:"stand"};
                        return;
                    }
                }
            break;
    }
},
```

We first try to stop at the destination if the vehicle is within 1 radius of the destination. We also stop if the vehicle is colliding and within a 3-radius distance of the destination. Finally, we stop if the vehicle has been colliding more than 30 times while being within a 5-radius distance of the destination. This last condition handles situations where the vehicle has been bumping around a crowded area for a while without finding a way to reach its destination.

If you run the game now and try to move multiple vehicles together, you will see that they intelligently stop near their destination even in crowded areas.

At this point, we have a reasonably good pathfinding and steering solution for intelligent unit movement. This system can be developed further to improve performance and add other intelligent behavior such as queuing, flocking, and leader following, depending on your game requirements. You should definitely research this topic further as you implement unit movement within your own games, starting with the work by Craig Reynolds (www.red3d.com/cwr/steer/).

Now that we have vehicle movement working, let's take the time to implement one more movement-related order: deploying the harvester.

Deploying the Harvester

We designed the harvester as a deployable vehicle that opened up into a harvester building when deployed on an oil field. We already set up the code to pass the deploy order to a harvester when the player right-clicks an oil field. Now we will implement the deploy case within the vehicle object's processOrders() method inside vehicles.js, as shown in Listing 7-22.

Listing 7-22. Implementation of the deploy Case Inside processOrders() (vehicles.js)

```
case "deploy":
    // If oilfield has been used already, then cancel order
    if(this.orders.to.lifeCode == "dead"){
        this.orders = {type:"stand"};
        return;
    }
    // Move to middle of oil field
    var target = {x:this.orders.to.x+1,y:this.orders.to.y+0.5,type:"terrain"};
    var distanceFromTargetSquared = (Math.pow(target.x-this.x,2) + Math.pow(target.y-this.y,2));
    if (distanceFromTargetSquared<Math.pow(this.radius*2/game.gridSize,2)) {
        // After reaching oil field, turn harvester to point towards left (direction 6)
        var difference = angleDiff(this.direction,6,this.directions);
        var turnAmount = this.turnSpeed*game.turnSpeedAdjustmentFactor;
        if (Math.abs(difference)>turnAmount){
            this.direction = wrapDirection(this.direction+turnAmount*Math.abs(difference)/
difference,this.directions);
        } else {
            // Once it is pointing to the left, remove the harvester and oil field and deploy a
harvester building
            game.remove(this.orders.to);
            this.orders.to.lifeCode="dead";
            game.remove(this);
            this.lifeCode="dead";
            game.add({type:"buildings", name:"harvester", x:this.orders.to.x,
y:this.orders.to.y, action:"deploy", team:this.team});
        }
    } else {
        var moving = this.moveTo(target);
        // Pathfinding couldn't find a path so stop
        if(!moving){
            this.orders = {type:"stand"};
        }
    }
    break;
```

We start by using the moveTo() method to move the harvester to the middle of the oil field. Once the harvester reaches the oil field, we use the angleDiff() method and turn the harvester toward the left (direction 6). Finally, we remove the harvester vehicle and oil field items from the game and add a harvester building at the oil field's location with the action set to deploy.

If we run our game, select the harvester vehicle, and then right-click an oil field, we should see the harvester move to the oil field and deploy into a building, as shown in Figure 7-5.

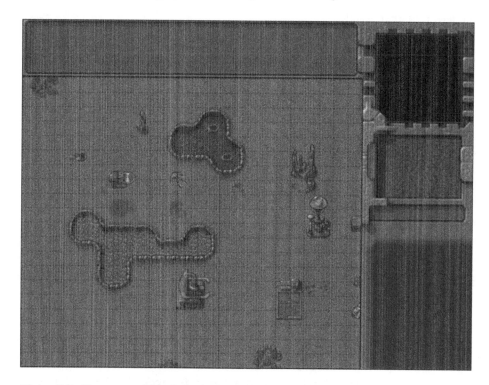

Figure 7-5. *Harvester vehicle deploying into a harvester building*

The harvester moves to the oil field, turns into position, and then seems to expand into a harvester building. As you can see, with the movement framework in place, handling different orders is very easy.

Before we wrap up unit movement, we will address one last thing. You may have noticed that the unit movement especially for fast units such as the wraith seems a little choppy. We will try to smoothen this unit movement.

Smoother Unit Movement

Our game animation loop currently runs at a steady 10 frames per second. Even though our drawing loop runs faster (typically 30 to 60 frames per second), it has no new information to draw during these extra loops, so effectively it too draws at 10 frames per second. This results in the choppy-looking movement that we see.

One simple way to make the animation look much smoother is interpolating the vehicle movement between animation frames. We can calculate the time since the last animation loop and use it to create an interpolation factor that is used to position the units during intermediate drawing loops. This little adjustment will make the units seem to move at a much higher frame rate, even though they are actually being moved only at 10 frames per second.

We will start by modifying the game object's animationLoop() method to save the last animation time and the drawingLoop() method to calculate an interpolation factor based on the current drawing time and the last animation time. The final version of animationLoop() and drawingLoop() will look like Listing 7-23.

Listing 7-23. Calculating a Movement Interpolation Factor (game.js)

```
animationLoop:function(){
    // Process orders for any item that handles it
    for (var i = game.items.length - 1; i >= 0; i--){
        if(game.items[i].processOrders){
            game.items[i].processOrders();
        }
    };

    // Animate each of the elements within the game
    for (var i = game.items.length - 1; i >= 0; i--){
        game.items[i].animate();
    };

    // Sort game items into a sortedItems array based on their x,y coordinates
    game.sortedItems = $.extend([],game.items);
    game.sortedItems.sort(function(a,b){
        return b.y-a.y + ((b.y==a.y)?(a.x-b.x):0);
    });

    //Save the time that the last animation loop completed
    game.lastAnimationTime = (new Date()).getTime();
},
drawingLoop:function(){
    // Handle Panning the Map
    game.handlePanning();

    // Check the time since the game was animated and calculate a linear interpolation factor (-1 to 0)
    // since drawing will happen more often than animation
    game.lastDrawTime = (new Date()).getTime();
        if (game.lastAnimationTime){
            game.drawingInterpolationFactor = (game.lastDrawTime-game.lastAnimationTime)/game.
animationTimeout - 1;
            if (game.drawingInterpolationFactor>0){ // No point interpolating beyond the next
animation loop ...
                game.drawingInterpolationFactor = 0;
            }
        } else {
          game.drawingInterpolationFactor = -1;

    }
```

```
    // Since drawing the background map is a fairly large operation,
    // we only redraw the background if it changes (due to panning)
    if (game.refreshBackground){
        game.backgroundContext.drawImage(game.currentMapImage, game.offsetX, game.offsetY,game.
canvasWidth, game.canvasHeight, 0, 0, game.canvasWidth, game.canvasHeight);
        game.refreshBackground = false;
    }

    // Clear the foreground canvas
    game.foregroundContext.clearRect(0,0,game.canvasWidth,game.canvasHeight);

    // Start drawing the foreground elements
    for (var i = game.sortedItems.length - 1; i >= 0; i--){
        game.sortedItems[i].draw();
    };

    // Draw the mouse
    mouse.draw();

    // Call the drawing loop for the next frame using request animation frame
    if (game.running){
        requestAnimationFrame(game.drawingLoop);
    }
},
```

We save the current time into game.lastAnimationTime at the end of the animationLoop() method. We then use this variable and the current time to calculate the game.drawingInterpolationFactor variable that is a number between -1 and 0. A value of -1 indicates that we draw the unit at the previous location, while a value of 0 means that we draw the unit at its present location. Any value between -1 and 0 means that we draw the unit at an intermediate location between the two points. We cap the value at 0 to prevent any extrapolation from happening (i.e., drawing the unit beyond the point that it has been animated).

■ **Note**   Using techniques such as extrapolation and client-side prediction to position units is much more common in multiplayer first-person shooter games to compensate for lag because of high latency.

Now that we have calculated the interpolation factor, we will use it along with the unit lastMovementX and lastMovementY values to position the element while drawing. First, we will modify the default draw() method for the aircrafts object inside aircraft.js, as shown in Listing 7-24.

Listing 7-24. Interpolating Movement While Drawing Aircraft (aircraft.js)

```
draw:function(){
    var x = (this.x*game.gridSize)-game.offsetX-this.pixelOffsetX +
this.lastMovementX*game.drawingInterpolationFactor*game.gridSize;
    var y = (this.y*game.gridSize)-game.offsetY-this.pixelOffsetY-this.pixelShadowHeight +
this.lastMovementY*game.drawingInterpolationFactor*game.gridSize;
    this.drawingX = x;
    this.drawingY = y;
    if (this.selected){
```

```
        this.drawSelection();
        this.drawLifeBar();
    }
    var colorIndex = (this.team == "blue")?0:1;
    var colorOffset = colorIndex*this.pixelHeight;
    var shadowOffset = this.pixelHeight*2; // The aircraft shadow is on the second row of the sprite sheet

    game.foregroundContext.drawImage(this.spriteSheet, this.imageOffset*this.
pixelWidth,colorOffset,this.pixelWidth,this.pixelHeight,x,y,this.pixelWidth,this.pixelHeight);
    game.foregroundContext.drawImage(this.spriteSheet, this.imageOffset*this.
pixelWidth,shadowOffset,this.pixelWidth,this.pixelHeight,x,y+this.pixelShadowHeight,this.
pixelWidth,this.pixelHeight);
}
```

The only change that we made is adding the extrapolation-related term to the x and y coordinate calculations. Next we will make the same change to the default draw() method for vehicles inside vehicles.js (see Listing 7-25).

Listing 7-25. Interpolating Movement While Drawing Vehicles (vehicles.js)

```
draw:function(){
    var x = (this.x*game.gridSize)-game.offsetX-this.pixelOffsetX + this.lastMovementX*game.
drawingInterpolationFactor*game.gridSize;
    var y = (this.y*game.gridSize)-game.offsetY-this.pixelOffsetY + this.lastMovementY*game.
drawingInterpolationFactor*game.gridSize;
    this.drawingX = x;
    this.drawingY = y;

    if (this.selected){
        this.drawSelection();
        this.drawLifeBar();
    }

    var colorIndex = (this.team == "blue")?0:1;
    var colorOffset = colorIndex*this.pixelHeight;

    game.foregroundContext.drawImage(this.spriteSheet, this.imageOffset*this.pixelWidth,colorOffset,
        this.pixelWidth,this.pixelHeight,x,y,this.pixelWidth,this.pixelHeight);
}
```

If we run the game and move the units around, the movement should now be visibly smoother than before. With this last change, we can now consider unit movement wrapped up.

Summary

In this chapter, we implemented intelligent unit movement for our game.

We started by developing a framework to give selected units commands and for the entities to then follow orders.

We implemented the move order for aircraft by moving them straight toward their destination and for vehicles by using a combination of A* for pathfinding and repulsive forces for steering. We then implemented the deploy order for harvesters using the movement code we developed.

Finally, we smoothened the unit movement by integrating an interpolation step within our drawing code.

In the next chapter, we will implement more of our game rules: creating and placing buildings, teleporting vehicles and aircraft from the starport, and harvesting for money. So, let's keep going.

CHAPTER 8

Adding More Game Elements

In the previous chapter, we developed a framework for unit movement that combined pathfinding and steering. We used this framework to implement move and deploy orders for the vehicles. Finally, we made our unit movement look smoother by interpolating the movement steps during intermediate drawing cycles.

We now have a game where the player can select units and command them to move around the map.

In this chapter, we will build upon this code by adding some more game elements. We will start by implementing an economy where the player can earn money by harvesting and then spend the money on creating buildings and units.

We will then build a framework to create scripted events within a game level, which we can use to control the game story line. We will also add the ability to display messages and notifications to the user. We will then use these elements to handle the completion of a mission within a level.

Let's get started. We will use the code from Chapter 7 as a starting point.

Implementing the Basic Economy

Our game will have a fairly simple economic system. Players will start each mission with an initial amount of money. They can then earn more by deploying a harvester at an oil field. Player will be able to see their cash balance in the sidebar. Once players have sufficient money, they can use it to purchase buildings and units using the sidebar.

The first thing we will do is modify the game to provide money to the player when the level starts.

Setting the Starting Money

We will start by removing some of the extra items in the items array and specifying the starting cash for both players in the first map inside maps.js, as shown in Listing 8-1.

Listing 8-1. Setting the Starting Cash Amount for the Level (maps.js)

```
/* Entities to be added */
"items":[
    {"type":"buildings","name":"base","x":11,"y":14,"team":"blue"},
    {"type":"buildings","name":"starport","x":18,"y":14,"team":"blue"},

    {"type":"vehicles","name":"harvester","x":16,"y":12,"team":"blue","direction":3, "uid":-1},
    {"type":"terrain","name":"oilfield","x":3,"y":5,"action":"hint"},

    {"type":"terrain","name":"bigrocks","x":19,"y":6},
    {"type":"terrain","name":"smallrocks","x":8,"y":3}
],
```

```
/* Economy Related*/
"cash":{
    "blue":5000,
    "green":1000
},
```

We removed all the unnecessary items from the items list. We also added a cash object that sets the starting cash for the blue team to 5000 and for the green team to 1000.

You may have noticed that we have specified a UID for the harvester vehicle. We will use this later in the chapter when we handle triggers and scripted events.

■ **Note**   We use negative values when we specify UIDs for an item so we can be sure that the UID will never clash with autogenerated UIDs, which are always positive.

Next, we will need to load these cash values inside the singleplayer object's startCurrentLevel() method, as shown in Listing 8-2.

Listing 8-2. Loading Cash Amount When Starting Level (singleplayer.js)

```
startCurrentLevel:function(){
    // Load all the items for the level
    var level = maps.singleplayer[singleplayer.currentLevel];

    // Don't allow player to enter mission until all assets for the level are loaded
    $("#entermission").attr("disabled", true);

    // Load all the assets for the level
    game.currentMapImage = loader.loadImage(level.mapImage);
    game.currentLevel = level;

    game.offsetX = level.startX * game.gridSize;
    game.offsetY = level.startY * game.gridSize;

    // Load level Requirements
    game.resetArrays();
    for (var type in level.requirements){
        var requirementArray = level.requirements[type];
        for (var i=0; i < requirementArray.length; i++) {
            var name = requirementArray[i];
            if (window[type]){
                window[type].load(name);
            } else {
                console.log('Could not load type :',type);
            }
        };
    };
```

```
    for (var i = level.items.length - 1; i >= 0; i--){
        var itemDetails = level.items[i];
        game.add(itemDetails);
    };

    // Create a grid that stores all obstructed tiles as 1 and unobstructed as 0
    game.currentMapTerrainGrid = [];
    for (var y=0; y < level.mapGridHeight; y++) {
        game.currentMapTerrainGrid[y] = [];
        for (var x=0; x< level.mapGridWidth; x++) {
            game.currentMapTerrainGrid[y][x] = 0;
        }
    };
    for (var i = level.mapObstructedTerrain.length - 1; i >= 0; i--){
        var obstruction = level.mapObstructedTerrain[i];
        game.currentMapTerrainGrid[obstruction[1]][obstruction[0]] = 1;
    };
    game.currentMapPassableGrid = undefined;

    // Load Starting Cash For Game
    game.cash = $.extend([],level.cash);

    // Enable the enter mission button once all assets are loaded
    if (loader.loaded){
        $("#entermission").removeAttr("disabled");
    } else {
        loader.onload = function(){
            $("#entermission").removeAttr("disabled");
        }
    }

    // Load the mission screen with the current briefing
    $('#missonbriefing').html(level.briefing.replace(/\n/g,'<br><br>'));
    $("#missionscreen").show();
},
```

At this point, the game should load the starting cash amount for both players when the level is loaded. However, before we can see the cash value, we need to implement the sidebar.

Implementing the Sidebar

We will implement the sidebar functionality within a `sidebar` object inside `sidebar.js`, as shown in Listing 8-3.

Listing 8-3. Creating the sidebar Object (sidebar.js)

```
var sidebar = {
    animate:function(){
        // Display the current cash balance value
        $('#cash').html(game.cash[game.team]);
    },
}
```

For now, the object has only the animate() method, which updates the sidebar cash value. We will call this method from within the game object's animationLoop() method, as shown in Listing 8-4.

Listing 8-4. Calling sidebar.animate() from game.animationLoop() (game.js)

```
animationLoop:function(){
    // Animate the Sidebar
    sidebar.animate();

    // Process orders for any item that handles it
    for (var i = game.items.length - 1; i >= 0; i--){
        if(game.items[i].processOrders){
            game.items[i].processOrders();
        }
    };

    // Animate each of the elements within the game
    for (var i = game.items.length - 1; i >= 0; i--){
        game.items[i].animate();
    };

    // Sort game items into a sortedItems array based on their x,y coordinates
    game.sortedItems = $.extend([],game.items);
    game.sortedItems.sort(function(a,b){
        return b.y-a.y + ((b.y==a.y)?(a.x-b.x):0);
    });

    game.lastAnimationTime = (new Date()).getTime();
},
```

Next, we will add a reference to sidebar.js inside the <head> section of index.html, as shown in Listing 8-5.

Listing 8-5. Adding a Reference to sidebar.js (index.html)

```
<script src="js/sidebar.js" type="text/javascript" charset="utf-8"></script>
```

If we run the code so far, we should see the player's cash balance in the sidebar area, as shown in Figure 8-1.

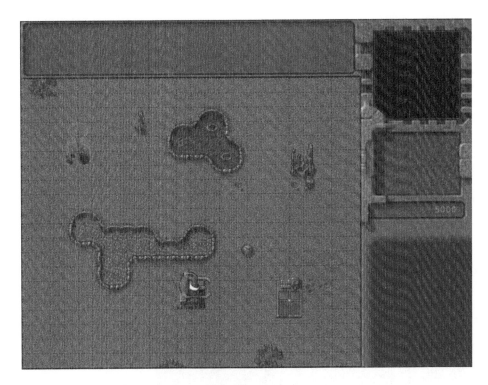

Figure 8-1. *Cash balance shown on sidebar*

Now that we have a basic sidebar with a cash balance, we will implement a way for the player to generate more money by harvesting.

Generating Money

We already implemented the ability to deploy a harvester in the previous chapter. To start earning money when harvesting, we will modify the deploy animation state and implement a new harvest animation state in the default animate() method inside buildings.js, as shown in Listing 8-6.

Listing 8-6. Implementing a New Harvest Animation State Inside animate() (buildings.js)

```
case "deploy":
    this.imageList = this.spriteArray["deploy"];
    this.imageOffset = this.imageList.offset + this.animationIndex;
    this.animationIndex++;
    // Once deploying is complete, go to harvest now
    if (this.animationIndex>=this.imageList.count){
        this.animationIndex = 0;
        this.action = "harvest";
    }
    break;
case "harvest":
    this.imageList = this.spriteArray[this.lifeCode];
    this.imageOffset = this.imageList.offset + this.animationIndex;
    this.animationIndex++;
```

199

```
if (this.animationIndex>=this.imageList.count){
    this.animationIndex = 0;
    if (this.lifeCode == "healthy"){
        // Harvesters mine 2 credits of cash per animation cycle
        game.cash[this.team] += 2;
    }
}
break;
```

The harvest case is similar to the stand case. However, every time the animation runs through one complete cycle, we add two credits to the player's cash balance. We do this only if the harvester building is not damaged.

We also modify the deploy state to roll over into the harvest state instead of the stand state. This way, once the harvester is deployed, it will automatically start earning money.

If we start the game and deploy the harvester into the oil field, we should see the cash balance slowly increasing, as shown in Figure 8-2.

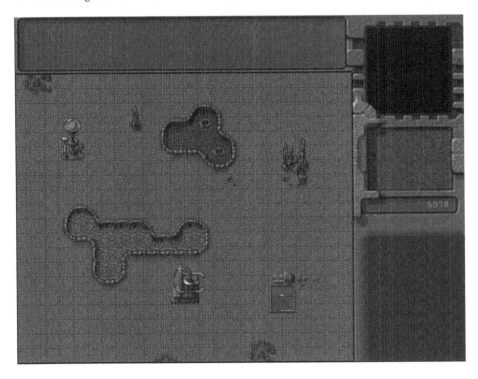

Figure 8-2. *Deployed harvester slowly earning money*

We now have a basic game economy set up. We are ready to implement the purchase of buildings and units.

Purchasing Buildings and Units

In our game, the base building is used to construct buildings, and the starport is used to construct vehicles and aircraft. Players will purchase items by selecting the building they want to construct from and then clicking the appropriate purchase button on the sidebar.

We will start by adding these purchase buttons to our sidebar.

Adding Sidebar Buttons

We will first add the HTML markup for the buttons to the gameinterfacescreen div inside index.html, as shown in Listing 8-7.

Listing 8-7. Adding the Sidebar Purchase Buttons to gameinterfacescreen (index.html)

```
<div id="gameinterfacescreen" class="gamelayer">
    <div id="gamemessages"></div>
    <div id="callerpicture"></div>
    <div id="cash"></div>
    <div id="sidebarbuttons">
        <input type="button" id="starportbutton" title = "Starport">
        <input type="button" id="turretbutton" title = "Turret">
        <input type="button" id="placeholder1" disabled>

        <input type="button" id="scouttankbutton" title = "Scout Tank">
        <input type="button" id="heavytankbutton" title = "Heavy Tank">
        <input type="button" id="harvesterbutton" title = "Harvester">

        <input type="button" id="chopperbutton" title = "Copter">
        <input type="button" id="wraithbutton" title = "Wraith">
        <input type="button" id="placeholder2" disabled>
    </div>
    <canvas id="gamebackgroundcanvas" height="400" width="480"></canvas>
    <canvas id="gameforegroundcanvas" height="400" width="480"></canvas>
</div>
```

Next we will add the appropriate CSS styles for these buttons to styles.css, as shown in Listing 8-8.

Listing 8-8. CSS Syles for Sidebar Buttons (styles.css)

```
/* Sidebar Buttons */
#gameinterfacescreen #sidebarbuttons {
    position:absolute;
    left:500px;
    top:305px;
    width:152px;
    height:148px;
    overflow:none;
}

#gameinterfacescreen #sidebarbuttons input[type="button"] {
    width:43px;
    height:35px;
    border-width:0px;
    padding:0px;
    background-image: url(images/buttons.png);
}

/* Grayed out state for buttons*/
#starportbutton:active, #starportbutton:disabled {
    background-position: -2px -305px;
}
```

```css
#placeholder1:active, #placeholder1:disabled {
    background-position: -52px -305px;
}
#turretbutton:active, #turretbutton:disabled {
    background-position: -100px -305px;
}
#scouttankbutton:active, #scouttankbutton:disabled {
    background-position: -2px -346px;
}
#heavytankbutton:active, #heavytankbutton:disabled {
    background-position: -52px -346px;
}
#harvesterbutton:active, #harvesterbutton:disabled {
    background-position: -102px -346px;
}
#chopperbutton:active, #chopperbutton:disabled {
    background-position: -2px -387px;
}
#placeholder2:active, #placeholder2:disabled {
    background-position: -52px -387px;
}
#wraithbutton:active, #wraithbutton:disabled {
    background-position: -102px -387px;
}

/* Regular state for buttons*/
#starportbutton {
    background-position: -167px -305px;
}
#placeholder1 {
    background-position: -216px -305px;
}
#turretbutton {
    background-position: -264px -305px;
}
#scouttankbutton {
    background-position: -167px -346px;
}
#heavytankbutton {
    background-position: -216px -346px;
}
#harvesterbutton {
    background-position: -264px -346px;
}
#chopperbutton {
    background-position: -167px -387px;
}
#placeholder2 {
    background-position: -216px -387px;
}
#wraithbutton {
    background-position: -264px -387px;
}
```

The HTML markup adds the buttons to the sidebar, while the CSS styles define images for these buttons using the `buttons.png` file.

If we run the game in the browser, we should see the purchase buttons in the sidebar, as shown in Figure 8-3.

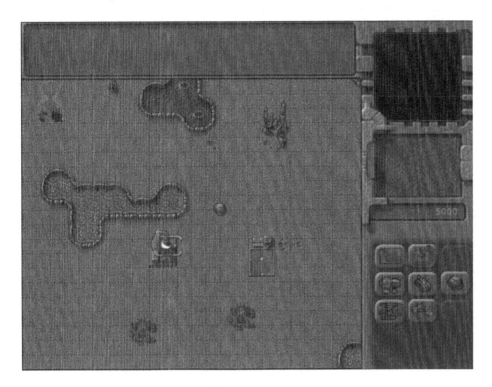

Figure 8-3. *Purchase buttons in the sidebar*

At this point, all of the buttons look enabled and active; however, clicking the buttons does not do anything. The buttons need to be enabled or disabled depending on whether the player is allowed to construct the items.

Enabling and Disabling Sidebar Buttons

The next thing we will do is to ensure that sidebar buttons are enabled only if the appropriate building is selected and the player has enough money to construct the item. We will do this by adding an `enableSidebarButtons()` method to `sidebar.js` and calling it from inside the `animate()` method, as shown in Listing 8-9.

Listing 8-9. Enabling and Disabling Sidebar Buttons (sidebar.js)

```
var sidebar = {
    enableSidebarButtons:function(){
        // Buttons only enabled when appropriate building is selected
        $("#gameinterfacescreen #sidebarbuttons input[type='button'] ").attr("disabled", true);

        // If no building selected, then no point checking below
        if (game.selectedItems.length==0){
            return;
        }
```

```
        var baseSelected = false;
        var starportSelected = false;
        // Check if base or starport is selected
        for (var i = game.selectedItems.length - 1; i >= 0; i--){
            var item = game.selectedItems[i];
            //  Check If player selected a healthy,inactive building (damaged buildings can't produce)
    if (item.type == "buildings" && item.team == game.team && item.lifeCode == "healthy" && item.
action=="stand"){
                if(item.name == "base"){
                    baseSelected = true;
                } else if (item.name == "starport"){
                    starportSelected = true;
                }
            }
        };

        var cashBalance = game.cash[game.team];
        /* Enable building buttons if base is selected,building has been loaded in requirements, not
in deploy building mode and player has enough money*/
        if (baseSelected && !game.deployBuilding){
            if(game.currentLevel.requirements.buildings.indexOf('starport')>-1 &&
cashBalance>=buildings.list["starport"].cost){
                $("#starportbutton").removeAttr("disabled");
            }
            if(game.currentLevel.requirements.buildings.indexOf('ground-turret')>-1 &&
cashBalance>=buildings.list["ground-turret"].cost){
                $("#turretbutton").removeAttr("disabled");
            }
        }

        /* Enable unit buttons if starport is selected, unit has been loaded in requirements, and
player has enough money*/
        if (starportSelected){
            if(game.currentLevel.requirements.vehicles.indexOf('scout-tank')>-1 &&
cashBalance>=vehicles.list["scout-tank"].cost){
                $("#scouttankbutton").removeAttr("disabled");
            }
    if(game.currentLevel.requirements.vehicles.indexOf('heavy-tank')>-1 &&
cashBalance>=vehicles.list["heavy-tank"].cost){
                $("#heavytankbutton").removeAttr("disabled");
            }
            if(game.currentLevel.requirements.vehicles.indexOf('harvester')>-1 &&
cashBalance>=vehicles.list["harvester"].cost){
                $("#harvesterbutton").removeAttr("disabled");
            }
            if(game.currentLevel.requirements.aircraft.indexOf('chopper')>-1 &&
cashBalance>=aircraft.list["chopper"].cost){
                $("#chopperbutton").removeAttr("disabled");
            }
```

```
                if(game.currentLevel.requirements.aircraft.indexOf('wraith')>-1 &&
cashBalance>=aircraft.list["wraith"].cost){
                    $("#wraithbutton").removeAttr("disabled");
                }
            }
        },
    animate:function(){
        // Display the current cash balance value
        $('#cash').html(game.cash[game.team]);

        //  Enable or disable buttons as appropriate
        this.enableSidebarButtons();
        },
}
```

Within the enableSidebarButton() method, we first disable all the buttons by default. We then check whether a valid base or starport has been selected. A valid base or starport belongs to the player, is healthy, and is currently in stand mode, which means it is not currently constructing anything else.

We enable the button for a building if the base has been selected, the building type has been loaded in the level requirements, and the player has enough cash to buy the building. We do the same thing for vehicles and aircraft if a valid starport has been selected.

If we run the game now, the sidebar buttons will get enabled once we select a base or starport, as shown in Figure 8-4.

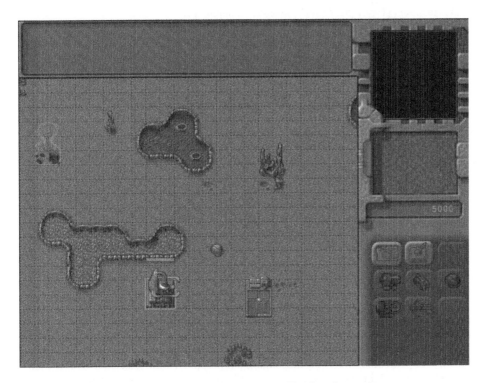

Figure 8-4. *Sidebar building construction buttons enabled by selecting base*

As you can see in the figure, the building buttons have been enabled while the vehicle and aircraft buttons are disabled because the base has been selected. We can similarly activate the vehicle and aircraft construction buttons by selecting the starport.

Now it's time to implement constructing vehicles and aircraft at the starport.

Constructing Vehicles and Aircraft at the Starport

The first thing we will do is modify the sidebar object to handle the click event for the buttons by adding the code in Listing 8-10.

Listing 8-10. Setting click Event for Sidebar Buttons (sidebar.js)

```
init:function(){
    $("#scouttankbutton").click(function(){
        sidebar.constructAtStarport({type:"vehicles","name":"scout-tank"});
    });
    $("#heavytankbutton").click(function(){
        sidebar.constructAtStarport({type:"vehicles","name":"heavy-tank"});
    });
    $("#harvesterbutton").click(function(){
        sidebar.constructAtStarport({type:"vehicles","name":"harvester"});
    });
    $("#chopperbutton").click(function(){
        sidebar.constructAtStarport({type:"aircraft","name":"chopper"});
    });
    $("#wraithbutton").click(function(){
        sidebar.constructAtStarport({type:"aircraft","name":"wraith"});
    });
},
constructAtStarport:function(unitDetails){
    var starport;
    // Find the first eligible starport among selected items
    for (var i = game.selectedItems.length - 1; i >= 0; i--){
        var item = game.selectedItems[i];
        if (item.type == "buildings" && item.name == "starport"
            && item.team == game.team && item.lifeCode == "healthy" && item.action=="stand"){
            starport = item;
            break;
        }
    };
    if (starport){
        game.sendCommand([starport.uid],{type:"construct-unit",details:unitDetails});
    }
},
```

We first declare an init() method that sets the click event for each of the vehicle and aircraft buttons to call the constructAtStarport() method with the appropriate unit details.

Within the constructAtStarport() method, we get the first eligible starport among the selected items. We then use the game.sendCommand() method to send the starport a construct-unit command with details of the unit to construct.

Next, we will call the `sidebar.init()` method from inside the `game.init()` method when the game is initialized, as shown in Listing 8-11.

Listing 8-11. Initializing the Sidebar from Inside game.init() (game.js)

```
// Start preloading assets
init: function(){
    loader.init();
    mouse.init();
    sidebar.init();

    $('.gamelayer').hide();
    $('#gamestartscreen').show();

    game.backgroundCanvas = document.getElementById('gamebackgroundcanvas');
    game.backgroundContext = game.backgroundCanvas.getContext('2d');

    game.foregroundCanvas = document.getElementById('gameforegroundcanvas');
    game.foregroundContext = game.foregroundCanvas.getContext('2d');

    game.canvasWidth = game.backgroundCanvas.width;
    game.canvasHeight = game.backgroundCanvas.height;
},
```

Next, we will create a `processOrder()` method for the starport building that implements the `construct-unit` order. We will add this method inside the starport definition, as shown in Listing 8-12.

Listing 8-12. Implementing processOrder() Inside the Starport Definition (buildings.js)

```
"starport":{
    name:"starport",
    pixelWidth:40,
    pixelHeight:60,
    baseWidth:40,
    baseHeight:55,
    pixelOffsetX:1,
    pixelOffsetY:5,
    buildableGrid:[
        [1,1],
        [1,1],
        [1,1]
    ],
    passableGrid:[
        [1,1],
        [0,0],
        [0,0]
    ],
    sight:3,
    cost:2000,
      hitPoints:300,
    spriteImages:[
        {name:"teleport",count:9},
```

```
            {name:"closing",count:18},
            {name:"healthy",count:4},
            {name:"damaged",count:1},
        ],
    processOrders:function(){
        switch (this.orders.type){
            case "construct-unit":
                if(this.lifeCode != "healthy"){
                    return;
                }
                // First make sure there is no unit standing on top of the building
                var unitOnTop = false;
                for (var i = game.items.length - 1; i >= 0; i--){
                    var item = game.items[i];
                    if (item.type == "vehicles" || item.type == "aircraft"){
                        if (item.x > this.x && item.x < this.x+2 && item.y> this.y &&
item.y<this.y+3){

                            unitOnTop = true;
                            break;
                        }
                    }
                };

                var cost = window[this.orders.details.type].list[this.orders.details.name].cost;
                if (unitOnTop){
                    if (this.team == game.team){
                        game.showMessage("system","Warning! Cannot teleport unit while landing bay
is occupied.");
                    }
                } else if(game.cash[this.team]<cost){
                    if (this.team == game.team){
                        game.showMessage("system","Warning! Insufficient Funds. Need "+cost+ "
credits.");
                    }
                } else {
                    this.action="open";
                    this.animationIndex = 0;
                    // Position new unit above center of starport
                    var itemDetails = this.orders.details;
                    itemDetails.x = this.x+0.5*this.pixelWidth/game.gridSize;
                    itemDetails.y = this.y+0.5*this.pixelHeight/game.gridSize;
                    // Teleport in unit and subtract the cost from player cash
                    itemDetails.action="teleport";
                    itemDetails.team = this.team;
                    game.cash[this.team] -= cost;
                    this.constructUnit = $.extend(true,[],itemDetails);

                }
```

```
                this.orders = {type:"stand"};
                break;
        }
    }
},
```

We start by checking whether any unit is already positioned above the starport, and if so, we use the
game.showMessage() method to notify the player that a unit cannot be teleported while the landing bay is occupied.
Next we check whether we have sufficient funds and, if not, notify the user.

Finally, we implement the actual purchase of the unit. We first set the animation action of the building to
open. We then set the position, action, and team properties for the item. We save the details of the new unit in the
constructUnit variable and finally subtract the cost of the item from the player's cash balance.

You may have noticed that we set a teleport action for the newly constructed unit. We will need to implement
this for both vehicles and aircraft.

Next we will modify the open animation state inside the buildings object's animate() method to add the unit to
the game, as shown in Listing 8-13.

Listing 8-13. Adding the Unit Once the Starport Opens (buildings.js)

```
case "open":
    this.imageList = this.spriteArray["closing"];
    // Opening is just the closing sprites running backwards
    this.imageOffset = this.imageList.offset + this.imageList.count - this.animationIndex;
    this.animationIndex++;
    // Once opening is complete, go back to close
    if (this.animationIndex>=this.imageList.count){
        this.animationIndex = 0;
        this.action = "close";
        // If constructUnit has been set, add the new unit to the game
        if(this.constructUnit){
            game.add(this.constructUnit);
            this.constructUnit = undefined;
        }
    }
     break;
```

Once the open animation is complete, we check whether the constructUnit property has been set, and if it has,
we add the unit to the game before unsetting the variable.

Next we will implement a showMessage() method inside the game object, as shown in Listing 8-14.

Listing 8-14. The game Object's showMessage() Method

```
// Functions for communicating with player
characters: {
    "system":{
        "name":"System",
        "image":"images/characters/system.png"
    }
},
showMessage:function(from,message){
    var character = game.characters[from];
    if (character){
        from = character.name;
```

```
        if (character.image){
            $('#callerpicture').html('<img src="'+character.image+'"/>');
            // hide the profile picture after six seconds
            setTimeout(function(){
                $('#callerpicture').html("");
            },6000)
        }
    }
    // Append message to messages pane and scroll to the bottom
    var existingMessage = $('#gamemessages').html();
    var newMessage = existingMessage+'<span>'+from+': </span>'+message+'<br>';
    $('#gamemessages').html(newMessage);
    $('#gamemessages').animate({scrollTop:$('#gamemessages').prop('scrollHeight')});
}
```

We first define a characters object that contains the name and the image for the system character. Within the showMessage() method, we check whether we have a character image for the from parameter and, if so, display the image for four seconds. Next, we append the message to the gamemessages div and scroll to the bottom of the div.

Whenever the showMessage() method is called, it will display the message in the messages window and the picture in the sidebar, as shown in Figure 8-5.

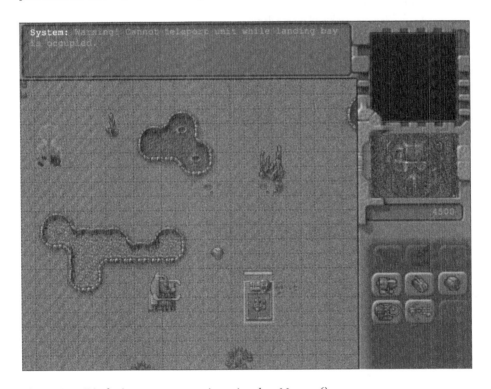

Figure 8-5. *Displaying a system warning using showMessage()*

We can use this mechanism to show the player dialogue from various game characters as we move the game story line forward. This will allow the single-player campaign to be more plot driven and make the game much more engaging.

Finally, we will modify the vehicles and aircraft objects to implement the new teleport action.

We will start by adding a case for the teleport action right below the stand action inside the vehicles object's animate() method, as shown in Listing 8-15.

Listing 8-15. Adding a Case for the Teleport Action inside animate() (vehicles.js)

```
case "teleport":
    var direction = wrapDirection(Math.round(this.direction),this.directions);
    this.imageList = this.spriteArray["stand-"+direction];
    this.imageOffset = this.imageList.offset + this.animationIndex;
    this.animationIndex++;

    if (this.animationIndex>=this.imageList.count){
        this.animationIndex = 0;
    }
    if (!this.brightness){
        this.brightness = 1;
    }
    this.brightness -= 0.05;
    if(this.brightness <= 0){
        this.brightness = undefined;
        this.action = "stand";
    }
    break;
```

We first set the imageOffset and the animationIndex just like we did for the default stand action. We then set a brightness variable to 1 and gradually reduce it to 0, at which point we switch the action state back to stand.

Next, we will modify the vehicles object's default draw() method to use the brightness property, as shown in Listing 8-16.

Listing 8-16. Modifying the draw() Method to Handle Teleport Brightness (vehicles.js)

```
draw:function(){
    var x = (this.x*game.gridSize)-game.offsetX-this.pixelOffsetX +
this.lastMovementX*game.drawingInterpolationFactor*game.gridSize;
    var y = (this.y*game.gridSize)-game.offsetY-this.pixelOffsetY +
this.lastMovementY*game.drawingInterpolationFactor*game.gridSize;
    this.drawingX = x;
    this.drawingY = y;

    if (this.selected){
        this.drawSelection();
        this.drawLifeBar();
    }

    var colorIndex = (this.team == "blue")?0:1;
    var colorOffset = colorIndex*this.pixelHeight;

    game.foregroundContext.drawImage(this.spriteSheet, this.imageOffset*this.pixelWidth,colorOffset,
            this.pixelWidth,this.pixelHeight,x,y,this.pixelWidth,this.pixelHeight);

    // Draw glow while teleporting in
    if(this.brightness){
```

211

```
        game.foregroundContext.beginPath();
        game.foregroundContext.arc(x+ this.pixelOffsetX, y+this.pixelOffsetY,
this.radius, 0 , Math.PI*2,false);
        game.foregroundContext.fillStyle = 'rgba(255,255,255,'+this.brightness+')';
        game.foregroundContext.fill();
    }
}
```

Within the newly added code, we check whether the vehicle has a brightness property set, and if so, we draw a filled white circle on top of the vehicle with a fill alpha value based on the brightness. Since the brightness property's value drops from 1 to 0, the circle will gradually shift from being bright white to completely transparent.

Next we will add a case for the teleport action right below the fly action inside the aircraft object's animate() method, as shown in Listing 8-17.

Listing 8-17. Adding a Case for the Teleport Action Inside animate() (aircraft.js)

```
case "teleport":
    var direction = wrapDirection(Math.round(this.direction),this.directions);
    this.imageList = this.spriteArray["fly-"+direction];
    this.imageOffset = this.imageList.offset + this.animationIndex;
    this.animationIndex++;

    if (this.animationIndex>=this.imageList.count){
        this.animationIndex = 0;
    }
    if (!this.brightness){
        this.brightness = 1;
    }
    this.brightness -= 0.05;
    if(this.brightness <= 0){
        this.brightness = undefined;
        this.action = "fly";
    }
    break;
```

Similar to what we did for vehicles, we set a brightness property, gradually drop it down to 0, and then set the action state to fly.

Finally, we will modify the aircraft object's default draw() method to use the brightness property just like we did for vehicles, as shown in Listing 8-18.

Listing 8-18. Modifying the draw() Method to Handle Teleport Brightness (aircraft.js)

```
draw:function(){
    var x = (this.x*game.gridSize)-game.offsetX-this.pixelOffsetX +
this.lastMovementX*game.drawingInterpolationFactor*game.gridSize;
    var y = (this.y*game.gridSize)-game.offsetY-this.pixelOffsetY-this.pixelShadowHeight +
this.lastMovementY*game.drawingInterpolationFactor*game.gridSize;
    this.drawingX = x;
    this.drawingY = y;
    if (this.selected){
        this.drawSelection();
        this.drawLifeBar();
    }
```

```
    var colorIndex = (this.team == "blue")?0:1;
    var colorOffset = colorIndex*this.pixelHeight;
    var shadowOffset = this.pixelHeight*2; // The aircraft shadow is on the second row of the sprite
sheet

    game.foregroundContext.drawImage(this.spriteSheet, this.imageOffset*this.pixelWidth,colorOffset,
this.pixelWidth, this.pixelHeight, x,y,this.pixelWidth,this.pixelHeight);
    game.foregroundContext.drawImage(this.spriteSheet, this.imageOffset*this.pixelWidth,
shadowOffset,this.pixelWidth, this.pixelHeight, x, y+this.pixelShadowHeight, this.pixelWidth,this.
pixelHeight);

    // Draw glow while teleporting in
    if(this.brightness){
        game.foregroundContext.beginPath();
        game.foregroundContext.arc(x+ this.pixelOffsetX,y+this.pixelOffsetY,this.radius,0,
Math.PI*2,false);
        game.foregroundContext.fillStyle = 'rgba(255,255,255,'+this.brightness+')';
        game.foregroundContext.fill();
    }
}
```

If you run the game in the browser, you should now be able to select the starport and construct a vehicle or aircraft, as shown in Figure 8-6.

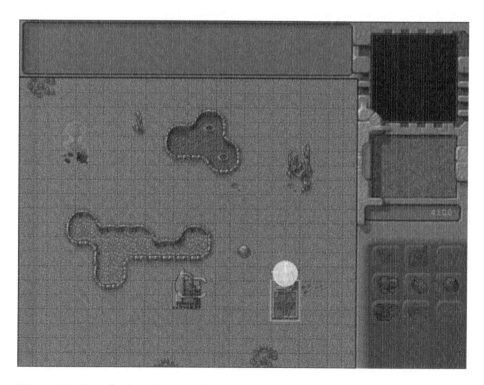

Figure 8-6. *Aircraft teleporting in at the starport*

The aircraft teleports right above the starport, inside a white glowing circle. You will notice that the sidebar buttons get disabled while the aircraft is being teleported in. Also, the cash balance decreases by the cost of the aircraft. When the player can no longer afford a unit, its button will automatically get disabled. Trying to construct a unit while the starport has another unit hovering over it will result in the system warning shown in Figure 8-5.

Now that we have implemented constructing vehicles and aircraft, it's time to implement constructing buildings at the base.

Constructing Buildings at the Base

We will start by setting the click event for the two building construction buttons in the sidebar object's init() method, as shown in Listing 8-19.

Listing 8-19. Setting click Event for the Building Buttons (sidebar.js)

```
init:function(){
    // Initialize unit construction buttons
    $("#scouttankbutton").click(function(){
        sidebar.constructAtStarport({type:"vehicles","name":"scout-tank"});
    });
    $("#heavytankbutton").click(function(){
        sidebar.constructAtStarport({type:"vehicles","name":"heavy-tank"});
    });
    $("#harvesterbutton").click(function(){
        sidebar.constructAtStarport({type:"vehicles","name":"harvester"});
    });
    $("#chopperbutton").click(function(){
        sidebar.constructAtStarport({type:"aircraft","name":"chopper"});
    });
    $("#wraithbutton").click(function(){
        sidebar.constructAtStarport({type:"aircraft","name":"wraith"});
    });

    //Initialize building construction buttons

    $("#starportbutton").click(function(){
        game.deployBuilding = "starport";
    });
    $("#turretbutton").click(function(){
        game.deployBuilding = "ground-turret";
    });
},
```

When either of the two building-construction buttons is clicked, we set the sidebar.deployBuilding property to the name of the building to be constructed.

Next, we will modify the sidebar animate() method to handle deploying a building, as shown in Listing 8-20.

Listing 8-20. Modifying the animate() Method to Handle Building Deployment (sidebar.js)

```
animate:function(){
    // Display the current cash balance value
    $('#cash').html(game.cash[game.team]);
```

```
    // Enable or disable buttons as appropriate
    this.enableSidebarButtons();

    if (game.deployBuilding){
        // Create the buildable grid to see where building can be placed
        game.rebuildBuildableGrid();
        // Compare with buildable grid to see where we need to place the building
        var placementGrid = buildings.list[game.deployBuilding].buildableGrid;
        game.placementGrid = $.extend(true,[],placementGrid);
        game.canDeployBuilding = true;
        for (var i = game.placementGrid.length - 1; i >= 0; i--){
            for (var j = game.placementGrid[i].length - 1; j >= 0; j--){
                if(game.placementGrid[i][j] &&
                    (mouse.gridY+i>= game.currentLevel.mapGridHeight ||
mouse.gridX+j>=game.currentLevel.mapGridWidth ||
game.currentMapBuildableGrid[mouse.gridY+i][mouse.gridX+j]==1)){
                        game.canDeployBuilding = false;
                        game.placementGrid[i][j] = 0;
                }
            };
        };
    }
},
```

If the game.deployBuilding variable has been set, we call the game.rebuildBuildableGrid() method to create the game.currentMapBuildableGrid array and then set the game.placementGrid variable using the buildableGrid property of the building being deployed.

We then iterate through the placement grid to check whether it is possible to deploy the building at the current mouse location. If any of the squares on which the building will be placed are outside the map bounds or marked as unbuildable in the currentMapBuildableGrid array, we mark the corresponding square on the placementGrid array as unbuildable and set the canDeployBuilding flag to false.

Next we will implement the rebuildBuildableGrid() method inside the game object, as shown in Listing 8-21.

Listing 8-21. Creating the buildableGrid in the rebuildBuildableGrid() Method (game.js)

```
rebuildBuildableGrid:function(){
    game.currentMapBuildableGrid = $.extend(true,[],game.currentMapTerrainGrid);
    for (var i = game.items.length - 1; i >= 0; i--){
        var item = game.items[i];
        if(item.type == "buildings" || item.type == "terrain"){
            for (var y = item.buildableGrid.length - 1; y >= 0; y--){
                for (var x = item.buildableGrid[y].length - 1; x >= 0; x--){
                    if(item.buildableGrid[y][x]){
                        game.currentMapBuildableGrid[item.y+y][item.x+x] = 1;
                    }
                };
            };
        } else if (item.type == "vehicles"){
            // Mark all squares under or near the vehicle as unbuildable
            var radius = item.radius/game.gridSize;
            var x1 = Math.max(Math.floor(item.x - radius),0);
            var x2 = Math.min(Math.floor(item.x + radius),game.currentLevel.mapGridWidth-1);
```

```
        var y1 = Math.max(Math.floor(item.y - radius),0);
        var y2 = Math.min(Math.floor(item.y + radius),game.currentLevel.mapGridHeight-1);
        for (var x=x1; x <= x2; x++) {
            for (var y=y1; y <= y2; y++) {
                game.currentMapBuildableGrid[y][x] = 1;
            };
        };
    }
};
},
```

We start by initializing the currentMapBuildableGrid to the currentMapTerrainGrid. We then mark out all squares under a building or terrain entity as unbuildable, just as we did when creating the passable array. Finally, we mark all grid squares next to a vehicle as unbuildable.

Next we will modify the draw() method of the mouse object to mark the grid location where the building will be deployed, as shown in Listing 8-22.

Listing 8-22. Drawing the Building Deploy Grid under the Mouse Cursor (mouse.js)

```
draw:function(){
    if(this.dragSelect){
        var x = Math.min(this.gameX,this.dragX);
        var y = Math.min(this.gameY,this.dragY);
        var width = Math.abs(this.gameX-this.dragX)
        var height = Math.abs(this.gameY-this.dragY)
        game.foregroundContext.strokeStyle = 'white';
        game.foregroundContext.strokeRect(x-game.offsetX,y-   game.offsetY, width, height);
    }
    if (game.deployBuilding && game.placementGrid){
        var buildingType = buildings.list[game.deployBuilding];
        var x = (this.gridX*game.gridSize)-game.offsetX;
        var y = (this.gridY*game.gridSize)-game.offsetY;
        for (var i = game.placementGrid.length - 1; i >= 0; i--){
            for (var j = game.placementGrid[i].length - 1; j >= 0; j--){
                if(game.placementGrid[i][j]){
                    game.foregroundContext.fillStyle = "rgba(0,0,255,0.3)";
                } else {
                    game.foregroundContext.fillStyle = "rgba(255,0,0,0.3)";
                }
                game.foregroundContext.fillRect(x+j*game.gridSize, y+i*game.gridSize, game.gridSize,
game.gridSize);
            };
        };
    }
},
```

We first check whether the deployBuilding and placementGrid variables have been set, and if so, we draw either blue or red squares depending on whether we can place the building at that grid location.

If you run the game now, select the main base, and try to create a building, you should see the building deploy grid at the mouse location, as shown in Figure 8-7.

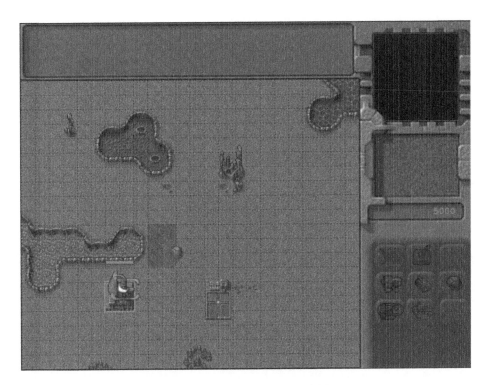

Figure 8-7. Building deploy grid with red marking unbuildable squares

Now that we can initiate building deploy mode, we will implement placing the building by left-clicking the mouse or canceling the mode by right-clicking the mouse. We will start by modifying the click() method of the mouse object, as shown in Listing 8-23.

Listing 8-23. Modifying mouse.click() to Complete or Cancel deploy Mode (mouse.js)

```
click:function(ev,rightClick){
    // Player clicked inside the canvas

    var clickedItem = this.itemUnderMouse();
    var shiftPressed = ev.shiftKey;

    if (!rightClick){ // Player left clicked
        // If the game is in deployBuilding mode, left clicking will deploy the building
        if (game.deployBuilding){
            if(game.canDeployBuilding){
                sidebar.finishDeployingBuilding();
            } else {
                game.showMessage("system","Warning! Cannot deploy building here.");
            }

            return;
        }
```

```
            if (clickedItem){
                // Pressing shift adds to existing selection. If shift is not pressed, clear existing
selection
                if(!shiftPressed){
                    game.clearSelection();
                }
                game.selectItem(clickedItem,shiftPressed);
            }
        } else { // Player right clicked
            // If the game is in deployBuilding mode, right clicking will cancel deployBuilding mode
            if (game.deployBuilding){
                sidebar.cancelDeployingBuilding();
                return;
            }
            // Handle actions like attacking and movement of selected units
            var uids = [];
            if (clickedItem){ // Player right clicked on something... Specific action
                if (clickedItem.type != "terrain"){
                    if (clickedItem.team != game.team){ // Player right clicked on an enemy item
                        for (var i = game.selectedItems.length - 1; i >= 0; i--){
                            var item = game.selectedItems[i];
                            // if selected item is from players team and can attack
                            if(item.team == game.team && item.canAttack){
                                uids.push(item.uid);
                            }
                        };
                        if (uids.length>0){
                            game.sendCommand(uids,{type:"attack",toUid:clickedItem.uid});
                        }
                    } else  { // Player right clicked on a friendly item
                        for (var i = game.selectedItems.length - 1; i >= 0; i--){
                            var item = game.selectedItems[i];
                            if(item.team == game.team && (item.type == "vehicles" ||
item.type == "aircraft")){
                                uids.push(item.uid);
                            }
                        };
                        if (uids.length>0){
                            game.sendCommand(uids,{type:"guard",toUid:clickedItem.uid});
                        }
                    }
                } else if (clickedItem.name == "oilfield"){
                    // Oilfield means harvesters go and deploy there
                    for (var i = game.selectedItems.length - 1; i >= 0; i--){
                        var item = game.selectedItems[i];
                        // pick the first selected harvester since only one can deploy at a time
                        if(item.team == game.team && (item.type == "vehicles" && item.name ==
"harvester")){
                            uids.push(item.uid);
                            break;
                        }
                    };
```

```
                if (uids.length>0){
                    game.sendCommand(uids,{type:"deploy",toUid:clickedItem.uid});
                }
            }
        } else { // Just try to move there
            // Get all UIDs that can be commanded to move
            for (var i = game.selectedItems.length - 1; i >= 0; i--){
                var item = game.selectedItems[i];
                if(item.team == game.team && (item.type == "vehicles" || item.type == "aircraft")){
                    uids.push(item.uid);
                }
            };
            if (uids.length>0){
                game.sendCommand(uids,{type:"move",  to:{x:mouse.gameX/game.gridSize,
y:mouse.gameY/game.gridSize}});
            }
        }
    }
},
```

If the player left-clicks when in deploy mode, we check the canDeployBuilding variable and call
sidebar.finishDeployingBuilding() if we can deploy the building, and we show a warning message using
game.showMessage() if we cannot.

If the player right-clicks when in deploy mode, we call the sidebar.cancelDeployingBuilding() method.

Next we will implement these two new methods, finishDeployBuilding() and cancelDeployBuilding(), inside
the sidebar object, as shown in Listing 8-24.

Listing 8-24. finishDeployingBuilding() and cancelDeployingBuilding() (sidebar.js)

```
cancelDeployingBuilding:function(){
    game.deployBuilding = undefined;
},
finishDeployingBuilding:function(){
    var buildingName= game.deployBuilding;
    var base;
    for (var i = game.selectedItems.length - 1; i >= 0; i--){
        var item = game.selectedItems[i];
        if (item.type == "buildings" && item.name == "base" && item.team == game.team &&
item.lifeCode == "healthy" && item.action=="stand"){
            base = item;
            break;
        }
    };
```

```
    if (base){
        var buildingDetails = {type:"buildings",name:buildingName,x:mouse.gridX,y:mouse.gridY};
        game.sendCommand([base.uid],{type:"construct-building",details:buildingDetails});
    }

    // Clear deployBuilding flag
    game.deployBuilding = undefined;
}
```

The cancelDeployingBuilding() method merely clears out the deployBuilding variable. The finishDeployingBuilding() method first selects the base and then uses the game.sendCommand() method to send it the construct-building order.

Next, we will create a processOrder() method for the base building that implements the construct-building order. We will add this method inside the base definition, as shown in Listing 8-25.

Listing 8-25. Implementing processOrder() Inside the Base Definition (buildings.js)

```
processOrders:function(){
    switch (this.orders.type){
        case "construct-building":
            this.action="construct";
            this.animationIndex = 0;
            var itemDetails = this.orders.details;
            // Teleport in building and subtract the cost from player cash
            itemDetails.team = this.team;
            itemDetails.action = "teleport";
            var item = game.add(itemDetails);
            game.cash[this.team] -= item.cost;
            this.orders = {type:"stand"};
            break;
    }
}
```

We first set the base entity's action state to construct. Next we add the building to the game with an action state of teleport. Finally, we subtract the cost of the building from the cash balance and set the base entity's orders property back to stand.

If you run the game now and try to deploy the building by left-clicking at a valid location on the map, the building should get teleported in at that location, as shown in Figure 8-8.

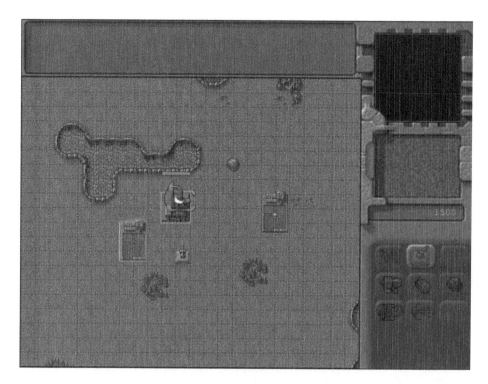

Figure 8-8. *Deployed building gets teleported in*

You will notice that the cash balance decreases by the cost of the building. When the player can no longer afford a building, its button will automatically get disabled. Also, if you try to deploy the building at an invalid location, you will see a system warning message telling you that the building cannot be deployed at that location.

We can now construct both units and buildings in our game. The last thing we will implement in this chapter is ending levels based on triggered events.

Ending a Level

Whenever players complete the objectives for a level successfully, we will show them a message box notifying them and then load the next level. If a player fails a mission, we will give the player the option of replaying the current level or leaving the single-player campaign.

We will check for the success and failure criteria by implementing a system of triggered events within our game. We will use this same event system to script story-based events in later chapters.

The first thing we will do is implement a message dialog box.

Implementing the Message Dialog Box

The message box will be a modal dialog box with only an OK button or with both OK and Cancel buttons.

We will start by adding the HTML markup for the message box screen to the body of index.html, as shown in Listing 8-26.

Listing 8-26. Adding HTML Markup for Message Box Inside the body Tag (index.html)

```
<body>
    <div id="gamecontainer">
        <div id="gamestartscreen" class="gamelayer">
            <span id="singleplayer" onclick = "singleplayer.start();">Campaign</span><br>
            <span id="multiplayer" onclick = "multiplayer.start();">Multiplayer</span><br>
        </div>
        <div id="missionscreen" class="gamelayer">
            <input type="button" id="entermission" onclick = "singleplayer.play();">
            <input type="button" id="exitmission" onclick = "singleplayer.exit();">
            <div id="missonbriefing">Welcome to your first mission.
            </div>
        </div>
        <div id="gameinterfacescreen" class="gamelayer">
            <div id="gamemessages"></div>
            <div id="callerpicture"></div>
            <div id="cash"></div>
            <div id="sidebarbuttons">
                <input type="button" id="starportbutton" title = "Starport">
                <input type="button" id="turretbutton" title = "Turret">
                <input type="button" id="placeholder1" disabled>

                <input type="button" id="scouttankbutton" title = "Scout Tank">
                <input type="button" id="heavytankbutton" title = "Heavy Tank">
                <input type="button" id="harvesterbutton" title = "Harvester">

                <input type="button" id="chopperbutton" title = "Copter">
                <input type="button" id="wraithbutton" title = "Wraith">
                <input type="button" id="placeholder2" disabled>
            </div>
            <canvas id="gamebackgroundcanvas" height="400" width="480"></canvas>
            <canvas id="gameforegroundcanvas" height="400" width="480"></canvas>
        </div>
        <div id="messageboxscreen" class="gamelayer">
            <div id="messagebox">
                <span id="messageboxtext"></span>
                <input type="button" id="messageboxok" onclick="game.messageBoxOK();">
                <input type="button" id="messageboxcancel" onclick="game.messageBoxCancel();">
            </div>
        </div>
        <div id="loadingscreen" class="gamelayer">
            <div id="loadingmessage"></div>
        </div>
    </div>
</body>
```

Next we will add the styles for the message box to styles.css, as shown in Listing 8-27.

Listing 8-27. Styles for Message Box (styles.css)

```css
/* Message Box Screen */
#messageboxscreen {
    background:rgba(0,0,0,0.7);
    z-index:20;
}
#messagebox {
    position:absolute;
    top:170px;
    left:140px;
    width:296px;
    height:178px;
    color:white;
    background:url(images/messagebox.png) no-repeat center;
    color:rgb(130,150,162);
    overflow:hidden;
    font-size: 13px;
    font-family: 'Courier New', Courier, monospace;
}
#messagebox span {
    position:absolute;
    top:30px;
    left:50px;
    width:200px;
    height:100px;
}

#messagebox input[type="button"]{
    background-image: url(images/buttons.png);
    position:absolute;
    border-width:0px;
    padding:0px;
}
#messageboxok{
    background-position: -2px -150px;
    top:126px;
    left:11px;
    width:74px;
    height:26px;
}
#messageboxok:active,#messageboxok:disabled{
    background-position: -2px -186px;
}
```

```
#messageboxcancel{
    background-position: -86px -150px;
    left:197px;
    top:129px;
    width:73px;
    height:24px;
}
#messageboxcancel:active,#messageboxcancel:disabled{
    background-position: -86px -184px;
}
```

Finally, we add some methods to the game object, as shown in Listing 8-28.

Listing 8-28. Adding Message Box Methods to the game Object (game.js)

```
/* Message Box related code*/
messageBoxOkCallback:undefined,
messageBoxCancelCallback:undefined,
showMessageBox:function(message,onOK,onCancel){
    // Set message box text
    $('#messageboxtext').html(message);

    // Set message box ok and cancel handlers and enable buttons
    if(!onOK){
        game.messageBoxOkCallback = undefined;
    } else {
        game.messageBoxOkCallback = onOK;
    }

    if(!onCancel){
        game.messageBoxCancelCallback = undefined;
        $("#messageboxcancel").hide();
    } else {
        game.messageBoxCancelCallback = onCancel;
        $("#messageboxcancel").show();
    }

    // Display the message box and wait for user to click a button
    $('#messageboxscreen').show();
},
messageBoxOK:function(){
    $('#messageboxscreen').hide();
    if(game.messageBoxOkCallback){
        game.messageBoxOkCallback()
    }
},
messageBoxCancel:function(){
    $('#messageboxscreen').hide();
    if(game.messageBoxCancelCallback){
        game.messageBoxCancelCallback();
    }
},
```

The showMessageBox() method first sets the message inside the messageboxtext element. Next it saves the onOK and onCancel callback method parameters into the messageBoxOkCallback and messageBoxCancelCallback variables. It shows or hides the Cancel button based on whether a cancel callback method parameter was passed. Finally, it shows the messageboxscreen layer.

The messageBoxOK() and messageBoxCancel() methods hide the messageboxscreen layer and then call their respective callback methods if they have been set.

When the showMessageBox() is called without specifying any callback methods, it will display the message box on a darkened screen with only an OK button, as shown in Figure 8-9.

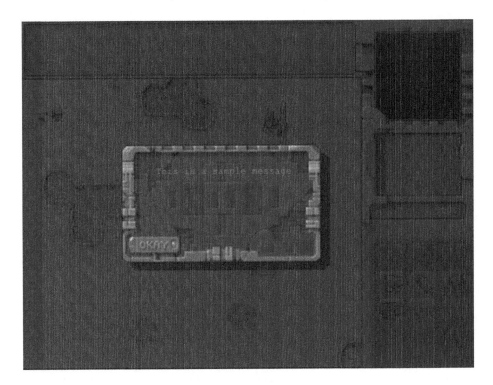

Figure 8-9. *A sample message shown in the message box*

Now that the code for the message box is in place, we will implement our game triggers.

Implementing Triggers

Our game will use two types of triggers.

- Timed triggers will execute an action after a specified time. They may also keep repeating at regular intervals.
- Conditional triggers will execute an action when a specified condition comes true.

We will start by adding a triggers array within our level inside the maps object, as shown in Listing 8-29.

Listing 8-29. Adding Triggers into the Level (maps.js)

```
/* Conditional and Timed Trigger Events */
"triggers":[
    /* Timed Events*/
    {"type":"timed","time":1000,
        "action":function(){
            game.showMessage("system","You have 20 seconds left.\nGet the harvester near the oil
field.");
        }
    },
    {"type":"timed","time":21000,
        "action":function(){
            singleplayer.endLevel(false);
        }
    },
    /* Conditional Event */
    {"type":"conditional",
        "condition":function(){
            var transport = game.getItemByUid(-1);
            return (transport.x <10 && transport.y <10);
        },
        "action":function(){
            singleplayer.endLevel(true);
        }
    }
],
```

All the triggers have a type and an action method. We have defined three triggers within the array.

The first trigger is a timed trigger with a time set to 1 second. In its action parameter, we call game.showMessage() and tell the player that he has 20 seconds to move the harvester near the oil field.

The second trigger, which is timed for 20 seconds later, calls the singleplayer.endLevel() method with a parameter of false, indicating the mission failed.

The final trigger is a conditional trigger. The condition method returns true when the transport is within the top-left quadrant of the map with x and y coordinates less than 10. When this condition is triggered, the action method calls the singleplayer.endLevel() method with a parameter of true indicating the mission was successfully completed.

Next we will implement the endLevel() method inside the singleplayer object, as shown in Listing 8-30.

Listing 8-30. Implementing the singleplayer endLevel() Method (singleplayer.js)

```
endLevel:function(success){
    clearInterval(game.animationInterval);
    game.end();

    if (success){
        var moreLevels = (singleplayer.currentLevel < maps.singleplayer.length-1);
        if (moreLevels){
            game.showMessageBox("Mission Accomplished.",function(){
                $('.gamelayer').hide();
                singleplayer.currentLevel++;
```

```
                singleplayer.startCurrentLevel();
            });
        } else {
            game.showMessageBox("Mission Accomplished.<br><br>This was the last mission in the
campaign.<br><br>Thank You for playing.",function(){
                $('.gamelayer').hide();
                $('#gamestartscreen').show();
            });
        }
    } else {
        game.showMessageBox("Mission Failed.<br><br>Try again?",function(){
            $('.gamelayer').hide();
            singleplayer.startCurrentLevel();
        }, function(){
            $('.gamelayer').hide();
            $('#gamestartscreen').show();
        });
    }
}
```

We first clear the game.animationInterval timer that calls the game.animationLoop() method. Next we call the game.end() method.

If the level was completed successfully, we check whether there are more levels in the map. If so, we notify the player that the mission was successful in a message box and then start the next level when the player clicks the OK button. If there are no more levels, we notify the player but go back to the game starting menu when the player clicks OK.

If the level was not completed successfully, we ask the player if he wants to try again. If the player clicks OK, we restart the current level. If instead the player clicks Cancel, we return to the game starting menu.

Next we will add a few trigger-related methods to the game object, as shown in Listing 8-31.

Listing 8-31. Adding Trigger-Related Methods to the game Object (game.js)

```
// Methods for handling triggered events within the game
initTrigger:function(trigger){
    if(trigger.type == "timed"){
        trigger.timeout = setTimeout (function(){
            game.runTrigger(trigger);
        },trigger.time)
    } else if(trigger.type == "conditional"){
        trigger.interval = setInterval (function(){
            game.runTrigger(trigger);
        },1000)
    }
},
runTrigger:function(trigger){
    if(trigger.type == "timed"){
        // Re initialize the trigger based on repeat settings
        if (trigger.repeat){
            game.initTrigger(trigger);
        }
        // Call the trigger action
        trigger.action(trigger);
    } else if (trigger.type == "conditional"){
```

```
            //Check if the condition has been satisfied
            if(trigger.condition()){
                // Clear the trigger
                game.clearTrigger(trigger);
                // Call the trigger action
                trigger.action(trigger);
            }
        }
    },
    clearTrigger:function(trigger){
        if(trigger.type == "timed"){
            clearTimeout(trigger.timeout);
        } else if (trigger.type == "conditional"){
            clearInterval(trigger.interval);
        }
    },
    end:function(){
        // Clear Any Game Triggers
        if (game.currentLevel.triggers){
            for (var i = game.currentLevel.triggers.length - 1; i >= 0; i--){
                game.clearTrigger(game.currentLevel.triggers[i]);
            };
        }
        game.running = false;
    }
```

The first method we implement is initTrigger(). We check whether the trigger is timed or conditional. For timed triggers, we call the runTrigger() method after the timeout specified in the time parameter. For conditional triggers, we call the runTrigger() method every second.

In the runTrigger() method, we check whether the trigger is timed or conditional. For timed triggers with the repeat parameter specified, we call initTrigger() again. We then execute the trigger action. For conditional triggers, we check whether the condition is true. If so, we clear the trigger and execute the action.

The clearTimeout() method just clears the timeout or interval for the triggers.

Finally, the end() method clears any triggers for a level and sets the game.running variable to false.

The last change we will make is to the game object's start() method, as shown in Listing 8-32.

Listing 8-32. Initializing the Triggers Inside the start() Method (game.js)

```
    start:function(){
        $('.gamelayer').hide();
        $('#gameinterfacescreen').show();
        game.running = true;
        game.refreshBackground = true;
        game.drawingLoop();

        $('#gamemessages').html("");
        // Initialize All Game Triggers
        for (var i = game.currentLevel.triggers.length - 1; i >= 0; i--){
            game.initTrigger(game.currentLevel.triggers[i]);
        };
    },
```

We initialize the gamemessages container when we start the level. Next we iterate through the current level's triggers array and call initTrigger() for each trigger.

If we run the game now, we should get a message asking us to take the harvester near the oil field within 20 seconds. If we do not do so in time, we will see a message box indicating that the mission failed, as shown in Figure 8-10.

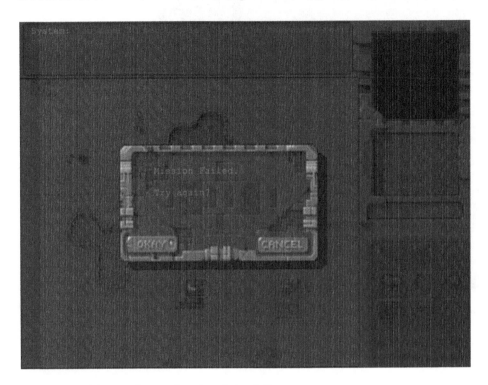

Figure 8-10. *Message shown when the mission fails*

If we click the Okay button, the level will restart, and we will be returned to the mission briefing screen. If we click the Cancel button instead, we will be taken back to the main menu.

If we move the harvester toward the oil field and reach there before the 20 seconds are up, we will see a message box indicating that the mission was accomplished, as shown in Figure 8-11.

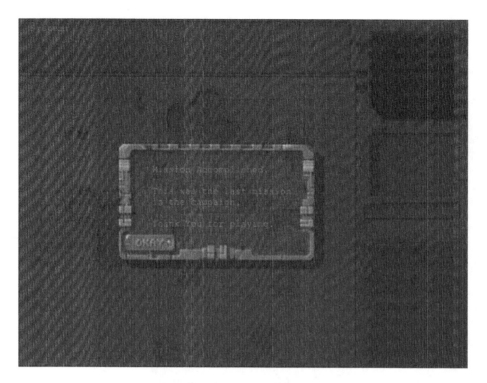

Figure 8-11. *Message shown when the mission is accomplished*

Since this is the only mission in our campaign, we will see the campaign ending message box. When we click Okay, we will be taken back to the main menu.

Summary

We accomplished a lot in this chapter. We started by creating a basic economy where we could earn cash by harvesting. We then implemented the ability to purchase units at the starport and buildings at the base using the buttons on the sidebar.

We developed a messaging system and a message dialog box to communicate with the player. We then built a system for trigger-based actions that handled both timed and conditional triggers. Finally, we used these triggers to create a simple mission objective and criteria for succeeding or failing the mission. Even though it was a fairly simple mission, we now have the infrastructure in place to build much more complex levels.

In the next chapter, we will handle another important component of our game: combat. We will implement different attack-based orders states for both units and turrets. We will use a combination of triggers and order states to make the units behave intelligently during combat. Finally, we will look at implementing a fog of war so that units cannot see or attack unexplored territory.

CHAPTER 9

Adding Weapons and Combat

Over the past few chapters, we built the basic framework for our game; added entities such as vehicles, aircraft, and buildings; implemented unit movement; and created a simple economy using the sidebar. We now have a game where we can start the level, earn money, purchase buildings and units, and move these units around to achieve simple goals.

In this chapter, we will implement weapons for vehicles, aircraft, and turrets. We will add the ability to process combat-based orders such as attacking, guarding, patrolling, and hunting to allow the units to fight in an intelligent way. Finally, we will implement a fog of war that limits visibility on the map, allowing for interesting strategies such as sneak attacks and ambushes.

Let's get started. We will use the code from Chapter 8 as a starting point.

Implementing the Combat System

Our game will have a fairly simple combat system. All units and turrets will have their own weapon and bullet type defined. When attacking an enemy, units will first get within range, turn toward the target, and then fire a bullet at them. Once the unit fires a bullet, it will wait until its weapon has reloaded before it fires again.

The bullet itself will be a separate game entity with its own animation logic. When fired, the bullet will fly toward its target and explode once it reaches its destination.

The first thing we will do is add bullets to our game.

Adding Bullets

We will start by defining a new `bullets` object inside `bullets.js`, as shown in Listing 9-1.

Listing 9-1. Defining the bullets Object (bullets.js)

```
var bullets = {
    list:{
        "fireball":{
            name:"fireball",
            speed:60,
            reloadTime:30,
            range:8,
            damage:10,
            spriteImages:[
                {name:"fly",count:1,directions:8},
                {name:"explode",count:7}
            ],
        },
```

```
        "heatseeker":{
            name:"heatseeker",
            reloadTime:40,
            speed:25,
            range:9,
            damage:20,
            turnSpeed:2,
            spriteImages:[
                {name:"fly",count:1,directions:8},
                {name:"explode",count:7}
            ],
        },
        "cannon-ball":{
            name:"cannon-ball",
            reloadTime:40,
            speed:25,
            damage:10,
            range:6,
            spriteImages:[
                {name:"fly",count:1,directions:8},
                {name:"explode",count:7}
            ],
        },
        "bullet":{
            name:"bullet",
            damage:5,
            speed:50,
            range:5,
            reloadTime:20,
            spriteImages:[
                {name:"fly",count:1,directions:8},
                {name:"explode",count:3}
            ],
        },
    },
    defaults:{
        type:"bullets",
        distanceTravelled:0,
        animationIndex:0,
        direction:0,
        directions:8,
        pixelWidth:10,
        pixelHeight:11,
        pixelOffsetX:5,
        pixelOffsetY:5,
        radius:6,
        action:"fly",
        selected:false,
        selectable:false,
        orders:{type:"fire"},
        moveTo:function(destination){
```

```
            // Weapons like the heatseeker can turn slowly toward target while moving
            if (this.turnSpeed){
                // Find out where we need to turn to get to destination
                var newDirection = findFiringAngle(destination,this,this.directions);
                // Calculate difference between new direction and current direction
                var difference = angleDiff(this.direction,newDirection,this.directions);
                // Calculate amount that bullet can turn per animation cycle
                var turnAmount = this.turnSpeed*game.turnSpeedAdjustmentFactor;
                if (Math.abs(difference)>turnAmount){
                    this.direction = wrapDirection(this.direction+turnAmount*Math.abs(difference)/
difference,this.directions);
                }
            }

            var movement = this.speed*game.speedAdjustmentFactor;
            this.distanceTravelled += movement;

            var angleRadians = -((this.direction)/this.directions)*2*Math.PI ;

            this.lastMovementX = - (movement*Math.sin(angleRadians));
            this.lastMovementY = - (movement*Math.cos(angleRadians));
            this.x = (this.x +this.lastMovementX);
            this.y = (this.y +this.lastMovementY);
        },
        reachedTarget:function(){
            var item = this.target;
            if (item.type=="buildings"){
                return (item.x<= this.x && item.x >= this.x - item.baseWidth/game.gridSize &&
item.y<= this.y && item.y >= this.y - item.baseHeight/game.gridSize);
            } else if (item.type=="aircraft"){
                return (Math.pow(item.x-this.x,2)+Math.pow(item.y-(this.y+item.pixelShadowHeight/
game.gridSize),2) < Math.pow((item.radius)/game.gridSize,2));
            } else {
                return (Math.pow(item.x-this.x,2)+Math.pow(item.y-this.y,2) <
 Math.pow((item.radius)/game.gridSize,2));
            }
        },
        processOrders:function(){
            this.lastMovementX = 0;
            this.lastMovementY = 0;
            switch (this.orders.type){
                case "fire":
                    // Move toward destination and stop when close by or if travelled past range
                    var reachedTarget = false;
                    if (this.distanceTravelled>this.range
                        || (reachedTarget = this.reachedTarget())) {
                        if(reachedTarget){
                            this.target.life -= this.damage;
                            this.orders = {type:"explode"};
                            this.action = "explode";
                            this.animationIndex = 0;
                        } else {
```

```
                            // Bullet fizzles out without hitting target
                            game.remove(this);
                        }
                    } else {
                        this.moveTo(this.target);
                    }
                    break;
                }
            },
            animate:function(){
                switch (this.action){
                    case "fly":
                        var direction = wrapDirection(Math.round(this.direction),this.directions);
                         this.imageList = this.spriteArray["fly-"+ direction];
                        this.imageOffset = this.imageList.offset;
                        break;
                    case "explode":
                        this.imageList = this.spriteArray["explode"];
                        this.imageOffset = this.imageList.offset + this.animationIndex;
                        this.animationIndex++;
                        if (this.animationIndex>=this.imageList.count){
                            // Bullet explodes completely and then disappears
                            game.remove(this);
                        }
                        break;
                }
            },
            draw:function(){
                var x = (this.x*game.gridSize)-game.offsetX-this.pixelOffsetX +
this.lastMovementX*game.drawingInterpolationFactor*game.gridSize;
                var y = (this.y*game.gridSize)-game.offsetY-this.pixelOffsetY +
this.lastMovementY*game.drawingInterpolationFactor*game.gridSize;
                var colorOffset = 0;
                game.foregroundContext.drawImage(this.spriteSheet, this.imageOffset*this.
pixelWidth,colorOffset, this.pixelWidth,this.pixelHeight, x,y,this.pixelWidth,this.pixelHeight);
            }
        },
        load:loadItem,
        add:addItem,
}
```

The bullets object follows the same pattern as all the other game entities. We start by defining a list of four bullet types: fireball, heatseeker, cannon-ball, and bullet. Each of the bullets has a common set of properties.

- speed: The speed at which the bullet travels

- reloadTime: The number of animation cycles after firing before the bullet can be fired again

- damage: The amount of damage to the target when the bullet explodes

- range: The maximum range that a bullet will fly before it loses momentum

The bullets also have two animation sequences defined: fly and explode. The fly state has eight directions similar to vehicles and aircraft. The explode state has only direction but has multiple frames.

We then define a default moveTo() method, which is similar to the aircraft moveTo() method. Within this method we first check whether the bullet can turn and, if so, gently turn the bullet toward its destination using the findFiringAngle() method to calculate the angle toward the center of the target. Next, we move the bullet forward along its current direction and update the bullet's distanceTravelled property.

Next we define a reachedTarget() method that checks whether the bullet has reached its target. We check whether the bullet's coordinates are inside the base area for buildings and within the item radius for vehicles and aircraft. If so, we return a value of true.

Within the processOrders() method, we implement the fire order. We check whether the bullet has either reached its target or traveled for more than its range. If not, we continue to move the bullet toward the target.

If the bullet travels beyond its range without hitting the target, we remove it from the game. If the bullet reaches its target, we first set the bullet's order and animation state to explode and reduce the life of its target by the damage amount.

Within the animate() method, we remove the bullet once the explode animation sequence completes.

Now that we have defined the bullets object, we will add a reference to bullets.js inside the <head> section of index.html, as shown in Listing 9-2.

Listing 9-2. Adding a Reference to the bullets Object (index.html)

```
<script src="js/bullets.js" type="text/javascript" charset="utf-8"></script>
```

We will also define the findFiringAngle() method inside common.js, as shown in Listing 9-3.

Listing 9-3. Defining the findFiringAngle() Method (common.js)

```
function findFiringAngle(target,source,directions){
    var dy = (target.y) - (source.y);
    var dx = (target.x) - (source.x);

    if(target.type=="buildings"){
        dy += target.baseWidth/2/game.gridSize;
        dx += target.baseHeight/2/game.gridSize;
    } else if(target.type == "aircraft"){
        dy -= target.pixelShadowHeight/game.gridSize;
    }

     if(source.type=="buildings"){
        dy -= source.baseWidth/2/game.gridSize;
        dx -= source.baseHeight/2/game.gridSize;
    } else if(source.type == "aircraft"){
        dy += source.pixelShadowHeight/game.gridSize;
    }

    //Convert Arctan to value between (0 - 7)
    var angle = wrapDirection(directions/2-(Math.atan2(dx,dy)*directions/(2*Math.PI)),directions);
    return angle;
}
```

The findFiringAngle() method is similar to the findAngle() method except we adjust the values of the dy and dx variables to point to the center of the source and target. For buildings, we adjust dx and dy using the baseWidth and baseHeight properties, and for aircraft we adjust dy by the pixelShadowHeight property. This way, bullets can be aimed at the center of the target.

We will also modify the loadItem() method inside common.js to load the bullet for an item when the item loads, as shown in Listing 9-4.

Listing 9-4. Loading the Bullets When Loading the Item (common.js)

```
/* The default load() method used by all our game entities*/
function loadItem(name){
    var item = this.list[name];
    // if the item sprite array has already been loaded then no need to do it again
    if(item.spriteArray){
        return;
    }
    item.spriteSheet = loader.loadImage('images/'+this.defaults.type+'/'+name+'.png');
    item.spriteArray = [];
    item.spriteCount = 0;

    for (var i=0; i < item.spriteImages.length; i++){
        var constructImageCount = item.spriteImages[i].count;
        var constructDirectionCount = item.spriteImages[i].directions;
        if (constructDirectionCount){
            for (var j=0; j < constructDirectionCount; j++) {
                var constructImageName = item.spriteImages[i].name +"-"+j;
                item.spriteArray[constructImageName] = {
                    name:constructImageName,
                    count:constructImageCount,
                    offset:item.spriteCount
                };
                item.spriteCount += constructImageCount;
            };
        } else {
            var constructImageName = item.spriteImages[i].name;
            item.spriteArray[constructImageName] = {
                name:constructImageName,
                count:constructImageCount,
                offset:item.spriteCount
            };
            item.spriteCount += constructImageCount;
        }
    };
    // Load the weapon if item has one
    if(item.weaponType){
        bullets.load(item.weaponType);
    }
}
```

When loading an item, we check whether it has a weaponType property defined and, if so, load the bullet for the weapon using the bullets.load() method. All entities that are capable of attacking will have a weaponType property.

The next change we will make is to modify the game object's drawingLoop() method to draw the bullets and explosions on top of all other items in the game. The updated drawingLoop() method will look like Listing 9-5.

Listing 9-5. Modifying drawingLoop() to Draw Bullets Above Other Items (game.js)

```
drawingLoop:function(){
    // Handle Panning the Map
    game.handlePanning();

    // Check the time since the game was animated and calculate a linear interpolation factor
(-1 to 0)
    // since drawing will happen more often than animation
    game.lastDrawTime = (new Date()).getTime();
    if (game.lastAnimationTime){
        game.drawingInterpolationFactor = (game.lastDrawTime -game.lastAnimationTime)/game.
animationTimeout - 1;
        if (game.drawingInterpolationFactor>0){ // No point interpolating beyond the next
animation loop...
            game.drawingInterpolationFactor = 0;
        }
    } else {
        game.drawingInterpolationFactor = -1;
    }

    // Since drawing the background map is a fairly large operation,
    // we only redraw the background if it changes (due to panning)
    if (game.refreshBackground){
        game.backgroundContext.drawImage(game.currentMapImage,game.offsetX,game.offsetY,
game.canvasWidth, game.canvasHeight, 0,0,game.canvasWidth,game.canvasHeight);
        game.refreshBackground = false;
    }

    // Clear the foreground canvas
    game.foregroundContext.clearRect(0,0,game.canvasWidth,game.canvasHeight);

    // Start drawing the foreground elements
    for (var i = game.sortedItems.length - 1; i >= 0; i--){
        if (game.sortedItems[i].type != "bullets"){
            game.sortedItems[i].draw();
        }
    };

    // Draw the bullets on top of all the other elements
    for (var i = game.bullets.length - 1; i >= 0; i--){
        game.bullets[i].draw();
    };

    // Draw the mouse
    mouse.draw()

    // Call the drawing loop for the next frame using request animation frame
    if (game.running){
        requestAnimationFrame(game.drawingLoop);
    }
},
```

We first draw all the items that are not bullets and finally draw the bullets. This way, bullets and explosions will always be clearly visible in the game.

Finally, we will modify the game object's resetArrays() method to also reset the game.bullets[] array, as shown in Listing 9-6.

Listing 9-6. Resetting the Bullets Array Inside resetArrays()(game.js)

```
resetArrays:function(){
    game.counter = 1;
    game.items = [];
    game.sortedItems = [];
    game.buildings = [];
    game.vehicles = [];
    game.aircraft = [];
    game.terrain = [];
    game.triggeredEvents = [];
    game.selectedItems = [];
    game.sortedItems = [];
    game.bullets = [];
},
```

Now that we have implemented the bullets object, it's time to implement combat-based orders for the turrets, vehicles, and aircraft.

Combat-Based Orders for Turrets

Ground turrets can fire cannonballs at any ground-based threat. When in guard or attack mode, they will search for a valid target that is in sight, aim the turret toward the target, and fire bullets until the target is either destroyed or out of range.

We will start by implementing the processOrders() method by modifying the ground-turret object inside buildings.js, as shown in Listing 9-7.

Listing 9-7. Modifying ground-turret Object to Implement Attack (buildings.js)

```
isValidTarget:isValidTarget,
findTargetsInSight:findTargetsInSight,
processOrders:function(){
    if(this.reloadTimeLeft){
        this.reloadTimeLeft--;
    }
    // damaged turret cannot attack
    if(this.lifeCode != "healthy"){
        return;
    }
    switch (this.orders.type){
        case "guard":
            var targets = this.findTargetsInSight();
            if(targets.length>0){
                this.orders = {type:"attack",to:targets[0]};
            }
            break;
```

```
        case "attack":
            if(!this.orders.to ||
                this.orders.to.lifeCode == "dead" ||
                !this.isValidTarget(this.orders.to) ||
                (Math.pow(this.orders.to.x-this.x,2) +
Math.pow(this.orders.to.y-this.y,2))>Math.pow(this.sight,2)
                ){

                var targets = this.findTargetsInSight();
                if(targets.length>0){
                    this.orders.to = targets[0];
                } else {
                    this.orders = {type:"guard"};
                }
            }

            if (this.orders.to){
                var newDirection = findFiringAngle(this.orders.to,this,this.directions);
                var difference = angleDiff(this.direction,newDirection,this.directions);
                var turnAmount = this.turnSpeed*game.turnSpeedAdjustmentFactor;
                if (Math.abs(difference)>turnAmount){
                    this.direction = wrapDirection(this.direction+turnAmount*Math.abs(difference)/
difference,this.directions);
                    return;
                } else {
                    this.direction = newDirection;
                    if(!this.reloadTimeLeft){
                        this.reloadTimeLeft = bullets.list[this.weaponType].reloadTime;
                        var angleRadians = -(Math.round(this.direction)/this.directions)*2*Math.PI ;
                        var bulletX = this.x+0.5- (1*Math.sin(angleRadians));
                        var bulletY = this.y+0.5- (1*Math.cos(angleRadians));
                        var bullet = game.add({name:this.weaponType,type:"bullets", x:bulletX,
y:bulletY, direction:this.direction, target:this.orders.to});
                    }
                }
            }
            break;
    }
}
```

We start by assigning two methods called isValidTarget() and findTargetInSight() inside the ground-turret object. We will need to define these methods. We then define the processOrders() method.

Within the processOrders() method, we decrease the value of the reloadTimeLeft property if the property is defined and is greater than 0. If the turret lifeCode is not healthy (it is damaged or dead), we do nothing and exit.

Next we define the behavior for both the guard and attack orders. In guard mode, we use the findTargetsInSight() method to find a target and, if we find one, attack it. In attack mode, if the current target of the turret is undefined, dead, or out of sight, we use findTargetsInSight() to find a new valid target and set an order to attack it. If we cannot find a valid target, we go back to guard mode.

If the turret does have a valid target, we turn it toward the target. Once the turret is facing the target and reloadTimeLeft is 0, we fire a bullet by adding it to the game using the game.add() method and reset the turret's reloadTimeLeft property to the bullet's reload time.

Next we will modify the guard animation case inside the default animate() method to handle directions, as shown in Listing 9-8.

Listing 9-8. Modifying the Guard Case Inside animate() (buildings.js)

```
case "guard":
    if (this.lifeCode == "damaged"){
        // The damaged turret has no directions
        this.imageList = this.spriteArray[this.lifeCode];
    } else {
        // The healthy turret has 8 directions
        var direction = wrapDirection(Math.round(this.direction),this.directions);
        this.imageList = this.spriteArray[this.lifeCode+"-"+ direction];
    }
    this.imageOffset = this.imageList.offset;
    break;
```

Next, we will add two methods called isValidTarget() and findTargetInSight() inside common.js, as shown in Listing 9-9.

Listing 9-9. Adding isValidTarget() and findTargetInSight() Methods (common.js)

```
// Common Functions related to combat
function isValidTarget(item){
    return item.team != this.team &&
(this.canAttackLand && (item.type == "buildings" || item.type == "vehicles")||
(this.canAttackAir && (item.type == "aircraft")));
}

function findTargetsInSight(increment){
    if(!increment){
        increment=0;
    }
    var targets = [];
    for (var i = game.items.length - 1; i >= 0; i--){
        var item = game.items[i];
        if (this.isValidTarget(item)){
            if(Math.pow(item.x-this.x,2) + Math.pow(item.y-this.y,2)<Math.pow(this.
sight+increment,2)){
                targets.push(item);
            }
        }
    };

    // Sort targets based on distance from attacker
    var attacker = this;
    targets.sort(function(a,b){
        return (Math.pow(a.x-attacker.x,2) + Math.pow(a.y-attacker.y,2))-(Math.pow(b.x-attacker.x,2)
+ Math.pow(b.y-attacker.y,2));
    });

    return targets;
}
```

The isValidTarget() method returns true if the target item is from the opposite team, and it can be attacked.

The findTargetsInSight() method checks all the items in the game.items() array to see whether they are valid targets and within range, and if so, it adds them to the targets array. It then sorts the targets array by distance of each target from the attacker. The method also accepts an optional increment parameter that allows us to find targets beyond the range of the item. These two common methods will be used by turrets, vehicles, and aircraft.

Before we see the results of our code, we will update our map from the last level by modifying the triggers and items arrays, as shown in Listing 9-10.

Listing 9-10. Updating the Map Items and Triggers (maps.js)

```
/* Entities to be added */
"items":[
    {"type":"buildings","name":"base","x":11,"y":14,"team":"blue"},
    {"type":"buildings","name":"starport","x":18,"y":14,"team":"blue"},

    {"type":"vehicles","name":"harvester","x":16,"y":12,"team":"blue","direction":3},
    {"type":"terrain","name":"oilfield","x":3,"y":5,"action":"hint"},

    {"type":"terrain","name":"bigrocks","x":19,"y":6},
    {"type":"terrain","name":"smallrocks","x":8,"y":3},

    {"type":"vehicles","name":"scout-tank","x":26,"y":14,"team":"blue","direction":4},
    {"type":"vehicles","name":"heavy-tank","x":26,"y":16,"team":"blue","direction":5},
    {"type":"aircraft","name":"chopper","x":20,"y":12,"team":"blue","direction":2},
    {"type":"aircraft","name":"wraith","x":23,"y":12,"team":"blue","direction":3},

    {"type":"buildings","name":"ground-turret","x":15,"y":23,"team":"green"},
    {"type":"buildings","name":"ground-turret","x":20,"y":23,"team":"green"},

    {"type":"vehicles","name":"scout-tank","x":16,"y":26,"team":"green","direction":4},
    {"type":"vehicles","name":"heavy-tank","x":18,"y":26,"team":"green","direction":6},
    {"type":"aircraft","name":"chopper","x":20,"y":27,"team":"green","direction":2},
    {"type":"aircraft","name":"wraith","x":22,"y":28,"team":"green","direction":3},

    {"type":"buildings","name":"base","x":19,"y":28,"team":"green"},
    {"type":"buildings","name":"starport","x":15,"y":28,"team":"green"},
],

/* Conditional and Timed Trigger Events */
"triggers":[
],
```

We removed the triggers that we defined in the previous chapter so the level doesn't end after 30 seconds. Now, if we run the game in the browser and move a vehicle close to the enemy turrets, the turrets should start attacking the vehicle, as shown in Figure 9-1.

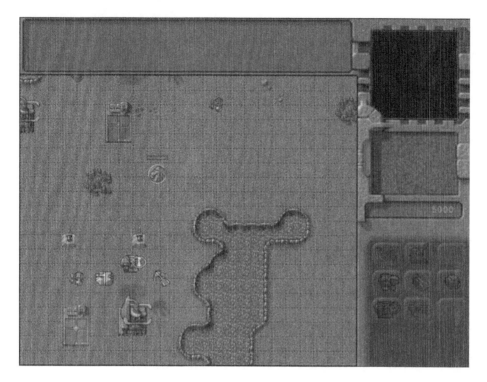

Figure 9-1. *Turret firing at a vehicle within range*

The bullets explode when they hit the vehicle and decrease the vehicle's life. Once the vehicle loses all its life, it disappears from the game. The turret stops shooting at a target if the target goes out of range and moves onto the next target.

Next we will implement combat-based orders for aircraft.

Combat-Based Orders for Aircraft

We will define several basic combat-based order states for aircraft.

- attack: Move within range of a target and shoot at it.

- float: Stay in one place and attack any enemy that comes close.

- guard: Follow a friendly unit and shoot at any enemy that comes close.

- hunt: Actively seek out enemies anywhere on the map and attack them.

- patrol: Move between two points and shoot at any enemy that comes within range.

- sentry: Stay in one place and attack enemies slightly more aggressively than in float mode.

We will implement these states by modifying the default processOrders() method inside the aircraft object, as shown in Listing 9-11.

Listing 9-11. Implementing Combat Orders for Aircraft (aircraft.js)

```
isValidTarget:isValidTarget,
findTargetsInSight:findTargetsInSight,
processOrders:function(){
    this.lastMovementX = 0;
    this.lastMovementY = 0;
    if(this.reloadTimeLeft){
        this.reloadTimeLeft--;
    }
    switch (this.orders.type){
        case "float":
            var targets = this.findTargetsInSight();
            if(targets.length>0){
                this.orders = {type:"attack",to:targets[0]};
            }
            break;
        case "sentry":
            var targets = this.findTargetsInSight(2);
            if(targets.length>0){
                this.orders = {type:"attack",to:targets[0],nextOrder:this.orders};
            }
            break;
        case "hunt":
            var targets = this.findTargetsInSight(100);
            if(targets.length>0){
                this.orders = {type:"attack",to:targets[0],nextOrder:this.orders};
            }
            break;
        case "move":
            // Move toward destination until distance from destination is less than aircraft radius
            var distanceFromDestinationSquared = (Math.pow(this.orders.to.x-this.x,2) +
Math.pow(this.orders.to.y-this.y,2));
            if (distanceFromDestinationSquared < Math.pow(this.radius/game.gridSize,2)) {
                this.orders = {type:"float"};
            } else {
                this.moveTo(this.orders.to);
            }
            break;
        case "attack":
            if(this.orders.to.lifeCode == "dead" || !this.isValidTarget(this.orders.to)){
                if (this.orders.nextOrder){
                    this.orders = this.orders.nextOrder;
                } else {
                    this.orders = {type:"float"};
                }
                return;
            }
            if ((Math.pow(this.orders.to.x-this.x,2) +
Math.pow(this.orders.to.y-this.y,2))<Math.pow(this.sight,2)) {
```

```
                //Turn toward target and then start attacking when within range of the target
                var newDirection = findFiringAngle(this.orders.to,this,this.directions);
                var difference = angleDiff(this.direction,newDirection,this.directions);
                var turnAmount = this.turnSpeed*game.turnSpeedAdjustmentFactor;
                if (Math.abs(difference)>turnAmount){
                    this.direction = wrapDirection(this.direction+ turnAmount*Math.abs(difference)/
difference, this.directions);
                    return;
                } else {
                    this.direction = newDirection;
                    if(!this.reloadTimeLeft){
                        this.reloadTimeLeft = bullets.list[this.weaponType].reloadTime;
                        var angleRadians = -(Math.round(this.direction)/this.directions)*2*Math.PI ;
                        var bulletX = this.x- (this.radius*Math.sin(angleRadians)/game.gridSize);
                        var bulletY = this.y- (this.radius*Math.cos(angleRadians)/game.gridSize)-
this.pixelShadowHeight/game.gridSize;
                        var bullet = game.add({name:this.weaponType, type:"bullets",x:bulletX,
y:bulletY, direction:newDirection, target:this.orders.to});
                    }
                }

            } else {
                var moving = this.moveTo(this.orders.to);
            }
            break;
        case "patrol":
            var targets = this.findTargetsInSight(1);
            if(targets.length>0){
                this.orders = {type:"attack",to:targets[0],nextOrder:this.orders};
                return;
            }
            if ((Math.pow(this.orders.to.x-this.x,2) + Math.pow(this.orders.to.y-
this.y,2))<Math.pow(this.radius/game.gridSize,2)) {
                var to = this.orders.to;
                this.orders.to = this.orders.from;
                this.orders.from = to;
            } else {
                this.moveTo(this.orders.to);
            }
            break;
        case "guard":
            if(this.orders.to.lifeCode == "dead"){
                if (this.orders.nextOrder){
                    this.orders = this.orders.nextOrder;
                } else {
                    this.orders = {type:"float"};
                }
                return;
            }
```

```
            if ((Math.pow(this.orders.to.x-this.x,2) + Math.pow(this.orders.to.y-
this.y,2))<Math.pow(this.sight-2,2)) {
                var targets = this.findTargetsInSight(1);
                if(targets.length>0){
                    this.orders = {type:"attack",to:targets[0],nextOrder:this.orders};
                    return;
                }
            } else {
                this.moveTo(this.orders.to);
            }
            break;

    }
},
```

We start by assigning the isValidTarget() and findTargetInSight() methods. We then define all the states inside the processOrders() method.

Within the processOrders() method, we decrease the value of the reloadTimeLeft property just like we did for turrets. We then define cases for each of the order states.

If the order type is float, we use findTargetsInSight() to check whether a target is nearby and, if so, attack it. We do the same thing when the order type is sentry, except we pass a range increment parameter of 2 so that the aircraft attacks units slightly beyond its typical range.

The hunt case is very similar except the range increment parameter is 100, which should ideally cover the entire map. This means the aircraft will attack any enemy unit or vehicle on the map starting with the nearest one.

For the attack case, we first check whether the target is still alive. If not, we either set orders to orders.nextOrder if it is defined or go back to float mode.

Next we check whether the target is within range, and if not, we move closer to the target. Next, we make sure that the aircraft is pointing toward the target. Finally, we wait until the reloadTimeLeft variable is 0 and then shoot a bullet at the target.

The patrol case is a combination of the move and sentry cases. We move the aircraft to the location defined in the to property and, once it reaches the location, turn around and move toward the from location. In case a target comes within range, we set the order to attack with the nextOrder set to the current order. This way, if the aircraft sees an enemy while patrolling, it will first attack the enemy and then go back to patrolling once the enemy has been destroyed.

Finally, in the case of guard mode, we move the aircraft within sight of the unit the aircraft is guarding and attack any enemy that comes close.

If you run the code we have so far, you should be able to see the different aircraft attacking each other, as shown in Figure 9-2.

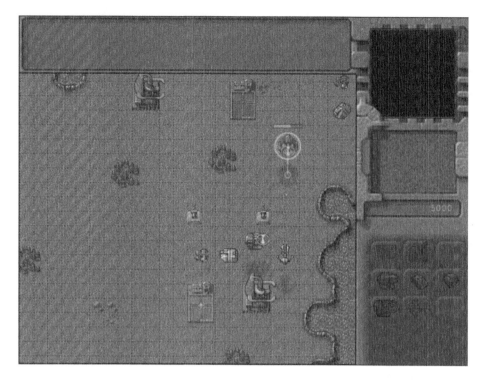

Figure 9-2. *Aircraft attacking each other*

You can command an aircraft to attack an enemy or guard a friend by right-clicking after selecting the aircraft. The chopper can attack both land and air units, while the wraith can attack only air units.

We will typically use the sentry, hunt, and patrol orders to give the computer AI a slight advantage and make the game more challenging for the player. The player will not have access to these orders.

■ **Tip** We can easily implement patrol for the player by modifying the click method to send a patrol command if a modifier key (such as Ctrl or Shift) is pressed when the player right-clicks the ground.

Next we will implement combat-based orders for vehicles.

Combat-Based Orders for Vehicles

The combat-based order states for vehicles will be very similar to the order states for aircraft.

- attack: Move within range of a target and shoot at it.

- stand: Stay in one place and attack any enemy that comes close.

- guard: Follow a friendly unit and shoot at any enemy that comes close.

- hunt: Actively seek out enemies anywhere on the map and attack them.

- patrol: Move between two points and shoot at any enemy that comes within range.

- sentry: Stay in one place an attack enemies slightly more aggressively than in stand mode.

We will implement these states by modifying the default processOrders() method inside the vehicles object, as shown in Listing 9-12.

Listing 9-12. Implementing Combat Orders for vehicles (vehicles.js)

```
isValidTarget:isValidTarget,
findTargetsInSight:findTargetsInSight,
processOrders:function(){
    this.lastMovementX = 0;
    this.lastMovementY = 0;
    if(this.reloadTimeLeft){
        this.reloadTimeLeft--;
    }
    var target;
    switch (this.orders.type){
        case "move":
            // Move toward destination until distance from destination is less than vehicle radius
            var distanceFromDestinationSquared = (Math.pow(this.orders.to.x-this.x,2) +
Math.pow(this.orders.to.y-this.y,2));
            if (distanceFromDestinationSquared < Math.pow(this.radius/game.gridSize,2)) {
                //Stop when within one radius of the destination
                this.orders = {type:"stand"};
                return;
            } else if (distanceFromDestinationSquared <Math.pow(this.radius*3/game.gridSize,2)) {
                //Stop when within 3 radius of the destination if colliding with something
                this.orders = {type:"stand"};
                return;
            } else {
                if (this.colliding && (Math.pow(this.orders.to.x-this.x,2) +
Math.pow(this.orders.to.y-this.y,2))<Math.pow(this.radius*5/game.gridSize,2)) {
                    // Count collsions within 5 radius distance of goal
                    if (!this.orders.collisionCount){
                        this.orders.collisionCount = 1
                    } else {
                        this.orders.collisionCount ++;
                    }
                    // Stop if more than 30 collisions occur
                    if (this.orders.collisionCount > 30) {
                        this.orders = {type:"stand"};
                        return;
                    }
                }
                var moving = this.moveTo(this.orders.to);
                // Pathfinding couldn't find a path so stop
                if(!moving){
                    this.orders = {type:"stand"};
                    return;
                }
            }
```

247

```
                    break;
            case "deploy":
                // If oilfield has been used already, then cancel order
                if(this.orders.to.lifeCode == "dead"){
                    this.orders = {type:"stand"};
                    return;
                }
                // Move to middle of oil field
                var target = {x:this.orders.to.x+1,y:this.orders.to.y+0.5,type:"terrain"};
                var distanceFromTargetSquared = (Math.pow(target.x-this.x,2) +
Math.pow(target.y-this.y,2));
                    if (distanceFromTargetSquared<Math.pow(this.radius*2/game.gridSize,2)) {
                        // After reaching oil field, turn harvester to point toward left (direction 6)
                        var difference = angleDiff(this.direction,6,this.directions);
                        var turnAmount = this.turnSpeed*game.turnSpeedAdjustmentFactor;
                        if (Math.abs(difference)>turnAmount){
                            this.direction = wrapDirection(this.direction+turnAmount*Math.abs(difference)/
difference,this.directions);
                        } else {
                            // Once it is pointing to the left, remove the harvester and oil field and
deploy a harvester building
                            game.remove(this.orders.to);
                            this.orders.to.lifeCode="dead";
                            game.remove(this);
                            this.lifeCode="dead";
                            game.add({type:"buildings", name:"harvester", x:this.orders.to.x,
y:this.orders.to.y, action:"deploy", team:this.team});
                        }
                    } else {
                        var moving = this.moveTo(target);
                        // Pathfinding couldn't find a path so stop
                        if(!moving){
                            this.orders = {type:"stand"};
                        }
                    }
                break;
            case "stand":
                var targets = this.findTargetsInSight();
                if(targets.length>0){
                    this.orders = {type:"attack",to:targets[0]};
                }
                break;
            case "sentry":
                var targets = this.findTargetsInSight(2);
                if(targets.length>0){
                    this.orders = {type:"attack",to:targets[0],nextOrder:this.orders};
                }
                break;
```

```
        case "hunt":
            var targets = this.findTargetsInSight(100);
            if(targets.length>0){
                this.orders = {type:"attack",to:targets[0],nextOrder:this.orders};
            }
            break;
        case "attack":
            if(this.orders.to.lifeCode == "dead" || !this.isValidTarget(this.orders.to)){
                if (this.orders.nextOrder){
                    this.orders = this.orders.nextOrder;
                } else {
                    this.orders = {type:"stand"};
                }
                return;
            }
            if ((Math.pow(this.orders.to.x-this.x,2) + Math.pow(this.orders.to.y-this.y,2))
<Math.pow(this.sight,2)) {
                //Turn toward target and then start attacking when within range of the target
                var newDirection = findFiringAngle(this.orders.to,this,this.directions);
                var difference = angleDiff(this.direction,newDirection,this.directions);
                var turnAmount = this.turnSpeed*game.turnSpeedAdjustmentFactor;
                if (Math.abs(difference)>turnAmount){
                    this.direction = wrapDirection(this.direction + turnAmount*Math.abs(difference)/
difference, this.directions);
                    return;
                } else {
                    this.direction = newDirection;
                    if(!this.reloadTimeLeft){
                        this.reloadTimeLeft = bullets.list[this.weaponType].reloadTime;
                        var angleRadians = -(Math.round(this.direction)/this.directions)*2*Math.PI ;
                        var bulletX = this.x- (this.radius*Math.sin(angleRadians)/game.gridSize);
                        var bulletY = this.y- (this.radius*Math.cos(angleRadians)/game.gridSize);
                        var bullet = game.add({name:this.weaponType,type:"bullets",x:bulletX,y:
bulletY, direction:newDirection, target:this.orders.to});
                    }
                }
            } else {
                var moving = this.moveTo(this.orders.to);
                // Pathfinding couldn't find a path so stop
                if(!moving){
                    this.orders = {type:"stand"};
                    return;
                }
            }
            break;
        case "patrol":
            var targets = this.findTargetsInSight(1);
            if(targets.length>0){
                this.orders = {type:"attack",to:targets[0],nextOrder:this.orders};
                return;
            }
```

```
            if ((Math.pow(this.orders.to.x-this.x,2) +
Math.pow(this.orders.to.y-this.y,2))<Math.pow(this.radius*4/game.gridSize,2)) {
                var to = this.orders.to;
                this.orders.to = this.orders.from;
                this.orders.from = to;
            } else {
                this.moveTo(this.orders.to);
            }
            break;
        case "guard":
            if(this.orders.to.lifeCode == "dead"){
                if (this.orders.nextOrder){
                    this.orders = this.orders.nextOrder;
                } else {
                    this.orders = {type:"stand"};
                }
                return;
            }
            if ((Math.pow(this.orders.to.x-this.x,2) + Math.pow(this.orders.to.y-this.y,2))
<Math.pow(this.sight-2,2)) {
                var targets = this.findTargetsInSight(1);
                if(targets.length>0){
                    this.orders = {type:"attack",to:targets[0],nextOrder:this.orders};
                    return;
                }
            } else {
                this.moveTo(this.orders.to);
            }
            break;
    }
},
```

The implementation of the states is almost the same as for aircraft. If we run the code now, we should be able to attack with the vehicles, as shown in Figure 9-3.

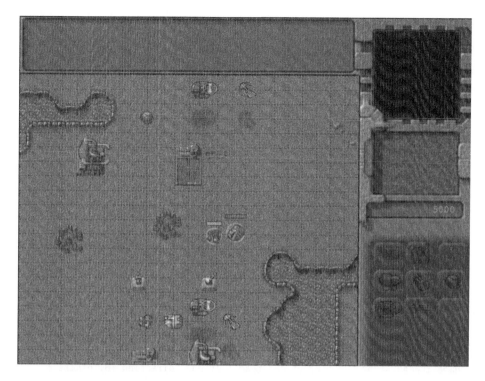

Figure 9-3. *Attacking with the vehicles*

We can now attack with vehicles, aircraft, or turrets.

You may have noticed that while the opposing team's units attack when you come close, they are still very easily defeated. Now that the combat system is in place, we will explore ways to make the enemy more intelligent and the game more challenging.

Building Intelligent Enemy

The primary goal in building an intelligent enemy AI is to make sure that the person playing the game finds it reasonably challenging and has a fun experience completing the level. An important thing to realize about RTS games, especially the single-player campaign, is that the enemy AI doesn't need to be a grandmaster-level chess player. The fact is, we can provide the player with a very compelling experience using only a combination of combat order states and conditional scripted events.

Typically, the "intelligent" way to behave for the AI will vary with each level.

In a simple level where there are no production facilities and only ground units, the only possible behavior is to drive up to the enemy units and attack them. A combination of patrol and sentry orders is usually more than enough to achieve this. We could also make the level interesting by attacking the player at a specific time or when a certain event occurs (for example, when the player arrives at a certain location or constructs a particular building).

In a more complex level, we might make the enemy challenging by constructing and sending in waves of enemies at specific intervals using timed triggers and the hunt order.

We can see some of these ideas at work by adding a few more items and triggers to the map, as shown in Listing 9-13.

Listing 9-13. Adding Triggers and Items to Make the Level Challenging (maps.js)

```
/* Entities to be added */
"items":[
    {"type":"buildings","name":"base","x":11,"y":14,"team":"blue"},
    {"type":"buildings","name":"starport","x":18,"y":14,"team":"blue"},

    {"type":"vehicles","name":"harvester","x":16,"y":12,"team":"blue","direction":3},
    {"type":"terrain","name":"oilfield","x":3,"y":5,"action":"hint"},

    {"type":"terrain","name":"bigrocks","x":19,"y":6},
    {"type":"terrain","name":"smallrocks","x":8,"y":3},

    {"type":"vehicles","name":"scout-tank","x":26,"y":14,"team":"blue","direction":4},
    {"type":"vehicles","name":"heavy-tank","x":26,"y":16,"team":"blue","direction":5},
    {"type":"aircraft","name":"chopper","x":20,"y":12,"team":"blue","direction":2},
    {"type":"aircraft","name":"wraith","x":23,"y":12,"team":"blue","direction":3},


    {"type":"buildings","name":"ground-turret","x":15,"y":23,"team":"green"},
    {"type":"buildings","name":"ground-turret","x":20,"y":23,"team":"green"},

    {"type":"vehicles","name":"scout-tank","x":16,"y":26,"team":"green","direction":4,"orders":
{"type":"sentry"}},
    {"type":"vehicles","name":"heavy-tank","x":18,"y":26,"team":"green","direction":6,"orders":
{"type":"sentry"}},

    {"type":"aircraft","name":"chopper","x":20,"y":27,"team":"green","direction":2,"orders":
{"type":"hunt"}},

    {"type":"aircraft","name":"wraith","x":22,"y":28,"team":"green","direction":3,"orders":
{"type":"hunt"}},

    {"type":"buildings","name":"base","x":19,"y":28,"team":"green"},
    {"type":"buildings","name":"starport","x":15,"y":28,"team":"green","uid":-1},
],

/* Economy Related*/
"cash":{
    "blue":5000,
    "green":5000
},

/* Conditional and Timed Trigger Events */
"triggers":[
/* Timed Events*/
    {"type":"timed","time":1000,
        "action":function(){
            game.sendCommand([-1],{type:"construct-unit",details:{type:"aircraft",name:"wraith",orde
rs:{"type":"patrol","from":{"x":22,"y":30},"to":{"x":15,"y":21}}}});
        }
    },
```

```
        {"type":"timed","time":5000,
            "action":function(){
                game.sendCommand([-1],{type:"construct-unit", details:{type:"aircraft",name:"chopper",
orders:{"type":"patrol","from":{"x":15,"y":30},"to":{"x":22,"y":21}}}});
            }
        },
        {"type":"timed","time":10000,
            "action":function(){
                game.sendCommand([-1],{type:"construct-unit",details:{type:"vehicles",name:"heavy-tank",
orders:{"type":"patrol","from":{"x":15,"y":30},"to":{"x":22,"y":21}}}});
            }
        },
        {"type":"timed","time":15000,
            "action":function(){
                game.sendCommand([-1],{type:"construct-unit",details:{type:"vehicles",name:"scout-tank",
orders:{"type":"patrol","from":{"x":22,"y":30},"to":{"x":15,"y":21}}}});
            }
        },
        {"type":"timed","time":60000,
            "action":function(){
                game.showMessage("AI","Now every enemy unit is going to attack you in a wave.");
                var units = [];
                for (var i=0; i < game.items.length; i++) {
                    var item = game.items[i];
                    if (item.team == "green" && (item.type == "vehicles"|| item.type == "aircraft")){
                        units.push(item.uid);
                    }
                };
                game.sendCommand(units,{type:"hunt"});
            }
        },
    ],
```

The first thing we do is order an enemy chopper and a wraith to hunt as soon as the game starts. Next, we assign a UID of –1 to the enemy starport and set a few timed triggers to build different types of patrolling units every few seconds.

Finally, after 60 seconds, we command all enemy units to hunt and notify the player using the showMessage() method.

If we run the code now, we can expect the AI to defend itself fairly well and attack very aggressively at the end of 60 seconds, as shown in Figure 9-4.

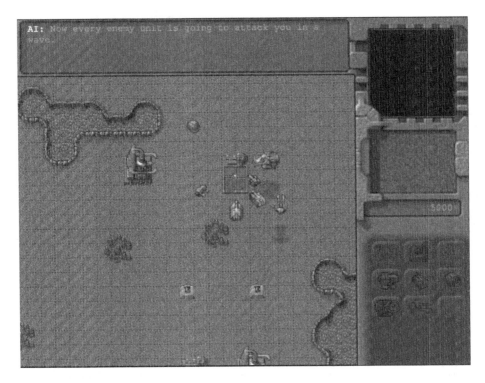

Figure 9-4. *Computer AI aggressively attacking player*

Obviously, this is a fairly contrived example. No one will want to play a game where they get attacked this brutally within the first minute of playing. However, as this example illustrates, we can make the game as easy or as challenging as we need just by adjusting these triggers and orders.

■ **Tip** You can implement separate sets of triggers and starting items depending on a difficulty setting so that the player can play easy or challenging versions of the same campaign based on the setting selected.

Now that we have implemented the combat system and explored ways to make the game AI challenging, the last thing we will look at in this chapter is adding a fog of war.

Adding a Fog of War

The fog of war is typically a dark, colored shroud that covers all unexplored terrain within the map. As player units move around the map, the fog is cleared anywhere that the unit can see.

This introduces elements of exploration and intrigue to the game. The ability to hide under the fog allows the use of strategies such as hidden bases, ambushes, and sneak attacks.

Some RTS games permanently remove the fog once an area is explored, while others clear the fog only in areas within sight of a player unit and bring back the fog once the unit leaves the area. For our game, we will be using the second implementation.

Defining the Fog Object

We will start by defining a new fog object inside fog.js, as shown in Listing 9-14.

Listing 9-14. Implementing the fog Object (fog.js)

```
var fog = {
    grid:[],
    canvas:document.createElement('canvas'),
    initLevel:function(){
        // Set fog canvas to the size of the map
        this.canvas.width = game.currentLevel.mapGridWidth*game.gridSize;
        this.canvas.height = game.currentLevel.mapGridHeight*game.gridSize;

        this.context = this.canvas.getContext('2d');

        // Set the fog grid for the player to array with all values set to 1
        this.defaultFogGrid = [];
        for (var i=0; i < game.currentLevel.mapGridHeight; i++) {
            this.defaultFogGrid[i] = [];
            for (var j=0; j < game.currentLevel.mapGridWidth; j++) {
                this.defaultFogGrid[i][j] = 1;
            };
        };

    },
    isPointOverFog:function(x,y){
        // If the point is outside the map bounds consider it fogged
        if(y<0 || y/game.gridSize >= game.currentLevel.mapGridHeight || x<0 || x/game.gridSize >=
game.currentLevel.mapGridWidth ){
             return true;
            }
        // If not, return value based on the player's fog grid
        return this.grid[game.team][Math.floor(y/game.gridSize)][Math.floor(x/game.gridSize)] == 1;
    },
    animate:function(){
        // Fill fog with semi solid black color over the map
        this.context.drawImage(game.currentMapImage,0,0)
        this.context.fillStyle = 'rgba(0,0,0,0.8)';
        this.context.fillRect(0,0,this.canvas.width,this.canvas.height);

        // Initialize the players fog grid
        this.grid[game.team] = $.extend(true,[],this.defaultFogGrid);

        // Clear all areas of the fog where a player item has vision
        fog.context.globalCompositeOperation = "destination-out";
        for (var i = game.items.length - 1; i >= 0; i--){
            var item = game.items[i];
            var team = game.team;
                if (item.team == team && !item.keepFogged){
                    var x = Math.floor(item.x );
                    var y = Math.floor(item.y );
```

```
                        var x0 = Math.max(0,x-item.sight+1);
                        var y0 = Math.max(0,y-item.sight+1);
                        var x1 = Math.min(game.currentLevel.mapGridWidth-1, x+item.sight-1+
(item.type=="buildings"?item.baseWidth/game.gridSize:0));
                        var y1 = Math.min(game.currentLevel.mapGridHeight-1, y+item.sight-1+
(item.type=="buildings"?item.baseHeight/game.gridSize:0));
                    for (var j=x0; j <= x1; j++) {
                        for (var k=y0; k <= y1; k++) {
                            if ((j>x0 && j<x1) || (k>y0 && k<y1)){
                                if(this.grid[team][k][j]){
                                    this.context.fillStyle = 'rgba(100,0,0,0.9)';
                                    this.context.beginPath();
                                    this.context.arc(j*game.gridSize+12, k*game.gridSize+12,
16, 0, 2*Math.PI, false);
                                    this.context.fill();
                                    this.context.fillStyle = 'rgba(100,0,0,0.7)';
                                    this.context.beginPath();
                                    this.context.arc(j*game.gridSize+12,
k*game.gridSize+12,18, 0, 2*Math.PI, false);
                                    this.context.fill();

                                    this.context.fillStyle = 'rgba(100,0,0,0.5)';
                                    this.context.beginPath();
                                    this.context.arc(j*game.gridSize+12, k*game.gridSize+12,
24, 0, 2*Math.PI, false);
                                    this.context.fill();

                                }
                                this.grid[team][k][j] = 0;
                            }
                        };
                    };
                }
            };
        fog.context.globalCompositeOperation = "source-over";
    },
    draw:function(){
        game.foregroundContext.drawImage(this.canvas,game.offsetX, game.offsetY, game.canvasWidth,
game.canvasHeight, 0,0,game.canvasWidth,game.canvasHeight);
    }
}
```

We start by defining a canvas inside the fog object. The initLevel() method resizes the canvas object to the size of the current map and defines a fogGrid array that has the same dimensions as the map with all its elements set to 1.

Within the animate() method, we first initialize the fog to the map background with a semi-transparent black layer over it. This way, fogged areas of the map show up as darkened background terrain.

We then iterate through each of the items in the game and clear the fog array and the fog canvas around the player's items based on their sight property. We do not clear the fog for items that are the opposing player's or that have a keepFogged attribute set to true.

Finally, the draw() method draws the fog canvas onto the game.foregroundContext context using the same offsets that we used when drawing the map onto the game.backgroundContext context.

Drawing the Fog

Now that we have defined the fog object, we will start by adding a reference to fog.js inside the head section of index.html, as shown in Listing 9-15.

Listing 9-15. Adding a Reference to the fog Object (index.html)

```
<script src="js/fog.js" type="text/javascript" charset="utf-8"></script>
```

Next, we need to initialize the fog once the level is loaded. We will do this by calling the fog.initLevel() method inside the singleplayer object's play() method, as shown in Listing 9-16.

Listing 9-16. Initializing the fog Object for the Level (singleplayer.js)

```
play:function(){
    fog.initLevel();
    game.animationLoop();
    game.animationInterval = setInterval(game.animationLoop,game.animationTimeout);
    game.start();
},
```

Next we need to modify the game object's animationLoop() and drawingLoop() methods to call fog.animate() and fog.draw() respectively, as shown in Listing 9-17.

Listing 9-17. Calling fog.animate() and fog.draw() (game.js)

```
animationLoop:function(){
    // Animate the Sidebar
    sidebar.animate();

    // Process orders for any item that handles it
    for (var i = game.items.length - 1; i >= 0; i--){
        if(game.items[i].processOrders){
            game.items[i].processOrders();
        }
    };

    // Animate each of the elements within the game
    for (var i = game.items.length - 1; i >= 0; i--){
        game.items[i].animate();
    };

    // Sort game items into a sortedItems array based on their x,y coordinates
    game.sortedItems = $.extend([],game.items);
    game.sortedItems.sort(function(a,b){
        return b.y-a.y + ((b.y==a.y)?(a.x-b.x):0);
    });

    fog.animate();
```

```
        game.lastAnimationTime = (new Date()).getTime();
},
drawingLoop:function(){
    // Handle Panning the Map
    game.handlePanning();

    // Check the time since the game was animated and calculate a linear interpolation factor
(-1 to 0)
    // since drawing will happen more often than animation
    game.lastDrawTime = (new Date()).getTime();
        if (game.lastAnimationTime){
            game.drawingInterpolationFactor = (game.lastDrawTime-game.lastAnimationTime)/
game.animationTimeout - 1;
            if (game.drawingInterpolationFactor>0){ // No point interpolating beyond the next
animation loop...
                game.drawingInterpolationFactor = 0;
            }
        } else {
          game.drawingInterpolationFactor = -1;

    }

    // Since drawing the background map is a fairly large operation,
    // we only redraw the background if it changes (due to panning)
    if (game.refreshBackground){
        game.backgroundContext.drawImage(game.currentMapImage,game.offsetX, game.offsetY,
game.canvasWidth, game.canvasHeight, 0,0,game.canvasWidth,game.canvasHeight);
        game.refreshBackground = false;
    }

    // Clear the foreground canvas
    game.foregroundContext.clearRect(0,0,game.canvasWidth,game.canvasHeight);

    // Start drawing the foreground elements
    for (var i = game.sortedItems.length - 1; i >= 0; i--){
        if (game.sortedItems[i].type != "bullets"){
            game.sortedItems[i].draw();
        }
    };

    // Draw the bullets on top of all the other elements
    for (var i = game.bullets.length - 1; i >= 0; i--){
        game.bullets[i].draw();
    };

    fog.draw();

    // Draw the mouse
    mouse.draw()
```

```
    // Call the drawing loop for the next frame using request animation frame
    if (game.running){
        requestAnimationFrame(game.drawingLoop);
    }
},
```

If we run the code now, we should see the entire map shrouded in a fog of war, as shown in Figure 9-5.

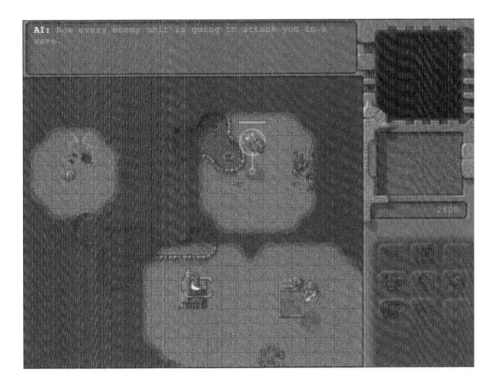

Figure 9-5. *Map shrouded in fog of war*

You will see that the fog is uncovered around friendly units and buildings. Also, the fogged area shows the original terrain but does not show any units under it.

The same enemy attack feels much scarier when we have no idea about the size or the location of the opposing army. Before we wrap up the chapter, we will make a few additions, starting with making the fogged areas unbuildable.

Making Fogged Areas Unbuildable

The first change we will make is to prevent the deploying of buildings on fogged areas by making fogged areas unbuildable. We will modify the sidebar object's animate() method, as shown in Listing 9-18.

Listing 9-18. Making Fogged Areas Unbuildable (sidebar.js)

```
animate:function(){
    // Display the current cash balance value
    $('#cash').html(game.cash[game.team]);

    //  Enable or disable buttons as appropriate
    this.enableSidebarButtons();

    if (game.deployBuilding){
        // Create the buildable grid to see where building can be placed
        game.rebuildBuildableGrid();
        // Compare with buildable grid to see where we need to place the building
        var placementGrid = buildings.list[game.deployBuilding].buildableGrid;
        game.placementGrid = $.extend(true,[],placementGrid);
        game.canDeployBuilding = true;
        for (var i = game.placementGrid.length - 1; i >= 0; i--){
            for (var j = game.placementGrid[i].length - 1; j >= 0; j--){
                if(game.placementGrid[i][j] &&
                    (mouse.gridY+i>= game.currentLevel.mapGridHeight || mouse.gridX+j>=
game.currentLevel.mapGridWidth
                        || game.currentMapBuildableGrid[mouse.gridY+i][mouse.gridX+j]==1 ||
fog.grid[game.team][mouse.gridY+i][mouse.gridX+j]==1)){
                    game.canDeployBuilding = false;
                    game.placementGrid[i][j] = 0;
                }
            };
        };
    }
},
```

We add an extra condition for testing the fog grid when creating the placementGrid array so that a fogged grid square is no longer buildable. If we run the game and try to build on a fogged area, we should see a warning, as shown in Figure 9-6.

Figure 9-6. *Cannot deploy buildings on fogged areas*

As you can see, the building deploy grid turns red on fogged areas to indicate that the player cannot build there. If you still try to click a fogged area, you will get a system warning.

Next we will make sure that the player cannot select or detect a building or unit that is under the fog. We do this by modifying the mouse object's pointUnderFog() method, as shown in Listing 9-19.

Listing 9-19. Hiding Objects Under the Fog (mouse.js)

```
itemUnderMouse:function(){
    if(fog.isPointOverFog(mouse.gameX,mouse.gameY)){
        return;
    }
    for (var i = game.items.length - 1; i >= 0; i--){
        var item = game.items[i];
        if (item.type=="buildings" || item.type=="terrain"){
            if(item.lifeCode != "dead"
                && item.x<= (mouse.gameX)/game.gridSize
                && item.x >= (mouse.gameX - item.baseWidth)/game.gridSize
                && item.y<= mouse.gameY/game.gridSize
                && item.y >= (mouse.gameY - item.baseHeight)/game.gridSize
                ){
                    return item;
            }
        } else if (item.type=="aircraft"){
            if (item.lifeCode != "dead" &&
```

```
            Math.pow(item.x-mouse.gameX/game.gridSize,2)+Math.pow(item.y-
(mouse.gameY+item.pixelShadowHeight)/game.gridSize,2) < Math.pow((item.radius)/game.gridSize,2)){
                return item;
            }
        }else {
            if (item.lifeCode != "dead" && Math.pow(item.x-mouse.gameX/game.gridSize,2) +
Math.pow(item.y-mouse.gameY/game.gridSize,2) < Math.pow((item.radius)/game.gridSize,2)){
                return item;
            }
        }
    }
},
```

We check whether the point under the mouse is fogged and, if so, return nothing. With this last change, we now have a working fog of war in our game.

Summary

In this chapter, we implemented a combat system for our game. We started by defining a bullets object with different types of bullets. We then added several combat-based order states to our turrets, aircraft, and vehicles. We used these orders along with the triggers system we defined in the previous chapter to create a fairly challenging enemy. Finally, we implemented a fog of war.

Our game now has most of the essential elements of an RTS. In the next chapter, we will polish our game framework by adding sound. We will then use this framework to build a few interesting levels and wrap up our single-player campaign.

CHAPTER 10

Wrapping Up the Single-Player Campaign

Our game framework now has almost everything we need to build a very nice single-player campaign: a level system, various units and buildings, intelligent movement using pathfinding, an economy, and finally combat.

Now it's time to add the finishing touches and wrap up our single-player campaign. We will first add sound effects such as explosions and voices to our game. We will then build several levels by combining and using the various elements that we developed over the past few chapters. You will see how these building blocks fall into place to create a complete game.

Let's get started. We will continue where we left off at the end of Chapter 9.

Adding Sound

RTS games have a lot more happening at the same time than games in other genres such as the physics game we developed in the first few chapters. If we are not careful, there is a possibility of overwhelming a player with so much audio input that it becomes a distraction and takes away from their immersion. For our game, we will focus on sounds that will make the player aware of essential events within the game.

- *Acknowledging commands*: Any time the player selects a unit and gives it a command, we will have the unit acknowledge that it received the command.

- *Messages*: Whenever the player receives either a system warning or a story line–driven notification, we will alert the player with a sound.

- *Combat*: We will add sounds during combat so that players instantly know that they are under attack somewhere on the map.

Setting Up Sounds

We will start by creating a sounds object inside sounds.js, as shown in Listing 10-1.

Listing 10-1. Creating a sounds Object (sounds.js)

```
var sounds = {
    list:{
        "bullet":["bullet1","bullet2"],
        "heatseeker":["heatseeker1","heatseeker2"],
        "fireball":["laser1","laser2"],
```

```
            "cannon-ball":["cannon1","cannon2"],
            "message-received":["message"],
            "acknowledge-attacking":["engaging"],
            "acknowledge-moving":["yup","roger1","roger2"],
        },
        loaded:{},
        init: function(){
            for(var soundName in this.list){
                var sound = {};
                sound.audioObjects = [];
                for (var i=0; i < this.list[soundName].length; i++) {
                    sound.audioObjects.push(loader.loadSound('audio/' + this.list[soundName][i]));
                };
                this.loaded [soundName] = sound;
            }
        },
        play:function(soundName){
            var sound = sounds.loaded[soundName];
            if(sound && sound.audioObjects && sound.audioObjects.length>0){
                if(!sound.counter || sound.counter>= sound.audioObjects.length){
                    sound.counter = 0;
                }
                var audioObject = sound.audioObjects[sound.counter];
                sound.counter++;
                audioObject.play();
            }
        }
    }
};
```

Within the sound object, we start by declaring a list, which maps a sound name to one or more sound files. For example, the bullet sound maps to two files: bullet1 and bullet2. You will notice that we don't specify the file extension (.ogg or .mp3). We let the loader object handle selecting the appropriate audio file extension for the browser.

Next we declare an init() method that iterates through the list of sounds, uses the loader.loadSound() method to load each audio file, and then creates an audioObjects array for each sound name. We then add this sound object to the loaded object.

Finally, we declare a play() method that looks up the appropriate sound object from the loaded array and then plays the audio object using its play() method. You will notice that we use a counter for each sound object to ensure that we iterate through the sounds for a given sound name so that a different sound is played each time play() is called. This allows us to play different versions of sounds for an event instead of hearing the same monotonous sound each time.

Next, we will add a reference to sounds.js inside the <head> section of index.html, as shown in Listing 10-2.

Listing 10-2. Referring to sounds.js (index.html)

```
<script src="js/sounds.js" type="text/javascript" charset="utf-8"></script>
```

Finally, we will load all these sounds when the game is initialized by calling the init() method from inside the game object's init() method, as shown in Listing 10-3.

Listing 10-3. Initializing the sounds Object Inside the game.init() Method (game.js)

```
init:function(){
    loader.init();
    mouse.init();
    sidebar.init();
    sounds.init();

    $('.gamelayer').hide();
    $('#gamestartscreen').show();

    game.backgroundCanvas = document.getElementById('gamebackgroundcanvas');
    game.backgroundContext = game.backgroundCanvas.getContext('2d');

    game.foregroundCanvas = document.getElementById('gameforegroundcanvas');
    game.foregroundContext = game.foregroundCanvas.getContext('2d');

    game.canvasWidth = game.backgroundCanvas.width;
    game.canvasHeight = game.backgroundCanvas.height;
},
```

Now that the sounds object is in place, we can start adding sounds for each event, starting with acknowledging commands.

Acknowledging Commands

We allow the player to give units several types of commands: attack, move, deploy, and guard. Any time a unit is sent an attack command, we will play the acknowledge-attacking sound. When the unit is sent any other command such as move or guard, we will play the acknowledge-moving sound.

We will do this by calling sounds.play() from inside the click() method of the mouse object, as shown in Listing 10-4.

Listing 10-4. Acknowledging Commands Inside the click() Method (mouse.js)

```
click:function(ev,rightClick){
    // Player clicked inside the canvas
    var clickedItem = this.itemUnderMouse();
    var shiftPressed = ev.shiftKey;

    if (!rightClick){ // Player left clicked
        // If the game is in deployBuilding mode, left clicking will deploy the building
        if (game.deployBuilding){
            if(game.canDeployBuilding){
                sidebar.finishDeployingBuilding();
            } else {
                game.showMessage("system","Warning! Cannot deploy building here.");
            }
            return;
        }
```

```
            if (clickedItem){
                // Pressing shift adds to existing selection. If shift is not pressed, clear
existing selection
                if(!shiftPressed){
                    game.clearSelection();
                }
                game.selectItem(clickedItem,shiftPressed);
            }
        } else { // Player right clicked
            // If the game is in deployBuilding mode, right clicking will cancel deployBuilding mode
            if (game.deployBuilding){
                sidebar.cancelDeployingBuilding();
                return;
            }
            // Handle actions like attacking and movement of selected units
            var uids = [];
            if (clickedItem){ // Player right clicked on something
                if (clickedItem.type != "terrain"){
                    if (clickedItem.team != game.team){ // Player right clicked on an enemy item
                        // identify selected items from players team that can attack
                        for (var i = game.selectedItems.length - 1; i >= 0; i--){
                            var item = game.selectedItems[i];
                            if(item.team == game.team && item.canAttack){
                                uids.push(item.uid);
                            }
                        };
                        // then command them to attack the clicked item
                        if (uids.length>0){
                            game.sendCommand(uids,{type:"attack", toUid:clickedItem.uid});
                            sounds.play("acknowledge-attacking");
                        }
                    } else  { // Player right clicked on a friendly item
                        //identify selected items from players team that can move
                        for (var i = game.selectedItems.length - 1; i >= 0; i--){
                            var item = game.selectedItems[i];
                            if(item.team == game.team && (item.type == "vehicles" || item.type ==
"aircraft")){
                                uids.push(item.uid);
                            }
                        };
                        // then command them to guard the clicked item
                        if (uids.length>0){
                            game.sendCommand(uids,{type:"guard", toUid:clickedItem.uid});
                            sounds.play("acknowledge-moving");
                        }
                    }
                } else if (clickedItem.name == "oilfield"){ // Player right clicked on an oilfield
                    // identify the first selected harvester from players team (since only one can
deploy at a time)
                    for (var i = game.selectedItems.length - 1; i >= 0; i--){
                        var item = game.selectedItems[i];
```

```
                    // pick the first selected harvester since only one can deploy at a time
                    if(item.team == game.team && (item.type == "vehicles" && item.name ==
"harvester")){
                            uids.push(item.uid);
                            break;
                    }
                };
                // then command it to deploy on the oilfield
                if (uids.length>0){
                    game.sendCommand(uids,{type:"deploy", toUid:clickedItem.uid});
                    sounds.play("acknowledge-moving");
                }
            }
        } else { // Player right clicked on the ground
            //identify selected items from players team that can move
            for (var i = game.selectedItems.length - 1; i >= 0; i--){
                var item = game.selectedItems[i];
                if(item.team == game.team && (item.type == "vehicles" || item.type == "aircraft")){
                    uids.push(item.uid);
                }
            };
            // then command them to move to the clicked location
            if (uids.length>0){
                game.sendCommand(uids,{type:"move", to:{x:mouse.gameX/game.gridSize, y:mouse.gameY/
game.gridSize}});
                sounds.play("acknowledge-moving");
            }
        }
    }
},
```

We call the sounds.play() method with the appropriate sound name whenever we send a game command.

One interesting thing to point out is that we play the sound when the command is sent out, not when it is received and processed. While this makes very little difference during the single-player campaign, it becomes important during multiplayer.

Usually, network latency and other issues can cause a lag of up to few hundred milliseconds between the sending of a command and it actually being received by all the players. By playing the sound as soon as the mouse is clicked, we give the player the illusion that the command has been executed immediately and make the effect of lag less noticeable.

▨ **Note** Some games use animation sequences in addition to sounds to indicate to the player that the unit is processing the command. Games such as first-person shooters often attempt to predict the unit movement and start moving the unit before receiving the server acknowledgment.

If you open and run the game now, you should hear the units acknowledge the command before they start moving or attacking. Next, let's add the message sound.

Messages

We will play a short beeping sound to notify players whenever they are shown a message. We will do this by playing the message-received sound from inside the game object's showMessage() method, as shown in Listing 10-5.

Listing 10-5. Message Notification Sound Inside the showMessage() Method (game.js)

```
showMessage:function(from,message){
    sounds.play('message-received');
    var character = game.characters[from];
    if (character){
        from = character.name;
        if (character.image){
            $('#callerpicture').html('<img src="'+character.image+'"/>');
            // hide the profile picture after six seconds
            setTimeout(function(){
                $('#callerpicture').html("");
            },6000)
        }
    }
    // Append message to messages pane and scroll to the bottom
    var existingMessage = $('#gamemessages').html();
    var newMessage = existingMessage+'<span>'+from+': </span>'+message+'<br>';
    $('#gamemessages').html(newMessage);
    $('#gamemessages').animate( {scrollTop:$('#gamemessages').prop('scrollHeight')});
},
```

If you play the game now, you should hear beeping whenever a new message is displayed.
The last set of sounds we will implement is for combat.

Combat

You may have noticed that we declared four different sound types within our sounds list: bullet, heatseeker, cannon-ball, and fireball. These four sounds correspond to the four bullet types that we declared in the previous chapter. Any time we fire a bullet, we will play the sound for the appropriate bullet.

We can easily do this by modifying the add() method inside game.js to play the appropriate sound whenever a bullet is added, as shown in Listing 10-6.

Listing 10-6. Playing Sound When a Bullet Is Added (game.js)

```
add:function(itemDetails) {
    // Set a unique id for the item
    if (!itemDetails.uid){
        itemDetails.uid = game.counter++;
    }

    var item = window[itemDetails.type].add(itemDetails);

    // Add the item to the items array
    game.items.push(item);
    // Add the item to the type specific array
    game[item.type].push(item);
```

```
    if(item.type == "buildings" || item.type == "terrain"){
        game.currentMapPassableGrid = undefined;
    }

    if (item.type == "bullets"){
        sounds.play(item.name);
    }
    return item;
},
```

If you play the game now, you should hear the distinct sounds of the different weapons as they are being fired.

We could keep adding more sound to our game if we wanted, such as explosions, construction noises, conversation, and even background music. The process would remain the same. However, the sounds we have implemented so far are sufficient for now.

Now that we have sound in our game, it's time to start building the actual levels for our single-player campaign.

Building the Single-Player Campaign

We will build three levels in our game campaign. Each of the levels will get progressively harder, while building upon the story from the previous levels. These levels will illustrate the typical types of levels you would find in an RTS game.

The Rescue

The introductory level in our game will be a relatively easy mission so that the player can get comfortable with moving units around the map and attacking enemy units.

The player will need to navigate across a map populated with easily defeated enemies and then escort a convoy of transport vehicles back to that player's starting location. After the mission briefing, we will move the story line forward using character dialogue that is triggered by timed and conditional triggers.

We will start with a completely fresh map object inside maps.js, as shown in Listing 10-7.

Listing 10-7. Creating the First Level (maps.js)

```
var maps = {
    "singleplayer":[
        {
            "name":"Rescue",
            "briefing": "In the months since the great war, mankind has fallen into chaos. Billions
are dead with cities in ruins.\nSmall groups of survivors band together to try and survive as best
as they can.\nWe are trying to reach out to all the survivors in this sector before we join back
with the main colony.",

            /* Map Details */
            "mapImage":"images/maps/level-one.png",
            "startX":36,
            "startY":0,

            /* Map coordinates that are obstructed by terrain*/
            "mapGridWidth":60,
            "mapGridHeight":40,
            "mapObstructedTerrain":[
```

[49,8], [50,8], [51,8], [51,9], [52,9], [53,9], [53,10], [53,11], [53,12], [53,13],
[53,14], [53,15], [53,16], [52,16], [52,17], [52,18], [52,19], [51,19], [50,19], [50,18], [50,17],
[49,17], [49,18], [48,18], [47,18], [47,17], [47,16], [48,16], [49,16], [49,15], [49,14], [48,14],
[48,13], [48,12], [49,12], [49,11], [50,11], [50,10], [49,10], [49,9], [44,0], [45,0], [45,1],
[45,2], [46,2], [47,2], [47,3], [48,3], [48,4], [48,5], [49,5], [49,6], [49,7], [50,7], [51,7],
[51,6], [51,5], [51,4], [52,4], [53,4], [53,3], [54,3], [55,3], [55,2], [56,2], [56,1], [56,0],
[55,0], [43,19], [44,19], [45,19], [46,19], [47,19], [48,19], [48,20], [48,21], [47,21], [46,21],
[45,21], [44,21], [43,21], [43,20], [41,22], [42,22], [43,22], [44,22], [45,22], [46,22], [47,22],
[48,22], [49,22], [50,22], [50,23], [50,24], [49,24], [48,24], [47,24], [47,25], [47,26], [47,27],
[47,28], [47,29], [47,30], [46,30], [45,30], [44,30], [43,30], [43,29], [43,28], [43,27], [43,26],
[43,25], [43,24], [42,24], [41,24], [41,23], [48,39], [49,39], [50,39], [51,39], [52,39], [53,39],
[54,39], [55,39], [56,39], [57,39], [58,39], [59,39], [59,38], [59,37], [59,36], [59,35], [59,34],
[59,33], [59,32], [59,31], [59,30], [59,29], [0,0], [1,0], [2,0], [1,1], [2,1], [10,3], [11,3],
[12,3], [12,2], [13,2], [14,2], [14,3], [14,4], [15,4], [15,5], [15,6], [14,6], [13,6], [13,5],
[12,5], [11,5], [10,5], [10,4], [3,9], [4,9], [5,9], [5,10], [6,10], [7,10], [8,10], [9,10], [9,11],
[10,11], [11,11], [11,10], [12,10], [13,10], [13,11], [13,12], [12,12], [11,12], [10,12], [9,12],
[8,12], [7,12], [7,13], [7,14], [6,14], [5,14], [5,13], [5,12], [5,11], [4,11], [3,11], [3,10],
[33,33], [34,33], [35,33], [35,34], [35,35], [34,35], [33,35], [33,34], [27,39], [27,38], [27,37],
[28,37], [28,36], [28,35], [28,34], [28,33], [28,32], [28,31], [28,30], [28,29], [29,29], [29,28],
[29,27], [29,26], [29,25], [29,24], [29,23], [30,23], [31,23], [32,23], [32,22], [32,21], [31,21],
[30,21], [30,22], [29,22], [28,22], [27,22], [26,22], [26,21], [25,21], [24,21], [24,22], [24,23],
[25,23], [26,23], [26,24], [25,24], [25,25], [24,25], [24,26], [24,27], [25,27], [25,28], [25,29],
[24,29], [23,29], [23,30], [23,31], [24,31], [25,31], [25,32], [25,33], [24,33], [23,33], [23,34],
[23,35], [24,35], [24,36], [24,37], [23,37], [22,37], [22,38], [22,39], [23,39], [24,39], [25,39],
[26,0], [26,1], [25,1], [25,2], [25,3], [26,3], [27,3], [27,2], [28,2], [29,2], [29,3], [30,3],
[31,3], [31,2], [31,1], [32,1], [32,0], [33,0], [32,8], [33,8], [34,8], [34,9], [34,10], [33,10],
[32,10], [32,9], [8,29], [9,29], [9,30], [17,32], [18,32], [19,32], [19,33], [18,33], [17,33],
[18,34], [19,34], [3,27], [4,27], [4,26], [3,26], [2,26], [3,25], [4,25], [9,20], [10,20], [11,20],
[11,21], [10,21], [10,19], [19,7], [15,7], [29,12], [30,13], [20,14], [21,14], [34,13], [35,13],
[36,13], [36,14], [35,14], [34,14], [35,15], [36,15], [16,18], [17,18], [18,18], [16,19], [17,19],
[18,19], [17,20], [18,20], [11,19], [58,0], [59,0], [58,1], [59,1], [59,2], [58,3], [59,3], [58,4],
[59,4], [59,5], [58,6], [59,6], [58,7], [59,7], [59,8], [58,9], [59,9], [58,10], [59,10], [59,11],
[52,6], [53,6], [54,6], [52,7], [53,7], [54,7], [53,8], [54,8], [44,17], [46,32], [55,32], [54,28],
[26,34], [34,34], [4,10], [6,11], [6,12], [6,13], [7,11], [8,11], [12,11], [27,0], [27,1], [26,2],
[28,1], [28,0], [29,0], [29,1], [30,2], [30,1], [30,0], [31,0], [33,9], [46,0], [47,0], [48,0],
[49,0], [50,0], [51,0], [52,0], [53,0], [54,0], [55,1], [54,1], [53,1], [52,1], [51,1], [50,1],
[49,1], [48,1], [47,1], [46,1], [48,2], [49,2], [50,2], [51,2], [52,2], [53,2], [54,2], [52,3],
[51,3], [50,3], [49,3], [49,4], [50,4], [50,5], [50,6], [50,9], [51,10], [52,10], [51,11], [52,11],
[50,12], [51,12], [52,12], [49,13], [50,13], [51,13], [52,13], [50,14], [51,14], [52,14], [50,15],
[51,15], [52,15], [50,16], [51,16], [51,17], [48,17], [51,18], [44,20], [45,20], [46,20], [47,20],
[42,23], [43,23], [44,23], [45,23], [46,23], [47,23], [48,23], [49,23], [44,24], [45,24], [46,24],
[44,25], [45,25], [46,25], [44,26], [45,26], [46,26], [44,27], [45,27], [46,27], [44,28], [45,28],
[46,28], [44,29], [45,29], [46,29], [11,4], [12,4], [13,4], [13,3], [14,5], [25,22], [31,22],
[27,23], [28,23], [27,24], [28,24], [26,25], [27,25], [28,25], [25,26], [26,26], [27,26], [28,26],
[26,27], [27,27], [28,27], [26,28], [27,28], [28,28], [26,29], [27,29], [24,30], [25,30], [26,30],
[27,30], [26,31], [27,31], [26,32], [27,32], [26,33], [27,33], [24,34], [25,34], [27,34], [25,35],
[26,35], [27,35], [25,36], [26,36], [27,36], [25,37], [26,37], [23,38], [24,38], [25,38], [26,38],
[26,39], [2,25], [9,19], [36,31]
                ],

```
            /* Entities to be loaded */
            "requirements":{
                "buildings":["base"],
                "vehicles":["transport","scout-tank","heavy-tank"],
                "aircraft":[],
                "terrain":[]
            },

            /* Economy Related*/
            "cash":{
                "blue":0,
                "green":0
            },

            /* Entities to be added */
            "items":[
                /* Slightly damaged base */
                {"type":"buildings","name":"base","x":55,"y":6,"team":"blue","life":100},

                {"type":"vehicles","name":"heavy-tank","x":57,"y":12,"direction":4,"team":
"blue","uid":-1},

                /* Two transport vehicles waiting just outside the visible map */
                {"type":"vehicles","name":"transport","x":-3,"y":2,"direction":2,"team":"blue",
"uid":-3,"selectable":false},
                {"type":"vehicles","name":"transport","x":-3,"y":4,"direction":2,"team":"blue",
"uid":-4,"selectable":false},

                /* Two damaged enemy scout-tanks patroling the area*/
                {"type":"vehicles","name":"scout-tank","x":40,"y":20,"direction":4,"team":"green",
"uid":-2,"life":20,"orders":{"type":"patrol","from":{"x":34,"y":20},"to":{"x":42,"y":25}}},
                {"type":"vehicles","name":"scout-tank","x":14,"y":0,"direction":4,"team":"green",
"uid":-5,"life":20,"orders":{"type":"patrol","from":{"x":14,"y":0},"to":{"x":14,"y":14}}},

            ],

            /* Conditional and Timed Trigger Events */
            "triggers":[
                {"type":"timed","time":3000,
                    "action":function(){
                        game.showMessage("op", "Commander!! We haven't heard from the last convoy in
over two hours. They should have arrived by now.");
                    }
                },
                {"type":"timed","time":10000,
                    "action":function(){
                        game.showMessage("op", "They were last seen in the North West Sector.
Could you investigate?");
                    }
                },
                {"type":"conditional",
                    "condition":function(){
```

271

```
                            return(isItemDead(-1)||isItemDead(-3)||isItemDead(-4));
                        },
                        "action":function(){
                            singleplayer.endLevel(false);
                        }
                    },
                ],
            }
        ]
    }
}
```

The first portion of the level consists of the same basic metadata that we saw in earlier levels. We start with the mission briefing, which gives the player a little background on the map. We then set the map image to the final version of the map instead of the debug version we have been using to build the game so far. We also set the map starting position to the top-right corner of the map. Finally, we set the map size and the mapObstructedTerrain properties.

Next we load a few essential items in the requirements array and set the starting cash balance for both players to 0.

Within the level's items array, we add a damaged base, a heavy-tank that the player will control, two enemy scout-tanks that patrol the area, and two transports. We set UIDs for each of them so that we can refer to them from the triggers.

Since this is the first level, we set the life of the scout-tanks so the player will find it easy to destroy them. The transports are positioned slightly outside the bounds of the top-left corner of the map so that they do not become visible to the player until the right time.

Within the triggers array, we define our first few triggers. The first two timed triggers show players a message from the operator, asking them to find the missing transport. The third is a conditional trigger that will end the mission as a failure if either the transports or the heavy tank get destroyed by using the isItemDead() method.

Next, we will add a few new characters to the characters object inside the game object, as shown in Listing 10-8.

Listing 10-8. Adding New Characters (game.js)

```
characters: {
    "system":{
        "name":"System",
        "image":"images/characters/system.png"
    },
    "op":{
        "name":"Operator",
        "image":"images/characters/girl1.png"
    },
    "pilot":{
        "name":"Pilot",
        "image":"images/characters/girl2.png"
    },
    "driver":{
        "name":"Driver",
        "image":"images/characters/man1.png"
    }
},
```

■ **Note**   These new character images are Creative Commons–licensed artwork found at http://opengameart.org.

We will also define the isItemDead() method inside common.js, as shown in Listing 10-9.

Listing 10-9. *The isItemDead() Method (common.js)*

```
function isItemDead(uid){
    var item = game.getItemByUid(uid);
    return (!item || item.lifeCode == "dead");
}
```

We consider an item dead if we can no longer find it in the game.items array or if its lifeCode property is set to dead.

If you run the game so far, you should see the operator giving you your first mission task by asking you to investigate the situation, as shown in Figure 10-1.

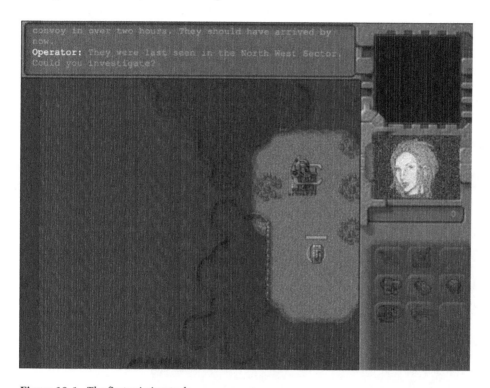

Figure 10-1. *The first mission task*

You should be able to select the tank and move it around, with the fog of war slowly clearing up as you explore the map.

Now, we will introduce the enemy and the convoy by adding a few more triggers to the first map, as shown in Listing 10-10.

Listing 10-10. *Introducing the Enemy and the Convoy (maps.js)*

```
{"type":"conditional",
    "condition":function(){
        // Check if first enemy is dead
```

```
        return isItemDead(-2);
    },
    "action":function(){
        game.showMessage("op", "The rebels have been getting very aggressive lately. I hope the
convoy is safe. Find them and escort them back to the base.");
    }
},
{"type":"conditional",
    "condition":function(){
        var hero = game.getItemByUid(-1);
        return(hero && hero.x<30 && hero.y<30);
    },
    "action":function(){
        game.showMessage("driver", "Can anyone hear us? Our convoy has been pinned down by rebel
tanks. We need help.");
    }
},
```

In the first conditional trigger, we show a message from the operator discussing the rebels once the first enemy scout tank is destroyed. In the second conditional trigger, we show a message from the convoy driver once we enter the top-left corner of the map.

If we run the game now, we should see the operator urging us to hurry after the first fight with the rebels and the convoy driver calling for help when we approach the convoy location, as shown in Figure 10-2.

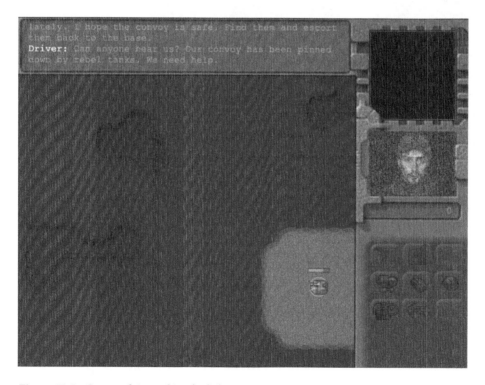

Figure 10-2. *Convoy driver asking for help*

Finally, we will add a few triggers to implement rescuing the convoy and completing the mission, as shown in Listing 10-11.

Listing 10-11. Rescuing the Convoy and Completing the Mission (maps.js)

```
{"type":"conditional",
    "condition":function(){
        var hero = game.getItemByUid(-1);
        return(hero && hero.x<10 && hero.y<10);
    },
    "action":function(){
        var hero = game.getItemByUid(-1);
        game.showMessage("driver", "Thank you. We thought we would never get out of here alive.");
        game.sendCommand([-3,-4],{type:"guard",to:hero});
    }
},
{"type":"conditional",
    "condition":function(){
        var transport1 = game.getItemByUid(-3);
        var transport2 = game.getItemByUid(-4);
        return(transport1 && transport2 && transport1.x>52 && transport2.x>52 && transport2.y<18
&& transport1.y<18);
    },
    "action":function(){
        singleplayer.endLevel(true);
    }
},
```

In the first conditional trigger, we show another message from the driver when the hero tank reaches the top-left corner of the map. We then command both the transports to guard the tank, which means they will follow the tank wherever it goes.

In the second conditional trigger, we end the game once both the transports reach the top-right corner of the map where the base is located.

If you run the game now, you should see the convoy driver thanking you for saving the convoy and then following you back to the base, as shown in Figure 10-3.

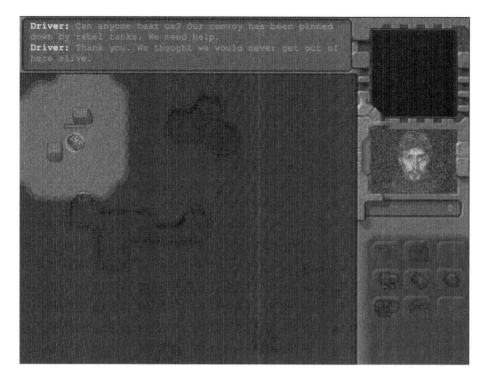

Figure 10-3. *Rescuing the convoy*

The return journey should be uneventful since all the enemies in this level are dead. Once the two transports reach the base, the mission will end. You have just completed your first mission in the single-player campaign.

Now it's time to make the next level, Assault.

Assault

The second level in our game will be a little more challenging than the first one. This time we will introduce the player to the idea of micromanaging units to attack the enemy, without having to worry about managing resources or the production of units.

Players will be provided a steady stream of reinforcements that they will need to use to locate and capture a small enemy base across the map. The enemy base will keep sending out steady waves of attacking units to make the mission more challenging.

We will create a new level object inside the singleplayer array of the map object, as shown in Listing 10-12. This new level will automatically be loaded once the first mission has been completed.

Listing 10-12. Creating the Second Level (maps.js)

```
{
    "name":"Assault",
    "briefing": "Thanks to the supplies from the convoy, we now have the base up and running.\n
The rebels nearby are proving to be a problem. We need to take them out. \n First set up the
base defences. Then find and destroy all rebels in the area.\n The colony will be sending us
reinforcements to help us out.",
```

```
/* Map Details */
"mapImage":"images/maps/level-one.png",
"startX":36,
"startY":0,

/* Map coordinates that are obstructed by terrain*/
"mapGridWidth":60,
"mapGridHeight":40,
"mapObstructedTerrain":[
     [49,8], [50,8], [51,8], [51,9], [52,9], [53,9], [53,10], [53,11], [53,12], [53,13],
[53,14], [53,15], [53,16], [52,16], [52,17], [52,18], [52,19], [51,19], [50,19], [50,18], [50,17],
[49,17], [49,18], [48,18], [47,18], [47,17], [47,16], [48,16], [49,16], [49,15], [49,14], [48,14],
[48,13], [48,12], [49,12], [49,11], [50,11], [50,10], [49,10], [49,9], [44,0], [45,0], [45,1],
[45,2], [46,2], [47,2], [47,3], [48,3], [48,4], [48,5], [49,5], [49,6], [49,7], [50,7], [51,7],
[51,6], [51,5], [51,4], [52,4], [53,4], [53,3], [54,3], [55,3], [55,2], [56,2], [56,1], [56,0],
[55,0], [43,19], [44,19], [45,19], [46,19], [47,19], [48,19], [48,20], [48,21], [47,21], [46,21],
[45,21], [44,21], [43,21], [43,20], [41,22], [42,22], [43,22], [44,22], [45,22], [46,22], [47,22],
[48,22], [49,22], [50,22], [50,23], [50,24], [49,24], [48,24], [47,24], [47,25], [47,26], [47,27],
[47,28], [47,29], [47,30], [46,30], [45,30], [44,30], [43,30], [43,29], [43,28], [43,27], [43,26],
[43,25], [43,24], [42,24], [41,24], [41,23], [48,39], [49,39], [50,39], [51,39], [52,39], [53,39],
[54,39], [55,39], [56,39], [57,39], [58,39], [59,39], [59,38], [59,37], [59,36], [59,35], [59,34],
[59,33], [59,32], [59,31], [59,30], [59,29], [0,0], [1,0], [2,0], [1,1], [2,1], [10,3], [11,3],
[12,3], [12,2], [13,2], [14,2], [14,3], [14,4], [15,4], [15,5], [15,6], [14,6], [13,6], [13,5],
[12,5], [11,5], [10,5], [10,4], [3,9], [4,9], [5,9], [5,10], [6,10], [7,10], [8,10], [9,10], [9,11],
[10,11], [11,11], [11,10], [12,10], [13,10], [13,11], [13,12], [12,12], [11,12], [10,12], [9,12],
[8,12], [7,12], [7,13], [7,14], [6,14], [5,14], [5,13], [5,12], [5,11], [4,11], [3,11], [3,10],
[33,33], [34,33], [35,33], [35,34], [35,35], [34,35], [33,35], [33,34], [27,39], [27,38], [27,37],
[28,37], [28,36], [28,35], [28,34], [28,33], [28,32], [28,31], [28,30], [28,29], [29,29], [29,28],
[29,27], [29,26], [29,25], [29,24], [29,23], [30,23], [31,23], [32,23], [32,22], [32,21], [31,21],
[30,21], [30,22], [29,22], [28,22], [27,22], [26,22], [26,21], [25,21], [24,21], [24,22], [24,23],
[25,23], [26,23], [26,24], [25,24], [25,25], [24,25], [24,26], [24,27], [25,27], [25,28], [25,29],
[24,29], [23,29], [23,30], [23,31], [24,31], [25,31], [25,32], [25,33], [24,33], [23,33], [23,34],
[23,35], [24,35], [24,36], [24,37], [23,37], [22,37], [22,38], [22,39], [23,39], [24,39], [25,39],
[26,0], [26,1], [25,1], [25,2], [25,3], [26,3], [27,3], [27,2], [28,2], [29,2], [29,3], [30,3],
[31,3], [31,2], [31,1], [32,1], [32,0], [33,0], [32,8], [33,8], [34,8], [34,9], [34,10], [33,10],
[32,10], [32,9], [8,29], [9,29], [9,30], [17,32], [18,32], [19,32], [19,33], [18,33], [17,33],
[18,34], [19,34], [3,27], [4,27], [4,26], [3,26], [2,26], [3,25], [4,25], [9,20], [10,20], [11,20],
[11,21], [10,21], [10,19], [19,7], [15,7], [29,12], [30,13], [20,14], [21,14], [34,13], [35,13],
[36,13], [36,14], [35,14], [34,14], [35,15], [36,15], [16,18], [17,18], [18,18], [16,19], [17,19],
[18,19], [17,20], [18,20], [11,19], [58,0], [59,0], [58,1], [59,1], [59,2], [58,3], [59,3], [58,4],
[59,4], [59,5], [58,6], [59,6], [58,7], [59,7], [59,8], [58,9], [59,9], [58,10], [59,10], [59,11],
[52,6], [53,6], [54,6], [52,7], [53,7], [54,7], [53,8], [54,8], [44,17], [46,32], [55,32], [54,28],
[26,34], [34,34], [4,10], [6,11], [6,12], [6,13], [7,11], [8,11], [12,11], [27,0], [27,1], [26,2],
[28,1], [28,0], [29,0], [29,1], [30,2], [30,1], [30,0], [31,0], [33,9], [46,0], [47,0], [48,0],
[49,0], [50,0], [51,0], [52,0], [53,0], [54,0], [55,1], [54,1], [53,1], [52,1], [51,1], [50,1],
[49,1], [48,1], [47,1], [46,1], [48,2], [49,2], [50,2], [51,2], [52,2], [53,2], [54,2], [52,3],
[51,3], [50,3], [49,3], [49,4], [50,4], [50,5], [50,6], [50,9], [51,10], [52,10], [51,11], [52,11],
[50,12], [51,12], [52,12], [49,13], [50,13], [51,13], [52,13], [50,14], [51,14], [52,14], [50,15],
[51,15], [52,15], [50,16], [51,16], [51,17], [48,17], [51,18], [44,20], [45,20], [46,20], [47,20],
[42,23], [43,23], [44,23], [45,23], [46,23], [47,23], [48,23], [49,23], [44,24], [45,24], [46,24],
[44,25], [45,25], [46,25], [44,26], [45,26], [46,26], [44,27], [45,27], [46,27], [44,28], [45,28],
```

```
[46,28], [44,29], [45,29], [46,29], [11,4], [12,4], [13,4], [13,3], [14,5], [25,22], [31,22],
[27,23], [28,23], [27,24], [28,24], [26,25], [27,25], [28,25], [25,26], [26,26], [27,26], [28,26],
[26,27], [27,27], [28,27], [26,28], [27,28], [28,28], [26,29], [27,29], [24,30], [25,30], [26,30],
[27,30], [26,31], [27,31], [26,32], [27,32], [26,33], [27,33], [24,34], [25,34], [27,34], [25,35],
[26,35], [27,35], [25,36], [26,36], [27,36], [25,37], [26,37], [23,38], [24,38], [25,38], [26,38],
[26,39], [2,25], [9,19], [36,31]
    ],

    /* Entities to be loaded */
    "requirements":{
        "buildings":["base","ground-turret","starport","harvester"],
        "vehicles":["transport","scout-tank","heavy-tank"],
        "aircraft":["chopper"],
        "terrain":[]
    },

    /* Economy Related*/
    "cash":{
        "blue":0,
        "green":0
    },

    /* Entities to be added */
    "items":[
        {"type":"buildings","name":"base","x":55,"y":6,"team":"blue","uid":-1},
        {"type":"buildings","name":"ground-turret","x":53,"y":17,"team":"blue"},
        {"type":"vehicles","name":"heavy-tank","x":55,"y":16,"direction":4,"team":"blue",
"uid":-2,"orders":{"type":"sentry"}},

        /* The first wave of attacks*/
        {"type":"vehicles","name":"scout-tank","x":55,"y":36,"direction":4,"team":"green","orders":
{"type":"hunt"}},
        {"type":"vehicles","name":"scout-tank","x":53,"y":36,"direction":4,"team":"green","orders":
{"type":"hunt"}},

        /* Enemies patroling the area */
        {"type":"vehicles","name":"scout-tank","x":5,"y":5,"direction":4,"team":"green","orders":
{"type":"patrol","from":{"x":5,"y":5},"to":{"x":20,"y":20}}},
        {"type":"vehicles","name":"scout-tank","x":5,"y":15,"direction":4,"team":"green","orders":
{"type":"patrol","from":{"x":5,"y":15},"to":{"x":20,"y":30}}},
        {"type":"vehicles","name":"scout-tank","x":25,"y":5,"direction":4,"team":"green","orders":
{"type":"patrol","from":{"x":25,"y":5},"to":{"x":25,"y":20}}},
        {"type":"vehicles","name":"scout-tank","x":35,"y":5,"direction":4,"team":"green","orders":
{"type":"patrol","from":{"x":35,"y":5},"to":{"x":35,"y":30}}},

        /* The Evil Rebel Base*/
        {"type":"buildings","name":"base","x":5,"y":36,"team":"green","uid":-11},
        {"type":"buildings","name":"starport","x":1,"y":30,"team":"green","uid":-12},
        {"type":"buildings","name":"starport","x":4,"y":32,"team":"green","uid":-13},
        {"type":"buildings","name":"harvester","x":1,"y":38,"team":"green","action":"deploy"},
        {"type":"buildings","name":"ground-turret","x":5,"y":28, "team":"green"},
```

```
            {"type":"buildings","name":"ground-turret","x":7,"y":33, "team":"green"},
            {"type":"buildings","name":"ground-turret","x":8,"y":37, "team":"green"},
        ],

    /* Conditional and Timed Trigger Events */
    "triggers":[
        {"type":"timed","time":8000,
            "action":function(){
                // Send in reinforcements to defend the base from the first wave
                game.showMessage("op", "Commander!! Reinforcements have arrived from the colony.");
                var hero = game.getItemByUid(-2);
                game.add ({"type":"vehicles","name":"scout-tank","x":61,"y":22, "team":"blue",
"orders":{"type":"guard","to":hero}});
                game.add ({"type":"vehicles","name":"scout-tank","x":61,"y":21, "team":"blue",
"orders":{"type":"guard","to":hero}});
                }
        },
        {"type":"timed","time":25000,
            "action":function(){
                // Supply extra cash
                game.cash["blue"] = 1500;
                game.showMessage("op", "Commander!! We have enough resources for another ground
turret. Set up the turret to keep the base safe from any more attacks.");
                }
        },
    ]
},
```

The first portion of the level has nearly the same metadata as the previous level. We are reusing the map from level 1. The only thing that changes is the mission briefing.

Next, we load all the essential items in the requirements array, and set the starting cash balance for both players to 0.

This time, we add a lot more items in the level's items array. We start with the base, a heavy tank that the player will control, and a ground turret to protect the base.

Next, we add two enemy scout tanks that are set to hunt mode so they will attack our base as soon as the game starts. We then add several more scout tanks that are set to patrol all around the map.

Finally, we add an enemy base that has two starports and a refinery. It is also well defended with several ground turrets and scout tanks patrolling nearby.

The triggers array contains two timed triggers that are set off within the first few seconds of the game. Within the first trigger, we add two friendly scout tanks to the game and notify the player that reinforcements have arrived.

In the second trigger, we give players 1,500 credits and tell them they have enough resources to build one ground turret. Placing this turret will be the only sidebar-related task players will perform in this game.

If you run the game, you will find that the second level starts in a much more exciting way than the first level. You will see that the base is under attack within the first few seconds and reinforcements arrive in the nick of time to save you, as shown in Figure 10-4.

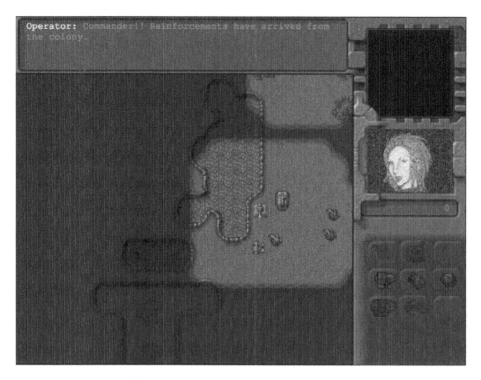

Figure 10-4. *Saved by reinforcements*

Once the attack has been stopped, the operator will notify you that you have enough resources to build one more turret.

Now we will add a few more triggers to add waves of attacking units and reinforcements, as shown in Listing 10-13.

Listing 10-13. Adding Enemy Waves and Reinforcements (maps.js)

```
// Construct a couple of bad guys to hunt the player every time enemy has enough money
{"type":"timed","time":60000,"repeat":true,
    "action":function(){
        if(game.cash["green"]>1000){
            game.sendCommand([-12,-13],{type:"construct-unit", details:{type:"vehicles",
name:"scout-tank", oders:{"type":"hunt"}}});
        }
    }
},
// Send in some reinforcements every three minutes
{"type":"timed","time":180000,"repeat":true,
    "action":function(){
        game.showMessage("op", "Commander!! More Reinforcments have arrived.");
        game.add ({"type":"vehicles","name":"scout-tank","x":61,"y":22, "team":"blue","orders":
{"type":"move","to":{"x":55,"y":21}}});
        game.add ({"type":"vehicles","name":"heavy-tank","x":61,"y":23, "team":"blue","orders":
{"type":"move","to":{"x":56,"y":23}}});
    }
},
```

In the first timed trigger, we check whether the green player has enough money every 60 seconds, and if the green player does, we construct a couple of scout tanks in hunt mode. In the second timed trigger, we send the hero two reinforcing units every 180 seconds.

Unlike the first level, the enemy has a lot more units and turret defenses. A direct frontal assault on the enemy base will not work because the player is likely to lose all the units. The player also cannot wait too long since the enemy will keep sending out waves of enemies every few minutes.

A player's best strategy will be to make small attacks, chipping away at the opposition and then falling back to the base for reinforcements until ready to make the final attack.

Finally, we will add triggers to provide the player with air support and to complete the mission, as shown in Listing 10-14.

Listing 10-14. Adding Air Support and Completing the Mission(maps.js)

```
// Send in air support after 10 minutes
{"type":"timed","time":600000,
    "action":function(){
        game.showMessage("pilot", "Close Air Support en route. Will try to do what I can.");
        game.add ({"type":"aircraft","name":"chopper","x":61, "y":22,"selectable":false,
"team":"blue", "orders":{"type":"hunt"}});
    }
},
/* Lose if our base gets destroyed  */
{"type":"conditional",
    "condition":function(){
        return isItemDead(-1);
    },
    "action":function(){
        singleplayer.endLevel(false);
    }
},
/* Win if enemy base gets at least half destroyed */
{"type":"conditional",
    "condition":function(){
        var enemyBase = game.getItemByUid(-11);
        return(!enemyBase || (enemyBase.life<=enemyBase.hitPoints/2));
    },
    "action":function(){
        singleplayer.endLevel(true);
    }
},
```

In the first timed trigger, we release a friendly chopper on hunt mode, ten minutes after the game starts. The next two conditional triggers set the conditions for successfully completing or failing the mission.

If we run the game now, we should see the chopper pilot coming in to give us a helping hand after some time, as shown in Figure 10-5.

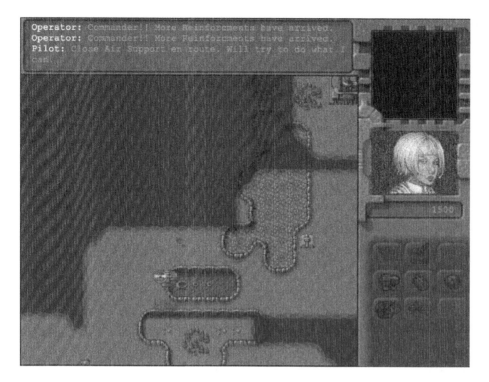

Figure 10-5. *Pilot flying in chopper for air support*

If you have trouble completing the mission, the extra air support should help. Again, we introduce a new character, the pilot, who will stay with us for the next mission. With the assistance of the chopper, we can capture the enemy base and complete the mission so we can go on to the final mission.

Now it's time to build our final mission: Under Siege.

Under Siege

The final level in our game will be the most challenging. The player will need to constantly build units to fight off several waves of enemy units.

This time, the player will take over the enemy base captured after the last mission. The player will be provided some initial supplies to help get started. After that, the player will need to fend off several waves of units and protect the transport vehicles filled with refugees until the colony reinforcements arrive to help them.

We will create a new level object inside the `singleplayer` array of the `map` object, as shown in Listing 10-15. This new level will automatically be loaded once the second mission has been completed.

Listing 10-15. Creating the Third Level (maps.js)

```
{
    "name":"Under Siege",
    "briefing": "Thanks to the attack led by you, we now have control of the rebel base. We can
expect the rebels to try to retaliate.\n The colony is sending in aircraft to help us evacuate back
to the main camp. All we need to do is hang tight until the choppers get here. \n Luckily, we have
```

some supplies and ammunition to defend ourselves with until they get here. \n Protect the transports at all costs.",

```
    /* Map Details */
    "mapImage":"images/maps/level-one.png",
    "startX":0,
    "startY":20,

    /* Map coordinates that are obstructed by terrain*/
    "mapGridWidth":60,
    "mapGridHeight":40,
    "mapObstructedTerrain":[
        [49,8], [50,8], [51,8], [51,9], [52,9], [53,9], [53,10], [53,11], [53,12], [53,13],
[53,14], [53,15], [53,16], [52,16], [52,17], [52,18], [52,19], [51,19], [50,19], [50,18], [50,17],
[49,17], [49,18], [48,18], [47,18], [47,17], [47,16], [48,16], [49,16], [49,15], [49,14], [48,14],
[48,13], [48,12], [49,12], [49,11], [50,11], [50,10], [49,10], [49,9], [44,0], [45,0], [45,1],
[45,2], [46,2], [47,2], [47,3], [48,3], [48,4], [48,5], [49,5], [49,6], [49,7], [50,7], [51,7],
[51,6], [51,5], [51,4], [52,4], [53,4], [53,3], [54,3], [55,3], [55,2], [56,2], [56,1], [56,0],
[55,0], [43,19], [44,19], [45,19], [46,19], [47,19], [48,19], [48,20], [48,21], [47,21], [46,21],
[45,21], [44,21], [43,21], [43,20], [41,22], [42,22], [43,22], [44,22], [45,22], [46,22], [47,22],
[48,22], [49,22], [50,22], [50,23], [50,24], [49,24], [48,24], [47,24], [47,25], [47,26], [47,27],
[47,28], [47,29], [47,30], [46,30], [45,30], [44,30], [43,30], [43,29], [43,28], [43,27], [43,26],
[43,25], [43,24], [42,24], [41,24], [41,23], [48,39], [49,39], [50,39], [51,39], [52,39], [53,39],
[54,39], [55,39], [56,39], [57,39], [58,39], [59,39], [59,38], [59,37], [59,36], [59,35], [59,34],
[59,33], [59,32], [59,31], [59,30], [59,29], [0,0], [1,0], [2,0], [1,1], [2,1], [10,3], [11,3],
[12,3], [12,2], [13,2], [14,2], [14,3], [14,4], [15,4], [15,5], [15,6], [14,6], [13,6], [13,5],
[12,5], [11,5], [10,5], [10,4], [3,9], [4,9], [5,9], [5,10], [6,10], [7,10], [8,10], [9,10], [9,11],
[10,11], [11,11], [11,10], [12,10], [13,10], [13,11], [13,12], [12,12], [11,12], [10,12], [9,12],
[8,12], [7,12], [7,13], [7,14], [6,14], [5,14], [5,13], [5,12], [5,11], [4,11], [3,11], [3,10],
[33,33], [34,33], [35,33], [35,34], [35,35], [34,35], [33,35], [33,34], [27,39], [27,38], [27,37],
[28,37], [28,36], [28,35], [28,34], [28,33], [28,32], [28,31], [28,30], [28,29], [29,29], [29,28],
[29,27], [29,26], [29,25], [29,24], [29,23], [30,23], [31,23], [32,23], [32,22], [32,21], [31,21],
[30,21], [30,22], [29,22], [28,22], [27,22], [26,22], [26,21], [25,21], [24,21], [24,22], [24,23],
[25,23], [26,23], [26,24], [25,24], [25,25], [24,25], [24,26], [24,27], [25,27], [25,28], [25,29],
[24,29], [23,29], [23,30], [23,31], [24,31], [25,31], [25,32], [25,33], [24,33], [23,33], [23,34],
[23,35], [24,35], [24,36], [24,37], [23,37], [22,37], [22,38], [22,39], [23,39], [24,39], [25,39],
[26,0], [26,1], [25,1], [25,2], [25,3], [26,3], [27,3], [27,2], [28,2], [29,2], [29,3], [30,3],
[31,3], [31,2], [31,1], [32,1], [32,0], [33,0], [32,8], [33,8], [34,8], [34,9], [34,10], [33,10],
[32,10], [32,9], [8,29], [9,29], [9,30], [17,32], [18,32], [19,32], [19,33], [18,33], [17,33],
[18,34], [19,34], [3,27], [4,27], [4,26], [3,26], [2,26], [3,25], [4,25], [9,20], [10,20], [11,20],
[11,21], [10,21], [10,19], [19,7], [15,7], [29,12], [30,13], [20,14], [21,14], [34,13], [35,13],
[36,13], [36,14], [35,14], [34,14], [35,15], [36,15], [16,18], [17,18], [18,18], [16,19], [17,19],
[18,19], [17,20], [18,20], [11,19], [58,0], [59,0], [58,1], [59,1], [59,2], [58,3], [59,3], [58,4],
[59,4], [59,5], [58,6], [59,6], [58,7], [59,7], [58,9], [59,9], [58,10], [59,10], [59,11],
[52,6], [53,6], [54,6], [52,7], [53,7], [54,7], [53,8], [54,8], [44,17], [46,32], [55,32], [54,28],
[26,34], [34,34], [4,10], [6,11], [6,12], [6,13], [7,11], [8,11], [12,11], [27,0], [27,1], [26,2],
[28,1], [28,0], [29,0], [29,1], [30,2], [30,1], [30,0], [31,0], [33,9], [46,0], [47,0], [48,0],
[49,0], [50,0], [51,0], [52,0], [53,0], [54,0], [55,1], [54,1], [53,1], [52,1], [51,1], [50,1],
[49,1], [48,1], [47,1], [46,1], [48,2], [49,2], [50,2], [51,2], [52,2], [53,2], [54,2], [52,3],
[51,3], [50,3], [49,3], [49,4], [50,4], [50,5], [50,6], [50,9], [51,10], [52,10], [51,11], [52,11],
[50,12], [51,12], [52,12], [49,13], [50,13], [51,13], [52,13], [50,14], [51,14], [52,14], [50,15],
```

```
[51,15], [52,15], [50,16], [51,16], [51,17], [48,17], [51,18], [44,20], [45,20], [46,20], [47,20],
[42,23], [43,23], [44,23], [45,23], [46,23], [47,23], [48,23], [49,23], [44,24], [45,24], [46,24],
[44,25], [45,25], [46,25], [44,26], [45,26], [46,26], [44,27], [45,27], [46,27], [44,28], [45,28],
[46,28], [44,29], [45,29], [46,29], [11,4], [12,4], [13,4], [13,3], [14,5], [25,22], [31,22],
[27,23], [28,23], [27,24], [28,24], [26,25], [27,25], [28,25], [25,26], [26,26], [27,26], [28,26],
[26,27], [27,27], [28,27], [26,28], [27,28], [28,28], [26,29], [27,29], [24,30], [25,30], [26,30],
[27,30], [26,31], [27,31], [26,32], [27,32], [26,33], [27,33], [24,34], [25,34], [27,34], [25,35],
[26,35], [27,35], [25,36], [26,36], [27,36], [25,37], [26,37], [23,38], [24,38], [25,38], [26,38],
[26,39], [2,25], [9,19], [36,31]
    ],

    /* Entities to be loaded */
    "requirements":{
        "buildings":["base","ground-turret","starport","harvester"],
        "vehicles":["transport","scout-tank","heavy-tank"],
        "aircraft":["chopper","wraith"],
        "terrain":[]
    },

    /* Economy Related*/
    "cash":{
        "blue":0,
        "green":0
    },

    /* Entities to be added */
    "items":[
        /* The Rebel Base now in our hands */
        {"type":"buildings","name":"base","x":5,"y":36,"team":"blue","uid":-11},
        {"type":"buildings","name":"starport","x":1,"y":28,"team":"blue","uid":-12},
        {"type":"buildings","name":"starport","x":4,"y":32,"team":"blue","uid":-13},
        {"type":"buildings","name":"harvester","x":1,"y":38,"team":"blue","action":"deploy"},
        {"type":"buildings","name":"ground-turret","x":7,"y":28,"team":"blue"},
        {"type":"buildings","name":"ground-turret","x":8,"y":32,"team":"blue"},
        {"type":"buildings","name":"ground-turret","x":11,"y":37,"team":"blue"},

        /* The transports that need to be protected*/
        {"type":"vehicles","name":"transport","x":2,"y":33,"team":"blue","direction":2,
"selectable":false, "uid":-1},
        {"type":"vehicles","name":"transport","x":1,"y":34,"team":"blue","direction":2,
"selectable":false,"uid":-2},
        {"type":"vehicles","name":"transport","x":2,"y":35,"team":"blue","direction":2,
"selectable":false,"uid":-3},
        {"type":"vehicles","name":"transport","x":1,"y":36,"team":"blue","direction":2,
"selectable":false,"uid":-4},

        /* The chopper pilot from the last mission */

{"type":"aircraft","name":"chopper","x":15,"y":40,"team":"blue","selectable":false,
"uid":-5,"orders":{"type":"patrol","from":{"x":15,"y":40},"to":{"x":0,"y":25}}},
```

```
        /* The first wave of attacks*/
        {"type":"vehicles","name":"scout-tank","x":15,"y":16,"direction":4,"team":"green",
"orders":{"type":"hunt"}},
        {"type":"vehicles","name":"scout-tank","x":17,"y":16,"direction":4,"team":"green",
"orders":{"type":"hunt"}},

        /* Secret Rebel bases*/

        {"type":"buildings","name":"starport","x":35,"y":37,"team":"green","uid":-23},
        {"type":"buildings","name":"starport","x":33,"y":37,"team":"green","uid":-24},
        {"type":"buildings","name":"harvester","x":28,"y":39,"team":"green","action":"deploy"},
        {"type":"buildings","name":"harvester","x":30,"y":39,"team":"green","action":"deploy"},

        {"type":"buildings","name":"starport","x":3,"y":0,"team":"green","uid":-21},
        {"type":"buildings","name":"starport","x":6,"y":0,"team":"green","uid":-22},
        {"type":"buildings","name":"harvester","x":0,"y":2,"team":"green","action":"deploy"},
        {"type":"buildings","name":"harvester","x":0,"y":4,"team":"green","action":"deploy"},

    ],

    /* Conditional and Timed Trigger Events */
    "triggers":[
        /* Lose if even one transport gets destroyed  */
        {"type":"conditional",
            "condition":function(){
                return isItemDead(-1)||isItemDead(-2)||isItemDead(-3)||isItemDead(-4);
            },
            "action":function(){
                singleplayer.endLevel(false);
            }
        },
        {"type":"timed","time":5000,
            "action":function(){
                game.showMessage("op", "Commander!! The rebels have started attacking. We need to
protect the base at any cost.");
            }
        },
    ],
}
```

Again, we are reusing the map from level 1. The first portion of the level has nearly the same metadata as the previous levels. The only thing that changes is the mission briefing.

Next we load all the essential items in the requirements array and set the starting cash balance for both players to 0.

This time, we add a lot more items to the map. First, we re-create the entire enemy base, but for the player team. Next, we add several transport vehicles that we will be protecting in this mission and add the chopper from the last mission on patrol mode to protect the base. Next, we add a few enemy units for a first wave of attacks. Finally, we define several starports and refineries for two secret enemy bases that will be attacking the player.

Within the triggers, we define one conditional trigger that ends the mission in case even one of the transports dies. The second timed trigger just displays a message from the operator.

If we run the game and start the third level, we should see the rebels attacking the base and the patrolling chopper fending them off, as shown in Figure 10-6.

Figure 10-6. *Patrolling chopper defending the base*

Now that the first wave of attacks has been fended off, we will build a little drama with a small cinematic story line within the mission by adding a few creative triggers to the map, as shown in Listing 10-16.

Listing 10-16. Adding a Little Drama to the Level (maps.js)

```
{"type":"timed","time":20000,
    "action":function(){
        game.add({"type":"vehicles","name":"transport","x":57,"y":3,"team":"blue","direction":4,
"selectable":false,"uid":-6});
        game.sendCommand([-5],{"type":"guard","toUid":-6})
        game.showMessage("driver", "Commander!! The colony has sent some extra supplies. We are
coming in from the North East sector through rebel territory. We could use a little protection.");
    }
},
//Have the pilot offer to assist and get some villains in to make it interesting
{"type":"timed","time":28000,
    "action":function(){
        game.showMessage("pilot", "I'm on my way.");
        game.add({"type":"vehicles","name":"scout-tank","x":57,"y":28,"team":"green","orders":
{"type":"hunt"}});
        game.add({"type":"aircraft","name":"wraith","x":55,"y":33,"team":"green",
"orders":{"type":"sentry"}});
        game.add({"type":"aircraft","name":"wraith","x":53,"y":33,"team":"green",
"orders":{"type":"sentry"}});
```

```
                game.add({"type":"vehicles","name":"scout-tank","x":35,"y":25,"life":20,"direction":4,"team"
    :"green", "orders":{"type":"patrol","from":{"x":35,"y":25},"to":{"x":35,"y":30}}}});
        }
    },
    // Start moving the transport,
    {"type":"timed","time":48000,
        "action":function(){
            game.showMessage("driver", "Thanks! Appreciate the backup. All right. Off we go.");
            game.sendCommand([-6],{"type":"move","to":{"x":0,"y":39,}});
        }
    },
    // Pilot asks for help when attacked
    {"type":"conditional",
        "condition":function(){
            var pilot = game.getItemByUid(-5);
            return pilot.life<pilot.hitPoints;
        },
        "action":function(){
            game.showMessage("pilot", "We are under attack! Need assistance. This doesn't look good.");
        }
    },
    // Extra supplies from new transport
    {"type":"conditional",
        "condition":function(){
            var driver = game.getItemByUid(-6);
            return driver && driver.x < 2 && driver.y>37;
        },
        "action":function(){
            game.showMessage("driver", "The rebels came out of nowhere. There was nothing we could do.
    She saved our lives. Hope these supplies were worth it.");
            game.cash["blue"] += 1200;
        }
    },
```

In the first timed trigger, the driver from the first mission asks for assistance while standing at the top-right corner of the map. We then command the pilot to guard the transport.

In the second timed trigger, the pilot announces she is on her way. We also add several enemy units to the map.

In the third timed trigger, which will be set off around the time the pilot arrives at the transport's location, we command the transport to start moving toward the base.

In the fourth conditional trigger—which is set off if the pilot's chopper gets attacked—the pilot messages asking for help.

In the final conditional trigger, which is set off if the transport reaches its destination, the driver talks about his experience, and the player's cash resources are increased.

If you run the game now, you should see a fairly interesting scene play out. You will see the pilot going out to help the driver when he calls for help. The pilot then protects the transport before getting ambushed by several enemy aircraft.

The transport continues to drive toward the base while under enemy fire. Once the driver reaches the base, the driver provides the player with some supplies and describes the experience, as shown in Figure 10-7.

Figure 10-7. *Driver describes the ordeal after getting back*

At the end of the whole experience, the player now has some extra cash to start building units.

Even though the story in our game is a little rushed, as you can see, this trigger mechanism can be used to tell a fairly interesting story. Obviously, the game framework can be extended to use a combination of video, audio, or animated GIFs to make the experience even more immersive.

Now let's add a trigger to set up the waves of enemy units, as shown in Listing 10-17.

Listing 10-17. Adding Enemy Waves (maps.js)

```
// Send in waves of enemies every 150 seconds
{"type":"timed","time":150000,"repeat":true,
    "action":function(){
        // Count aircraft and tanks already available to bad guys
        var wraithCount = 0;
        var chopperCount = 0;
        var scoutTankCount = 0;
        var heavyTankCount = 0;
        for (var i = game.items.length - 1; i >= 0; i--){
            var item = game.items[i];
            if(item.team=="green"){
                switch(item.name){
                    case "chopper":
                        chopperCount++;
                        break;
                    case "wraith":
```

```
                    wraithCount++;
                    break;
                case "scout-tank":
                    scoutTankCount++;
                    break;
                case "heavy-tank":
                    heavyTankCount++;
                    break;
            }
        }
    };

    // Make sure enemy has atleast two wraiths and two heavy tanks, and use the remaining
starports to build choppers and scouts
    if(wraithCount==0){
        // No wraiths alive. Ask both starports to make wraiths
        game.sendCommand([-23,-24],{type:"construct-unit",details:{type:"aircraft",name:
"wraith","orders":{"type":"hunt"}}});
    } else if (wraithCount==1){
        // One wraith alive. Ask starports to make one wraith and one chopper
        game.sendCommand([-23],{type:"construct-unit",details:{type:"aircraft",name:"wraith",
"orders":{"type":"hunt"}}});
        game.sendCommand([-24],{type:"construct-unit",details:{type:"aircraft",name:"chopper",
"orders":{"type":"hunt"}}});
    } else {
        // Two wraiths alive. Ask both starports to make choppers
        game.sendCommand([-23,-24],{type:"construct-unit",details:{type:"aircraft",name:
"chopper","orders":{"type":"hunt"}}});
    }

    if(heavyTankCount==0){
        // No heavy-tanks alive. Ask both starports to make heavy-tanks
        game.sendCommand([-21,-22],{type:"construct-unit",details:{type:"vehicles",name:
"heavy-tank","orders":{"type":"hunt"}}});
    } else if (heavyTankCount==1){
        // One heavy-tank alive. Ask starports to make one heavy-tank and one scout-tank
        game.sendCommand([-21],{type:"construct-unit",details:{type:"vehicles",name:
"heavy-tank","orders":{"type":"hunt"}}});
        game.sendCommand([-22],{type:"construct-unit",details:{type:"vehicles",name:
"scout-tank","orders":{"type":"hunt"}}});
    } else {
        // Two heavy-tanks alive. Ask both starports to make scout-tanks
        game.sendCommand([-21,-22],{type:"construct-unit",details:{type:"vehicles",name:
"scout-tank","orders":{"type":"hunt"}}});
    }
    // Ask any units on the field to attack
    var uids = [];
    for (var i=0; i < game.items.length; i++) {
        var item = game.items[i];
```

```
            if(item.team == "green" && item.canAttack){
                uids.push(item.uid);
            }
        };
        game.sendCommand(uids,{"type":"hunt"});
    }
},
```

Unlike the previous level, the enemy waves trigger is a little more intelligent. The timed trigger runs every 150 seconds. It first counts the number of enemy units of each type. It then decides which units to build based on what units are available. In this simple example, we first make sure that the green team has at least two wraiths to control the sky and two heavy tanks to control the ground, and if not, we build them at the starports. We build choppers and scout tanks on any remaining starports. Finally, we command all green team units that can attack to go on hunt mode.

If you run the game now, the enemy will send out waves every few minutes. This time, the composition of the enemy units will vary with each attack. If you don't plan your defense properly, you can expect to get overwhelmed by the enemy.

Obviously, this AI can be improved further by tweaking the enemy composition based on the player's composition or selecting the targets to attack intelligently. However, as you can see, even this simple set of instructions provides us with a fairly challenging enemy.

Now that we have a challenging enemy in the level, we will implement triggers for ending the mission, as shown in Listing 10-18.

Listing 10-18. Implementing the Ending (maps.js)

```
//After 8 minutes, start waiting for the end
{"type":"timed","time":480000,
    "action":function(){
        game.showMessage("op", "Commander! The colony air fleet is just a few minutes away.");
    }
},
//After 10 minutes send in reinforcements
{"type":"timed","time":600000,
    "action":function(){
        game.showMessage("op", "Commander! The colony air fleet is approaching");
        game.add({"type":"aircraft","name":"wraith","x":-1,"y":30, "team":"blue","orders":
{"type":"hunt"}});
        game.add({"type":"aircraft","name":"chopper","x":-1,"y":31, "team":"blue","orders":
{"type":"hunt"}});
        game.add({"type":"aircraft","name":"wraith","x":-1,"y":32, "team":"blue","orders":
{"type":"hunt"}});
        game.add({"type":"aircraft","name":"chopper","x":-1,"y":33, "team":"blue","orders":
{"type":"hunt"}});
        game.add({"type":"aircraft","name":"wraith","x":-1,"y":34, "team":"blue","orders":
{"type":"hunt"}});
        game.add({"type":"aircraft","name":"chopper","x":-1,"y":35, "team":"blue","orders":
{"type":"hunt"}});
        game.add({"type":"aircraft","name":"wraith","x":-1,"y":36, "team":"blue","orders":
{"type":"hunt"}});
        game.add({"type":"aircraft","name":"chopper","x":-1,"y":37, "team":"blue","orders":
{"type":"hunt"}});
```

```
        game.add({"type":"aircraft","name":"wraith","x":-1,"y":38, "team":"blue","orders":
{"type":"hunt"}});
        game.add({"type":"aircraft","name":"chopper","x":-1,"y":39, "team":"blue","orders":
{"type":"hunt"}});
    }
},
// And a minute after, end the level
{"type":"timed","time":660000,
    "action":function(){
        singleplayer.endLevel(true);

    }
},
```

The first trigger, eight minutes into the game, is the operator announcing that the colony air fleet has almost arrived. In the second trigger, two minutes later, we add an entire fleet of friendly aircraft in hunt mode. Finally, one minute after the fleet arrival we end the level.

Obviously, the only goal of this mission is to survive and protect the transport until the fleet arrives. If you play the mission now and survive that long, you should see the large fleet flying in and destroying the enemy, as shown in Figure 10-8.

Figure 10-8. *The colony air fleet flying in to save the day*

Once the fleet flies in, we have an extra minute to enjoy watching them attack and destroy the enemy before completing the last level in our single-player campaign.

Summary

In this chapter, we finally completed the entire single-player campaign of our RTS game. We started by adding sound to the game. We then used the framework that we built over the past few chapters to develop several levels for the campaign. We looked at ways to make the levels challenging and interesting by creatively using triggered events. We also learned how to weave a complete story into the game.

At this point, you have a complete, working, single-player RTS game that you can either extend or use for your own ideas. A good way to go forward from here is to try developing your own interesting levels for this campaign.

After that, if you are ready for something more challenging, you should try building your own game. You can use this code to prototype new game ideas fairly quickly by just modifying the artwork and adjusting the settings. If the feedback on your prototype is encouraging, you can then invest more time and effort to build a complete game.

Of course, while playing against the computer is fun, it can be a lot more fun challenging your friends. In the next two chapters, we will look at the HTML5 WebSocket API and how we can use it to build a multiplayer game so you can play against your friends over the network. So, once you have spent some time enjoying the single-player game, proceed on to the next chapter so that we can get started with multiplayer.

CHAPTER 11

Multiplayer with WebSockets

No matter how challenging we make a single-player game, it will always lack the challenge of competing against another human being. Multiplayer games allow players to either compete against each other or work cooperatively toward a common goal.

Now that we have a working single-player campaign, we will look at how we can add multiplayer support to our RTS game by using the HTML5 WebSocket API.

Before we start adding multiplayer to our game, let's first take a look at some networking basics using the WebSocket API with Node.js.

Using the WebSocket API with Node.js

The heart of our multiplayer game is the new HTML5 WebSocket API. Before WebSockets came along, the only way browsers could interact with a server was by polling and long-polling the server with a steady stream of requests. These methods, while they worked, had a very high network latency as well as high-bandwidth usage, making them unsuitable for real-time multiplayer games.

All of this changed with the arrival of the WebSocket API. The API defines a bidirectional, full-duplex communications channel over a single TCP socket, providing us with an efficient, low-latency connection between browser and server.

In simple terms, we can now create a single, persistent connection between a browser and server and send data back and forth much faster than before. You can read more about the benefits of WebSockets at www.websocket.org/. Let's take a look at a simple example of communication between the browser and the server using WebSockets.

WebSockets on the Browser

Using WebSockets to communicate with a server involves the following steps:

1. Instantiating a WebSocket object by providing the server URL

2. Implementing the onopen, onclose, and onerror event handlers as needed

3. Implementing the onmessage event handler to handle actions when a message is received from the server

4. Sending messages to the server by using the send() method

5. Closing the connection to the server by using the close() method

We can create a simple WebSocket client in a new HTML file, as shown in Listing 11-1. We will place this new file inside the websocketdemo folder to keep it separate from our game code.

Listing 11-1. A Simple WebSocket Client (websocketclient.html)

```
<!DOCTYPE html>
<html>
    <head>
        <meta http-equiv="Content-type" content="text/html; charset=utf-8">
        <title>WebSocket Client</title>
        <script type="text/javascript" charset="utf-8">

            var websocket;
            var serverUrl = "ws://localhost:8080/";

            function displayMessage(message){
                document.getElementById("displaydiv").innerHTML += message +"<br>";
            }

            // Initialize the WebSocket object and setup Event Handlers
            function initWebSocket(){
                // Check if browser has an implementation of WebSocket (older Mozilla browsers
used MozWebSocket)
                var WebSocketObject = window.WebSocket || window.MozWebSocket;
                if(WebSocketObject){
                    // Create the WebSocket object
                    websocket = new WebSocketObject(serverUrl);

                    // Setup the event handlers
                    websocket.onopen = function(){
                        displayMessage("WebSocket Connection Opened");
                        document.getElementById("sendmessage").disabled = false;
                    };

                    websocket.onclose = function(){
                        displayMessage("WebSocket Connection Closed");
                        document.getElementById("sendmessage").disabled = true;
                    };

                    websocket.onerror = function(){
                        displayMessage("Connection Error Occured");
                    };

                    websocket.onmessage = function(message){
                        displayMessage("Received Message: <i>"+message.data+"</i>");
                    };

                } else {
                    displayMessage("Your Browser does not support WebSockets");
                }
            }
```

```
            // Send a message to the server using the WebSocket
            function sendMessage(){
                // readyState can be CONNECTING,OPEN,CLOSING,CLOSED
                if (websocket.readyState = websocket.OPEN){
                    var message = document.getElementById("message").value;
                    displayMessage("Sending Message: <i>"+message+"</i>");
                    websocket.send(message);
                } else {
                    displayMessage("Cannot send message. The WebSocket connection isn't open");
                }
            }


        </script>
    </head>
    <body onload="initWebSocket();">
        <label for="message">Message</label><input type="text" value="Simple Message" size="40"
id="message">
        <input type="button" value="Send" id="sendmessage" onclick="sendMessage()" disabled="true">
        <div id="displaydiv" style="border:1px solid black;width:600px; height:400px;
font-size:14px;"></div>
    </body>
</html>
```

The body tag of the HTML file contains a few basic elements: an input box for a message, a button for sending messages, and a div to display all messages.

Within the script tag, we start by declaring a server URL that points to the WebSocket server using the WebSocket protocol (ws://).

We then declare a simple displayMessage() method that appends a given message to the displaydiv div element.

Next we declare the initWebSocket() method that initializes the WebSocket connection and sets up the event handlers.

Within this method, we first check for the existence of the WebSocket or MozWebSocket object to verify that the browser supports WebSockets and save it to WebSocketObject. This is because older versions of the Mozilla browser named their implementation MozWebSocket before shifting to WebSocket.

We then initialize the WebSocket object by calling the constructor of WebSocketObject and saving it to the websocket variable.

Finally, we define handlers for the onopen, onclose, onerror, and onmessage event handlers, where we display appropriate messages to the user. We also enable the sendmessage button when the connection is opened and disable it when the connection is closed.

In the sendMessage() method, we check that connection is open using the readyState property and then use the send() method to send the contents of the message input box to the server.

Our browser client needs a server that it can commmunicate with using the WebSocket protocol. There are already several WebSocket server implementations available for most popular languages such as jWebSocket (http://jwebsocket.org/) and Jetty (http://jetty.codehaus.org/jetty/) for Java, Socket.io (http://github.com/LearnBoost/Socket.IO-node) and WebSocket-Node (https://github.com/Worlize/WebSocket-Node) for Node.js, and WebSocket++ (https://github.com/zaphoyd/websocketpp) for C++.

In this book, we will be using WebSocket-Node for Node.js. We will start by setting up Node.js and creating an HTTP server and then add WebSocket support to it.

Creating an HTTP Server in Node.js

Node.js (http://nodejs.org/) is a server-side platform consisting of several libraries built on top of Google's JavaScript V8 engine. Originally created by Ryan Dahl starting in 2009, Node.js was designed for easily building fast, scalable network applications. Programs are written in JavaScript using an event-driven, nonblocking I/O model that is lightweight and efficient. Node.js has gained a lot of popularity in a relatively short time and is used by a large number of companies, including LinkedIn, Microsoft, and Yahoo.

Before you can start writing Node.js code, you will need to install Node.js on your computer. Implementations of Node.js are available for most operating systems, such as Windows, Mac OS X, Linux, and SunOS, and detailed instructions for setting up Node.js on your specific operating system are available at https://github.com/joyent/node/wiki/Installation. For Windows and Mac OS X, the simplest installation method is to run the ready-made installer files downloadable at http://nodejs.org/download/.

Once Node.js has been set up correctly, you will be able to run Node.js programs from the command line by calling the node executable and passing the program name as a parameter.

After setting up Node.js, we can create a simple HTTP web server inside a new JavaScript file, as shown in Listing 11-2. We will place this file inside the websocketdemo folder.

Listing 11-2. A Simple HTTP Web Server in Node.js (websocketserver.js)

```
// Create an HTTP Server
var http = require('http');

// Create a simple web server that returns the same response for any request
var server = http.createServer(function(request,response){
    console.log('Received HTTP request for url ', request.url);
    response.writeHead(200, {'Content-Type': 'text/plain'});
    response.end("This is a simple node.js HTTP server.");
});

// Listen on port 8080
server.listen(8080,function(){
    console.log('Server has started listening on port 8080');
});
```

The code for building a simple web server in Node.js is surprisingly small using the Node.js HTTP library. You can find detailed documentation on this library at http://nodejs.org/api/http.html.

We first refer to the HTTP library using the require() method and save it to the http variable. We then create an HTTP server by calling the createServer() method and passing it a method that will handle all HTTP requests. In our case, we send back the same text response for any HTTP request to the server. Finally, we tell the server to start listening on port 8080.

If you run the code in websocketserver.js from the command line and try to access the web server's URL (http://localhost:8080) from the browser, you should see the output shown in Figure 11-1.

Figure 11-1. *A simple HTTP server in Node.js*

We have our HTTP server up and running. This server will return the same page no matter what path we pass after the server name in the URL. This server also does not yet support WebSockets.

Next, we will add WebSocket support to this server by using the WebSocket-Node package.

Creating a WebSocket Server

The first thing you will need to do is install the WebSocket-Node package using the `npm` command. Detailed instructions for installation along with sample code is available at `https://github.com/Worlize/WebSocket-Node`.

If Node.js is set up correctly, you should be able to set up WebSocket by running the following command from the command line:

`npm install websocket`

■ **Tip**   In case you have previously installed Node.JS and WebSocket-Node, you should ensure that you are using the latest version by running the `npm update` command.

Once the WebSocket package has been installed, we will add WebSocket support by modifying `websocketserver.js`, as shown in Listing 11-3.

Listing 11-3. Implementing a Simple WebSocket Server (websocketserver.js)

```
// Create an HTTP Server
var http = require('http');

// Create a simple web server that returns the same response for any request
var server = http.createServer(function(request,response){
  console.log('Received HTTP request for url', request.url);
```

```javascript
  response.writeHead(200, {'Content-Type': 'text/plain'});
  response.end("This is a simple node.js HTTP server.");
});

// Listen on port 8080
server.listen(8080,function(){
  console.log('Server has started listening on port 8080');
});

// Attach WebSocket Server to HTTP Server
var WebSocketServer = require('websocket').server;
var wsServer = new WebSocketServer({
  httpServer:server
});

// Logic to determine whether a specified connection is allowed.
function connectionIsAllowed(request){
  // Check criteria such as request.origin, request.remoteAddress
  return true;
}

// Handle WebSocket Connection Requests
wsServer.on('request',function(request){
  // Reject requests based on certain criteria
  if(!connectionIsAllowed(request)){
     request.reject();
     console.log('WebSocket Connection from' + request.remoteAddress + 'rejected.');
     return;
  }
  // Accept Connection
  var websocket = request.accept();
  console.log('WebSocket Connection from' + request.remoteAddress + 'accepted.');
  websocket.send ('Hi there. You are now connected to the WebSocket Server');

  websocket.on('message', function(message) {
   if (message.type === 'utf8') {
      console.log('Received Message:' + message.utf8Data);
      websocket.send('Server received your message:'+ message.utf8Data);
   }
});

    websocket.on('close', function(reasonCode, description) {
     console.log('WebSocket Connection from' + request.remoteAddress + 'closed.');
    });
});
```

The first part of the code where we create the HTTP server remains the same. In the newly added code, we start by using the require() method to save a reference to the WebSocket server. We then create a new WebSocketServer object by passing the HTTP server that we created earlier as a configuration option. You can read about the different WebSocketServer configuration options as well as details on the WebSocketServer API at https://github.com/Worlize/WebSocket-Node/wiki/Documentation.

Next we implement the handler for the request event of the server. We first check whether the connection request should be rejected and, if so, call the `reject()` method of the request.

We use a method called `connectionIsAllowed()` to filter connections that need to be rejected. Right now we approve all connections; however, this method can use information such as the connection request's IP address and origin to intelligently filter requests.

If the connection is allowed, we accept the request using the `accept()` method and save the resulting WebSocket connection to the `websocket` variable. This `websocket` variable is the server-side equivalent of the `websocket` variable that we created in the client HTML file earlier.

Once we create the connection, we use the `websocket` object's `send()` method to send the client a welcome message notifying it that the connection has been made.

Next we implement the handler for the `message` event of the `websocket` object. Every time a message arrives, we send back a message to the client saying the server just received the message and then log the message to the console.

■ **Note** The WebSocket API allows for multiple message data types such as UTF8 text, binary, and blob data. Unlike on the browser, the `message` object on the server side stores the message data using different properties (such as `utf8Data`, `binaryData`) based on the data type.

Finally, we implement the handler for the `close` event, where we just log the fact that the connection was closed.

If you run the `websocketserver.js` code from the command line and open `websocketclient.html` in the browser, you should see the interaction between the client and the server, as shown in Figure 11-2.

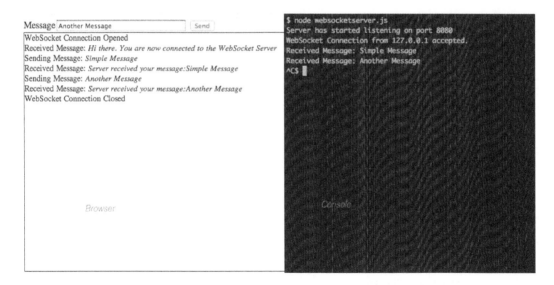

Figure 11-2. *Interaction between client and server*

As soon as the WebSocket connection is established, the browser receives a welcome message from the server. The Send button also gets enabled on the client. If you type a message and click Send, the server displays the message in the console and sends back a response to the client. Finally, if you shut down the server, the client displays a message that the connection has been closed.

We now have a working example of transmitting plain-text messages back and forth between the client and the server.

■ **Note**   It is possible to reduce the message size and optimize bandwidth usage by using binary data instead of plain text. However, we will continue to use UTF8 text even in our game implementation to keep the code simple.

Now that we have looked at the basics of WebSocket communication, it is time to add multiplayer to our game. We will continue from where we left off at the end of Chapter 10.

The first thing we will build is a multiplayer game lobby.

Building the Multiplayer Game Lobby

Our game lobby will display a list of game rooms. Players can join or leave these rooms from the game lobby screen. Once two players join a room, the multiplayer game will start, and the two players can compete with each other.

Defining the Multiplayer Lobby Screen

We will start by adding the HTML code for the multiplayer lobby screen into the gamecontainer div in index.html, as shown in Listing 11-4.

Listing 11-4. HTML Code for the Multiplayer Lobby Screen (index.html)

```
<div id="multiplayerlobbyscreen" class="gamelayer">
    <select id="multiplayergameslist" size="10">
    </select>
    <input type="button" id="multiplayerjoin" onclick="multiplayer.join();">
    <input type="button" id="multiplayercancel" onclick="multiplayer.cancel();">
</div>
```

The layer contains a select element to display the list of game rooms along with two buttons. We will also add the CSS code for the lobby screen to styles.css, as shown in Listing 11-5.

Listing 11-5. CSS Code for the Multiplayer Lobby Screen (styles.css)

```
/* Multiplayer Lobby Screen */
#multiplayerlobbyscreen {
    background:url(images/multiplayerlobbyscreen.png) no-repeat center;
}
#multiplayerlobbyscreen input[type="button"]{
    background-image: url(images/buttons.png);
    position:absolute;
    border-width:0px;
    padding:0px;
}
#multiplayerjoin{
    background-position: -2px -212px;
    top:400px;
```

```css
    left:21px;
    width:74px;
    height:26px;
}
#multiplayerjoin:active,#multiplayerjoin:disabled{
    background-position: -2px -247px;
}
#multiplayercancel{
    background-position: -86px -150px;
    left:545px;
    top:400px;
    width:73px;
    height:24px;
}
#multiplayercancel:active,#multiplayercancel:disabled{
    background-position: -86px -184px;
}
#multiplayergameslist {
    padding:20px;
    position:absolute;
    width:392px;
    height:270px;
    top:98px;
    left:124px;
    background:rgba(0,0,0,0.7);
    border:none;
    color:gray;
    font-size: 15px;
    font-family: 'Courier New', Courier, monospace;
}
#multiplayergameslist:focus {
    outline:none;
}
#multiplayergameslist option.running{
    color:gray;
}
#multiplayergameslist option.waiting{
    color:green;
}
#multiplayergameslist option.empty{
    color:lightblue;
}
```

Now that the lobby screen is in place, we will build the code to connect the browser to the server and populate the games list.

Populating the Games List

We will start by defining a new multiplayer object inside multiplayer.js, as shown in Listing 11-6.

Listing 11-6. Defining the Multiplayer Object (multiplayer.js)

```javascript
var multiplayer = {
    // Open multiplayer game lobby
    websocket_url:"ws://localhost:8080/",
    websocket:undefined,
    start:function(){
        game.type = "multiplayer";
        var WebSocketObject = window.WebSocket || window.MozWebSocket;
        if (!WebSocketObject){
            game.showMessageBox("Your browser does not support WebSocket. Multiplayer
will not work.");
            return;
        }
        this.websocket = new WebSocketObject(this.websocket_url);
        this.websocket.onmessage = multiplayer.handleWebSocketMessage;
        // Display multiplayer lobby screen after connecting
        this.websocket.onopen = function(){
            // Hide the starting menu layer
            $('.gamelayer').hide();
            $('#multiplayerlobbyscreen').show();
        }
    },
    handleWebSocketMessage:function(message){
        var messageObject = JSON.parse(message.data);
        switch (messageObject.type){
            case "room_list":
                multiplayer.updateRoomStatus(messageObject.status);
                break;
        }
    },
    statusMessages:{
        'starting':'Game Starting',
        'running':'Game in Progress',
        'waiting':'Awaiting second player',
        'empty':'Open'
    },
    updateRoomStatus:function(status){
        var $list = $("#multiplayergameslist");
        $list.empty(); // remove old options
        for (var i=0; i < status.length; i++) {
            var key = "Game "+(i+1)+". "+this.statusMessages[status[i]];
            $list.append($("<option></option>").attr("disabled",status[i]== "running"||status[i]==
"starting").attr("value", (i+1)).text(key).addClass(status[i]).attr("selected",
(i+1)== multiplayer.roomId));
        };
    },
};
```

Inside the multiplayer object, we first define a start() method that tries to initialize a WebSocket connection to the server and saves it in the websocket variable. We then set the websocket object's onmessage event handler to call the handleWebSocketMessage() method and use the onopen event handler to display the lobby screen once the connection is opened.

Next we define the handleWebSocketMessage() method to handle the message data. Instead of passing strings like we did in our WebSocket example earlier, we are going to be passing complete objects between the server and the browser by using JSON.parse() and JSON.stringify() to convert between objects and strings. We start by parsing the message data into a messageObject variable and then use the parsed object's type property to decide how to handle the message.

If the type property is set to room_list, we call the updateRoomStatus() method and pass it the status property.

Finally, we define an updateRoomStatus() method that takes an array of status messages and populates the multiplayergameslist select element. We disable any options that have a status of starting or running and also set the CSS class of the option to the status.

Next, we will need to add a reference to multiplayer.js inside the head section of index.html, as shown in Listing 11-7.

Listing 11-7. Adding Reference to multiplayer.js (index.html)

```
<script src="js/multiplayer.js" type="text/javascript" charset="utf-8"></script>
```

Finally, we will define our multiplayer WebSocket server inside a new file called server.js, as shown in Listing 11-8.

Listing 11-8. Defining the Multiplayer Server (server.js)

```
var WebSocketServer = require('websocket').server;
var http = require('http');

// Create a simple web server that returns the same response for any request
var server = http.createServer(function(request,response){
    response.writeHead(200, {'Content-Type': 'text/plain'});
    response.end("This is the node.js HTTP server.");
});

server.listen(8080,function(){
    console.log('Server has started listening on port 8080');
});

var wsServer = new WebSocketServer({
    httpServer:server,
    autoAcceptConnections: false
});

// Logic to determine whether a specified connection is allowed.
function connectionIsAllowed(request){
    // Check criteria such as request.origin, request.remoteAddress
    return true;
}
```

```javascript
// Initialize a set of rooms
var gameRooms = [];
for (var i=0; i < 10; i++) {
    gameRooms.push({status:"empty",players:[],roomId:i+1});
};

var players = [];
wsServer.on('request',function(request){
    if(!connectionIsAllowed(request)){
        request.reject();
        console.log('Connection from' + request.remoteAddress + 'rejected.');
        return;
    }

    var connection = request.accept();
    console.log('Connection from' + request.remoteAddress + 'accepted.');

    // Add the player to the players array
    var player = {
        connection:connection
    }
    players.push(player);

    // Send a fresh game room status list the first time player connects
    sendRoomList(connection);

    // On Message event handler for a connection
    connection.on('message', function(message) {
        if (message.type === 'utf8') {
            var clientMessage = JSON.parse(message.utf8Data);
            switch (clientMessage.type){
                // Handle different message types
            }
        }
    });

    connection.on('close', function(reasonCode, description) {
        console.log('Connection from' + request.remoteAddress + 'disconnected.');
        for (var i = players.length - 1; i >= 0; i--){
            if (players[i]==player){
                players.splice(i,1);
            }
        };
    });
});

function sendRoomList(connection){
    var status = [];
    for (var i=0; i < gameRooms.length; i++) {
        status.push(gameRooms[i].status);
    };
```

```
    var clientMessage = {type:"room_list",status:status};
    connection.send(JSON.stringify(clientMessage));
}
```

We start by defining the HTTP server and the WebSocketServer like we did in our earlier websocketdemo example. Next, we define a rooms array and fill it with ten room objects that have a status property set to empty.

Finally, we implement the connection request event handler. We start by creating a player object for the connection and adding it to the players array. We then call the sendRoomList() method for the connection.

Next, we implement the message event handler for the connection to parse the message data and respond based on the type property just like we did on the client. We aren't processing any message types yet.

Next, we implement the close event handler where we remove the player from the players array once the connection closes.

Finally, we create a sendRoomList() method that sends a status array inside a message object of type room_list. This is the same message that we will be parsing on the client side.

If we run the newly created server.js and then open our game in the browser, we should be able to click the Multiplayer menu option and arrive at the multiplayer game lobby screen, as shown in Figure 11-3.

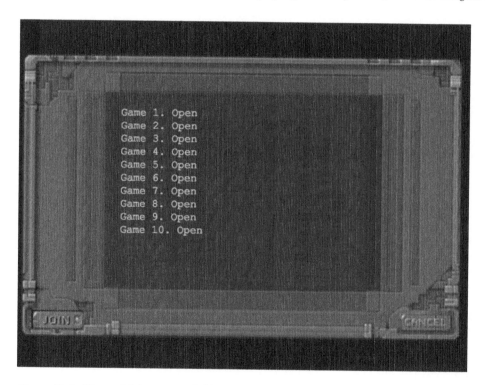

Figure 11-3. *The multiplayer game lobby screen*

Behind the scenes, the client is creating a socket connection to the server, and the server is sending back a room_list message to the client, which is then used to populate the list.

You should be able to select any of the game rooms but cannot join or leave these rooms. We will now implement joining and leaving a game room.

Joining and Leaving a Game Room

We will start by implementing join() and cancel() methods inside the multiplayer object, as shown in Listing 11-9.

Listing 11-9. Implementing join() and cancel() (multiplayer.js)

```
join:function(){
    var selectedRoom = document.getElementById('multiplayergameslist').value;
    if(selectedRoom){
        multiplayer.sendWebSocketMessage({type:"join_room",roomId:selectedRoom});
        document.getElementById('multiplayergameslist').disabled = true;
        document.getElementById('multiplayerjoin').disabled = true;
    } else {
        game.showMessageBox("Please select a game room to join.");
    }
},
cancel:function(){
    // Leave any existing game room
    if(multiplayer.roomId){
        multiplayer.sendWebSocketMessage({type:"leave_room",roomId:multiplayer.roomId});
        document.getElementById('multiplayergameslist').disabled = false;
        document.getElementById('multiplayerjoin').disabled = false;
        delete multiplayer.roomId;
        delete multiplayer.color;
        return;
    } else {
        // Not in a room, so leave the multiplayer screen itself
        multiplayer.closeAndExit();
    }
},
closeAndExit:function(){
    // clear handlers and close connection
    multiplayer.websocket.onopen = null;
    multiplayer.websocket.onclose = null;
    multiplayer.websocket.onerror = null;
    multiplayer.websocket.close();

    document.getElementById('multiplayergameslist').disabled = false;
    document.getElementById('multiplayerjoin').disabled = false;
    // Show the starting menu layer
    $('.gamelayer').hide();
    $('#gamestartscreen').show();
},
sendWebSocketMessage:function(messageObject){
    this.websocket.send(JSON.stringify(messageObject));
},
```

In the join() method, we check whether a room has been selected and, if it has, send a join_room WebSocket message to the server with the roomId property. We then disable the Join button and the games list. If no room is selected, we ask the player to select a room first.

In the cancel() method, we first check whether the player is in a room using the multiplayer.roomId property. If so, we send a leave_room WebSocket message to the server, delete the roomId and color properties, and enable the Join button and the games list select element. If not, we close the socket connection and return to the game start screen using the closeAndExit() method.

In the closeAndExit() method, we first clear the websocket object's event handlers and close the connection. We then enable the Join button and games list and return to the game start screen.

Finally, we define a sendWebSocketMessage() that converts the messageObject into a string and sends it to the server.

Next, we will modify the server to handle the join_room and leave_room message types by modifying the message event handler in server.js, as shown in Listing 11-10.

Listing 11-10. Handling join_room and leave_room Messages (server.js)

```
// On Message event handler for a connection
connection.on('message', function(message) {
    if (message.type === 'utf8') {
        var clientMessage = JSON.parse(message.utf8Data);
        switch (clientMessage.type){
            case "join_room":
                var room = joinRoom(player,clientMessage.roomId);
                sendRoomListToEveryone();
                break;
            case "leave_room":
                leaveRoom(player,clientMessage.roomId);
                sendRoomListToEveryone();
                break;
        }
    }
});
```

When a join_room message comes in, we first call the joinRoom() method and then send the room list to all players using the sendRoomListToEveryone() method. Similarly, when a leave_room message comes in, we first call the leaveRoom() method and then call the sendRoomListToEveryone() method.

Next, we will define these three new methods inside server.js, as shown in Listing 11-11.

Listing 11-11. The joinRoom(), leaveRoom(), and sendRoomListToEveryone() Methods (server.js)

```
function sendRoomListToEveryone(){
    // Notify all connected players of the room status changes
    var status = [];
    for (var i=0; i < gameRooms.length; i++) {
        status.push(gameRooms[i].status);
    };
    var clientMessage = {type:"room_list",status:status};
    var clientMessageString = JSON.stringify(clientMessage);
    for (var i=0; i < players.length; i++) {
        players[i].connection.send(clientMessageString);
    };
}
```

```
function joinRoom(player,roomId){
    var room = gameRooms[roomId-1];
    console.log("Adding player to room",roomId);
    // Add the player to the room
    room.players.push(player);
    player.room = room;
    // Update room status
    if(room.players.length == 1){
        room.status = "waiting";
        player.color = "blue";
    } else if (room.players.length == 2){
        room.status = "starting";
        player.color = "green";
    }
    // Confirm to player that he was added
    var confirmationMessageString = JSON.stringify({type:"joined_room", roomId:roomId,
color:player.color});
    player.connection.send(confirmationMessageString);
    return room;
}

function leaveRoom(player,roomId){
    var room = gameRooms[roomId-1];
    console.log("Removing player from room",roomId);

    for (var i = room.players.length - 1; i >= 0; i--){
        if(room.players[i]==player){
            room.players.splice(i,1);
        }
    };
    delete player.room;
    // Update room status
    if(room.players.length == 0){
        room.status = "empty";
    } else if (room.players.length == 1){
        room.status = "waiting";
    }
}
```

In the sendRoomListToEveryone() method, we iterate through all the players in the players array and send them a room_list message with the list of rooms.

In the joinRoom() method, we first get the room object using roomId and add the player to the room object's players array. We then set the room's status to waiting or starting depending on how many players are in the room. We also set the player's color to blue or green based on whether the player is the first or second player to join the room. Finally, we send a joined_room message back to the player, with details of the room ID and player color.

In the leaveRoom() method, we first get the room object using roomId and remove the player from the room object's players array. We then set the room object's status to empty or waiting depending on how many players are in the room.

The next change we will make is to handle the joined_room confirmation message inside multiplayer.js, as shown in Listing 11-12.

Listing 11-12. Handling the joined_room Message (multiplayer.js)

```
handleWebSocketMessage:function(message){
    var messageObject = JSON.parse(message.data);
    switch (messageObject.type){
        case "room_list":
            multiplayer.updateRoomStatus(messageObject.status);
            break;
        case "joined_room":
            multiplayer.roomId = messageObject.roomId;
            multiplayer.color = messageObject.color;
            break;
    }
},
```

When a joined_room message comes in, we save the roomId and color properties inside the multiplayer object.

Finally, we will ensure that a player is removed from a game room if the player is disconnected by modifying the close event handler on the server, as shown in Listing 11-13.

Listing 11-13. Handling Player Disconnects (server.js)

```
connection.on('close', function(reasonCode, description) {
    console.log('Connection from' + request.remoteAddress + 'disconnected.');

    for (var i = players.length - 1; i >= 0; i--){
        if (players[i]==player){
            players.splice(i,1);
        }
    };

    // If the player is in a room, remove him from room and notify everyone
    if(player.room){
        var status = player.room.status;
        var roomId = player.room.roomId;
        // If the game was running, end the game as well
        leaveRoom(player,roomId);
        sendRoomListToEveryone();
    }
});
```

In the newly added code, we check whether the disconnected player is in a room, and if so, we remove the player from the room using the leaveRoom() method and then notify everyone using the sendRoomListToEveryone() method.

If we restart the server and run the game in more than one browser window, we should be able to join a room in one window and see the status change in both the windows, as shown in Figure 11-4.

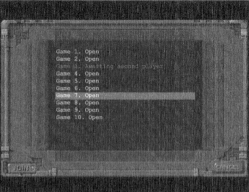

Figure 11-4. *Room status updated on both browsers when joining a room*

You will notice that the Join button and the list get disabled once you join a room. If you join the same room on both browsers, the room status changes to starting and no one else can join the room.

If you click Cancel, you will leave the room, and the Join button will be reenabled. If you click Cancel again, you are taken back to the main menu. If you disconnect from the server by closing the browser window, you will be removed from the room.

We now have a working game lobby where players can join and leave game rooms. Next we will start the multiplayer game once the players join the game room.

Starting the Multiplayer Game

Our multiplayer game will start once two players join a game room. We will need to tell both the clients to load the same level. Once the level has loaded on both browsers, we will then start the game. The first thing we need to do is define a new multiplayer level.

Defining the Multiplayer Level

The multiplayer level, while being similar to the single-player levels, will contain some extra information such as the starting location for each player and the starting items for each team. We will start by defining a simple level inside a new multiplayer array in the maps object, as shown in Listing 11-14.

Listing 11-14. A Multiplayer Level Inside the Multiplayer Array (maps.js)

```
"multiplayer":[
    {
        /* Map Details */
        "mapImage":"images/maps/level-one.png",

        /* Map coordinates that are obstructed by terrain*/
        "mapGridWidth":60,
        "mapGridHeight":40,
        "mapObstructedTerrain":[
            [49,8], [50,8], [51,8], [51,9], [52,9], [53,9], [53,10], [53,11], [53,12], [53,13],
[53,14], [53,15], [53,16], [52,16], [52,17], [52,18], [52,19], [51,19], [50,19], [50,18], [50,17],
```

```
[49,17], [49,18], [48,18], [47,18], [47,17], [47,16], [48,16], [49,16], [49,15], [49,14], [48,14],
[48,13], [48,12], [49,12], [49,11], [50,11], [50,10], [49,10], [49,9], [44,0], [45,0], [45,1],
[45,2], [46,2], [47,2], [47,3], [48,3], [48,4], [48,5], [49,5], [49,6], [49,7], [50,7], [51,7],
[51,6], [51,5], [51,4], [52,4], [53,4], [53,3], [54,3], [55,3], [55,2], [56,2], [56,1], [56,0],
[55,0], [43,19], [44,19], [45,19], [46,19], [47,19], [48,19], [48,20], [48,21], [47,21], [46,21],
[45,21], [44,21], [43,21], [43,20], [41,22], [42,22], [43,22], [44,22], [45,22], [46,22], [47,22],
[48,22], [49,22], [50,22], [50,23], [50,24], [49,24], [48,24], [47,24], [47,25], [47,26], [47,27],
[47,28], [47,29], [47,30], [46,30], [45,30], [44,30], [43,30], [43,29], [43,28], [43,27], [43,26],
[43,25], [43,24], [42,24], [41,24], [41,23], [48,39], [49,39], [50,39], [51,39], [52,39], [53,39],
[54,39], [55,39], [56,39], [57,39], [58,39], [59,39], [59,38], [59,37], [59,36], [59,35], [59,34],
[59,33], [59,32], [59,31], [59,30], [59,29], [0,0], [1,0], [2,0], [1,1], [2,1], [10,3], [11,3],
[12,3], [12,2], [13,2], [14,2], [14,3], [14,4], [15,4], [15,5], [15,6], [14,6], [13,6], [13,5],
[12,5], [11,5], [10,5], [10,4], [3,9], [4,9], [5,9], [5,10], [6,10], [7,10], [8,10], [9,10], [9,11],
[10,11], [11,11], [11,10], [12,10], [13,10], [13,11], [13,12], [12,12], [11,12], [10,12], [9,12],
[8,12], [7,12], [7,13], [7,14], [6,14], [5,14], [5,13], [5,12], [5,11], [4,11], [3,11], [3,10],
[33,33], [34,33], [35,33], [35,34], [35,35], [34,35], [33,35], [33,34], [27,39], [27,38], [27,37],
[28,37], [28,36], [28,35], [28,34], [28,33], [28,32], [28,31], [28,30], [28,29], [29,29], [29,28],
[29,27], [29,26], [29,25], [29,24], [29,23], [30,23], [31,23], [32,23], [32,22], [32,21], [31,21],
[30,21], [30,22], [29,22], [28,22], [27,22], [26,22], [26,21], [25,21], [24,21], [24,22], [24,23],
[25,23], [26,23], [26,24], [25,24], [25,25], [24,25], [24,26], [24,27], [25,27], [25,28], [25,29],
[24,29], [23,29], [23,30], [23,31], [24,31], [25,31], [25,32], [25,33], [24,33], [23,33], [23,34],
[23,35], [24,35], [24,36], [24,37], [23,37], [22,37], [22,38], [22,39], [23,39], [24,39], [25,39],
[26,0], [26,1], [25,1], [25,2], [25,3], [26,3], [27,3], [27,2], [28,2], [29,2], [29,3], [30,3],
[31,3], [31,2], [31,1], [32,1], [32,0], [33,0], [32,8], [33,8], [34,8], [34,9], [34,10], [33,10],
[32,10], [32,9], [8,29], [9,29], [9,30], [17,32], [18,32], [19,32], [19,33], [18,33], [17,33],
[18,34], [19,34], [3,27], [4,27], [4,26], [3,26], [2,26], [3,25], [4,25], [9,20], [10,20], [11,20],
[11,21], [10,21], [10,19], [19,7], [15,7], [29,12], [30,13], [20,14], [21,14], [34,13], [35,13],
[36,13], [36,14], [35,14], [34,14], [35,15], [36,15], [16,18], [17,18], [18,18], [16,19], [17,19],
[18,19], [17,20], [18,20], [11,19], [58,0], [59,0], [58,1], [59,1], [59,2], [58,3], [59,3], [58,4],
[59,4], [59,5], [58,6], [59,6], [58,7], [59,7], [59,8], [58,9], [59,9], [58,10], [59,10], [59,11],
[52,6], [53,6], [54,6], [52,7], [53,7], [54,7], [53,8], [54,8], [44,17], [46,32], [55,32], [54,28],
[26,34], [34,34], [4,10], [6,11], [6,12], [6,13], [7,11], [8,11], [12,11], [27,0], [27,1], [26,2],
[28,1], [28,0], [29,0], [29,1], [30,2], [30,1], [30,0], [31,0], [33,9], [46,0], [47,0], [48,0],
[49,0], [50,0], [51,0], [52,0], [53,0], [54,0], [55,1], [54,1], [53,1], [52,1], [51,1], [50,1],
[49,1], [48,1], [47,1], [46,1], [48,2], [49,2], [50,2], [51,2], [52,2], [53,2], [54,2], [52,3],
[51,3], [50,3], [49,3], [49,4], [50,4], [50,5], [50,6], [50,9], [51,10], [52,10], [51,11], [52,11],
[50,12], [51,12], [52,12], [49,13], [50,13], [51,13], [52,13], [50,14], [51,14], [52,14], [50,15],
[51,15], [52,15], [50,16], [51,16], [51,17], [48,17], [51,18], [44,20], [45,20], [46,20], [47,20],
[42,23], [43,23], [44,23], [45,23], [46,23], [47,23], [48,23], [49,23], [44,24], [45,24], [46,24],
[44,25], [45,25], [46,25], [44,26], [45,26], [46,26], [44,27], [45,27], [46,27], [44,28], [45,28],
[46,28], [44,29], [45,29], [46,29], [11,4], [12,4], [13,4], [13,3], [14,5], [25,22], [31,22],
[27,23], [28,23], [27,24], [28,24], [26,25], [27,25], [28,25], [25,26], [26,26], [27,26], [28,26],
[26,27], [27,27], [28,27], [26,28], [27,28], [28,28], [26,29], [27,29], [24,30], [25,30], [26,30],
[27,30], [26,31], [27,31], [26,32], [27,32], [26,33], [27,33], [24,34], [25,34], [27,34], [25,35],
[26,35], [27,35], [25,36], [26,36], [27,36], [25,37], [26,37], [23,38], [24,38], [25,38], [26,38],
[26,39], [2,25], [9,19], [36,31]
    ],

    /* Entities to be loaded */
    "requirements":{
        "buildings":["base","harvester","starport","ground-turret"],
        "vehicles":["transport","scout-tank","heavy-tank","harvester"],
```

```
            "aircraft":["wraith","chopper"],
            "terrain":["oilfield"]
        },

        /* Economy Related*/
        "cash":{
            "blue":1000,
            "green":1000
        },

        /* Entities to be added */
        "items":[
            {"type":"terrain","name":"oilfield","x":16,"y":4,"action":"hint"},
            {"type":"terrain","name":"oilfield","x":34,"y":12,"action":"hint"},
            {"type":"terrain","name":"oilfield","x":1,"y":30,"action":"hint"},
            {"type":"terrain","name":"oilfield","x":38,"y":38,"action":"hint"},
        ],

        /* Entities for each starting team */
        "teamStartingItems":[
            {"type":"buildings","name":"base","x":0,"y":0},
            {"type":"vehicles","name":"harvester","x":2,"y":0},
            {"type":"vehicles","name":"heavy-tank","x":2,"y":1},
            {"type":"vehicles","name":"scout-tank","x":3,"y":0},
            {"type":"vehicles","name":"scout-tank","x":3,"y":1},
        ],
        "spawnLocations":[
            { "x":48, "y":36,"startX":36,"startY":20},
            { "x":3,  "y":36,"startX":0,"startY":20},
            { "x":36, "y":3,"startX":32,"startY":0},
            { "x":3,  "y":3,"startX":0,"startY":0},
        ],
        /* Conditional and Timed Trigger Events */
        "triggers":[
        ]
    }
]
```

The two new elements that we have introduced in the multiplayer level are the teamStartingItems and spawnLocations arrays.

The teamStartingItems array contains a list of items that each team will have at the beginning of the level. The x and y coordinates will be relative to the location where the team is spawned.

The spawnLocations array contains a few spots on the map where each player team can start. Each object contains the x and y coordinates of the location, as well as the starting panning offset for the location.

Now that we have defined the multiplayer level, we need to load the level once the two players join a game room.

Loading the Multiplayer Level

When two players join a room, we will tell them both to initialize the level and wait for both to confirm that the level has been initialized. Once this happens, we need to tell them both to start the game.

We will start by adding a few new methods to server.js to handle initializing and starting the game, as shown in Listing 11-15.

Listing 11-15. Initializing and Starting the Game (server.js)

```
function initGame(room){
    console.log("Both players Joined. Initializing game for Room "+room.roomId);

    // Number of players who have loaded the level
    room.playersReady = 0;

    // Load the first multiplayer level for both players
    // This logic can change later to let the players pick a level
    var currentLevel = 0;

    // Randomly select two spawn locations between 0 and 3 for both players.
    var spawns = [0,1,2,3];
    var spawnLocations = {"blue":spawns.splice(Math.floor(Math.random()*spawns.length),1),
"green":spawns.splice(Math.floor(Math.random()*spawns.length),1)};

    sendRoomWebSocketMessage(room,{type:"init_level", spawnLocations:spawnLocations,
level:currentLevel});
}

function startGame(room){
    console.log("Both players are ready. Starting game in room",room.roomId);
    room.status = "running";
    sendRoomListToEveryone();
    // Notify players to start the game
    sendRoomWebSocketMessage(room,{type:"start_game"});
}

function sendRoomWebSocketMessage(room,messageObject){
    var messageString = JSON.stringify(messageObject);
    for (var i = room.players.length - 1; i >= 0; i--){
        room.players[i].connection.send(messageString);
    };
}
```

In the initGame() method, we initialize the playersReady variable, select two random spawn locations for both the players, and send the location to both the players inside an init_level message using the sendRoomWebSocketMessage() method.

In the startGame() method, we set the room status to running, update every player's room list, and finally send both players the start_game message using the sendRoomWebSocketMessage() method.

Finally, in the sendRoomWebSocketMessage() method we iterate through the players in a room and send each of them a given message.

Next, we will modify the message event handler in server.js to initialize and start the game, as shown in Listing 11-16.

Listing 11-16. Modifying the Message Event Handler (server.js)

```
// On Message event handler for a connection
connection.on('message', function(message) {
    if (message.type === 'utf8') {
        var clientMessage = JSON.parse(message.utf8Data);
```

```
        switch (clientMessage.type){
            case "join_room":
                var room = joinRoom(player,clientMessage.roomId);
                sendRoomListToEveryone();
                if(room.players.length == 2){
                    initGame(room);
                }
                break;
            case "leave_room":
                leaveRoom(player,clientMessage.roomId);
                sendRoomListToEveryone();
                break;
            case "initialized_level":
                player.room.playersReady++;
                if (player.room.playersReady==2){
                    startGame(player.room);
                }
                break;
        }
    }
});
```

When a player joins a room and the player count reaches two, we call the initGame() method. When we receive an initialized_level message from a player, we increment the playersReady variable. Once the count reaches two, we call the startGame() method.

Next we will add two new methods to the multiplayer object to initialize the multiplayer level and start the game, as shown in Listing 11-17.

Listing 11-17. Initializing and Starting the Multiplayer Game (multiplayer.js)

```
currentLevel:0,
initMultiplayerLevel:function(messageObject){
    $('.gamelayer').hide();
    var spawnLocations = messageObject.spawnLocations;

    // Initialize multiplayer related variables
    multiplayer.commands = [[]];
    multiplayer.lastReceivedTick = 0;
    multiplayer.currentTick = 0;

    game.team = multiplayer.color;

    // Load all the items for the level
    multiplayer.currentLevel = messageObject.level;
    var level = maps.multiplayer[multiplayer.currentLevel];

    // Load all the assets for the level
    game.currentMapImage = loader.loadImage(level.mapImage);
    game.currentLevel = level;

    // Setup offset based on spawn location sent by server
```

```
// Load level Requirements
game.resetArrays();
for (var type in level.requirements){
      var requirementArray = level.requirements[type];
      for (var i=0; i < requirementArray.length; i++) {
          var name = requirementArray[i];
          if (window[type]){
              window[type].load(name);
          } else {
              console.log('Could not load type :',type);
          }
      };
 }

for (var i = level.items.length - 1; i >= 0; i--){
    var itemDetails = level.items[i];
    game.add(itemDetails);
};

// Add starting items for both teams at their respective spawn locations
for (team in spawnLocations){
    var spawnIndex = spawnLocations[team];
    for (var i=0; i < level.teamStartingItems.length; i++) {
        var itemDetails = $.extend(true,{},level.teamStartingItems[i]);
        itemDetails.x += level.spawnLocations[spawnIndex].x+itemDetails.x;
        itemDetails.y += level.spawnLocations[spawnIndex].y+itemDetails.y;
        itemDetails.team = team;
        game.add(itemDetails);
    };

    if (team==game.team){
        game.offsetX = level.spawnLocations[spawnIndex].startX*game.gridSize;
        game.offsetY = level.spawnLocations[spawnIndex].startY*game.gridSize;
    }
}


// Create a grid that stores all obstructed tiles as 1 and unobstructed as 0
game.currentMapTerrainGrid = [];
for (var y=0; y < level.mapGridHeight; y++) {
    game.currentMapTerrainGrid[y] = [];
      for (var x=0; x< level.mapGridWidth; x++) {
      game.currentMapTerrainGrid[y][x] = 0;
    }
};
for (var i = level.mapObstructedTerrain.length - 1; i >= 0; i--){
    var obstruction = level.mapObstructedTerrain[i];
    game.currentMapTerrainGrid[obstruction[1]][obstruction[0]] = 1;
};
game.currentMapPassableGrid = undefined;
```

```
        // Load Starting Cash For Game
        game.cash = $.extend([],level.cash);

        // Enable the enter mission button once all assets are loaded
        if (loader.loaded){
            multiplayer.sendWebSocketMessage({type:"initialized_level"});

        } else {
            loader.onload = function(){
                multiplayer.sendWebSocketMessage({type:"initialized_level"});
            }
        }
    },
    startGame:function(){
        fog.initLevel();
        game.animationLoop();
        game.start();
    },
```

In the `initMultiplayerLevel()` method, we start by initializing a few multiplayer-related variables that we will need later. We then initialize the `game.team` and `multiplayer.currentLevel` variables. We then load the multiplayer map like we did for the single-player campaign.

Next, we place all the starting items for both the players at their respective spawn locations and set the offset location for each player based on their spawn locations.

We then load the terrain grid like we did for single player, and finally we send the `initialized_level` message back to the server once the map has loaded completely to let the server know that the client has finished loading the level.

In the `startGame()` method, we initialize the fog, call the `animationLoop()` once, and finally call `game.start()`.

Next, we will modify the `handleWebSocketMessage()` method in `multiplayer.js` to call these newly created methods, as shown in Listing 11-18.

Listing 11-18. Modifying Message Handler to Initialize and Start Game (multiplayer.js)

```
handleWebSocketMessage:function(message){
    var messageObject = JSON.parse(message.data);
    switch (messageObject.type){
        case "room_list":
            multiplayer.updateRoomStatus(messageObject.status);
            break;
        case "joined_room":
            multiplayer.roomId = messageObject.roomId;
            multiplayer.color = messageObject.color;
            break;
        case "init_level":
            multiplayer.initMultiplayerLevel(messageObject);
            break;
        case "start_game":
            multiplayer.startGame();
            break;
    }
},
```

We merely call the `initMultiplayerLevel()` method when we receive an `init_level` message and the `startGame()` method when we receive a `start_game` message.

If we restart the server and run the game in two browser windows, we should be able to join the same room from both browsers and see the game load in both, as shown in Figure 11-5.

Figure 11-5. Multiplayer game loading in both browser windows

Once the two players join the room, the server automatically assigns both the players different colors and spawn locations. When the game loads, both players are placed at their respective spawn locations with the same starting team: two scout tanks, a heavy tank, and a harvester.

We can scroll around the map and even select units; however, we still can't play the game by giving these units commands. This is what we will implement in the next chapter.

Summary

In this chapter, we looked at using the WebSocket API with Node.js for a simple client-server architecture. First we installed Node.js and the WebSocket-Node package and used it to build a simple WebSocket server. Then we built a simple WebSocket-based browser client and sent messages back and forth between the browser and the server.

We used this same architecture to implement a multiplayer game lobby with rooms that players could join and leave. We designed a multiplayer level with spawn locations and starting teams. Finally, we loaded and started the same level on two different browsers, while placing the two players at different spawn locations.

In the next chapter, we will implement the actual multiplayer gameplay by passing commands between the browsers and server. We will use triggers to implement winning and losing a game. Finally, we will add some finishing touches and wrap up the multiplayer section of our game.

CHAPTER 12

Multiplayer Gameplay

In the previous chapter, we saw how the WebSocket API could be used with a Node.js server to implement a simple client–server networking architecture. We used this to build a simple game lobby, so two players can now join a game room on a server and start a multiplayer game against each other.

In this chapter, we will continue where we left off at the end of Chapter 11 and implement a framework for the actual multiplayer gameplay using the lock-step networking model. We will look at ways to handle typical game networking problems such as latency and game synchronization. We will then use the sendCommand() architecture that we designed in earlier chapters to ensure that the players' commands are executed on both the browsers so that the games stay in sync. We will then implement winning and losing in the game by using triggers like we did in Chapter 10. Finally, we will implement a chat system for our game.

Let's get started.

The Lock-Step Networking Model

So far, we used the Node.js server to communicate simple messages such as the game lobby status and joining or leaving a room. These messages were independent of each other, and one player's messages did not affect another player. However, when it comes to the gameplay, this communication is going to get a little more complex.

One of the most important challenges in building a multiplayer game is to ensure that all the players are in sync. This means every time a change occurs in any of the games (for example, a player issues a move or attack command), the change is communicated to the other players so that they too can make the same change.

What is even more important is that the action or change occurs at the same moment in both the players' machines. If there is a delay in executing these changes, subtle differences in unit positions will eventually build up, resulting in noticeable divergences between the game states.

For example, a unit that is just half a second late in arriving at an enemy location might avoid an enemy attack and survive in one browser, while the same unit may have been destroyed on the other player's browser. The moment something like this happens, the two players are now playing two completely different games instead of the same one.

To ensure that both players are completely in sync, we will implement an architecture known as the *lock-step* networking model. Both players will start with the same game state. When the player gives a unit a command, we will send the command to the server instead of executing it immediately. The server will then send the same command to the connected players with instructions on when to execute the command. Once the players receive the command, they will execute it at the same time, ensuring that the games stay synchronized.

The server will achieve this behavior by running its own game timer, at 10 clock ticks per second. When a player sends the server a command, the server will record the clock tick when it received the command. The server will then send the command to the players, while specifying the game tick to execute the command. The players in turn will keep track of the current game tick and execute the command at the right tick.

One thing to remember is that since the server needs to execute the commands for all the players at the same time, it will need to wait for the commands from all the players to arrive before stepping ahead to the next game tick, which is why it's called *lock-step*.

This process is further complicated by the fact that network latency can cause communication delays, with messages sometimes taking several hundred milliseconds to travel between client and server. Our networking model will need to measure and take this latency into account to ensure smooth gameplay.

We will start by modifying our game code to measure the network latency for each player when the player first connects to the server.

Measuring Network Latency

For our purposes, we will define the latency as the time taken by a message to travel from the server to the client. We will measure this latency by sending several messages back and forth between the server and the client and then taking an average of the time used for each trip.

We will start by defining two new methods for measuring the latency inside server.js, as shown in Listing 12-1.

Listing 12-1. Methods for Measuring Network Latency (server.js)

```
function measureLatency(player){
    var connection = player.connection;
    var measurement = {start:Date.now()};
    player.latencyTrips.push(measurement);
    var clientMessage = {type:"latency_ping"};
    connection.send(JSON.stringify(clientMessage));
}
function finishMeasuringLatency(player,clientMessage){
    var measurement = player.latencyTrips[player.latencyTrips.length-1];
    measurement.end = Date.now();
    measurement.roundTrip = measurement.end - measurement.start;
    player.averageLatency = 0;
    for (var i=0; i < player.latencyTrips.length; i++) {
        player.averageLatency += measurement.roundTrip/2;
    };
    player.averageLatency = player.averageLatency/player.latencyTrips.length;
    player.tickLag = Math.round(player.averageLatency * 2/100)+1;
    console.log("Measuring Latency for player. Attempt", player.latencyTrips.length, "-
Average Latency:",player.averageLatency, "Tick Lag:", player.tickLag);
}
```

In the measureLatency() method, we first create a new measurement object with a start property set to the current time and add the object to the player.latencyTrips array. We then send a message of type latency_ping to the player. The player will respond to this message by sending back a message of type latency_pong.

In the finishMeasuringLatency() method, we take the last measurement from the player.latencyTrips array and set its end property to the current time and its roundTrip property to the difference between the end and start times.

We then calculate the average latency for the player by adding up all the roundTrip values and then dividing the sum by the number of trips.

Finally, we use averageLatency to calculate a tickLag property for the player. This is the number of ticks after sending a command that the player can be safely expected to have received the command. The heuristic uses a value that is 200 percent of the typical latency, with a minimum value of one game tick.

You can play around with this heuristic and fine-tune it for accuracy if you like; however, for the purposes of smooth gameplay, it is safer to have a high value. It has been found that players are able to get used to network lag and automatically adjust for it as long as the delay is consistent. Any time the lag varies too much, players tend to get frustrated by it.

Next we will modify the multiplayer object's handleWebSocketMessage() method to respond to the server's latency_ping message, as shown in Listing 12-2.

Listing 12-2. Responding to latency_ping with a latency_pong (multiplayer.js)

```
handleWebSocketMessage:function(message){
    var messageObject = JSON.parse(message.data);
    switch (messageObject.type){
        case "room_list":
            multiplayer.updateRoomStatus(messageObject.status);
            break;
        case "joined_room":
            multiplayer.roomId = messageObject.roomId;
            multiplayer.color = messageObject.color;
            break;
        case "init_level":
            multiplayer.initMultiplayerLevel(messageObject);
            break;
        case "start_game":
            multiplayer.startGame();
            break;
        case "latency_ping":
            multiplayer.sendWebSocketMessage({type:"latency_pong"});
            break;
    }
},
```

When the browser receives a latency_ping message from the server, it immediately sends back a latency_pong message to the server.

Finally, we will modify the request event handler for the websocket object on the server to start measuring latency when a player connects and to finish measuring latency when the player sends back a latency_pong response, as shown in Listing 12-3.

Listing 12-3. Starting and Finishing Latency Measurement (server.js)

```
wsServer.on('request',function(request){
    if(!connectionIsAllowed(request)){
        request.reject();
        console.log('Connection from ' + request.remoteAddress + ' rejected.');
        return;
    }

    var connection = request.accept();
    console.log('Connection from ' + request.remoteAddress + ' accepted.');

    // Add the player to the players array
    var player = {
        connection:connection,
        latencyTrips:[]
    }
    players.push(player);
```

```
        // Send a fresh game room status list the first time player connects
        sendRoomList(connection);

        // Measure latency for player
        measureLatency(player);

        // On Message event handler for a connection
        connection.on('message', function(message) {
            if (message.type === 'utf8') {
                var clientMessage = JSON.parse(message.utf8Data);
                switch (clientMessage.type){
                    case "join_room":
                        var room = joinRoom(player,clientMessage.roomId);
                        sendRoomListToEveryone();
                        if(room.players.length == 2){
                            initGame(room);
                        }
                        break;
                    case "leave_room":
                        leaveRoom(player,clientMessage.roomId);
                        sendRoomListToEveryone();
                        break;
                    case "initialized_level":
                        player.room.playersReady++;
                        if (player.room.playersReady==2){
                            startGame(player.room);
                        }
                        break;
                    case "latency_pong":
                        finishMeasuringLatency(player,clientMessage);
                        // Measure latency at least thrice
                        if(player.latencyTrips.length<3){
                            measureLatency(player);
                        }
                        break;
                }
            }
        });

        connection.on('close', function(reasonCode, description) {
            console.log('Connection from ' + request.remoteAddress + ' disconnected.');
            for (var i = players.length - 1; i >= 0; i--){
                if (players[i]==player){
                    players.splice(i,1);
                }
            };

            // If the player is in a room, remove him from room and notify everyone
            if(player.room){
                var status = player.room.status;
                var roomId = player.room.roomId;
```

```
            leaveRoom(player,roomId);

            sendRoomListToEveryone();
        }
    });
});
```

We start by adding a `latencyTrips` array to the `player` object and calling `measureLatency()` once the player has connected.

We then modify the message handler to handle messages of type `latency_pong`. When the player responds to a `latency_ping` message with a `latency_pong` message, we call the `finishMeasuringLatency()` method that we defined earlier. We then check whether we have at least three latency measurements and, if not, call the `measureLatency()` method again.

Now, if you start the server and run the game, the server will make three attempts to measure the latency. You can see the Websocket communication using the browser's developer console, as shown in Figure 12-1.

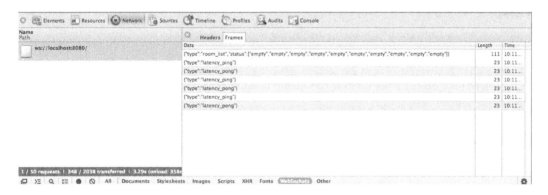

Figure 12-1. *Observing the websocket communication in the developer console*

Now that we have measured latency for the players, it's time to implement sending commands.

Sending Commands

Once the game starts, we will maintain a game clock with a game tick number on both the server and the clients. When a player sends a command to the server, we will send the command back to the clients with instructions to execute the command at a later tick calculated by using `tickLag`.

We will start by modifying the `multiplayer` object's `handleWebSocketMessage()` method to receive commands within a `game_tick` message, as shown in Listing 12-4.

Listing 12-4. Receiving Commands in game_tick Message (multiplayer.js)

```
handleWebSocketMessage:function(message){
    var messageObject = JSON.parse(message.data);
    switch (messageObject.type){
        case "room_list":
            multiplayer.updateRoomStatus(messageObject.status);
            break;
```

```
        case "joined_room":
            multiplayer.roomId = messageObject.roomId;
            multiplayer.color = messageObject.color;
            break;
        case "init_level":
            multiplayer.initMultiplayerLevel(messageObject);
            break;
        case "start_game":
            multiplayer.startGame();
            break;
        case "latency_ping":
            multiplayer.sendWebSocketMessage({type:"latency_pong"});
            break;
        case "game_tick":
            multiplayer.lastReceivedTick = messageObject.tick;
            multiplayer.commands[messageObject.tick] = messageObject.commands;
            break;
    }
},
```

When we receive a game_tick message from the server containing a list of commands and the tick number on which the commands need to be executed, we save the commands in the multiplayer.commands array and then update the lastReceivedTick variable.

Next we will implement the game loop and handle sending commands, as shown in Listing 12-5.

Listing 12-5. Sending Commands from the Client (multiplayer.js)

```
startGame:function(){
    fog.initLevel();
    game.animationLoop();
    multiplayer.animationInterval = setInterval(multiplayer.tickLoop, game.animationTimeout);
    game.start();
},
sendCommand:function(uids,details){
    multiplayer.sentCommandForTick = true;
    multiplayer.sendWebSocketMessage({type:"command",uids:uids,
details:details,currentTick:multiplayer.currentTick});
},
tickLoop:function(){
    // if the commands for that tick have been received
    // execute the commands and move on to the next tick
    // otherwise wait for server to catch up
    if(multiplayer.currentTick <= multiplayer.lastReceivedTick){
        var commands = multiplayer.commands[multiplayer.currentTick];
        if(commands){
            for (var i=0; i < commands.length; i++) {
                game.processCommand(commands[i].uids,commands[i].details);
            };
        }
```

```
    game.animationLoop();

    // In case no command was sent for this current tick, send an empty command to the server
    // So that the server knows that everything is working smoothly
    if (!multiplayer.sentCommandForTick){
        multiplayer.sendCommand();
    }
    multiplayer.currentTick++;
    multiplayer.sentCommandForTick = false;
    }
},
```

First, in the startGame() method, we set an interval to call the tickLoop() method every 100 milliseconds when the game starts.

Next, in the sendCommand() method, we send a message of type command to the server with the details of the command as well as the UIDs for the command.

The command message also contains the current game tick. This way, the command message acts as a heartbeat to let the server know what game tick the client is currently on. We also set the sendCommandForTick flag to true.

In the tickLoop() method, we check to see whether we have received commands for the current tick. In case we have not, we will wait for the commands to arrive from the server.

If we have received the commands for the tick, we process all the received commands using the game.processCommand() method. We then call the game.animationLoop() method.

In case we have not sent out any commands so far, we also send an empty command to the server.

Finally, we increment the game tick number and clear the sentCommandForTick flag.

Now that the client has been modified to send and receive commands, we will modify the server to handle these commands as well.

We will start by modifying the message event handler on the server to handle messages of type command, as shown in Listing 12-6.

Listing 12-6. Handing Messages of Type command (server.js)

```
// On Message event handler for a connection
connection.on('message', function(message) {
    if (message.type === 'utf8') {
        var clientMessage = JSON.parse(message.utf8Data);
        switch (clientMessage.type){
            case "join_room":
                var room = joinRoom(player,clientMessage.roomId);
                sendRoomListToEveryone();
                if(room.players.length == 2){
                    initGame(room);
                }
                break;
            case "leave_room":
                leaveRoom(player,clientMessage.roomId);
                sendRoomListToEveryone();
                break;
            case "initialized_level":
                player.room.playersReady++;
                if (player.room.playersReady==2){
                    startGame(player.room);
                }
```

```
                 break;
         case "latency_pong":
             finishMeasuringLatency(player,clientMessage);
             // Measure latency at least thrice
             if(player.latencyTrips.length<3){
                 measureLatency(player);
             }
             break;
         case "command":
             if (player.room && player.room.status=="running"){
                 if(clientMessage.uids){
                     player.room.commands.push({uids:clientMessage.uids,
details:clientMessage.details}));
                 }
                 player.room.lastTickConfirmed[player.color] = clientMessage.currentTick +
player.tickLag;
             }
             break;
     }
   }
});
```

When the server receives a message of type command, we check whether the message has UIDs. If so, we store the commands in the room's commands array. If not, the message is just a heartbeat message with no command that needs saving. We then update the lastTickConfirmed property for the player.

Next, we will modify the startGame() method in server.js, as shown in Listing 12-7.

Listing 12-7. Modifying the startGame() Method (server.js)

```
function startGame(room){
    console.log("Both players are ready. Starting game in room",room.roomId);
    room.status = "running";
    sendRoomListToEveryone();
    // Notify players to start the game
    sendRoomWebSocketMessage(room,{type:"start_game"});

    room.commands = [];
    room.lastTickConfirmed = {"blue":0,"green":0};
    room.currentTick = 0;

    // Calculate tick lag for room as the max of both player's tick lags
    var roomTickLag = Math.max(room.players[0].tickLag,room.players[1].tickLag);

    room.interval = setInterval(function(){
        // Confirm that both players have send in commands for up to present tick
        if(room.lastTickConfirmed["blue"] >= room.currentTick &&
room.lastTickConfirmed["green"] >= room.currentTick){
            // Commands should be executed after the tick lag
            sendRoomWebSocketMessage(room,{type:"game_tick",
tick:room.currentTick+roomTickLag, commands:room.commands}));
            room.currentTick++;
            room.commands = [];
```

```
        } else {
            // One of the players is causing the game to lag. Handle appropriately
            if(room.lastTickConfirmed["blue"] < room.currentTick){
                console.log ("Room",room.roomId,"Blue is lagging on
Tick:",room.currentTick,"by", room.currentTick-room.lastTickConfirmed["blue"]);
            }
            if(room.lastTickConfirmed["green"] < room.currentTick){
                console.log ("Room",room.roomId,"Green is lagging on Tick:",
room.currentTick, "by", room.currentTick-room.lastTickConfirmed["green"]);
            }
        }
    },100);
}
```

When the game starts, we initialize the commands array, currentTick, and the lastTickConfirmed object for the room. We then calculate the tick lag for the room as the maximum of the tick lag for the two players and save it in the roomTickLag variable.

We then start the timer loop for the game using setInterval(). Within this loop, we first check that both players have caught up with the server by sending commands for the present game tick.

If so, we send out a game_tick message to the message to the players with a list of commands and ask them to execute the commands roomTickLag ticks after the current tick. This way, both the players will execute the command at the same time, even if the message takes a little time to reach the players.

We then clear the commands array on the server and increase the currentTick variable for the room.

If the server hasn't received confirmation for the current tick from both the clients, we log a message to the console and do not increment the tick. You can modify this code to check whether the server has been waiting for a long time and, if so, send the players a notification that the server is experiencing lag.

If you start the server and run the game on two different browsers, you should be able to command the units and have your first multiplayer battle, as shown in Figure 12-2.

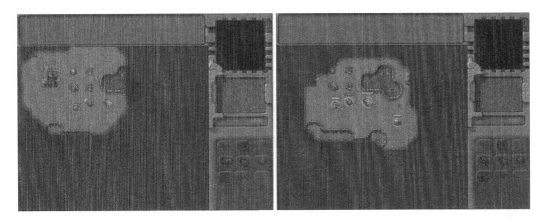

Figure 12-2. *Commanding units in a multiplayer battle*

The multiplayer portion of our game is now working. Right now both the browsers are on the same machine. You can move the server code onto a separate Node.js machine and modify the multiplayer object to point to this new server instead of localhost. If you want to move to a public server, you can find several hosting providers that provide Node.js support such as Nodester (http://nodester.com) and Nodejitsu (http://nodejitsu.com/).

Now that we have implemented sending commands, we will implement ending the multiplayer game.

Ending the Multiplayer Game

The multiplayer game can be ended in two ways. The first is if one of the players defeats the other by satisfying the requirements for the level. The other is if a player either closes the browser or gets disconnected from the server.

Ending the Game When a Player Is Defeated

We will implement ending the game using triggered events just like we did in Chapter 10. This gives us the flexibility to design different types of multiplayer levels such as capture the flag or death match. We are limited only by our imagination.

For now, we will make the level end when one side is completely destroyed. We will start by creating a simple triggered event in the multiplayer map, as shown in Listing 12-8.

Listing 12-8. Trigger for Ending the Multiplayer Level (maps.js)

```
/* Conditional and Timed Trigger Events */
"triggers":[
    /* Lose if not even one item is left */
    {"type":"conditional",
        "condition":function(){
            for (var i=0; i < game.items.length; i++) {
                if(game.items[i].team == game.team){
                    return false;
                }
            };
            return true;
        },
        "action":function(){
            multiplayer.loseGame();
        }
    },
]
```

In the conditional trigger, we check whether the game.items array contains at least one item belonging to the player. If the player has no items left, we call the loseGame() method.

Next we will add the loseGame() and endGame() methods to the multiplayer object, as shown in Listing 12-9.

Listing 12-9. Adding loseGame() and endgame() Methods (multiplayer.js)

```
// Tell the server that the player has lost
loseGame:function(){
    multiplayer.sendWebSocketMessage({type:"lose_game"});
},
endGame:function(reason){
    game.running = false
    clearInterval(multiplayer.animationInterval);
    // Show reason for game ending, and on OK, exit multiplayer screen
    game.showMessageBox(reason,multiplayer.closeAndExit);
}
```

In the loseGame() method, we send a message of type lose_game to the server to let it know that the player has lost the game.

In the endGame() method, we clear the game.running flag and the multiplayer.animationInterval interval. We then show a message box with the reason for ending the game and finally call the multiplayer.closeAndExit() method once the OK button on the message box is clicked.

Next, we will define a new endGame() method in server.js, as shown in Listing 12-10.

Listing 12-10. The Server endGame() Method (server.js)

```
function endGame(room,reason){
    clearInterval(room.interval);
    room.status = "empty";
    sendRoomWebSocketMessage(room,{type:"end_game",reason:reason})
    for (var i = room.players.length - 1; i >= 0; i--){
        leaveRoom(room.players[i],room.roomId);
    };
    sendRoomListToEveryone();
}
```

We start by clearing the interval for the game loop. We then send the end_game message to all the players in the room with the reason provided as a parameter. We then set the room to empty and remove all the players from the room using the leaveRoom() method. Finally, we send the updated room list to all connected players.

Next, we will modify the message event handler on the server to handle messages of type lose_game, as shown in Listing 12-11.

Listing 12-11. Handing Messages of Type lose_game (server.js)

```
// On Message event handler for a connection
connection.on('message', function(message) {
    if (message.type === 'utf8') {
        var clientMessage = JSON.parse(message.utf8Data);
        switch (clientMessage.type){
            case "join_room":
                var room = joinRoom(player,clientMessage.roomId);
                sendRoomListToEveryone();
                if(room.players.length == 2){
                    initGame(room);
                }
                break;
            case "leave_room":
                leaveRoom(player,clientMessage.roomId);
                sendRoomListToEveryone();
                break;
            case "initialized_level":
                player.room.playersReady++;
                if (player.room.playersReady==2){
                    startGame(player.room);
                }
                break;
            case "latency_pong":
                finishMeasuringLatency(player,clientMessage);
```

```
                // Measure latency at least thrice
                if(player.latencyTrips.length<3){
                    measureLatency(player);
                }
                break;
            case "command":
                if (player.room && player.room.status=="running"){
                    if(clientMessage.uids){
                        player.room.commands.push({uids:clientMessage.uids,
details:clientMessage.details});
                    }
                    player.room.lastTickConfirmed[player.color] = clientMessage.currentTick +
player.tickLag;
                }
                break;
            case "lose_game":
                endGame(player.room, "The "+ player.color +" team has been defeated.");
                break;
        }
    }
});
```

When we receive a lose_game message from one of the players, we call the endGame() method with the reason for ending the game.

Finally, we will modify the multiplayer object's handleWebSocketMessage() method to receive messages of type end_game, as shown in Listing 12-12.

Listing 12-12. Receiving Messages of Type end_game (multiplayer.js)

```
handleWebSocketMessage:function(message){
    var messageObject = JSON.parse(message.data);
    switch (messageObject.type){
        case "room_list":
            multiplayer.updateRoomStatus(messageObject.status);
            break;
        case "joined_room":
            multiplayer.roomId = messageObject.roomId;
            multiplayer.color = messageObject.color;
            break;
        case "init_level":
            multiplayer.initMultiplayerLevel(messageObject);
            break;
        case "start_game":
            multiplayer.startGame();
            break;
        case "latency_ping":
            multiplayer.sendWebSocketMessage({type:"latency_pong"});
            break;
        case "game_tick":
            multiplayer.lastReceivedTick = messageObject.tick;
            multiplayer.commands[messageObject.tick] = messageObject.commands;
            break;
```

```
    case "end_game":
        multiplayer.endGame(messageObject.reason);
        break;
    }
},
```

When the client receives an end_game message, we call `multiplayer.endGame()` with the reason provided in the message.

If you start the server and run the game, you should see a message box when one of the players destroys all of the other players units and buildings, as shown in Figure 12-3.

Figure 12-3. *Game ends when one player defeats the other*

If you click the Okay button, you should be taken back to the main game menu. You will notice that when a game ends, the lobby automatically shows the room as empty so that the next set of players can join the room.

We will also end the game when a player closes the browser or is disconnected from the server.

Ending the Game When a Player Is Disconnected

Whenever a player disconnects from the server while playing a game, it will trigger a websocket close event on the server. We will handle this disconnect by modifying the close event handler on the server, as shown in Listing 12-13.

Listing 12-13. Handling Player Disconnects (server.js)

```
connection.on('close', function(reasonCode, description) {
    console.log('Connection from ' + request.remoteAddress + ' disconnected.');
```

```
    for (var i = players.length - 1; i >= 0; i--){
        if (players[i]==player){
            players.splice(i,1);
        }
    };

    // If the player is in a room, remove him from room and notify everyone
    if(player.room){
        var status = player.room.status;
        var roomId = player.room.roomId;
        // If the game was running, end the game as well
        if(status=="running"){
            endGame(player.room, "The "+ player.color +" player has disconnected.");
        } else {
            leaveRoom(player,roomId);
        }
        sendRoomListToEveryone();
    }
});
```

If the player is in a room, we remove the player from the room and send the updated room list to everyone. If the game was running, we also call the endgame() method with the reason that the player has disconnected.

If you start the server and begin a multiplayer game, you should see a disconnect message when either of the players gets disconnected, as shown in Figure 12-4.

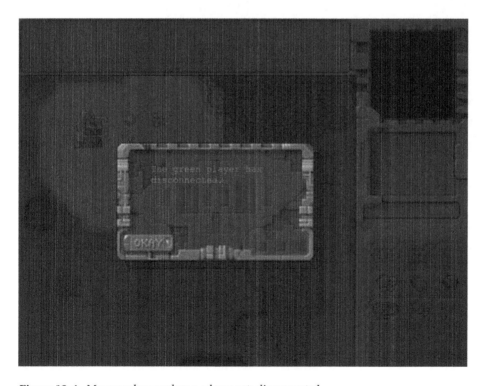

Figure 12-4. *Message shown when a player gets disconnected*

Clicking the Okay button will take you back to the main menu screen. Again, the lobby automatically shows the room as empty so that the next set of players can join the room.

The last thing we will handle is ending the game if a connection error occurs and the connection is lost.

Ending the Game When a Connection Is Lost

Whenever the client gets disconnected from the server or an error occurs, it will trigger either an error or a close event on the client. We will handle this by implementing these event handlers within the start() method of the multiplayer object, as shown in Listing 12-14.

Listing 12-14. Handling Connection Errors (multiplayer.js)

```
start:function(){
    game.type = "multiplayer";
    var WebSocketObject = window.WebSocket || window.MozWebSocket;
    if (!WebSocketObject){
        game.showMessageBox("Your browser does not support WebSocket. Multiplayer will not work.");
        return;
    }
    this.websocket = new WebSocketObject(this.websocket_url);
    this.websocket.onmessage = multiplayer.handleWebSocketMessage;
    // Display multiplayer lobby screen after connecting
    this.websocket.onopen = function(){
        // Hide the starting menu layer
        $('.gamelayer').hide();
        $('#multiplayerlobbyscreen').show();
    }

    this.websocket.onclose = function(){
        multiplayer.endGame("Error connecting to server.");
    }

    this.websocket.onerror = function(){
        multiplayer.endGame("Error connecting to server.");
    }
},
```

For both the events, we call the endGame() method with an error message. If you run the game now and shut down the server to re-create a server disconnect, you should see an error message, as shown in Figure 12-5.

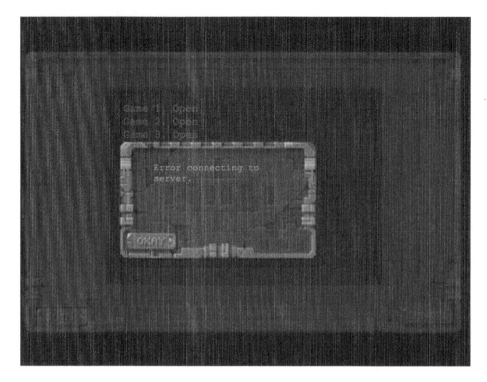

Figure 12-5. Message shown in case of a connection error

If there is a problem with the connection while the player is either in the lobby or playing a game, the browser will now display this error message and then return to the main game screen.

A more robust implementation would include trying to reconnect to the server within a timeout period and then resuming the game. We can achieve this by passing a reconnect message with a unique player ID to the server and handling the message appropriately on the server side. However, we will stick with this simpler implementation for our game.

Before we wrap up the multiplayer portion of our game, we will implement one last feature in our game: player chat.

Implementing Player Chat

We will start by defining an input box for chat messages inside the gameinterfacescreen layer in index.html, as shown in Listing 12-15.

Listing 12-15. Adding Input Box for Chat Message (index.html)

```
<div id="gameinterfacescreen" class="gamelayer">
    <div id="gamemessages"></div>
    <div id="callerpicture"></div>
    <div id="cash"></div>
    <div id="sidebarbuttons">
        <input type="button" id="starportbutton" title = "Starport">
        <input type="button" id="turretbutton" title = "Turret">
        <input type="button" id="placeholder1" disabled>
```

```
        <input type="button" id="scouttankbutton" title = "Scout Tank">
        <input type="button" id="heavytankbutton" title = "Heavy Tank">
        <input type="button" id="harvesterbutton" title = "Harvester">

        <input type="button" id="chopperbutton" title = "Copter">
        <input type="button" id="wraithbutton" title = "Wraith">
        <input type="button" id="placeholder2" disabled>

    </div>
    <canvas id="gamebackgroundcanvas" height="400" width="480"></canvas>
    <canvas id="gameforegroundcanvas" height="400" width="480"></canvas>
    <input type="text" id="chatmessage"></input>
</div>
```

Next we will add some extra styles for the chat message input to styles.css, as shown in Listing 12-16.

Listing 12-16. Styles for Chat Message Input Box (styles.css)

```
#chatmessage{
    position:absolute;
    top:460px;
    width:479px;
    background:rgba(0,255,0,0.1);
    color:green;
    border:1px solid green;
    display:none;
}
#chatmessage:focus {
    outline:none;
}
```

Next we will add an event handler for keydown events inside multiplayer.js, as shown in Listing 12-17.

Listing 12-17. Handing Keydown Events to Handle the Chat Message Input (multiplayer.js)

```
$(window).keydown(function(e){
    // Chatting only allowed in multiplayer when game is running
    if(game.type != "multiplayer" || !game.running){
        return;
    }

    var keyPressed = e.which;
    if (e.which == 13){ // Enter key pressed
        var isVisible = $('#chatmessage').is(':visible');
        if (isVisible){
            // if chat box is visible, pressing enter sends the message and hides the chat box
            if ($('#chatmessage').val()!= ''){

                multiplayer.sendWebSocketMessage({type:"chat",message:$('#chatmessage').val()});
                $('#chatmessage').val('');
            }
            $('#chatmessage').hide();
        } else {
```

```
            // if chat box is not visible, pressing enter shows the chat box
            $('#chatmessage').show();
            $('#chatmessage').focus();
        }
        e.preventDefault();
    } else if (e.which==27){ // Escape key pressed
        // Pressing escape hides the chat box
        $('#chatmessage').hide();
        $('#chatmessage').val('');
        e.preventDefault();
    }
});
```

Whenever a key is pressed, we first confirm that the game is a multiplayer game and it is running and exit if it is not. If the key pressed is the Enter key (key code 13), we first check whether the chatmessage input box is visible. If it is visible, we send the contents of the message box to the server inside a message of type chat. We then clear the contents of the input box and hide it. If the input box is not already visible, we display the chat input box and set the focus to it. If the key pressed is Escape (key code 27), we clear the contents of the input box and hide it. Next, we will modify the message event handler on the server to handle messages of type chat, as shown in Listing 12-18.

Listing 12-18. Handing Messages of Type chat (server.js)

```
// On Message event handler for a connection
connection.on('message', function(message) {
    if (message.type === 'utf8') {
        var clientMessage = JSON.parse(message.utf8Data);
        switch (clientMessage.type){
            case "join_room":
                var room = joinRoom(player,clientMessage.roomId);
                sendRoomListToEveryone();
                if(room.players.length == 2){
                    initGame(room);
                }
                break;
            case "leave_room":
                leaveRoom(player,clientMessage.roomId);
                sendRoomListToEveryone();
                break;
            case "initialized_level":
                player.room.playersReady++;
                if (player.room.playersReady==2){
                    startGame(player.room);
                }
                break;
            case "latency_pong":
                finishMeasuringLatency(player,clientMessage);
                // Measure latency at least thrice
                if(player.latencyTrips.length<3){
                    measureLatency(player);
                }
                break;
```

```
        case "command":
            if (player.room && player.room.status=="running"){
                if(clientMessage.uids){
                    player.room.commands.push({uids:clientMessage.uids,
details:clientMessage.details});
                }
                player.room.lastTickConfirmed[player.color] = clientMessage.currentTick +
player.tickLag;
            }
            break;
        case "lose_game":
            endGame(player.room, "The "+ player.color +" team has been defeated.");
            break;
        case "chat":
            if (player.room && player.room.status=="running"){
                var cleanedMessage = clientMessage.message.replace(/[<>]/g,"");
                sendRoomWebSocketMessage(player.room,{type:"chat", from:player.color,
message:cleanedMessage});
            }
            break;
        }
    }
});
```

When we receive a message of type chat from a player, we send back a message of type chat to all the players in the room, with a from property set to the player's color and a message property set to the message we just received.

Ideally, you should validate the chat message so that a player cannot send malicious HTML and script tags inside chat messages. For now, we use a simple regular expression to strip out any HTML tags from the message before sending it back.

Finally, we will modify the multiplayer object's handleWebSocketMessage() method to receive messages of type chat, as shown in Listing 12-19.

Listing 12-19. Receiving Messages of Type chat (multiplayer.js)

```
handleWebSocketMessage:function(message){
    var messageObject = JSON.parse(message.data);
    switch (messageObject.type){
        case "room_list":
            multiplayer.updateRoomStatus(messageObject.status);
            break;
        case "joined_room":
            multiplayer.roomId = messageObject.roomId;
            multiplayer.color = messageObject.color;
            break;
        case "init_level":
            multiplayer.initMultiplayerLevel(messageObject);
            break;
        case "start_game":
            multiplayer.startGame();
            break;
```

```
        case "latency_ping":
            multiplayer.sendWebSocketMessage({type:"latency_pong"});
            break;
        case "game_tick":
            multiplayer.lastReceivedTick = messageObject.tick;
            multiplayer.commands[messageObject.tick] = messageObject.commands;
            break;
        case "end_game":
            multiplayer.endGame(messageObject.reason);
            break;
        case "chat":
            game.showMessage(messageObject.from,messageObject.message);
            break;
    }
},
```

If you start the server and play a multiplayer game now, you should be able to send chat messages from one player to the other, as shown in Figure 12-6.

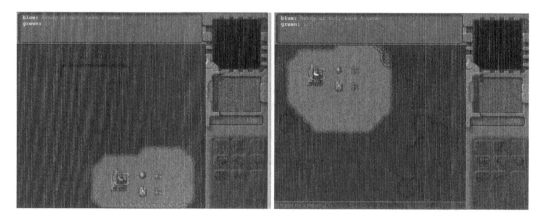

Figure 12-6. *Chat between players during multiplayer*

We now have a working player chat for multiplayer. With this last change, we can consider our multiplayer game wrapped up.

Summary

We have come a long way over the course of this book. We started by looking at the basic elements of HTML5 needed to build games, such as drawing and animating on the canvas, playing audio, and using sprite sheets.

We then used these basics to build a Box2D physics engine–based game called *Froot Wars*. In the process, we looked at creating splash screens, asset loaders, and customizable levels. We then examined the building blocks of the Box2D engine and integrated Box2D with the game to create realistic-looking physics. We then added sound effects and background music to create a very polished game.

After that, we built a complete real-time strategy game called *Lost Colony*. Building upon ideas from the previous chapters, we first created a single-player game world with large pannable levels and different types of entities. We added intelligent movement using pathfinding and steering, combat using states and triggers, and even a game economy. We then saw how this framework could be used to tell a compelling story over several levels of a single-player campaign.

Finally, over the last two chapters, we used Node.js and WebSockets to add multiplayer support to our game. We started by looking at the basics of WebSocket communication and using it to create a multiplayer game lobby.

We then implemented a framework for multiplayer gameplay using the lock-step networking model, which also compensated for network latency while maintaining game synchronization. We handled connection errors as well as game completion using triggered events. Finally, we built a chat system to send messages between the players.

If you have been following along, you should now have the knowledge, resources, and confidence to build your own amazing games in HTML5.

My goal in writing this book was to demystify the process of building complex games in HTML5 and provide you with everything that you would need to build such games on your own.

If you have questions or feedback, you can reach me using the dedicated page for this book on my website at `www.adityaravishankar.com/pro-html5-games/`. I would love to hear about how you used this book as a starting point for your own projects.

I wish you all the best in your game-programming journey.

Index

■ H

■ I, J, K

■ S, T, U, V

■ W, X, Y, Z

CPSIA information can be obtained at www.ICGtesting.com
Printed in the USA
LVOW020042141212

311598LV00015B/211/P